THE L
OF

Lady Arbella Stuart

WOMEN WRITERS IN ENGLISH
1350–1850

GENERAL EDITORS

Susanne Woods and Elizabeth H. Hageman

MANAGING EDITOR

Julia Flanders

SECTION EDITORS

Patricia Caldwell

Stuart Curran

Margaret J. M. Ezell

Elizabeth H. Hageman

WOMEN WRITERS PROJECT

Brown University

THE LETTERS
OF
Lady Arbella Stuart

EDITED BY

Sara Jayne Steen

New York   Oxford

OXFORD UNIVERSITY PRESS

1994

OXFORD UNIVERSITY PRESS

Oxford   New York

Athens   Auckland   Bangkok   Bombay
Calcutta   Cape Town   Dar es Salaam   Delhi
Florence   Hong Kong   Istanbul   Karachi
Kuala Lumpur   Madras   Madrid   Melbourne
Mexico City   Nairobi   Paris   Singapore
Taipei   Tokyo   Toronto
and associated companies in
Berlin   Ibadan

Published by Oxford University Press, Inc.,
200 Madison Avenue, New York, New York 10016

Oxford is a registered trademark of Oxford University Press

Library of Congress Cataloging-in-Publication Data

Stuart, Arabella, Lady, 1575–1615.
[Correspondence]
The letters of Lady Arbella Stuart / edited by Sara Jayne Steen.
p.   cm.   -- (Women writers in English 1350–1850)
Includes bibliographical references and index.
1. Stuart, Arabella, Lady, 1575–1615—Correspondence.   2. Women
political prisoners—Great Britain—Correspondence.   3. Great Britain—History—
Elizabeth, 1558–1603.   4. Great Britain—Kings and rulers—Succession.
5. Great Britain—History—James I, 1603–1625.
6. Nobility—Great Britain—Correspondence.
I. Steen, Sara Jayne, 1949– .   II. Title.   III. Series.
DA391.1.S9A4   1994   942.06'092--dc20   94-18536
ISBN 0-19-508057-2 (cloth)
ISBN 0-19-508718-6 (paper)

This volume was supported in part by the National Endowment
for the Humanities, an independent federal agency.

Printing (last digit):   9   8   7   6   5   4   3   2   1

Printed in the United States of America
on acid-free paper

*To Opal Marie Singleton Steen
and Forrest Martin Steen*

CONTENTS

*A genealogical chart of the descendants of Henry VII
and Elizabeth of York appears on page 106.
Examples of Lady Arbella Stuart's handwriting appear
after the Textual Introduction, on pages 112 and 113.*

FOREWORD

Women Writers in English 1350–1850 presents texts of cultural and literary interest in the English-speaking tradition, often for the first time since their original publication. Most of the writers represented in the series were well known and highly regarded until the professionalization of English studies in the later nineteenth century coincided with their excision from canonical status and from the majority of literary histories.

The purpose of this series is to make available a wide range of unfamiliar texts by women, thus challenging the common assumption that women wrote little of real value before the Victorian period. While no one can doubt the relative difficulty women experienced in writing for an audience before that time, or indeed have encountered since, this series shows that women nonetheless had been writing from early on and in a variety of genres, that they maintained a clear eye to readers, and that they experimented with an interesting array of literary strategies for claiming their authorial voices. Despite the tendency to treat the powerful fictions of Virginia Woolf's *A Room of One's Own* (1928) as if they were fact, we now know, against her suggestion to the contrary, that there were many "Judith Shakespeares," and that not all of them died lamentable deaths before fulfilling their literary ambitions.

This series is unique in at least two ways. It offers, for the first time, concrete evidence of a rich and lively heritage of women writing in English before the mid-nineteenth century, and it is based on one of the most sophisticated and forward-looking electronic resources in the world: the Brown University Women Writers Project textbase (full text database) of works by early women writers. The Brown University Women Writers Project (WWP) was established in 1988 with a grant from the National Endowment for the Humanities, which continues to assist in its development.

Women Writers in English 1350–1850 is a print publication project derived from the WWP. It offers lightly annotated versions based on single good copies or, in some cases, collated versions of texts with more complex editorial histories, normally in their original spelling. The editions are aimed at a wide audience, from the informed under-graduate through professional students of literature, and they attempt to include the general reader who is interested in exploring a fuller tradition of early texts in English than has been available through the almost exclusively male canonical tradition.

SUSANNE WOODS
ELIZABETH H. HAGEMAN
General Editors

ACKNOWLEDGMENTS

The tremendous collaborative effort that is the Women Writers Project thrives on the contributions of all its members; I can hardly say enough here to acknowledge everyone who deserves recognition and thanks. In particular the students whose energy and enthusiasm have sustained the Project over the years are by now far too numerous to list by name.

Ongoing thanks are due to Brown University and to its administrators for their continued support, especially President Vartan Gregorian, Provost Frank Rothman, Dean of the Faculty Bryan Shepp, and Vice President Brian Hawkins. We are also very grateful to the Brown English Department and in particular to Elizabeth Kirk, Stephen Foley, and Marilyn Netter. In Brown's Computing and Information Services Don Wolfe and Geoffrey Bilder have helped and sustained the Project as well.

I have been delighted to work with our associates at Oxford University Press, Elizabeth Maguire, Jeff Edelstein, Claude Conyers, and Ellen Barrie, who have been so generous with their creativity and patience.

It is hard to imagine a more committed set of colleagues than the Women Writers Project staff. Carole Mah, Maria Fish, and Elizabeth Adams have been true comrades, tireless and inspiring in their efforts. Many thanks are due to Syd Bauman, who continues to guide us expertly through the intricacies of the computer. Thanks go as well to Elaine Brennan for her work in establishing this volume and the series itself, and for bringing the Women Writers Project so far. Others who have helped make this series possible include Anthony Arnove, Rebecca Bailey, Kim Bordner, Susie Castellanos, Cathleen Drake, Faye Halpern, John Marx, Jennifer Reid, Caleb Rounds, Elizabeth Terzakis, Andrea Weisman, and Kristen Whissel. Sarah Brown deserves special thanks for her help all along the way. Finally, all of us owe a great debt of affection and gratitude to our local co-director Allen Renear, whose energy and vision inspire us all.

JULIA FLANDERS
Managing Editor

ACKNOWLEDGMENTS

Like most projects that have continued over years, this one has involved many other people—the friends and colleagues who have generously offered suggestions and commented on papers and articles, and the librarians and archivists who have become friends and far exceeded in kindness the responsibilities of their positions.

I would like to thank the Duke of Norfolk, the Duke of Northumberland, the Marquess of Bath, and the Marquess of Salisbury for allowing me to visit their libraries and to publish the texts of manuscripts in their possession. The staffs of the following libraries, archives, houses, and offices were unfailingly helpful and thoughtful: the Alnwick Castle Archives, the Arundel Castle Library, the Beinecke Rare Book and Manuscript Library, the Biblioteca Apostolica Vaticana, the Bodleian Library, the British Library, Chatsworth House, the Courtauld Institute of Art, the Dean and Chapter Library of Durham Cathedral, the Folger Shakespeare Library, the Government Art Collection, Hardwick Hall, Hatfield House, the Huntington Library, Lambeth Palace Library, the Library of Congress, Longleat House, the National Trust, the Public Record Office, the Royal Commission on Historical Manuscripts, the Royal Danish Embassy Information Office, the University of London Library, and the University of Nottingham Library. Nearly two hundred archivists and librarians in Belgium, Canada, Denmark, England, France, Ireland, Italy, Scotland, the United States, and Wales answered queries, as did many scholars; and the interlibrary-loan personnel at Montana State University's Renne Library were, as always, prompt and attentive.

During my research, B. S. Benedikz of the University of Birmingham offered helpful suggestions on manuscript locations; Christine Maria Grafinger of the Vatican Library searched the collections there for useful information; Ian St. C. Hughes, administrator at Hardwick Hall, guided me through Hardwick Hall; Brigadier Kenneth Mears, with the kind permission of the governor of the Tower of London, conducted me through the Lennox Room and the Bell Tower, where Stuart is believed to have been imprisoned; and Roger C. Norris, deputy chapter librarian of Durham Chapter Library, notified me of the existence of Stuart's Hebrew/Syriac/Greek Bible, with a cover said to have been embroidered by Stuart. Among the archivists, curators, and librarians with whom I have worked, I owe special thanks to R. H. Harcourt Williams, librarian and archivist to the Marquess of Salisbury, Hatfield House; Kate Harris, librarian and archivist to the Marquess of Bath, Longleat House; W. H. Kelliher, curator of manuscripts at the British Library; Sara Rodger, assistant librarian to the Duke of Norfolk, Arundel Castle; and Colin Shrimpton, archivist to the Duke of Northumberland, Alnwick Castle.

Some of the documents related to Stuart were written in Latin and Italian, and some of Stuart's letters were penned in a highly abbreviated court Latin that presented special problems. Clayton Miles Lehmann translated items ranging from pamphlets to book dedications into splendid English prose, instructed me in basic Latin, and translated Stuart's letters from my initial transcripts of the Latin texts. Margaret J. Arnold generously interrupted her own work at the British Library to aid me in further transcribing Stuart's secretaries' Latin. Jane Woodruff elegantly reworked translations of the letters as I revised the Latin transcripts, answered numerous questions, and deserves much of the credit for the edited Latin texts that appear in Appendix A. Ada Giusti kindly translated into English the Italian letter from Stuart's creditor Prospero Gorges that appears in Appendix B.

Sections of this manuscript were originally presented as papers at meetings of the Modern Language Association, the Rocky Mountain Medieval and Renaissance Association, the Sixteenth Century Studies Conference, and the Pacific Northwest Renaissance Conference, in sessions chaired by Sharon A. Beehler, James B. Fitzmaurice, Elizabeth McCutcheon, Josephine A. Roberts, and Linda Woodbridge. Other sections were presented as lectures at Montana State University, Northern Arizona University, Arizona State University, the College of Physicians of Philadelphia, and the University of South Dakota. Some materials in this volume also appeared in earlier form in essays originally published in *English Literary Renaissance, The Sixteenth Century Journal,* and *Voices of Silence: Editing the Letters of Renaissance Women* (edited by Josephine A. Roberts, Renaissance English Text Society Proceedings, 1991); I am grateful to the editors and publishers for use of these materials.

I benefited from a seminar in paleography led by Laetitia Yeandle at a conference of the Shakespeare Association of America; from conversations about Stuart's mental state with psychologist Barbara Honeyman; and from discussions of Stuart's health and early modern medicine with professor Pierce Mullen and physicians Robert J. Flaherty and John M. Opitz, chairman of the Department of Medical Genetics at Shodair Hospital. For other help, I am indebted to Liahna Babener, Peter Beal, John C. Bean, David Cherry, Clifford Davidson, James B. Fitzmaurice, James L. Harner, Harrison T. Meserole, David Metzger, Oliver Phillips, Christopher Pinet, Josephine A. Roberts, and Bruce Selyem. I am grateful to Montana State University for a sabbatical leave and to the National Endowment for the Humanities, the Folger Shakespeare Library, and the College of Letters and Sciences at Montana State University for the grants, stipends, and fellowships that in part funded this study.

Among those to whom I am most deeply indebted are Elizabeth H. Hageman, my section editor, and Elizabeth McCutcheon, each of whom read this manuscript in its entirety and made thoughtful and detailed suggestions; Julia Flanders of the Women Writers Project, who carefully coordinated the production of a complex text; and Joseph Bourque, writer, computer expert, and spouse, who saved my prose and computer files from many a glitch.

SARA JAYNE STEEN

INTRODUCTION

I. The Legends and the Letters

Unlike most women of early modern England, Lady Arbella Stuart has not been invisible. On the contrary, she has accumulated layers of legend. From the seventeenth through the twentieth centuries, her story has been told and retold in ballad, poetry, novel, drama, and biography. To romantics, she was the woman who never desired the throne she could have claimed, but who fervently desired love; the woman whose hope to live with her husband led her to make a daring escape from confinement disguised as a man, with doublet, wig, and rapier; the woman who allowed herself to be captured off the coast of France and returned to England rather than land safely without the man she had chosen as husband; the woman who risked all for love and lost. In this view, Stuart was a steadfast heroine[1] victimized by her selfish and craven cousin King James. Writers celebrating romantic love and marriage extended heroism to sainthood and made Stuart a martyr to the cause of marital devotion: in 1828, the popular poet Felicia Dorothea Hemans put into verse what she imagined to have been Stuart's feelings when the imprisoned Stuart found her "woman's heart" could "wake a spirit and a power to bless, / Ev'n in this hour's o'ershadowing fearfulness."[2] Other writers of fiction and history have taken a more pragmatic approach, presenting Stuart's story instead as a deplorable drama, a mirthless comedy of errors. According to this alternative legend, Stuart was hysterical, vain, indecisive, easily manipulated, and incapable of parlaying her birth into the crown. She was a woman who lacked the

---

1. The female form is used here deliberately because by the early nineteenth century the legend focused on her sex.

2. "Arabella Stuart," *Records of Woman* (rpt. New York: Garland, 1978), 19. For other romantic views, see the art ballad attributed to William Mickle (Elizabeth Cooper, *The Life and Letters of Lady Arabella Stuart* [London: Hurst and Blackett, 1866], 2:254–59) and George Payne Rainsford James, *Arabella Stuart: A Romance from English History* (London: Richard Bentley, 1844).

strength of mind and character for command, and who, like her aunt
Mary Queen of Scots, in every crisis of her life made an unreasonable
choice; a woman whose marriage demonstrated her inability to face the
political realities of her high birth and to acknowledge her king's and
country's need for an uncomplicated succession; a woman who twice
suffered emotional and physical breakdowns and finally died insane, the
culmination of weaknesses evident throughout her life. To these observers, her fate was perhaps pitiful, but not tragic; in 1868, James Spedding
concluded that Stuart was only one of many women whose marriages
were not altogether their "own business," and if she had had the good
sense to "have submitted, as other people do, to what was inevita-
ble...she might have done well enough."[1]

Both interpretations emerge from traditional stereotypes of womanhood. Lady Arbella Stuart was woman on a pedestal, the ideal of tenderness and self-sacrifice, or woman off the pedestal, inadequate and out of
her domain in the public arena—domestic saint or political sinner. The
underlying message might be phrased as, "Woman's proper role is as
wife and if in defense of family she displays strengths beyond those
usual to her sex, she should be lauded, but in the political realm, her
natural female frailties predictably lead to failure." If Stuart was openly
angry, she was hysterical, either finally and sadly driven beyond the limits of her endurance (the first legend), or demonstrating her deficiencies
of mind and character (the second). If she chose death over a life of
imprisonment in the Tower of London, she was insane.

Until recently these cultural paradigms have been pervasive, and students of early modern England necessarily have read and rewritten Stuart's story by their light, sometimes defending one characterization and
disputing the other, sometimes interweaving the two. Certainly the
writers have differed in the points they have emphasized and in the
vigor and flamboyance of their rhetoric; the dual legends summarize
their positions. In critiquing those stances, I do not mean to suggest

---

1. *The Letters and the Life [of Francis Bacon]*, vol. 4, *The Works of Francis Bacon,* ed. James
Spedding (London: Longmans et al.), 294–95. Such views are particularly prevalent among
political historians.

that even the most extreme of the early promoters of the Stuart legends should be condemned. As historians and as writers of fiction, these authors read and composed from perspectives that reflected the cultural assumptions of their eras; in fact, their attitudes persist enough in our society that their reasoning and responses are hardly foreign. Often their work deserves much credit. Victorian women such as Louisa Stuart Costello, Elizabeth Cooper, and Emily Tennyson Bradley did substantial research on Stuart's life and located copies of many of her letters. Mid-twentieth-century biographers such as Phyllis Margaret Handover and David N. Durant tried to resituate Stuart in the historical context of Elizabethan and Jacobean England.[1] These writers have countered various points of the legends and contributed significantly to our understanding of Stuart's life, writing, and era. But the assumptions about women that have underlain the vast majority of interpretations over centuries are no longer those of a growing community of scholars.

Recent scholars have been increasingly conscious of the preconceptions readers bring to their reading and of gender as a category of analysis. Our understanding of Renaissance stereotypes of women and their effect on the lives of living women has radically shifted our perceptions of early modern England, as have economic and demographic studies of women as producers and consumers, wives and mothers.[2] Texts written by aristocratic and middle-class women are being made available, and previously canonized and lesser-known texts are being reinterpreted

---

1. *Memoirs of Eminent Englishwomen* (London: Richard Bentley, 1844), 1:197–333; *The Life and Letters of Lady Arabella Stuart* (1866); *Life of the Lady Arabella Stuart* (London: Richard Bentley, 1889); *Arbella Stuart: Royal Lady of Hardwick and Cousin to King James* (London: Eyre and Spottiswoode, 1957); *Arbella Stuart: A Rival to the Queen* (London: Weidenfeld and Nicolson, 1978).

2. For books and articles published through early 1990 on women in relation to early modern culture, see Elizabeth H. Hageman's bibliographies in *Women in the Renaissance: Selections from "English Literary Renaissance,"* ed. Kirby Farrell, Elizabeth H. Hageman, and Arthur F. Kinney (Amherst: Univ. of Massachusetts Press, 1990), 228–44, 258–64, 269–309. Among books published since early 1990 are Valerie Fildes, ed., *Women as Mothers in Pre-Industrial England: Essays in Memory of Dorothy McLaren* (London: Routledge, 1990); Constance Jordan, *Renaissance Feminism: Literary Texts and Political Models* (Ithaca: Cornell Univ. Press, 1990); and Margaret L. King, *Women of the Renaissance*, Women in Culture and Society (Chicago: Univ. of Chicago Press, 1991).

within the context of what women read and wrote.[1] As a result, we are beginning to glimpse Renaissance women's lives, to learn what they thought about themselves and what they saw as constraints and freedoms, and to trace a female literary tradition. This study is an attempt to situate Lady Arbella Stuart's letters within that scholarship.

Stuart is unlike many Renaissance women in that her life was more directly defined by contemporary politics, more determined by circumstances of birth that made her religion and health consequential to the courts of Europe as well as to Elizabethan and Jacobean England. The weighting of public versus private life is different for a woman who is a ranking member of the royal family than it is for most women in her culture; Stuart's letters offer an opportunity to observe the intricate dynamics of power exercised at the highest social and political levels. But while Stuart's public importance lay in what she was—a marriageable female claimant to the throne—her private life was as influenced by her friends, family, and residences as the lives of women whose public personas were less obviously and confusingly intertwined with their daily existence. To read Stuart's letters is to explore her social milieu and physical surroundings, the country house in Derbyshire where she ate, slept, and studied, the gallery where she walked; it is to learn of the grandmother with whom Stuart had a difficult and volatile alliance, the aunt to whom she turned for advice, and the uncle whom she teased, as well as to examine the entangled relationship between personality and political situation.

Stuart's letters contribute to our developing understanding of the roles of and pressures on upper-class Englishwomen in the late sixteenth and early seventeenth centuries. Stuart was one of the last of the aristocratic Englishwomen to be formally educated in the classical tradition

---

1. Copies of writings in English by women, 1330-1830, are available through the Women Writers Project at Brown University, Providence, R.I. For books and articles published through early 1990 on women writers, see Hageman's bibliographies, noted above, and, in the same volume, Josephine A. Roberts's bibliographies of works on Mary Sidney, 245–58, 265–69. Among books published since early 1990, see Charlotte F. Otten, ed., *English Women's Voices, 1540–1700* (Miami: Florida International Univ. Press, 1992).

of Greek and Roman learning and languages, an education normally reserved for men but that had been extended to women by the early Renaissance humanists.[1] As a learned woman who enjoyed and maintained her studies, Stuart was an anomaly at King James's masculine and sportive court. An unmarried woman without significant independent means, since Queen Elizabeth and King James between them had absorbed her inheritance, Stuart was economically dependent and found it difficult to pay for the style of life she and others considered appropriate to her royal rank. In an era when the ideal woman was expected to be chaste, silent, and obedient, Stuart was educated for command, and the women of rank around her in her youth—Mary of Scots, Queen Elizabeth, and Bess of Hardwick—were active and aggressive role models. The paradox of the aristocratic woman whose sex signified subordination, but whose class signified authority was more extreme in Stuart's case because of her birth and upbringing. Her letters reflect the tensions among these social forces.

Although the letters indicate that Stuart understood her culture's ideal of femininity, she did not fulfill it. She hated being the subservient poor relation, said so directly, and, like other women of her class, sought patents and monopolies in an effort to improve her financial position. She fought for a measure of independence, to "be my owne woman," as she put it (letter 16), and her actions in marrying against the declared edict of her male relative and king and then attempting to escape to France made her, from King James's perspective, subversive. The governmental and popular responses to her defiance of the patriarchal and political hierarchy provide useful gauges of how far a woman could go in challenging authority and for what reasons. In the court letters, Stuart demonstrates both her awareness of the stereotypes of womanhood as conventions and her ability to manipulate them to her advantage, which suggests that they did not altogether govern her sense of self. As I shall discuss in Part VI below, documents that re-emerged only in 1984,

---

1. On this tradition of education, see Elizabeth McCutcheon, "The Learned Woman in Tudor England: Margaret More Roper," in *Women Writers of the Renaissance and Reformation*, ed. Katharina M. Wilson (Athens: Univ. of Georgia Press, 1987), 449–80.

and thus were unavailable to previous scholars, indicate that during her last imprisonment Stuart was working on her own behalf.[1] Even during her final illness in the Tower of London, Stuart strove to retain a measure of control over her life and body.[2] That Stuart was active—willing to take risks when the alternatives were unpalatable, and sometimes frankly angry, rather than quiet and passive—is an important aspect of her story for modern readers.

Literary critics long have been aware of Stuart as someone who, because she was the dedicatee and subject of literary works, tangentially influenced the literature of her own day and later centuries. More importantly, however, Stuart is an author and thus directly in our literary tradition. For many years, letters were seen primarily as historical documents to be examined for background information about prominent figures or notable political and religious movements or events. Stuart's letters were preserved because of her historical importance; as claimant to the throne of England, niece to Mary Queen of Scots, and cousin to King James, she was of sufficient interest that some of her letters and drafts were retained in private collections or became government papers. Recent critical thought, however, has blurred those distinctions between history and literature and profitably asked "literary" questions of what used to be seen as exclusively historical texts.[3] And current scholars have argued convincingly that letters are more than sources of information about how women and men "really" lived, that the letter was an important genre in early modern England, and that the texts were shaped and involved the creation of personas, the

---

1. BL Add. MS 63543.

2. According to the post-mortem report, Stuart refused remedies and would not allow her physicians even to take her pulse (HMC Appendix to Eighth Report, *MSS of the College of Physicians*, 229).

3. See, for example, Margreta de Grazia, "What is a Work? What is a Document?" *The New Historicism and the Editing of English Renaissance Texts*, ed. Thomas L. Berger, Renaissance English Text Society Proceedings, 1990; rpt. in *New Ways of Looking at Old Texts: Papers of the Renaissance English Text Society, 1985–91*, ed. W. Speed Hill, Medieval and Renaissance Texts and Studies, in conjunction with the Renaissance English Text Society (Binghamton, N.Y.: 1993), 199–207.

handling of rhetoric, and the establishment of tone.[1] Dr. Nathaniel Johnson, a respected mid-seventeenth-century physician and antiquarian, indicated one Renaissance reader's criteria for the genre when he praised Stuart's familial letters: she "hath left a very well Enameld Picture of her self drawn by her own pen, wherein Equal Commendation is to be given to the Easiness of stile, and the quickness of her invention and phancy."[2]

This is not to suggest that Stuart saw herself as a writer in the public or professional sense. Stuart belonged to an extraordinary and extended family of women writers: her grandmother Margaret Stuart, Countess of Lennox, had been a poet;[3] her cousin Elizabeth Grey, Countess of Kent, composed a medical text that would be published in 1653, after Grey's death;[4] by marriage Stuart was related to authors Mary Sidney, Countess of Pembroke, and her niece Lady Mary Wroth; Stuart's cousin Sir William Cavendish's daughters Lady Jane Cavendish and Lady Elizabeth Brackley, born in the 1620s, would be poets and playwrights; and their step-mother was Margaret Cavendish, Duchess of Newcastle, who at mid-century would publish works such as *Natures Pictures* and *The Description of a New World.*[5] But the notion of a *woman* of letters was only incipient in the late sixteenth and early seventeenth centuries when Stuart wrote. Many men of Stuart's class were reluctant to publish or to indicate that they considered themselves authors; even fewer women did so. It would have been difficult for "writer" to have been a

---

1. See, for example, Claudio Guillén, "Notes Toward the Study of the Renaissance Letter," *Renaissance Genres: Essays on Theory, History, and Interpretation*, ed. Barbara Kiefer Lewalski (Cambridge: Harvard Univ. Press, 1986), 70–101.

2. Chatsworth MS "Lives of the Earls of Shrewsbury" (1693), 7:2.

3. Antonia Fraser, *Mary Queen of Scots* (New York: Delacorte Press, 1969), 222.

4. *A Choice Manuall of Rare and Select Secrets in Physick and Chirurgery.*

5. For brief discussions of the Sidneys and Cavendishes, see Virginia Blain, Patricia Clements, and Isobel Grundy, eds., *The Feminist Companion to Literature in English: Women Writers from the Middle Ages to the Present* (New Haven: Yale Univ. Press, 1990). Margaret J. M. Ezell discusses the Cavendish sisters' manuscript volume in "'To Be Your Daughter in Your Pen': The Social Functions of Literature in the Writings of Lady Elizabeth Brackley and Lady Jane Cavendish," *Huntington Library Quarterly* 51 (1988): 281–96.

component of Stuart's self-image. At the same time, writing was an important part of her life. It could provide psychological release, as I shall argue below that it did in 1603 when she was under close confinement at Hardwick Hall just before Queen Elizabeth's death, or it could offer her the pleasure of giving a valued gift, since her letters were presents she could afford to give family members who she knew enjoyed her keen observations on the court. And from her late twenties until her death, serious matters rested on her ability to use words to obtain the good offices of those who had more power than she did. At court, she was acknowledged to be a fine writer, one whose words were read aloud in the king's Privy Council and commended.[1]

Stuart's extant letters can be divided into three forms of writing: loosely structured letters from Hardwick Hall, informal letters from James's court, and formal Jacobean court letters. Stuart's 1603 letters from Hardwick Hall were written when she was in her late twenties, after her attempt to take charge of her life by contracting an unauthorized marriage had been disclosed to Queen Elizabeth and her counselors. Sometimes letters that begin conventionally shift into writing that is an outpouring of fears, recriminations, justifications, hopes, and rage rarely seen in women's writings until the twentieth century.[2] Anger and defensiveness prevail, until even the pretense of politeness is gone. Stuart lashes out at her enemies, bemoans her situation, tries to exonerate herself, and even develops a fictional lover to force waning court attention to her plight, using personas by turns evasive, arrogant, submissive, and flamboyant. She recognizes that this "scribling melancholy," so far from the (male) model of detachment and distance, will be perceived as

---

1. Virginia Woolf commented about the importance of letter-writing for Renaissance women: "Had she been born in 1827, Dorothy Osborne would have written novels....But she was born in 1627, and at that date though writing books was ridiculous for a woman there was nothing unseemly in writing a letter." Letter-writing was "an art that a woman could practice without unsexing herself," into which "went powers of observation and of wit that were later to take rather a different shape in *Evelina* and in *Pride and Prejudice*" (*The Second Common Reader* [New York: Harcourt, Brace, 1932], 60).

2. Carolyn G. Heilbrun, *Writing a Woman's Life* (New York: Norton, 1988); she writes, "above all other prohibitions, what has been forbidden to women is anger, together with the open admission of the desire for power and control over one's life" (13).

a "kinde of madnesse" (letter 16); in one frame of mind, she thinks of it that way herself.

The second form of writing among her extant papers is the informal letter, usually written to her aunt and uncle, Mary and Gilbert Talbot, after James had succeeded to the throne and been convinced to bring his cousin to court. Stuart wanted to maintain contact with the relatives to whom she felt close. In these letters, the Arbella persona she creates is often at ease, allusive, teasing, affectionate, and, especially in the early letters, a perceptive recorder of court life. From these letters come glimpses of court activities—the plays performed during the Christmas season, the endless hunting, the lavish gifts presented by the Spanish ambassador at sumptuous dinners—and revelations that are the more interesting because they come from the perspective of a well-educated woman of rank who was not always pleased with what she saw. The informal letters contain court news and political notes, as well as casual discussions of messengers and health and financial woes.

The formal court letters, the third form among Stuart's papers, were written both during the years of relative calm from 1603 through 1609, when Stuart was acknowledged a ranking member of the royal family, and during the years of crisis, from her betrothal in 1610 until her death in the Tower of London in 1615. The court letters show a woman handling the patronage network, offering favors and requesting others, in the early letters attempting to establish herself more firmly economically and politically at court and in the later letters attempting to regain favor and liberty. These letters are written with a high degree of structure and formality, and Stuart's persona is humble, in accordance with the modes of the day. On occasion, she calls attention to herself as a woman, shaping a vision of herself at her needlework (letter 84B) or troubling a busy man with her "womanish toyes" (letter 59A), at the same time that she uses the semblance of submissiveness to help achieve her own ends.

The court letters offer close readers a further benefit. Stuart's political importance meant that in some cases even the drafts of her letters were filed as state papers, and the drafts demonstrate that Stuart frequently revised, carefully crafting the phraseology that might mean the difference between security and dependence or between freedom and continued imprisonment. These multiple drafts, incidentally, refute the occasionally expressed argument that Renaissance women only wrote spontaneously and are therefore less worthy of study than writers who shaped their words. Through examining Stuart's revisions, we can see when she decided to flatter someone or tone down her anger or alter her entire rhetorical strategy. We can see the process by which she resolved contradictions in her thinking and rhetorically defined herself for formal presentation. Extending to women Stephen Greenblatt's thesis about male power to fashion a self,[1] we can watch an intelligent and well-educated Renaissance woman fashion a self in prose.

Like most of us, Lady Arbella Stuart was a person of contradictions, living her life in the midst of shifting social paradigms of women, marriage, religion, and the state, sometimes confused and sometimes certain of what she probably should have doubted, her days occupied with reading, writing, conversation, family, friends, and tradespeople. The majority of women from Stuart's era are lost now as individuals, the papers that might have given shape and dimension to their lives irretrievably gone, if they ever existed. In Lady Arbella Stuart's case, thankfully, some of her letters are extant; and while few people would be happy to be interpreted on the basis of the letters that happened to survive, having some of Stuart's letters is a world apart from having none. With the help of her letters, we can brush aside the layers of legend and listen to Lady Arbella Stuart for ourselves.

II. The Most Renowned Stocke

I should have adjudged my selfe unworthy of life if I had degenerated from the most renowned stocke whearof it is my greatest honour to be a branch.

                    Lady Arbella Stuart to Queen Elizabeth (letter 6)

---

1. *Renaissance Self-Fashioning: From More to Shakespeare* (Chicago: Univ. of Chicago Press, 1980).

What we know about the childhood and adolescence that shaped Lady Arbella Stuart as a woman and writer is largely political. Of Stuart's extant letters, only two were written before she reached her mid-twenties, and she rarely (but tellingly) describes her youth in later letters. However, because Stuart was closely related to the reigning monarchs of England and Scotland, she was from birth an object of negotiation and subject of discussion; as a result, there exists for Stuart a body of evidence far larger than that for most Renaissance Englishwomen from which to discuss the political and, to a lesser degree, the personal context of her writing.

If Queen Elizabeth had had the choice, Stuart probably would not have been a branch of that "most renowned stocke" (letter 6). The queen was forty-two in 1575 when Stuart was born. Although Elizabeth continued to conduct marriage negotiations for another six years, she was approaching the age at which she no longer would be able physically to produce an heir; growing public apprehension that the house of Tudor might end had resulted in intense pressure for her to marry. The birth of another claimant would have reminded Elizabeth that many people thought she had not fulfilled her responsibility to the realm; at the same time, it provided a potential if distant threat, since disaffected subjects might rally behind any legitimate heir. The queen had no reason to be pleased about Stuart's birth.

Nor was she pleased that Stuart's parents had married without her approval. The union of Elizabeth Cavendish and Charles Stuart, Earl of Lennox, appears to have been arranged by their mothers, who brought the two together in late October 1574 at Rufford Abbey, on the edge of Sherwood Forest. Elizabeth was twenty and Charles nineteen; soon after they met, George Talbot, Earl of Shrewsbury, wrote the Earl of Leicester that the young couple "hath so tied themselves upon their own liking as cannot part" and that "the young man is so far in love that belike he is sick without her."[1] They were wedded well before 17 November, when the offenders were summoned to court.

---

1. 5 November 1574, quoted in Bradley, 1:27.

The women who projected this match, Stuart's grandmothers, were forceful personalities, both of whom had been imprisoned for their connections with the unapproved marriages of claimants and understood the potential consequences of their actions. Elizabeth Cavendish's mother was Elizabeth Talbot, Countess of Shrewsbury, known as Bess,[1] one of England's most well-to-do women. The daughter of a poor Derbyshire squire, she had risen through four marriages to become a countess with the independence to conduct business on a large scale. Eventually she would be reputed one of the finest English builders of the century.[2] Although she had supported Princess Elizabeth, Bess had been incarcerated early in Elizabeth's reign while her friend Catherine Grey's secret marriage to Edward Seymour was investigated. Bess was fully exonerated. (Ironically and appropriately, Catherine Grey had served as godmother to Bess's daughter Elizabeth.[3]) Bess's fourth marriage had been to the wealthy George Talbot, Earl of Shrewsbury, who soon after their wedding had been appointed guardian of the exiled Mary Stuart, Queen of Scotland.

Charles's mother was Lady Margaret Douglas, granddaughter of Henry VII, who as a young woman had been arrested twice for planning to marry without Henry VIII's consent. The husband arranged for her when she was in her late twenties had been Matthew Stuart, Earl of Lennox, a descendant of James II of Scotland. Their children, then, were claimants to the thrones of both England and Scotland, and it was the elder son Henry, Lord Darnley's marriage to Mary Queen of Scots for which his mother had been imprisoned. By the time of Charles's marriage, his brother Henry was dead, murdered in Scotland with the complicity, many people thought, of Mary Queen of Scots. Of Margaret

---

1. Although it seems overly familiar to address Elizabeth Talbot as Bess, the name usefully distinguishes her from her daughter and the queen, also Elizabeths. For more information on Bess, see discussions in Durant and in Emerson, 102–3.

2. Handover calls her "the greatest woman builder ever known" (77), and Mark Girouard describes her new Hardwick Hall as "the supreme triumph of Elizabethan architecture" (*Robert Smythson and the Elizabethan Country House* [New Haven: Yale Univ. Press, 1983], 146).

3. Handover, 24; Emerson, 44–45.

Stuart's eight children, Charles was the only one surviving.[1] Through the marriage of Charles and Elizabeth, the financially strapped Margaret Stuart allied her son with Talbot wealth, and the upwardly mobile Elizabeth Talbot allied her daughter with the royal house of Stuart.

Although the succession was a complex issue involving not only familial relationships, but also religious allegiances, wills, and decrees, Charles Stuart stood relatively high in the line of succession (see chart on page 106). If Queen Elizabeth did not bear a child, Henry VIII's direct line would end, and the most direct claimants would be his sisters' descendants. Of the English claimants derived from his younger sister, Mary Tudor, only one of the older branch's granddaughters, Bess's friend Catherine Grey, had been a birth mother, and Queen Elizabeth had had Catherine's marriage to Edward Seymour declared invalid and their two sons illegitimate. The other primary English claimants descended from Henry's older sister, Margaret Tudor, who had married twice. The granddaughter of the first marriage was Mary Stuart, Queen of Scotland, who was widely regarded as first in the succession, but as she was a Roman Catholic and under house arrest in England, her future was unclear. Her son James VI of Scotland was, to many, second in line and united the claims of Mary and Henry Stuart, but his Scottish birth was an impediment; because only those born in England could inherit English land, some people argued that no one foreign-born should inherit the kingdom. Margaret Stuart was the daughter of Margaret Tudor's second marriage and next in line, but she was unlikely to outlive Queen Elizabeth. Margaret Stuart's son Charles, then, could be considered third in the succession. His child would hold a lesser claim than the child's first cousin, James VI of Scotland, but these two would be the major claimants of their generation.

Queen Elizabeth's response to the Cavendish-Stuart marriage was mild by comparison to her reaction to earlier unapproved royal marriages. As soon as she learned of the alliance, she sent for Margaret

---

1. For more information on Margaret Stuart, see discussions in Handover; Durant; and Emerson, 73–74.

Stuart, Charles Stuart, and Elizabeth Cavendish, now Stuart. The brunt of the queen's anger fell on her Roman Catholic cousin Margaret Stuart. The critical issue was whether Margaret intended solely to effect an heir, which, although offensive to Elizabeth, entailed no near threat to her, or whether Margaret was conspiring with other Roman Catholics to remove Elizabeth from the throne. According to David N. Durant, Bess was the one person not commanded to the queen's presence, since Queen Elizabeth trusted that, while Bess might have seized the opportunity to make a royal marriage for her daughter, she would not have been disloyal;[1] it is a measure of the queen's confidence that the Shrewsburys remained guardians of Mary Queen of Scots. Margaret Stuart, by contrast, was sent to the Tower, but only for a short time. She was home by 10 November 1575, when she wrote to thank Mary Queen of Scots "for your good remembrance and bounty to our little daughter" Arbella, who was then probably a few weeks old.[2]

Little is known of Arbella Stuart's parents. Her father Charles is usually described as falling short of his brother Henry's good looks, although a portrait painted the year before his marriage suggests he was neither particularly striking nor unappealing.[3] He had spent some time apart from his family, while his father and brother were in Scotland and his mother imprisoned. When Charles was fifteen, Margaret wrote Lord Burghley that Charles was her greatest sorrow; unlike his brother, Charles had lacked a father's company and was "Somwayes unfurnished of Quallyties nedefull." Since Margaret was trying to advance her son by convincing Burghley to act as a surrogate father, she may have exaggerated her despair, but her comments are certainly unflattering.[4] From a modern perspective, the oft-repeated negative comparisons of Charles to his brother become wearisome; if Charles differed from his violent and sottish older brother, it is hard to imagine that he could have been

---

1. Durant, 2–4.

2. *CSP, Scottish*, 5:202.

3. The portrait is reproduced in Durant, illustrations.

4. 4 November 1571, SPD, Elizabeth, vol. 83, ff. 7–8.

anything but better. In any case, Charles had little time to influence his daughter. By April 1576, when Arbella was approximately six months old, he was dead of what was then called consumption.

Elizabeth Cavendish's letters offer the best extant evidence of Stuart's mother's personality. Nearly two years after Stuart's birth, Elizabeth wrote Bess about a misunderstanding: "I have not so evell deserved as your Ladyship hath made shewe, by your Lettrs to others whych maketh, me doutful that your Ladyship hath ben informed som great untruth of me…and I myght be so bould as to crave at your Ladyships hands that it wold pleas you to exteme [esteem] shuch falce bruts [rumors]…as lightly as you have don when others were in the like cas."[1] Elizabeth seems here to care about the relationship, and her language is deferential, but she feels her mother may have unfairly credited rumors and is "bould" enough to say so. A year later, Elizabeth urged Lord Burghley to fight for her daughter's Scottish inheritance: "I can assuer your Lordship therldome [the Earldom] of *Lennox* was graunted by acte of parlyment to my Lord my late husband and the heyres [heirs] of his body, so that they shuld offer great wronge in seekinge to take it from *arbela.*"[2] She appears straightforward in her suit, an affectionate mother concerned about her daughter's rights.

Those rights were at issue within months of Arbella Stuart's birth in the mid-autumn of 1575. When her father died, Stuart should have assumed his title and Scottish estates, which had been granted outright to him. James's regent, however, refused the title and seized the estates, and despite the battles fought through Lord Burghley and Queen Elizabeth, Stuart never won the dispute. On 3 May 1578 James revoked the earldom, ignoring his mother's command to the contrary from captivity,[3] and eventually made his favorite Esmé Stuart the Duke of Lennox. The portrait of Arbella Stuart at twenty-three months that hangs in Hardwick Hall, entitled in Latin *Arabella, Cometissa Levenox [Arbella,*

---

1. 25 July [1577?], Folger MS X.d.428 (51).
2. 15 August 1578, BL Lansdowne MS 27, ff. 9–10.
3. Handover, 54.

Countess of Lennox],[1] depicts a full-faced toddler in formal court dress. From her triple-stranded gold chain hangs a shield with a countess's coronet and the Lennox motto, *Pour parvenir, j'endure* [To achieve, I endure].[2]

Stuart soon was deprived of her English estates as well, a loss to which she repeatedly refers with resentment in her letters to the English court. After her father's death, Stuart and her mother apparently had continued to live with Margaret Stuart, Dowager Countess of Lennox. Margaret Stuart's financial situation was poor, since she had to pay the interest on a loan from Bess and on loans that had reverted to the crown. On 9 March 1578, when Arbella Stuart was two years old, her grandmother died, and the English Lennox estates were seized by the crown in payment of debts. The countess's funeral and monument in Westminster Abbey were suitable to her rank and thus costly, but the money came from her holdings. When James tried to claim the English Lennox lands, Queen Elizabeth told him nothing remained after debts and expenses. Margaret's jewels had been entrusted to her secretary Thomas Fowler to be held until Arbella was fourteen; Fowler left for Scotland, where he said he was robbed, but somehow the jewels made their way to the Scottish king. King James and Queen Elizabeth between them had appropriated Stuart's entire inheritance. Queen Elizabeth had allocated an annual pension of two hundred pounds for the care of the child, a small amount that satisfied only the queen, and Elizabeth Stuart was forced to return with Arbella to her mother's home.

Four years later, Stuart was orphaned. On 21 January 1582, her mother died after a short illness. George Talbot wrote that Bess

---

1. In this portrait's Latin title, Stuart's name is spelled *Arabella*, the Latinate form that coexisted with *Arbella* in the Renaissance; Stuart consistently signed herself *Arbella*.

2. Other contemporary portraits confirmed to be of Stuart include one painted when she was thirteen and a posthumous engraving issued by John Whittakers, Sr.; almost certainly of Stuart is the portrait now at Lancaster House, a copy of which may have belonged to Stuart's husband and which, according to librarian and archivist Kate Harris, has been in the Longleat inventory since 1718.   For reproductions and further discussion of the above, see Roy Strong, *Tudor and Jacobean Portraits* (London: Her Majesty's Stationery Office, 1969) 1:302–4; 2:601–3.

"neither dothe nor can thincke of any thinge but of Lamentinge and wepinge."[1] He made no mention of how Arbella responded. In her will, Elizabeth asked that Bess be made Stuart's guardian, which was granted, but the queen provided the guardian no additional money for the child's support. Bess had protested that the expenses associated with a royal heir were high; after all, "her better education her servauntes that are to loke to her, her masters that are to trayne her upp in all good Learninge and vertue will require no small charges."[2] From Queen Elizabeth's perspective, however, the child's guardian could afford to maintain Bess's "jewel" in style.[3]

Much has been speculated about Stuart's relationship with her aunt, the exiled Scottish queen, during the years that Stuart lived in that politically charged household. Some biographers have envisioned the child brightening Mary's lonely days, substituting for the son Mary had left in Scotland, while others have lamented the Scots queen's "malignant influence" on the young Arbella.[4] Little, however, is known of their association. Mary of Scots wrote affectionately of Arbella, supported her niece's claims, and in her will left Arbella her French Book of Hours, the unfilled pages of which she had covered with poetry and the names of friends.[5] (Stuart later sent the book to her husband on the continent.) Whatever their relationship may have been, personal contact between the guarded Scots queen and a primary English-born heir to the throne likely was well supervised.

Mary's captivity, however, affected Stuart's life in other indirect ways. Mary hated and fought her confinement; servants had to exercise extreme vigilance and be monitored; visitors were rarely permitted, and strangers were suspect. The Shrewsburys were loyal to Queen Elizabeth,

1. George Talbot to William Cecil, 21 January 1582, BL Lansdowne MS 34, ff. 2–3.

2. Elizabeth Talbot to William Cecil, 28 January 1582, BL Lansdowne MS 34, ff. 4–5.

3. Bess's term for her granddaughter; see, for example, her letters to William Cecil (28 January 1582, BL Lansdowne MS 34, ff. 4–5) and to Francis Walsingham (6 May 1582, SPD, Elizabeth, vol. 153, f. 84).

4. Antonia Fraser, for example, describes Mary's "pleasant quasi–maternal relationship" with Stuart (463–64); the quoted phrase is Durant's, 38.

5. Durant, 40.

but could not be harsh with the woman who might one day be their queen, and they argued often over her and the expenses they were forced to bear for her, since Queen Elizabeth allotted only about fifty pounds per week to support all of Mary's entourage and guards.[1] Eventually their marriage deteriorated beyond repair. Not long after Stuart's mother died, the Shrewsburys separated, with George taking the Queen of Scots to Sheffield Castle and Bess moving to Chatsworth.[2] Over the next few years, Stuart lived sometimes with Bess and sometimes with her godparents Mary and Gilbert Talbot (Bess's daughter and George's son, who had married in 1567), with whom Stuart later corresponded regularly. On occasion, Stuart appears to have been a pawn in her grandparents' dispute; in 1584 Bess complained that George had sent Arbella to her even though Bess wanted her to remain with Mary Talbot, and George complained to the court about Stuart's poor upbringing under Bess's supervision and wanted his son relieved of the charge of caring for her.[3]

Not surprisingly, Stuart's letters and actions suggest that she was influenced by Mary of Scots's trial and execution. In 1584, the Scottish queen was removed from the Earl of Shrewsbury's custody; two and a half years later, as Earl Marshal, he had to supervise the beheading of the woman who had been his charge for sixteen years. Stuart was eleven when her aunt was executed for conspiring with Catholics to replace Queen Elizabeth on the throne. Although Stuart does not specifically mention Mary in her extant letters, she occasionally alludes to events associated with the Queen of Scots, and her actions after her marriage suggest she saw death as the outcome of confinement in the north, where one could not talk to the monarch or effectively seek redress. Her aunt's execution removed the person first in the line of succession and before Mary died she had disinherited James (which mattered to no

1. Handover, 60.

2. Durant, 29–30.

3. Durant, 33–35; later copy of a letter from George Talbot to William Cecil, April 1584, Alnwick Castle MS 93A/35, Part 1.

one), but Stuart may have received a warning from her aunt's choices: during the months after James had acceded to the English throne, when others conspired to crown Arbella instead, she reassured Mary Talbot that she would not participate in treasonous activities: "when any great matter comes in question rest secure I beseech you, that I am not interessed in it as an Actour" (letter 35).

Until her late twenties, Stuart was an actor in little of the political activity swirling around her. As a claimant who could bring the dowry of a crown, she was a commodity, one of high worth on the matrimonial market, but whose value fluctuated with English and European politics and the rise and fall of Elizabeth's favor. From the time she was a child, Stuart was expected to marry advantageously, but she had nothing to say about when or whom she would marry. Before Stuart was eight, Bess promised or even betrothed Stuart to the four-year-old son of Robert Dudley, Earl of Leicester.[1] The boy died soon afterwards, the queen learned of the attempt, and Bess must have been warned, for her letters reflect her clear understanding that Stuart's consort would be chosen by the queen.[2]

As a marriageable property, Stuart was useful to Queen Elizabeth and her advisers. Had there not been an English heir with a claim nearly equal to his, James might have been more insistent in his demands. As it was, Elizabeth could pressure James by favoring Arbella, and she could use Arbella as a bargaining chip in foreign policy, tantalizing continental nobility with the prospect of marriage accompanied by the declaration of succession. In 1581, the queen weighed the possibility of betrothing Arbella to Esmé Stuart, to whom James had awarded Arbella's estates and the title Duke of Lennox, but Lennox was anti-English. In 1585, the queen discussed James of Scotland, but that choice would have made James and Arbella so surely the heirs that it might have invited invasion from the north. In the summer of 1587,

---

1. Handover, 62–65.

2. See, for example, her 9 January 1603 letter to Queen Elizabeth, Cecil Papers 135, f. 112; Hatfield House Library (hereafter cited as Cecil Papers).

the queen considered Rainutio Farnese, the son of the Duke of Parma, and summoned Stuart to court about a projected marriage that was to figure in Stuart's life for five years.[1]

By 1587, Elizabeth and her advisers knew that the Spanish Armada was being built, and they expected a Catholic offensive in retaliation for the execution of Mary Queen of Scots, who had been the Catholic hope for the conversion of England. Stuart's engagement to the Duke of Parma's son might have a dual benefit. Since Farnese was Catholic, an engagement might persuade Catholics that there was a possibility of converting England peaceably; and if Philip of Spain insisted on attacking England, he might lose the crucial support of the Duke of Parma, his lieutenant in the Spanish Netherlands. Bringing the eleven-year-old Stuart to court and showing her favor would underscore the likelihood of her accession and thus promote English diplomatic efforts.

The court was at Theobalds, Burghley's estate, when Stuart joined it in the summer of 1587. She spoke with Queen Elizabeth, dined in her presence, and was flattered and given precedence by everyone in attendance. Stuart's uncle Charles Cavendish wrote Bess that Lord Burghley had spoken to Sir Walter Ralegh "greatly in hir commendacion, as that she had the French th Italian[,] play of instruments, dansed wrough [wrought, sewed] and writt very fayre, wished she weare 15 years old." When Burghley whispered something to Ralegh, Ralegh responded "it would be a happy thing." According to Charles, Burghley "made exceeding much of hir."[2] The queen told the French ambassador's wife, Madame de Chateauneuf, that Stuart would "one day be even as I am."[3]

Attendance at court, however, was not always so happy. A year later, Stuart again was summoned to Elizabeth. It was Armada summer, and the atmosphere was tense. According to Venetian secretary Giovanni Carlo Scaramelli, writing fifteen years later to denigrate Stuart, she was dismissed from court for presumption: on the way to chapel she had

1. Durant, 41.

2. Undated, HMC Third Report, *Manuscripts of the Duke of Devonshire*, 42.

3. Bradley, 1:64–65; Handover, 77.

taken precedence as a princess, saying "by God's will that was the very lowest place that could possibly be given her."[1] For whatever reason, Stuart was disgraced, and the Earl of Essex, Queen Elizabeth's favorite, was kind. Stuart wrote later, "How dare others visit me in distresse when the Earle of Essex then in highest favour durst scarse steale a salutation in the Privy chamber wheare howsoever it pleased hir Majesty I should be disgraced in the Presence <at Greenwich>,[2] and discouraged in the Lobby at Whithall it pleased hir Majesty to give me leave to gaze on hir and by triall pronounce me an Eglett of hir owne kinde" (letter 16). Queen Elizabeth did not enjoy being reminded of the "eaglet" who could replace her, however, and the Earl of Essex's defenses of Stuart bred rumors of an affair between them (letter 16).[3] Perhaps as a result of Elizabeth's annoyance, perhaps as a matter of state policy, Stuart was returned to Derbyshire.

In 1591, the sixteen-year-old Stuart was brought once more to court about the Farnese marriage, which had involved countless coded letters entrusted to secret agents slipping across the continent. On this visit, Stuart was accompanied by her grandmother and an entourage, as though on a miniature state progress. She was in and out of court circles for eight months, over the Christmas holidays at Whitehall and through the spring and summer of 1592. She was favored by Queen Elizabeth and received the "faire words" of courtiers positioning themselves for the future (letter 16). But when the Duke of Parma died, negotiations to marry Stuart to his son ceased.

Others besides the queen were interested in Stuart as a marriageable property. English and foreign Catholics debated kidnapping and forcibly marrying the Protestant Stuart to Catholic nobles who would invade England at the head of continental armies. One such plot was uncovered not long after Stuart left court in 1592. A captured priest confessed that he had been party to a scheme to abduct Stuart to

---

1. *CSP, Venetian,* 9:541.

2. For an explanation of the editorial symbols, such as angle brackets, employed in Stuart's letters, see Textual Introduction, page 110.

3. John Harington suggests that Essex's words were misinterpreted (*A Tract on the Succession to the Crown [A.D. 1602],* ed. Clements R. Markham [London: J. B. Nichols, 1880], 42).

Brussels. Stuart was with her grandmother at the old Hardwick Hall when Burghley's warning letter came, but Bess reassured him that she had the matter in hand and described the young woman's restricted life: "I have litle resort to me, my house is furnished with sufficient company, Arbell walks not late, at such tyme as she shall take the ayre, yt shalbe nere the howse, and well attended on; she goeth not to any bodyes howse atall, I se hyr almost every howre in the day, she lyeth in my bed chamber." Bess added that, with this warning, she would be even "more precise then I have bene."[1]

Marital prospects included much of the eligible European nobility. King James suggested candidates loyal to him. Henry IV of France was a possibility, but would not negotiate unless Stuart were first declared heir.[2] Rumors abounded: Duke Mathias, the Earl of Gowrie, the Earl of Northumberland, Sir Robert Cecil, the Prince of Condé, the Duke of Nevers. In 1596 the Pope even offered to release Cardinal Farnese, Rainutio's brother, from his religious vows in order that he might marry Stuart.[3] By the time Stuart was in her twenties, the queen had established with Stuart a pattern much like the one she had established for herself when she was younger. A potential alliance was a wonderful diplomatic tool, but if a match were ever concluded, the game would be over. And thus no match was ever concluded. Bess reminded the queen that it was time Stuart was bestowed in marriage and was told only that her majesty "would be carefull of her."[4]

Beyond politics, little is known of Stuart's early years. She was frequently moved from house to house, both because the Shrewsburys' charge to care for Mary of Scots necessitated regular transitions among the Shrewsbury properties and, later, because Stuart's guardian was a busy woman who, while she oversaw Stuart's upbringing and education, had other interests as well. Stuart often appears to have been in the care of her godparents Mary and Gilbert Talbot. Sometimes Stuart appears

1. 21 September 1592, BL Lansdowne MS 71, f. 3.

2. Maximilian de Bethune, *Memoirs of Maximilian de Bethune, Duke of Sully,* trans. Charlotte Lennox (London: A. Millar, 1756), 1:463.

3. Durant, 85; Cardinal Dossat to Henry IV, 26 November 1601, BL Stowe MS 155, ff. 18–19.

4. Dorothy Stafford to Elizabeth Talbot, 13 January 1601, Folger MS X.d.428 (120).

to have been staying at one of the manors solely under the supervision of trusted retainers. When Stuart was thirteen, Nicholas Kynnersley, the steward of Wingfield Manor, wrote Bess that Stuart was merry and eating well, but had not been to school for six days, so he would be pleased if her grandmother would come to take charge.[1]

Wherever and with whomever she stayed, Stuart was the noble claimant in a wealthy household. From childhood, she had a servant of her own, and at some later point a small entourage. As a potential queen, she may have been treated with more deference than discipline by the Shrewsbury retainers, even by significant gentleman retainers such as Kynnersley, the steward who wanted her grandmother to correct Stuart's behavior. Stuart also found companionship among her attendants. (When Stuart was at James's court, one of Mary Talbot's retainers thought that Stuart permitted "much less awe" than was appropriate;[2] but some of Stuart's attendants were devoted to her, and several risked their lives on her behalf.) George Talbot, after he was estranged from Bess, said that Stuart had been as pampered by the family as by the servants until she was thirteen: she had been given the "upper hand" of Bess and Mary Talbot until her disgrace at court in 1588, after which she was less indulged, on the advice of friends.[3]

Although Stuart's letters reveal a consciousness of her rank, her youthful arrogance may have been overemphasized by those who, like George Talbot, were anxious to demonstrate her or her family's failings. Pride is absent from the two extant letters that were written before Stuart was in her mid-twenties. At age twelve, she sent her grandmother her hair trimmings and a pot of jelly and passed on recent family news (letter 1). A few months later, she offered in French her farewell from court to Lord Burghley (letter 2). In both cases, she was living with Mary and Gilbert Talbot, and the letters, although small evidence, suggest a bright, well-educated young woman mindful of appropriate forms and phrases. Sir John Harington described her as having been commended for "hir virtuous disposition, sometyme of hir choice education, hir rare skill in lan-

---

1. 5 November 1588, Folger MS X.d.428 (44).
2. Thomas Cooke to Mary Talbot, 12 February 1604, Lambeth Palace Library MS 3203, f. 182.
3. Quoted in Handover, 88.

guages, hir good judgement and sight in musick, and a mynde to all these, free frome pryde, vanitye and affectation," all of which he had been an eyewitness to, he said, at Hardwick, Chelsea, and Wingfield.[1]

A courtier like Harington might be expected to praise a female claimant in such fulsome and conventional terms, but Harington's admiration of Stuart's fine education and "rare skill in languages" is supported by evidence from a variety of sources. Stuart's letters demonstrate that she was intelligent, verbal, and well-read. Unlike those for whom study was a necessary evil, Stuart became one of the most learned women at James's court, where she maintained regular hours for scholarship (letter 28). When she was six, she was described by her proud grandmother as "of very greate towardnes" to learn;[2] and her grandmother's judgment was verified by Sir Walter Mildmay, Chancellor of the Exchequer, who visited Sheffield in connection with Mary Queen of Scots and was impressed enough to pass on with his good words a letter Stuart had written to Queen Elizabeth.[3] Stuart also was lucky in her education. Even as an aristocratic woman, she would not necessarily have received a thorough classical education; but Bess, although she lacked that background herself, assured her granddaughter an education on the model of Queen Elizabeth's and provided her with excellent tutors.

Extant evidence suggests that Stuart was close to if not fully multilingual, which would mean she had learned at least one other language before age five. As an adult, she wrote in French and Latin, read literature in both, and was comfortable enough in Latin to dictate in it to a secretary. Lord Burghley commented on her Italian during her visit to court in 1587, and Sir John Harington, who translated Ariosto's *Orlando Furioso* from Italian to English, said when Stuart was thirteen that "shee did read French out of Italian, and English out of both, much better then I could."[4] Stuart was said to understand Spanish and to read Greek and Hebrew, the latter a rare accomplishment for either sex. Two

---

1. Harington, 45.

2. Elizabeth Talbot to Francis Walsingham, 6 May 1582, SPD, Elizabeth, vol. 153, f. 84.

3. *CSP, Scottish*, 6:505; Stuart's letter has been lost.

4. Harington, 45.

volumes of Latin poetry were dedicated to her, and Oxford scholar Richard Brett dedicated a Hebrew and Latin text to her as well.[1] A treatise entitled *Glossopaideia: That Is, The Ready Way of Teaching and Learning the Languages* was dedicated to "the most noble Ladie A," also called "Your H[ighnes]s"; the dedication likely refers to Stuart and compliments her well-known skill in language.[2] A cleric later inscribed Stuart's Hebrew/Syriac/Greek Bible with a note that Stuart had embroidered its cover because of her "singular knowledge in both the Hebrew and greek tongue and for her love thereunto."[3]

Stuart sought moral guidance and pleasure from reading; the authors of books were, she said, her "counsellers and comforters" (letter 15). Her curriculum is unknown, but her letters reveal a strong background in classical literature: she read Virgil, whose *Aeneid* she could quote in Latin while writing a letter in haste (letter 16); Lucan, whose *Pharsalia* she cites in the closing of another letter (letter 13); and Plutarch, whom she describes as her "disgraced frend" (letter 12). Her writing contains literary allusions and quotations as well as references to poetical conceits, allegories, the theater, and themes heroic and romantic. She once asked John Harington to read the tale of Drusilla from the *Orlando Furioso* and, according to Harington, "censured it with a gravitye beyond her years."[4] (Even allowing for a courtier's excessive praise, Harington's comment suggests Stuart may have given a thoughtful response.) She alludes to classical philosophers,

---

1. David Hume, *Davidis Humii Theagrii Lusus Poetici* (London: Richard Field, 1605); John Owen, *Epigrammatum Joannis Owen, Cambro-Britanni, Ad Excellentissimam et doctissimam Herionam, D. Arbellam Stuart, Liber Singularis* (London: Humphrey Lownes, 1607). Richard Brett's volume is described in William Macray, "The Manuscripts of Rev. William Dunn Macray, M.A., F.S.A., Ducklington Rectory, Witney," HMC *Thirteenth Report, Appendix, Part IV,* 507.

2. Hobbes MS B. 1, at Chatsworth House. I am grateful to Peter Beal for calling this treatise to my attention.

3. Durham Chapter Library B.III.31, inside cover. I am indebted to Roger C. Norris, deputy chapter librarian of Durham Chapter Library, for alerting me to this volume and to Jill Ivy for a discussion of the needlework cover. In the late seventeenth century, Nathaniel Johnson said Stuart had used this Bible at church (Chatsworth MS "Lives of the Earls of Shrewsbury" [1693], 7:23).

4. Harington, 45. In the tale, Drusilla is kidnapped and her husband murdered. First, overwhelmed with sorrow, she attempts suicide; then she seeks revenge. She feigns love to her captor in order to poison him and herself at their wedding and rejoin her husband in paradise.

and her prose resonates with biblical allusions, especially to the Psalms.

Stuart was not grim and passionless, however, as she was sometimes described by court contemporaries, in the non-booklover's stereotypical condemnation of the booklover.[1] She was often merry,[2] and her relaxed letters to her aunt Mary and uncle Gilbert Talbot are warm and teasing. She is said to have played the lute and the viol, among other instruments, with some expertise. In 1603, when her activities had been highly restricted, she wrote Lords Cecil and Stanhope that she wanted the "Schollers, Musick, hunting, hauking," and "variety of any lawfull disport" that she had had before (letter 8). Like most Renaissance women, she practiced dancing and sewing; in 1587 Burghley praised her ability in both, and in her letters Stuart repeatedly alludes to needlework.

The strongest sense of Stuart's daily life emerges from her years with her grandmother at Hardwick Hall from the late 1590s until 1603, when Stuart was no longer a girl, but a woman in her mid-twenties. In 1597, they moved into the mansion Bess had built next to the old Hardwick Hall. The new Hardwick Hall was a residence many would have envied—a three-story stone rectangle with three towers clustered around the short sides, each of the towers topped with an imposing "ES," for Elizabeth of Shrewsbury. The external walls held as many glass windows as could be accommodated with structural safety, and the interior and exterior masonry was impressive. Bess spared no expense to equip the building; the Hardwick embroideries are still considered among the best in all of Europe. In the Withdrawing Chamber hung a series of embroidered cloths depicting classical heroines and their virtues, including Penelope with Perseverance and Patience, and Lucretia with Chastity and Liberality. In the Best Bed Chamber hung panels depicting other allegorized ideal women, Faith with Mahomet at her feet and Temperance in victory. Portraits of the Tudor monarchs lined

---

1. Even Harington, who as a rule respected learning, scorned the learned lady as removed from life; in discussing the succession, he wrote, "wee ar not like to be governed by a ladye shut up in a chamber" (Harington, 51).

2. Nicholas Kynnersley's term in his letter to Elizabeth Talbot, 5 November 1588, Folger MS X.d.428 (44).

the High Great Chamber, a compliment should the queen deign to visit and perhaps a reminder that the next portrait might be of a Stuart woman. In the Gallery were alabaster statues of Justice and Mercy.[1] The atmosphere at Hardwick was that of a small court, with dozens of servants, and the continual small ceremonials associated with serving food and wine. Occasional diversions included seeing the touring players, like the Queen's players, Lord Thomas Howard's players, and the troupes of Lord Ogle and the Earls of Huntingdon and Pembroke. There were visits by musicians who were servants in other households or employed by local townships; there were household concerts.[2]

Stuart's 1603 letters suggest, however, that she saw herself as buried in the northern countryside, a virtual state prisoner. She despaired of being allowed by her grandmother to present her service to the queen at court (letter 6). The Hardwick Hall inventory of 1601 reveals that the twenty-five-year-old Stuart's bed, covered with "a Canopy of darnix blue and white with gilt knobs and blue and white fringe" was in her grandmother's bedroom with her grandmother's scarlet and silver bedstead and personal items.[3] Bess, now in her mid-seventies, failed to recognize that her granddaughter was grown, and antagonism between them developed and intensified. According to James Starkey, the chaplain at Hardwick Hall, Stuart said in 1602 that she could no longer endure being treated like a child and having her nose tweaked for punishment; he added, "oftentymes being at her booke she would breake forth into teares."[4]

By late 1602, Stuart was twenty-seven. She had not visited court in a decade, and Queen Elizabeth gave no indication that Stuart would be matched in marriage. Matrimony was Stuart's responsibility, not only because marriage in those years was Everywoman's role, but because

---

1. Mark Girouard, *Hardwick Hall, Derbyshire: A History and a Guide* (London: The National Trust, 1976), passim.

2. Durant, 82–83.

3. Mark Girouard, *A Country House Companion* (New Haven and London: Yale Univ. Press, 1987), 32–33.

4. From his January 1603 confession after Stuart's attempted marriage, Cecil Papers 135, f. 175/2.

Stuart would disappoint her family's hopes if she did not marry well. She had been denied her inheritance and awarded by the queen an inadequate pension that made her financially dependent on her relations. Unmarried, she was a liability when, were she but suitably wed, she could advance them. And marriage offered escape; she would no longer be forced to remain at Hardwick Hall. Thus Stuart's needs were directly opposed to those of Queen Elizabeth, for whom Stuart was valuable while she was unmarried and marketable. Stuart was female in an era when women were to be submissive—she regularly passed the praiseworthy Penelope figured with the virtue of Patience—but she also had been raised with a sense of her due. However her grandmother might say that Stuart must await the decision of the crown, Bess's behavior indicated otherwise, as did the actions of Stuart's paternal grandmother Margaret Stuart and her aunt Mary Queen of Scots, who were hardly acquiescent. Stuart's mother had taken a risk when she was much younger than twenty-seven. Stuart could not initiate foreign matrimonial negotiations; such a step would interfere with the queen's foreign policy and hazard execution. But an English marriage similar to her parents' was another question.

III. Till I Be My Owne Woman

> I thinck the time best spent in tiring you with the idle conceits of my travelling minde till it make you ashamed to see into what a scribling melancholy…you have brought me and leave me, if you leave me till I be my owne woman and then your trouble and mine too will cease.
>   Lady Arbella Stuart to Sir Henry Brounker (letter 16)

On Christmas Day in 1602, Stuart sent John Dodderidge, one of her grandmother's trusted retainers, to the Earl of Hertford with a message: if Hertford were still interested in a marriage between her and his older grandson Edward—she had been told of such a proposal—he should send the young man to her in disguise, that they first might "have had sight, the one of the other, to see how they could like." Dodderidge had been reluctant to make the journey without Bess's approval, but told that he represented Stuart and her uncles Henry and William Cavendish (the rising generation of employers), he rode away to Tottenham on a horse loaned by Henry Cavendish, who had come to Hardwick Hall for the Christmas holidays and apparently approved of Stuart's decision.[1]

The young man Stuart hoped to meet, Edward Seymour, was still considered a claimant in spite of Queen Elizabeth's having decreed that the marriage between his grandmother, Lady Catherine Grey, and his grandfather, the Earl of Hertford, had not occurred. In fact, the widely read *Conference About the Next Succession to the Crown of England* (1594), which had been intended to enhance the Roman Catholic cause and thus argued the Spanish Infanta's case, had noted that Burghley favored Stuart despite her sex, but called Hertford's son the popular candidate, which had revived interest in the Seymours as claimants.[2] Such a marriage, uniting two claims to the throne, doubtless would have been forbidden, which is why Stuart cautioned secrecy and disguise (letter 3).

Examined from Stuart's perspective, her decision seems more thoughtful than it might first appear. Given her background, Stuart could not have married beneath her class and rank; her sense of position and family obligation was too strong. The Seymours were among the few acceptable noble families. Beyond that, Stuart had reason to believe that Hertford would welcome the overture. She had been told some three or four years earlier that Hertford had caused his solicitor to speak to David Owen Tudor, whose son Richard was now Stuart's page, about such a match. Bess had rejected the idea unless it received the queen's approval, but Hertford might be willing to entertain now a proposal he had initiated not long before. Moreover, the Seymour family history was encouraging. The Earl of Hertford in his youth had married Lady

---

1. Dodderidge's confession, 2 January 1603, Cecil Papers 135, ff. 110–11.

2. The book was published in Antwerp under the pseudonym of R. Doleman. Although the author endorses the Infanta Isabel of Spain, who was descended from John of Gaunt, Duke of Lancaster (1340–99), few Protestants supported her candidacy. Interestingly, he objects to Stuart in part on the grounds "that she is a woman, who ought not to be preferred, before so many men as at this tyme do or may stand for the crowne: and that it were much to have three women to reigne in Ingland one after the other, wheras in the space of above a thousaid [*sic*] yeares before them, there hath not reigned so many of that sexe." The writer also suggests that Stuart would need to combine her title with another claimant's in order to have enough supporters to take the throne (128, 249). See Handover, 107, and Durant, 75–77.

Catherine Grey with only his sister Jane as a witness and without even ascertaining the name of the minister; Stuart's grandmother Bess had been imprisoned in connection with that episode. Hertford's son, Lord Beauchamp, had married without approval and been confined for three years to his father's house. Only two years earlier, Hertford had married for a third time, still without banns or witnesses.[1] And Stuart could believe that royal displeasure would be short-lived. Her parents had been allowed to live together, and the grandmother who had been blamed for the alliance had been free within a year. Queen Elizabeth was sixty-nine years old, so she might be tired enough or compassionate enough to let the offense pass; if she did not, her displeasure could last only as long as she lived, and it was frequently rumored that Elizabeth was unwell. Stuart probably did not know that James's succession already had been arranged with Robert Cecil, but should the queen succumb to one of her murmured illnesses, the likely candidates were James of Scotland, who had professed his loving kinship (see Appendix B, letters 1 and 2), or Stuart herself.

The obvious and unanswerable question is to what degree Stuart was positioning herself to take the crown when Queen Elizabeth died. Nothing in Stuart's writing demonstrates that she thought of this marriage as a step toward displacing the queen during her lifetime. Nothing in Stuart's writing argues that her primary goal was the throne. Her consistently stated objectives were freedom from her grandmother's domination, the right to live where she chose, and the opportunity to marry. On the other hand, gathered nearby were several of Stuart's supporters from neighboring counties, including John Hacker, to whom Stuart appealed for assistance in January (letter 5), and her uncle Henry Cavendish's friend Henry Stapleton, a Catholic whom the court already suspected of intrigue.[2] Although Stuart's exile from court meant that she

---

1. Handover, 111–12.

2. In a letter to Cecil, Henry Brounker listed the names of six men he had recognized from several counties (2 January 1603, Cecil Papers 91, f. 22). During these early months of 1603, William Cavendish also had one hundred muskets and one hundred pike-heads sent to Chatsworth (Lawrence Stone, *The Crisis of the Aristocracy, 1558–1641* [Oxford: Clarendon Press, 1965], 221). Although Stuart denied that her uncles were involved, it is likely that Henry Cavendish, at least, supported her decision.

had had little opportunity to build a large personal following, her letters reveal her awareness of herself as a claimant around whom others might rally, and she was proposing a match that would enhance her claim at a time when Elizabeth's health reportedly was weakening. Stuart's initial and conscious motivation may have been exactly what she wrote, that she wanted the rights of an adult woman and took action to obtain them. If she had greater designs, she was smart enough to convince the court otherwise.[1] It is also possible that she had ambitions that she could only partially acknowledge even to herself.

If Stuart's choice of Edward Seymour is understandable in this context, her choice of messenger is not, because it violated class decorum. Three weeks before Christmas, when Stuart first had talked with Dodderidge, she had asked him to speak with Hertford's lawyer, who then would have dealt with Hertford as a trusted friend. Had that plan been followed, or had Stuart's uncle Henry Cavendish as a nobleman and a family member privately met with Hertford, the outcome might have differed; at least the matter could have remained quiet. But Stuart asked Dodderidge, a retainer, to speak secretly with the Earl of Hertford himself, and the earl was so alarmed by a servant unaccountably demanding personal access to him that he refused to hear Dodderidge without witnesses.[2] Once Dodderidge had explained his mission publicly, Hertford had to reject the offer and exonerate himself. Stuart clearly believed that Hertford betrayed her by first suggesting and then revealing the proposal, but she may have been misinformed. The earlier proposal well could have been broached by Lord Beauchamp without his father's knowledge.

In any case, Hertford turned Stuart's message and messenger over to Sir Robert Cecil, Elizabeth's chief counselor, and within a few days, Sir Henry Brounker arrived at Hardwick Hall to investigate. Caught out

---

1. In her recent book chapter on Stuart, Barbara Kiefer Lewalski takes this position. She argues that in sending Dodderidge to Hertford, Stuart was attempting to claim the succession and that Stuart in her subsequent letters effectively disguised her intentions ("Writing Resistance in Letters: Arbella Stuart and the Rhetoric of Disguise and Defiance," in her *Writing Women in Jacobean England* [Cambridge: Harvard Univ. Press, 1993], 71–77).

2. Report of the Earl of Hertford's man, [January 1603], Cecil Papers 135, ff. 179–80.

and aware of the potential danger of Elizabeth's wrath, Stuart first denied and evaded and even blamed Dodderidge;[1] then, seemingly chastened, she apologized and acknowledged her grandmother's guardianship, saying, perhaps in echo of Bess's outraged words, that she hoped the queen would "signify your Majesties most gratious remission to me by your Highnesse letter to my Lady my Grandmother whose discomfort I shall be till then" (letter 4).

What had begun not as a passionate adventure, but as a struggle for independence (and perhaps a step toward the throne) had failed, with the result that Bess redoubled restrictions on the granddaughter who could not be trusted. Stuart's correspondence was intercepted. Even letters sent by Stuart's servants from villages beyond Hardwick Hall were stopped. Letters written by Mrs. Bridget Sherland, Stuart's gentlewoman, asking Stuart's friends to deliver messages or letters or to visit her were confiscated, and Bess also dictated feigned answers to stall Stuart and to encourage further correspondence with the supposed recipients. The seized letters and their false answers were copied by Bess's steward and forwarded to Cecil at court.[2]

Brounker and Cecil thought it best if Queen Elizabeth were told that Stuart had been deceived about Hertford's intentions by someone hoping to entrap and then blackmail him,[3] but not even after the queen's pardon was received did Bess relax her vigilance. Cecil and Stanhope insisted that the world must not see Stuart as a prisoner, but Bess argued that she could not both guarantee Stuart's safety and let her walk or ride, because Stuart and her friends were wary now; Bess would be unable to oversee their actions or intercept letters.[4] Stuart was denied hunting, music, scholars, visitors. Her conversations were fully monitored, her privacy nonexistent. Stuart swore that her sole motive had

---

1. Henry Brounker to Queen Elizabeth, [January 1603], Cecil Papers 135, ff. 113–14.

2. They comprise Cecil Papers 135, ff. 124–26.

3. Henry Brounker to Robert Cecil, 10 January 1603, Cecil Papers 135, f. 118; Robert Cecil and John Stanhope to Elizabeth Talbot, [January 1603], Cecil Papers 135, f. 128.

4. John Stanhope and Robert Cecil to Elizabeth Talbot, [January 1603], Cecil Papers 135, f. 128; the same to Elizabeth Talbot, 21 February 1603, Cecil Papers 135, f. 151; Elizabeth Talbot to Queen Elizabeth, 29 January 1603, Cecil Papers 135, f. 127.

been to end her northern exile at Hardwick (letter 6), and Bess also requested that her granddaughter be removed from her custody—even be given in marriage to someone of a far lesser rank if that would please the court[1]—but without effect. Cecil recommended Stuart remain with Bess. Educated for command, Stuart seemed powerless, politically and personally enclosed: chaste, with no opportunity to be otherwise; silenced, forbidden unmonitored conversations or letters; and obedient, under the very real threat of the Tower or death.

Stuart's response was to try to turn restriction to advantage. If her words were to be scrutinized, she would compose something to goad her scrutinizer into action. Under enormous pressure, Stuart risked lying to Queen Elizabeth and her counselors and toyed with the royal power by creating a fictional lover in order to force court attention to her plight. It was a desperate fiction indeed, given the potential consequences, but one perhaps natural to a committed reader.[2] The strategy must have seemed straightforward: if one potential lover had stirred up Elizabeth and her advisors, so would another. Stuart would create a lover whose discovery either would result in a command to appear at court, where she could talk to the queen directly, or would bring another emissary on a fast horse. An emissary would sympathize, as Brounker had pretended to, and carry Stuart's plea to Elizabeth without intermediaries like Bess or counselors Robert Cecil and John Stanhope. The queen would hear Stuart's words, understand her small, but necessary deception, and allow her to live elsewhere, perhaps even at court.

In a letter addressed to Bess and purporting to set down fully and finally the truth about what had occurred, Stuart asserts that she and her "dearest" had agreed that she should send someone of low degree in marriage negotiations to the Earl of Hertford so that the proposal could not be taken seriously and would be reported to the crown; in that way Queen Elizabeth would learn about the devious plots being laid for people who, like Stuart, were seen as having been unjustly exiled from

---

1. Elizabeth Talbot to Queen Elizabeth, 29 January 1603, Cecil Papers 135, f. 127.

2. Feigning was a common literary device, as well as the basis of literature. In the Drusilla episode of *Orlando Furioso* that Harington read to Stuart (*Tract*, 45), Drusilla feigned submission and love in order to achieve justice by poisoning her captor.

the court—jabs at Hertford and the queen and her counselors. The plan, Stuart says, worked beautifully. She describes her beloved warmly, how he has always put her needs and honor before his own, how high his reputation is with Elizabeth and the court, how many virtues he possesses, how he trusts her with his every thought, and how she came to accept his love, which she will never reject or regret and for which she is ready to abandon everything and everyone, except the queen (letter 7). Stuart could hope that this letter, too, would be read at court, perhaps even by Elizabeth. Her revisions suggest that the audience she kept in mind as she wrote was, at least in part, the queen; Stuart occasionally had to alter a phrase like "your Majesties knowledge" to "your Ladyships knowledge" as she recollected whom she was supposed to be addressing.

The letter was, as expected, forwarded to Cecil, and a subsequent letter in which Stuart feigned abashment at the discovery was converted into an opportunity to hint further about her lover: conscious device masquerades as maidenly embarrassment. But Stuart promised to be honest and implored Cecil and Stanhope to send down Henry Brounker, who would learn and faithfully deliver to Elizabeth the names of everyone involved, including the name of Stuart's lover, which she could not entrust to paper (letter 8). She wrote Edward Talbot, a half-uncle she hardly knew but whose difficulties with the crown might make him sympathetic to her cause, asking him to take a message to the queen (letter 9). Surprisingly, Talbot received his letter, but since he had been involved with the Earl of Essex's thwarted rebellion, he quickly sought exoneration by forwarding Stuart's letter to Cecil himself.[1]

While Stuart awaited response to the letters forwarded to court, she either deliberately began to starve herself, or became too ill to eat and drink. She then discovered that her illness gave her some control over her situation. By the second week of February, Stuart was reported to have had pains in her side and been "inforced to take much phisick." Bess saw Stuart's further actions as entirely conscious; on 21 February, Bess wrote Cecil that Stuart had been so "wilfully bent" that she had

---

1. Edward Talbot to Robert Cecil, 23 February 1603, Cecil Papers 91, f. 149.

taken a vow not to eat or drink at Hardwick Hall. In order to save Stuart's life, Bess wrote, she had capitulated and allowed Stuart to move to Owlcotes, another Shrewsbury home two miles away,[1] where she remained until the end of the month, when Brounker was again dispatched to Hardwick Hall. It was a small victory for Stuart, but a victory nonetheless. Fasting, like her fictional lover, forced others to react. Both stratagems argue Stuart's consciousness of herself as a political entity, a medium of exchange. If public opinion was important enough that the court wanted to ensure Stuart was not perceived as a prisoner, then self-destruction could be a powerful tool. The court would not want the world to think she had been forced to end her life.

When Brounker arrived, he came with a series of questions based on Stuart's fictional love affair, clearly intending to unmask a conspiracy if one existed, not to listen to complaints about Stuart's treatment and direct them to Queen Elizabeth, who was, in any case, by this point too ill with pneumonia to act on Stuart's guardianship. Cecil could not overlook clues to a north-country uprising that might complicate James's succession, but otherwise he planned to take little action while Elizabeth might be dying. Brounker forced Stuart to admit that she had lied, but her terminology was literary: one point was "but a poeticall fiction," she said, another was "one of her sole conceytes," and her lover was, surprise of surprises, an impossible fiction—the married King of Scots (letter 10). Brounker and Bess feared Stuart had intended to flee to Scotland, hoping, ironically in light of subsequent events, for better treatment from King James than she had received from Queen Elizabeth. Stuart's language suggests that she not only cast her letters as "poeticall fiction" by way of excuse, but that she saw her writing as fiction that could achieve a real-life goal. Her many references to acting and art indicate her awareness of her creation.

Stuart seems to have been disappointed and irritated that Brounker considered her concerns only tangential to her conspiracy and refused

---

1. Elizabeth Talbot to Robert Cecil, Cecil Papers 135, f. 150. A number of recent studies treat women's use of fasting as a tool to achieve control, including Rudolph M. Bell, *Holy Anorexia* (Chicago: Univ. of Chicago Press, 1985), and Joan Jacobs Brumberg, *Fasting Girls: The Emergence of Anorexia Nervosa as a Modern Disease* (Cambridge: Harvard Univ. Press, 1988).

to set a date for her removal from Hardwick Hall. To question after question about her beloved, Stuart answered "the Kinge of Scottes" (letter 10), until Brounker tired of the game. In a declaration that Brounker carried away with him, Stuart confessed that she was free from any contract or promise of marriage. Experience had taught her, she noted, that the only way to bring an important crown representative to Hardwick was to be suspected of something and since she had nothing to work with but a lover, she had created one (letter 11). Even after her admission, however, Stuart continued the fiction in letters to Brounker (letters 12, 13, 15, and 16), using it to argue for his return as though she still believed the lover a potentially effective ploy, or was reluctant or embarrassed to give up the fiction, or simply had run out of options. For the sake of that wonderful man, she says, she would endure ten years of pain rather than endanger him by releasing his name to someone who has treated her so badly (letter 12).

Cecil and Brounker, however, were no longer willing to credit Stuart's words. Cecil noted on letter 12, "by this Time you see I think that she hath some strange vapours to her braine." Brounker agreed and later told the Privy Council that "much writinge" had led to the "distempering of her braynes apparente enough by the multitude of her idle discourses."[1] He told Stuart, harking back to Aristotle's views on women, that the more she wrote, "to the lesse purpose it was" (letter 16). Historians have usually described the letters as "hysterical,"[2] an ironically appropriate word choice, since *hysteria* (from *hyster*, or the womb) was the diagnosis applied to women suffering from, among other symptoms, "choking, feelings of suffocation, [and] partial paralysis."[3] Cer-

---

1. Henry Brounker to the Privy Council, 19 March 1603, Cecil Papers 135, f. 174.

2. Bradley, 1:143; Francis Bickley, *The Cavendish Family* (Boston: Houghton Mifflin, 1914), 30; B[lanche] C[hristabel] Hardy, *Arbella Stuart: A Biography* (London: Constable, 1913), 115–16; M. Lefuse, *The Life and Times of Arabella Stuart* (London: Mills and Boon, 1913), 71; Ian McInnes, *Arabella: The Life and Times of Lady Arabella Seymour, 1575–1615* (London: W. H. Allen, 1968), 112–14; and Durant, who notes the usual charges and agrees they are possible, 106–7. Handover views the letters as distressed and indicative of a lack of composure, but rational (149–53), as does Lewalski, who describes Stuart as being in "great emotional distress," but "quite sane" ("Writing Resistance in Letters," 75).

3. Coppélia Kahn, "The Absent Mother in *King Lear*," *Rewriting the Renaissance: The Discourses of Sexual Difference in Early Modern Europe*, ed. Margaret W. Ferguson, Maureen Quilligan, and Nancy J. Vickers (Chicago: Univ. of Chicago Press, 1986), 33.

tainly the letters were rhetorically puzzling, and became increasingly so as weeks passed and Stuart remained her grandmother's ward. Biographer David N. Durant calls even Stuart's first description of her lover "six long pages of rambling obscurity." He notes, however, "[i]f the letter had not been so long, it might have been ingenious…a resourceful plan to escape from Hardwick"—she just kept on writing and writing until, as he puts it, "the message all but got lost."[1]

That Stuart kept on writing suggests that these letters were fulfilling a need besides that of addressing a specific audience in a brief, detached, and well-disciplined style, the dominant male model of letter-writing. It suggests they were fulfilling a need of which Stuart herself had some recognition when she wrote of "disburdn[ing]" her "weake body and travelling mind" (letter 16). In the same lengthy mid-March 1603 letter to Brounker, Stuart described her reason for writing as she did:

> being allowed no company to my likeing and finding this the best excuse to avoid the tedious conversation I am bound to, I thinck the time best spent in tiring you with the idle conceits of my travelling minde till it make you ashamed to see into what a scribling melancholy (which is a kinde of madnesse and theare are severall kindes of it) you have brought me and leave me, if you leave me till I be my owne woman and then your trouble and mine too will cease.

Her latter comment, by the way, was true: when Stuart finally was allowed to leave Hardwick Hall, her "hysterical" writing ceased.

What Stuart delineates in this letter is a woman who was intensely unhappy with the restrictions on her life, who was under tremendous tension without any other form of release, since she rarely was able to speak to anyone who would not betray the conversation, and who passed the time by letting her mind "travel" and writing where it went. In the context of Renaissance composition, that is "madness" of a kind, but it sounds remarkably akin to what the twentieth century knows as freewriting, which can be therapeutic and cathartic.[2] If Stuart's 1603

---

1. Durant, 105–6.

2. Jane Donawerth notes that Renaissance poets, too, accepted the idea that speech and writing could relieve an overflowing heart, although a character who spoke from passion would be perceived as "grand but self-indulgent," because reason and control were expected to predominate (*Shakespeare and the Sixteenth-Century Study of Language* [Urbana: Univ. of Illinois Press, 1984], 58–62).

letters are understood to be amalgams of controlled formal and familiar Renaissance letters and something closer to "disburdening," they begin to make psychological and rhetorical sense, as does the perplexity of those who received the letters and read them with very different expectations.

Sometimes Stuart's letters begin in a conventionally controlled fashion and shift into an outburst of apprehensions, evasions, or accusations, and then shift back again. Her anger may emerge for a phrase or many pages and then resubmerge. Stuart's persona may change from submissive and humble to arrogant and demanding within half a sheet, which is likely what Brounker meant when he told her servant George Chaworth she was of "a hundred myndes" (Appendix B, letter 4), the disjunctions themselves indicative of Stuart's ambivalences and confusions. Her usual highly controlled syntax may become more relaxed, her punctuation drop away, and her structure of ideas become more associational, as though presenting a stream of consciousness. Even her handwriting may suggest shifts in emotion, as an elegant, upright presentation script (see Figure 3) becomes a plain, slanted informal hand, or a careful informal hand (see Figure 2) becomes a seemingly hurried, heavily blotted scrawl.

It is not so much, however, that Stuart loses all sense of an audience beyond herself, as that she periodically casts aside regard for propriety of tone, form, or subject matter, apparently impelled by a necessity that overshadows adherence to the conventions, and writes for herself as well as to her specified audience. The interplay between the formal, restrained prose and the startlingly open, more associational prose that yet is conscious of the "other" is dramatic and intriguing; and the situation is doubly complicated because Stuart sometimes intends to deceive with a fiction pretending not to be fiction. When is the humility genuine and when manipulative, a response to the game being played? To what extent is the fiction shaped and to what extent fulfilling a need for self-expression?

For example, in letter 16, the letter to Brounker mentioned earlier, Stuart begins politely: "Sir as you weare a private person I found all humanity and courtesy from you and whilest I live will thanckfully acknowledge it." Soon, however, Stuart's language, while it is rhetorically impressive, becomes politically inflammatory and insulting to the queen and her counselors:

> are the Stanhopes and Cecilles able to hinder or diminish the <good> reputation of a Stuart hir Majesty being judge? have I stained hir Majesties bloud with unworthy or doubtfull marriage? have I claimed my land <these .ii. yeares> though I had hir Majesties promise I should have it and hath my Lord of Hartford regarded hir Majesties expresse commaundment <and [been] threatned and felt indignation> so much? have I forborne so long to send to the King of Scots to expostulat his unkindnesse and declare my minde to him in many matters and have no more thanckes for my labour?

Her anger is open and straightforward and continues at length. Writing hurriedly and with virtually no revision, Stuart imagines the day when she and her enemies will be revealed for what they are:

> for these pleites and foldes and slight devises do but glitter in the ey and theyr small value is discerned who soever make them worne for fashion shake. wheras mine shall be strange, and new and richly worth more then I am worth or any Lady of a subject in this land. but you shall not know the devise at Court least you prevent me, or the foreknowledge take away the grace of the soudain and gorgeous change of my suite which how little so ever my mourning weede be respected will make <me> envied who am not pittied, but hard it will be for any of them all to follow me it will be so costly and yet to me so easy that they will at least for civility confesse them selves lesse worthy of that which theyr betters have had much a do to perswade me to take in free guift aknowledging me (in theyr partiall opinion) worthy of more then they can give which is more then incredulous you can beleeve should be offred much more so long unreceived by pore me.

To what extent is this passage a conscious continuation of her earlier fiction? Stuart may be enjoying a joke, believing an escape attempt set for the next day would succeed and her earlier fictions seem vindicated. Her words may reflect a longing to envision herself as supported and triumphant. Surely the suggestion that some people want her in regal robes is in part a conscious strategy, but Stuart seems to revel in her description, and the run-on syntax and fluid style are unlike her usual highly controlled prose—usual, that is, at any time other than the first three months of 1603. Stuart's abandonment of political caution is rarely more clear than in this letter where she suggests a parallel between her case and that of the Earl of Essex, who had been executed for treason in 1601 and was a particularly painful topic with Queen Elizabeth. Essex had been kind to Stuart, supported her claim to the throne, and perhaps corresponded with her for a time. Now her good friend Essex is gone, Stuart laments, also victimized by enemies, and she has never more needed a friend than now, when she is so miserable that she has spent the day verbally portraying her unhappiness.

In addition to providing an emotional outlet, the letters from Hardwick allow Stuart to formulate on paper an identity she can accept. Letter-writing under any circumstances involves modeling a self in prose, but these letters are unusually self-focused, and in them Stuart often casts herself in two related literary roles, the beloved woman and the heroic victim. Not surprisingly, Bess, Cecil, and Brounker came to doubt the existence of Stuart's love affair; Stuart's description of her lover is vague, but hyperbolically romantic and self-glorifying, and as such counterproductive to her fiction's plausibility. The man she loves has been forced to hide his affection by seeming to be against her at court, but she generously and freely forgives him these necessary wrongs. Many things she has rudely demanded of him, and he never resents her commands, as long as she will not reject him. His love is like pure gold. His only fault, she says, is jealousy, which implies a woman of such worth that a wonderful man would fear losing her; and she weaves a tale of how she has treated him unkindly and proudly—even though loving him too well to conceal any thought from him—once when she wrongly thought that he no longer loved her and again when she needed to make him realize that his jealousy deeply injured her and would provoke a quarrel (letter 7). It is understandable that a woman in her later twenties, denied any opportunity for a romantic relationship and feeling deeply betrayed by a relative she had trusted, would tend to the rhetorical excesses of popular romance in portraying herself as cherished by a man to whom she could confide her every thought, even be rude and still be loved; but the excesses violated her audience's expectations at a time when marriage among the upper classes was likely to be a mixture of affection and more pragmatic concerns like estates. In Stuart's fiction, the idea of a conspiracy only enlarges the number of those who love her: when the truth is revealed, she says, her friends will confess "how farre they have offended hir Majesty for my sake and if they receive the sentence of death out of hir Majesties mouth I dare answer for them they shall dy content" (letter 7). Stuart had attendants who were nearly that loyal, like George Chaworth, whose letter from London well expresses the uncertainties Stuart and her friends faced during these politically tumultuous months and is signed "Your honores true servant to death" (Appendix B, letter 4). But only in her letters was Stuart so widely beloved.

Stuart emphasizes the extent to which she deserves love and respect by depicting herself as heroic in the face of unjustly inflicted suffering. No matter how extraordinarily Queen Elizabeth punishes her, Stuart says, she will be grieved by the queen's displeasure, but she can endure, because she has had long experience of heavy crosses (letter 8). If the queen's counselors think to make her despair and take her own life, like the tragic Mr. Starkey,[1] they will discover she is too strong to be defeated that way (letter 15). In order to achieve victory over hard-heartedness, she can survive the worst pain they can inflict; she would rather spit out her tongue than utter a true word under coercion. Her heart would break before she submitted and the worse the torture the greater her achievement (letter 16). Stuart's self-idealization is a composite of qualities stereotypically male and stereotypically female; she has the inner strength and invincibility of a stoic Christian hero

---

1. The Reverend Mr. James Starkey had been employed at Hardwick as tutor to William Cavendish's sons and left after being denied both payment and an expected living. He had been a confidant of Stuart's and was suspected of having been complicitous in a plot to free her from Hardwick the previous spring. He had delivered gifts to London for her, and his name had been linked with hers romantically, which distressed him. (Instead of printing "Ja.S." on a Bible, a stationer had printed "J.A.S.," which was rumored to mean "James and Arbella Starkey.") Already deeply depressed, Starkey hanged himself in February after he was questioned about the Hertford proposal. Before he committed suicide, he wrote a note in which he argued his innocence; and although he somehow had come to believe that Stuart had implicated him in revenge for the stationer's error, he praised her virtue and intelligence and asked her and her friends' pardon for having unwittingly offered her the indignity of pairing her name with his (Cecil Papers 135, f. 175/2). Obviously, Stuart was aware that actions taken by her and the court could result, and had resulted, in someone's death.

combined with the grace and lovability of a woman—an ideal female ruler, according to Renaissance thought, or perhaps a warrior woman like Ariosto's Bradamante or Spenser's Britomart. The writer, however, doth protest too much; to this modern reader at least, her words more argue loneliness and powerlessness than the image she likely hoped to convey to others and herself.

In early 1603, it would have been hard for Stuart to face reality as the powerful others in her life constructed it. Stuart heard every day how foolish her grandmother and the court thought her, how rash her actions had been and how unbecoming; she ran from a "voley of most bitter and injurious words" (letter 12). It must have been nearly unbearable for a bright, spirited, class-conscious woman to be told that her struggle for independence had made her an object of scorn and derision. Stuart's repeated hints of suicide are more than a convenient political weapon; starvation requires resolve, and suicide threats, even if partially a ploy, suggest genuine distress.

Letter-writing offered Stuart an opportunity to deny that negative vision of herself and replace it with another, to rework her actions on paper until she was as innocent as she needed to see herself. Writing was a mechanism to maintain self-respect. Sending Dodderidge as the messenger to Hertford was not rash, and thus dishonorable, but a carefully executed plan (letter 7); and although she admits some guilt in saying that never before had she had to "accuse my selfe…of giving hir Majesty the least colour of just offence," she follows immediately with "and I protest my conscience doth not accuse me of any fault hearin but a small, honest necessary and consequently most pardonable presumption…the smallest [offence] that ever was made" (letter 11). To Brounker, she says that she knows he will argue the fault is hers, but her conscience is clear, and eventually he, too, will understand how the queen has been deceived and Stuart wronged (letter 16). We will never know how far she believed her words, but these letters, so puzzling to their recipients, probably offered Stuart refuge. In the world she created on paper, a strong and beloved woman rightfully raged against her oppressors.

On Ash Wednesday, while Stuart wrote letter 16, her longest letter to Brounker, she was under particular tension; that day, she had sent her page Richard to conclude arrangements for a Thursday escape. Stuart's uncle Henry Cavendish, formerly a soldier in the Low Countries, would meet her at the gates of Hardwick with only one or two men in sight and approximately forty others, armed and on horseback, hidden nearby. But according to Bess's description of what followed, on Thursday afternoon when Stuart walked to the gate, Bess refused to allow the gate to be opened. Stuart asked if she was being held prisoner and demanded to leave, but Bess retained control of the situation: her guards obeyed her.[1] Henry Cavendish, although he was permitted inside the gates to consult with Stuart, could not lead his men to attack Hardwick Hall without potential injury to family members and servants he and Stuart cared about. The escape faltered and failed.

Only after Brounker had investigated this rebellion, which he viewed as local and personal, rather than as Catholic or regional, was Stuart removed from Hardwick Hall. Both Stuart and Brounker were still there when Queen Elizabeth died on 24 March 1603, and although Stuart was invited to be principal mourner at the funeral, she declined; she was said to have commented that since she had not been permitted access during Elizabeth's life, she would not now be brought on stage as a public spectacle.[2] James's succession clearly was settled. Stuart was removed from Hardwick Hall to Wrest Park in Bedfordshire, to the temporary custody of Henry Grey, the fifth Earl of Kent, whose nephew was married to Mary and Gilbert Talbot's daughter Elizabeth.[3]

It is easy to view Stuart's dramatic letters from Hardwick Hall as self-indulgent, self-centered, and arrogant. Like some of the later court letters, they have encouraged many readers to regard Stuart in the stereotypical ways discussed in Part I, as a romantic heroine or unrealistic fool. Certainly these letters are strikingly different from the objective, detached discourse that was then and is still our norm for judgment.

---

1. Elizabeth Talbot to Henry Brounker, 10 March 1603, Cecil Papers 135, f. 167.

2. From an account of Queen Elizabeth's reign said to have been written by one of Burghley's retainers, BL Sloane MS 718, f. 39.

3. Elizabeth, later Countess of Kent, was one of many talented Cavendish and Talbot women. Her *A Choice Manuall of Rare and Select Secrets in Physick and Chirurgery* was published in 1653, two years after her death, and was printed in nineteen editions over the next three and a half decades.

On the other hand, Stuart was a victim of her rank, of her sex, of a culture in which gender and politics were so confusingly intertwined. Surely she was justified in complaining "But I am growne a woman and…[yet] not allowed the liberty of graunting lawfull favors" (letter 16) and wondering if somehow "the running on of yeares be not discerned in me onely" (letter 8). Surely she was justified in wanting power to choose more than her day's dress. Lady Arbella Stuart had a right to the anger that so often comes through in these rhetorically complex letters, and it is gratifying that she was not passive in restraint, that, win or lose, she rejected resignation. Her fictional lover, however, failed to achieve the immediate goal of effecting her removal from her grandmother's custody. And, ironically, her fiction was less effective on that pragmatic level because the writing was fulfilling Stuart's need to see herself as capable of freeing herself with the aid of those who loved her, capable of some measure of control over her destiny. For a time, that may have been the greatest fiction of all.

IV. To Live Safe

[B]y the patronage of so worthy a Prince, so interested in them of whom my fortune depends, and so gratiously affected to me, I cannot doubt, but to live safe.

Lady Arbella Stuart to Sir Andrew Sinclair (letter 52)

Once James's succession was a *fait accompli*, Stuart gained some small degree of autonomy. The new King of England, informed of her acknowledgment of his authority, in May wrote the Earl of Kent that Stuart should be permitted to visit court.[1] King James met with her and afterwards was convinced by Robert Cecil, who was already a trusted advisor, that Stuart should be allowed more freedom, that she had been too long "tormented" by grief and should be treated more "tenderly"— or so Cecil reported the conversation to Stuart's grateful uncle Gilbert

---

1. 11 May 1603, Cecil Papers 135, f. 176/2.

Talbot.[1] Finally free of official custodians, Stuart stayed through June with the Marchioness of Northampton and in July joined the court for the coronation and summer progress.

In that first year after Stuart came to court, she received dedications, rode directly behind Queen Anna in the official state entry pageant,[2] was appointed to the office of queen's carver, attended plays and masques, and was sought after and praised. Some people envied her learning, it was said, but she also found friends.[3] Although James waited until September to reestablish Stuart's allowance, which had ceased on Queen Elizabeth's death, and the amount of eight hundred pounds per annum and diet was disappointing by comparison with the more lavish grants that others received, Stuart's letters indicate that she was often optimistic. She wrote her family when Cecil sent her a New Year's gift of bracelets, reassuring her of his friendship (letter 40). It was suggested that James might restore her patrimony, and, as rumors of marriage proposals circulated, Stuart joked with her uncle Gilbert Talbot about how he might "soone be dispatched" of her forever in "honorable sort" (letter 42).

On the other hand, the fragility of her political position was almost immediately made clear. In July, two plots against the king were uncovered. The Bye plot involved several Catholics and Puritans who had intended to kidnap King James until he agreed to allow greater religious diversity and pardon their act. In the Main Plot, Lords Cobham, Ralegh, and others were charged with having conspired to assassinate King James and Robert Cecil and place Stuart on the throne. Although Walter Ralegh probably was guilty only of having failed to acquaint James's ministers with what he suspected,[4] Cobham indeed had been in touch with Count d'Aremburg, the Spanish ambassador in the

---

1. Gilbert Talbot's account of his conversation with Robert Cecil, 18 May 1603, Lambeth Palace Library MS 709, f. 86.

2. Thomas Dekker, Ben Jonson, and Thomas Middleton's *The Magnificent Entertainment Given to King James* (1604).

3. Later copy of a letter from William Stewart to Gilbert Talbot, 16 September 1603, BL Althorp Papers F172, f. 115.

4. Durant, 127.

Netherlands, about the project. Cobham simply assumed that, in exchange for the crown, Stuart would write Philip III of Spain, the Duke of Savoy, and the Archduke of Austria promising to tolerate Roman Catholicism, make peace with Spain, and allow Philip III to approve any match she might negotiate. Except that she was said to have received a letter that she had turned over to James, Stuart was uninvolved.[1]

The treason trials were held in November at Winchester. Stuart was not charged, nor was her uncle Henry Cavendish, who was implicated and examined; but a family friend and former neighbor, Sir Griffin Markham, was a co-conspirator, and the potential danger Stuart posed to King James was emphasized to the court. Stuart was seated in the gallery next to the Earl of Nottingham when Sir Edward Coke, sensing his prosecution of Ralegh jeopardized by Ralegh's eloquent defense, began to denigrate Stuart; Cecil stood to remind his protegé that Stuart was innocent and should not be slandered. Although Stuart did not herself speak, she asked the Earl of Nottingham to speak for her: "The lady doth here protest upon her salvation, that she never dealt in any of these things, and so she willed me to tell the court."[2]

The outcomes were predictable: all guilty verdicts. Three men were executed. When Lord Cobham, Lord Grey, and Sir Griffin Markham were led to the scaffold, however, they were told King James had issued a reprieve to the remaining conspirators. Stuart wrote her uncle Gilbert Talbot, "I have reserved the best newes for the last, and that is the Kings pardon of <life to> the not-executed traitours. I dare not beginne to tell of the Royall and wise manner of the Kings proceeding thearin, least I should finde no ende of extolling him for it till I had written out a payre of badd eyes" (letter 36).

The contradictions of that first year foreshadow events of the years to follow. Stuart was publicly acknowledged as a royal princess and family member, and as such she had some influence and access to the king; but she was not fully trusted by James, who scorned learned women and did

---

1. Account of Ralegh's trial, BL Harley MS 39, ff. 275, 288.

2. Quoted in Handover, 186.

not enjoy Stuart's company, in spite of their shared interests in intellectual matters. She might be honored, as she was in 1605 by being asked
to serve as godparent to James's daughter Mary, along with the Duke of
Holstein, one of Anna's brothers; but others' acts and comments still
could cast doubt on her loyalty. Although she might one day marry well
and have great wealth, until then she was an unmarried dependent who
had to make her own way at court.

Both of the types of letters Stuart wrote from 1603 until early 1610,
when she and William Seymour were betrothed—her informal letters
to family and friends and her formal court letters—reflect the pervasive-
ness of the system of patronage at James's court and Stuart's continuing
attempts to advance herself and her family and to achieve security. Her
quest was not an easy one; the court Stuart joined was politically and
economically frantic. Many studies in the last decade have examined
patronage at James's court, where, far more than at Elizabeth's, it
seemed one could gain anything through the "good offices" of someone
with more power and influence. Courtiers who wanted the positions,
titles, patents, and monopolies that meant wealth and social and political advancement competed for the right patron in a furious jockeying
for reward. An illusion of noble generosity, bounty, even extravagant
affection, was predicated on an economic reality of obligation and self-
interest: the "freely" bestowed gift—of an office, for example—obli-
gated the recipient to flattery, secondary patronage to others, expendi-
ture, and reciprocation.[1] Politics and economics were intimately
intertwined.

Even Stuart's informal letters to her family, although they seem much
more casual than her formal court letters, should be read with Stuart's
political situation in mind. The early years were especially tense, given
the atmosphere of suspicion surrounding the treason trials. In the
autumn of 1603, Mary Talbot apparently hinted that Stuart should be

---

1. Coppélia Kahn, "'Magic of Bounty': *Timon of Athens*, Jacobean Patronage, and Maternal
Power," *Shakespeare Quarterly* 38 (1987): 42. For studies of patronage at James's court, see Guy
Fitch Lytle and Stephen Orgel, eds., *Patronage in the Renaissance* (Princeton: Princeton Univ.
Press, 1981) and Linda Levy Peck, *Northampton: Patronage and Policy at the Court of James I*
(London: George Allen and Unwin, 1982).

more circumspect in what she wrote (see Stuart's response in letter 26). Undelivered letters were a worry (letter 37), because they might fall into the hands of unfriendly factions. Trusted carriers were mentioned by name. Instructions from Mary and Gilbert were burned in the presence of the retainers who had delivered them.[1] Even a letter's address could cause confusion. A year after the treason trials, a half-drunk William Herbert, Earl of Pembroke, wrote his soon-to-be father-in-law Gilbert Talbot that an ambassador was coming from Poland to request Stuart in marriage: "so may our princesse of the blood grow a great Queene, and then wee shall be safe from the danger of missuperscribing letters,"[2] an allusion to an unidentified but apparently awkward political incident involving the wording of an address.

Despite the continual need for caution, Stuart's informal letters to her family are far more lively and open than her politically sensitive court letters. Through these informal letters, largely written to Mary and Gilbert Talbot, Stuart was maintaining her relationship with family members to whom she was close, and the Arbella persona she creates is often confident and teasing.[3] Because she passes on court news and gossip that she thinks might amuse her uncle, these letters are a wonderful introduction to daily life at James's court: the arriving ambassadors, trips by coach, and secret plans for Christmas masques. For the first time since her mid-teens, Stuart was at court, now a new court under a different monarch. Although pleased to be in attendance, she was not always pleased with what she saw, and said so directly, expressing her dismay at, for example, the general lack of courtesy or James's "eve[r]lasting hunting" (letters 25 and 27). She was equally direct about her feelings, like her relief at having been exonerated of guilt in the Main Plot: "I am a witnesse not onely of the rare guifte of speach which

1. Thomas Cooke to Mary Talbot, 12 February 1604, Lambeth Palace Library MS 3203, ff. 182–83.

2. 3 October [1604], Talbot Papers, Original Letters, 2, ff. 224–25; Longleat House Library (hereafter cited as Talbot Papers).

3. Letters written to Gilbert after Stuart's fall from grace in 1610 concern the disposition of servants she can no longer care for; in these letters, her persona is serious and concerned, but the tone of the letters is still informal.

God hath given him [Cecil], but of his excellent judgement in chusing most plausible and honorable Theames as The defending a wronged Lady" (letter 36).

In these informal letters, Stuart's affection is clear: she writes to Mary, "your love and judgement together makes me hope you know I can like nor love nothing better, then the love and kindnesse of so honorable frends as you and my uncle" (letter 35), and she urges Mary to "commend me to my uncle Charles and my Aunt, and my .2. prety cousins, I thinck I shall many times wish my selfe set by my cousin Charles at meales" (letter 68). In letter 42, she even tries to reconcile Gilbert and her grandmother Bess, whose former severity Stuart is willing to forgive, and her mock-threatening tone gives a good sense of the warm relationship she had with her uncle: "you know I have cause onely to be partiall on your side so many kindenesses and favours have I received from you and so many unkindenesses and disgraces have I received from the other party; yet will I not be restrained from chiding you (as great a Lord as you are), if I finde you either not willing to harken to this good motion, or to procede in it as I shall thinck reasonable." Her persona here is both respectful and affectionate as she banters with her uncle; her syntax is controlled, and her ideas are stated forthrightly.

These informal letters reveal much about the patronage network in which Stuart and her relatives were active participants. The frequent exchange of gifts was a notable feature of the system.[1] To Mary and Gilbert, Stuart sends thanks for gifts of hart's horn or red deer pies from the north—the latter were gifts of special importance among the aristocracy—and she hopes her aunt and uncle will like a new cheese or savory salad (letters 33, 46, and 69). Such gifts are a sign of love, as Stuart saw the letters themselves (letter 35), a reaffirmation of the bonds between giver and recipient, an indication of alliance. With Mary and Gilbert, Stuart discusses patronage straightforwardly: how Sir William Stewart has been lobbying her to lobby someone else but cannot persuade her to waste her efforts; when the Duke of Lennox is the only counselor who

---

1. On this point, see, for example, Barbara J. Harris, "Women and Politics in Early Tudor England," *Historical Journal* 33 (1990): 265–67.

can be moved on an issue; how Mary and Gilbert are to be congratulated on acquiring a powerful new ally when their daughter marries well (letters 35, 37, and 43).

That Stuart asks her uncle to employ on her behalf his influence as an earl and member of the Privy Council suggests that she believed his offices and wealth gave him more power than her close familial connection to King James gave her. She thanks Gilbert for thanking those who have aided her and letting them know that he considers himself a debtor who will reciprocate kindnesses to her (letter 36). Repeatedly she thanks him for letters written directly in her support or written for others at her request, the latter indirectly benefiting her, since by being a successful patron, her own influence and further effectiveness will be increased (letters 23, 24, and 36). She begs the disposition of ecclesiastical offices: in 1609 she hoped to determine the livings of the next two parsonages to become available to him (letter 71). Even though it is Gilbert whose influence and action she begs, however, Stuart is equally political in the early letters when she writes to Mary Talbot, who has influence both on Gilbert (letter 24) and in her own right. Mary was well known as a patron and benefactor and has been called "one of the most intellectual women of the time";[1] Stuart apparently valued her advice.

These letters indicate that Stuart worked not only for her individual advancement, but also for the wider network of her family and friends. She once intercedes with the Court of Requests for an old family friend, saying she will be the debtor should the case be decided in his favor (letter 61); she lobbies Gilbert to help members of the family he does not like, trying, for example, to persuade him to bring Henry and Grace Cavendish to London, because they have suits pending and they and she can't afford it—do it, she says, for me "and our families good" (letter 42). Stuart reciprocates Mary and Gilbert's help as much as an unmarried female without lands or sufficient income can, by cautioning them of political shifts at court, advising them about New Year's gifts, pro-

---

1. Violet A. Wilson, *Society Women of Shakespeare's Time* (1924; rpt. Port Washington, N.Y.: Kennikat Press, 1970), 178.

moting their causes, and passing on patents and letters (letters 34, 35, 37, and 38). Her greatest reciprocation, however, is always the potential one: the fruit of her favor with her paternal cousin King James and her royal marriage.[1]

The confident and lively persona that appears in Stuart's informal letters only rarely appears in her formal letters to those associated with James and his court. Stuart's court letters are written with a high degree of structure, guardedness, and formality, a formality to which her informal letters form an illuminating contrast. What in a newsy letter to her aunt or uncle would be the direct "Let me interrupt you with a request" becomes in a court letter "I acknowledge my selfe greatly bounde to your Lordship and have sent this bearer my servant to attend your pleasure, whose important affaires I am constrained to interrupt with this necessary importunity" (letter 21). What in an informal letter would be "I thank you for your help" becomes in a court letter "I aknowledge my selfe greatly bounden to your Lordship of whose patience I presume in reading these needlesse lines, rather then I would by omitting your due thanckes a short time, leave your Lordship in the least suspence of my thanckfulnesse to you, whose good opinion and favour I highly esteeme" (letter 22). Stuart had learned the value of discretion and appropriate rhetoric in her dealings with the court.

The persona she creates in the court letters is humble and lowly, in accordance with the conventions of the day; in fact, "humble" may be the adjective she most often applies to herself in these letters. She sends "humble thanckes," and "humbly" takes leave, and signs herself a "humble and dutifull" servant. Even for an age of flattery, Stuart's court letters sometimes are so deferential that we cringe at what seems to us obsequiousness. Not all Jacobean writers of Stuart's high rank would have carried the role of humility as far as this thank-you in letter 59 to King Christian's chamberlain Sir Andrew Sinclair for having served as messenger: "Sir you having not onely performed the kindnesse I required of you in delivering my letters to theyr Majesties but returned

---

1. Thomas Cooke wrote Mary Talbot what Stuart had said about the Talbots finding the "fruite" of her favor (12 February 1604, Lambeth Palace Library MS 3203, ff. 182–83).

me so great and unexpected a favour as his Majesties letters, have
doubly bounde me to you, and I yeild you thearfore many great
thanckes, beseeching you to continue in preserving theyr Majesties
favour to me, for which [*of*] good office I most desire to becomme
obliged to you so worthy and reverent a person." Nor were most people
of Stuart's high rank in so dependent a position: a single woman, the
second lady in the land and expected to conduct herself as such, but a
woman whose political future was uncertain and who had little income
beyond a diet from the king's table and her pension. Stuart's precarious
political and economic situation magnified the need for support from
others and therefore for flattery and self-deprecation.

Like many women in early modern England and in spite of her
struggle for personal autonomy, Stuart was not a proto-feminist in the
sense of envisioning women as a community. She once asserted, however seriously, that women as a sex are "the purer and more innocent
kinde" (letter 34), but she showed little understanding of the limita-
tions placed on Queen Anna and other women at court and little sense
of affinity with them; instead she criticized what she saw as their frivolous and thoughtless activities, such as playing children's games or
mocking the late Queen Elizabeth's gestures and faults (letters 34 and
24). It is all the more significant, then, that on occasion Stuart specifically calls attention to herself as a woman in the court letters. Sometimes she incorporates the vision of the ideal, submissive female into her
prose, crafting, for example, a picture of herself at her needlework—
women's work[1]—making "trifles" that others would honor her by
accepting. When Stuart asks Andrew Sinclair in 1607 to pass along a
small gift of needlework to James's sister-in-law, the Queen of Denmark, her draft emphasizes the degree to which she places herself below
him: "Thus am I bold to trouble you even with these womanish toyes

---

1. Needlework was one of the few occupations considered appropriate for a woman at court
and indeed for Renaissance women in general. Giovanni Michele Bruto, the Italian author
whose volume on female education, *La institutione di una fanciulla nata nobilmente* (1555),
was translated into French and English, urged parents to see that daughters plied the
respectable needle, not the dangerous pen (Ruth Kelso, *Doctrine for the Lady of the Renaissance*
[Urbana: Univ. of Illinois Press, 1956], 59–60).

whose serious minde must have somm relaxation and this may be one to vouchsafe to discend to these petty offices for one that will ever wish your happinesse [*and*] increase and continuance of honour" (letter 59A). She thanks Denmark's queen for accepting a gift which Stuart has given "with blushing at the unworthinesse thearof...onely out of the confidence of the Sympathy of your gratious disposition, with that I found in the most puissant and noble King your husband" (letter 56), a man whose drunken excesses she probably deplored. Stuart perpetuates the ideal of womanly submission even as she uses submissiveness to achieve her ends, in this case to improve her political position at James's court by a close relationship with his brother-in-law and sister-in-law.

Stuart had little choice but to employ others in her quest for security. The person upon whom Stuart was most dependent was King James, and while she could claim the ties of blood in her requests to him, she could not reciprocate his gifts; as a result of the loss of her Scottish and English lands and revenues, she had little with which to repay him. Even had she wanted to, she could not have charmed him, as could a male favorite such as Robert Carr. Instead, she tried to influence the king through intercessors who could make him a return: Sir Robert Cecil, for years her strongest ally with James, and King Christian and Queen Anna Cathrine of Denmark.

With Cecil, Stuart was dealing with a man to whom her cousin believed he owed his English throne (probably rightly), even his life (probably wrongly), but someone James enormously respected; and Stuart's carefully artistic, self-conscious letters reflect her ability to employ the vocabulary of patronage well, even in the early court letters, like letter 18, written in 1603:

> My good Lord./ I presume to trouble your Lordship in renewing that request, which when I last spake with you it would not please you to graunt; or at least to lett me know you would make me bound to you in that kinde; that is that it will please your Lordship to remember the Kings Majesty of my maintenance, which if it be not a matter fitt for you (as which your Lordship hath already dealt in) my uncle of Shrouesbury is greatly deceived or hath deceived me, but I suppose neither, and thearfore presume so much of your honorable disposition that you will indeavour to obtaine me that which it will be for his Majesties honour to graunt,

and thearfore your Lordship in that respect (if thear[e] weare no other) I
doubt not will performe more the[n] it was your pleasure to promise me,
I thinck because you would have the benifitt greater comming
unpromised.

The supplication is impressively worded, as it should be, since Stuart is
insistently repeating her request that Cecil remind James she needs
money, which might annoy Cecil. At the same time, she is deferential;
acknowledges his status by begging pardon for troubling someone so
important; notes that she will be in his debt—will be "bound" to him—
which suggests potential reward; refers to her uncle, a significant person
who favors her and might reciprocate; and, although she touches briefly
on her relationship to James, emphasizes Cecil's and James's honor and
beneficence, to the extent that should Cecil not grant her request and
serve as intercessor, it would seem to invalidate the honor she attributes
to him.[1] Cecil sometimes helped Stuart, but he received many requests,
and he was committed to trimming expenses that had doubled since
King James had taken the throne.

Stuart's letters to King Christian and Queen Anna Cathrine of Denmark[2] also emphasize her deference, her gratitude, and her subservi-
ence, as was appropriate in letters to Denmark's rulers and members of
the royal family who could, if they chose, make King James handsome
returns for his favors to Stuart. Stuart had met King Christian when he
had visited England; and after his departure, King Christian had initiated the correspondence by asking Stuart to defend his reputation,
damaged when he insulted Lady Nottingham. Soon afterwards, his
chamberlain Sir Andrew Sinclair wrote Stuart that King Christian
wanted her to consider him one of her best friends in the world (Appendix B, letter 7). As a result, and even though Stuart writes formally, she
is relatively straightforward in asking King Christian for "the power and
aid of your famous name in advancing my affairs" (letter 55). When she

1. On letters of supplication, see Frank Whigham, "The Rhetoric of Elizabethan Suitors'
Letters," *PMLA* 96 (1981): 864–82, and his *Ambition and Privilege: The Social Tropes of
Elizabethan Courtesy Theory* (Berkeley: Univ. of California Press, 1984).

2. King Christian IV reigned from 1588 until his death in 1648; the queen was the former
Anna Cathrine of Brandenburg.

writes Sinclair, she first employs the public fiction of mutual generosity—she would never deprive Christian and Anna Cathrine of the "honour and contentment they receive in well doing"—then turns to the mechanics of patronage: Sinclair, too, will partake of "the fruite of your paines" if he will be good enough to bring Christian's letters when she calls for them. In the meantime, Stuart says, she is consulting with friends about the best suits, since she would "rather loose time then not be in very assured hope to prevaile by these meanes when I imploy them" (letter 52). It is unclear whether King Christian ever helped Stuart, but through Queen Anna and Prince Henry, he asked that one of Stuart's lutenists be sent to his service, a request Stuart could not refuse.

Stuart's efforts to advance herself and her family and friends met with some success. She was able to promote family members, friends, and former attendants and neighbors; she achieved a baronetcy for her grandmother's favorite son and heir, William Cavendish. When Sir John Harington, to whom Princess Elizabeth had been entrusted, needed an intercessor with the queen, he called upon Stuart (Appendix B, letter 12), which argues that he thought Stuart's opinions carried some weight with Anna. And when in November 1609 Sir Henry Yelverton had offended King James by his speeches and conduct in Parliament, he appealed to Stuart for mediation. She recommended his suit of reconciliation to the Lord Chancellor of Scotland, who, for Stuart's sake, favorably promoted Yelverton to the king. The manuscript at Alnwick Castle in which the episode is recounted has a note saying the affair proves Stuart had "considerable Influence" until her marriage.[1] However, if Stuart's influence, and thus her power to reward her supporters, had been proportional to her rank, one would expect to find more extant evidence of her prestige as a mediator and patron.

Dedications and celebratory poems indicate that Stuart had a public image as a woman of the arts. Even before Stuart had come to court, Michael Cavendish had dedicated his book of songs and madrigals to her and commented on Stuart's "rare perfections in so many

---

1. Eighteenth-century copy of a narrative dated 10 January 1610, Alnwick Castle MS 93A/35, Part I.

knowledges," and Henry Constable had in sonnets praised her "wit," "phrase," and "judgment" and placed his book under the protection of Stuart, his Petrarchan "Mistrisse."[1] When Hugh Holland published *Pancharis* soon after James came to the throne, his presentation verses to Stuart were composed in Latin, a compliment to her learning. Richard Brett of Lincoln College, Oxford, dedicated his Hebrew and Latin *Ritus jejunii Judaici* to her; David Hume praised her erudition and literary understanding in the Latin dedication to *Davidis Humii Theagrii Lusus Poetici;* and John Owen described her in his 1607 *Epigrammatum Joannis Owen,* again in Latin, as a noble and learned heroine.[2] John Wilbye, one of the foremost English madrigalists, praised Stuart's "deepe understanding…in all the *Arts,* and perticular excellency in this of *Musicke"* and added that he had never thought of any other patron to whom to dedicate his *Second Set of Madrigales* (1609) than "your Honour, whose never-failing Judgement in the depth of *Musicke,* I do wish might be pleased with some of these."[3] In a dedicatory sonnet to his translation of Homer's *Iliad,* George Chapman called Stuart *"our English Athenia, Chaste Arbitresse of ver*tue and learning," and Aemilia Lanyer in *Salve Deus* described Stuart as a "Great learned Ladie," one accompanied by *"Pallas,* and the Muses."[4]

Lanyer's poem tantalizes because it suggests Stuart may have been a poet, or "maker" of fictions, as well as an informed patron. Lanyer says

---

1. "To the Honorable Protection of the Ladie Arbella," *14 Ayres in Tabletorie to the Lute* (1598; rpt. Menston, England: Scolar Press Limited, 1971); "To my Ladye Arbella. Sonet 4," "To the Ladye Arbella. Sonet 5," and "To the divine protection of the Ladie Arbella the author commendeth both his Graces honoure and his Muses aeternitye," *The Poems of Henry Constable,* ed. Joan Grundy (Liverpool: Liverpool Univ. Press, 1960), 148, 149, 179.

2. Hugh Holland, "Illustrissimae Dominae Arbellae Stuartae," *Pancharis: The First Booke* (1603; rpt. London: for John Payne Collier, 1866), 5; Richard Brett's manuscript volume is described in Macray, 507; David Hume, "Illustrissimae, et omni laudis genere Ornatissimae Dominae, D. Arabellae Stuartae," *Davidis Humii,* sig. A2; John Owen, "1. Ad Nobilissimam et Doctissimam Heroinam, Dominam Arbellam Stuartam," "2. Ad Eandem," and "276. Ad nobilissimam ac Illustriss. Dominam Arbellam Stuart," *Epigrammatum Joannis Owen,* sigs. B, D11.

3. John Wilbye, "To the Most Noble and Vertuous Lady, the Lady Arbella Stuart," *The Second Set of Madrigales* (London: Thomas Este for John Browne, 1609), sig. A4.

4. George Chapman, "To our English Athenia…the Ladie Arbella," *Homer Prince of Poets* (London: for Samuel Macham, c. 1609), sig. Ee; Aemilia Lanyer, "To the Ladie *Arabella,"* *Salve Deus Rex Judaeorum* (London: by Valentine Simmes for Richard Bonian, 1611), sig. C.

she has known Stuart long and yet not so well as she wishes, character-
izing Stuart as a "Rare *Phoenix*, whose faire feathers are your owne, /
With which you flie, and are so much admired," which could imply
original authorship of poetry or fiction, although admittedly the line is
ambiguous. Bathsua Makin in 1673 commended Stuart's "great faculty
in Poetry" and several later writers echoed this point, but no writing
beyond Stuart's letters has been clearly identified as hers.[1] Stuart's other
works may have been lost or, like many women's, subsumed under
"anonymous"; it is also possible that her reputation as a literary woman
was transformed over time into a reputation as a poet.

Given Stuart's interest in the arts, we might expect her to have been
an active patron; but of the dedications to Stuart, two were composed
by family friends or distant relatives and several by writers not closely
associated with the Jacobean court. Professional writers intimately tied
with the court only rarely dedicated works to Stuart, probably because
she lacked the wealth to commend their efforts. James had not accepted
any of the numerous marriages proposed for her, nor had he provided
her with an income equivalent to the inheritance he had taken from her.
In 1607, when the new Venetian ambassador reported home on the
state of England, he said that Stuart, the king's nearest relative, studied
much; that she was so poor she could not live "as magnificently nor
reward her attendants as liberally as she would"; and that although
James professed his love and had promised to restore her property when
he came to the throne, he had not done so, "saying that she shall have it
all and more on her marriage, but so far the husband has not been
found, and she remains without a mate and without estate."[2]

Stuart's attendance at court was an enormous economic drain. In
1603, Stuart received between twelve and fourteen hundred pounds
annually from resources Bess had assembled for her, and she maintained
a personal staff of at least ten servants. James awarded her an allowance
of eight hundred pounds a year, and he increased her allowance by a
thousand pounds in December 1604, for a total income of

---

1. Lanyer, sig. C; Bathsua Makin, *An Essay to Revive the Antient Education of Gentlewomen*
(London: by J.D., 1673), 20.
2. *CSP, Venetian*, 10:514.

approximately three thousand pounds. Such an income sounds acceptable, given that the annual rent for several manors might be only two or
three hundred pounds.[1] It was not sufficient, however, to maintain Stuart at court, where a presentation sword might cost three thousand
pounds or an evening's masque two thousand. When Pembroke became
Lord Chamberlain, his salary was nearly five thousand pounds, the
minimum amount Lawrence Stone estimates would have been necessary to maintain an establishment at the level of an earl. King James and
Queen Anna spent ten thousand pounds a year on the silks for their
clothes, and by 1610, they were committing over twenty-five thousand
pounds annually to their wardrobe. Robert Cecil's income from land
and office in 1608 was twenty-four thousand pounds; his expenditures
for the years 1608–1612 amounted to almost fifty thousand pounds.[2]
By comparison with those at court to whom Stuart would have compared herself, then, her income was small, and expenses were high. The
costumes for the masques in which Stuart was almost obliged to participate cost two or three hundred pounds each, a cost she had to bear—
up to a tenth of her annual income—for a dress that could never be
worn in that form again.[3] She was expected to provide royal gifts at
New Year's, weddings, and christenings, tip others' servants well, and
pay the salaries of an entourage appropriate to her station, which by
early 1610 included twenty-three servants.[4]

By insisting that Stuart remain in attendance at what was rapidly
becoming the most expensive court in Europe, James committed her to
spending beyond her income and kept her dependent on his occasional
gifts and what she could borrow. Like other courtiers, Stuart borrowed
heavily—Ben Jonson satirized the court as glittering with clothes and
jewelry "not paid for yet."[5] She tried to maintain the pretense of splen-

1. Durant, 125, 147; Handover, 177; Graham Parry, *The Golden Age Restor'd: The Culture of the Stuart Court, 1603–42* (New York: St. Martin's Press, 1981), 150.

2. Stone, 548, 563, 136, and Appendix 23.

3. Parry, 150; McInnes, 152.

4. Crompton's account book, Seymour Papers 22; Longleat House Library (hereafter cited as Seymour Papers).

5. "To Sir Robert Wroth," *Ben Jonson*, vol. 8, ed. C. H. Herford, Percy Simpson, and Evelyn Simpson (Oxford: Clarendon Press, 1947), 97.

dor, since, while James liked to see himself as a benefactor to his favorites and gave lavishly—ten thousand pounds in jewels to Lady Frances Howard when she married his favorite Robert Carr—the way to obtain the king's approval was to live magnificently.[1] Stuart shared in the excess that James's attitude promoted. When John Chamberlain passed on rumors to Dudley Carleton about Ben Jonson's *Masque of Beauty* (1608), which was to be performed the following Sunday, he said of the participants, "one Lady and that under a barronesse, is saide to be furnished for better then an hundred thousand pound [in jewels], and the Lady Arbella goes beyond her, and the Quene must not come behinde."[2] Chamberlain's sources may have exaggerated the worth of the jewels worn in that masque, but his comment gives some sense of the style of James's court. It was hard to live magnificently on three thousand pounds a year.

As a result, Stuart actively sought patents and monopolies and bought and sold lands. In October 1607, she bought a cottage with surrounding lands in Nottinghamshire from Sir Percival and Henry Willoughby, former neighbors, for one hundred pounds. During 1608 and the early months of 1609 she petitioned for the impost on oats, may have been involved in a dropped lawsuit for lands, bought for two hundred pounds a townhouse in Blackfriars that would allow her to retire from court occasionally, sold the manor of Smallwood in Chester county to Francis Bennett and Matthew Stock for an unnamed sum, and petitioned to import hides from Ireland.[3] Eventually, however, Stuart sank into debt until she was economically trapped at court as she had been physically trapped at Hardwick Hall.

Stuart's letters reflect her increasing frustration. She wrote Gilbert Talbot in November 1608 that she had temporarily retired from court and was "settling my selfe to follow the Lawyers most diligently," having

---

1. Kahn, "'Magic of Bounty'," 45–46.

2. 8 January 1608, in Chamberlain, 1:252–53.

3. Deed of sale, 31 October 1607, Univ. of Nottingham MS Mi 6/173/242; petition for an impost on oats, July 1608, Lambeth Palace Library MS 3202, ff. 158–60; John Chamberlain to Dudley Carleton, 28 October 1608, in Chamberlain, 1:266; Handover, 238, and Durant, 162; copy of Smallwood deed of sale, 5 December 1608, Univ. of Nottingham MS Mi 5/169b/7; petition on Irish hides, undated [February 1609?], Public Record Office, Irish Correspondence, vol. 226, no. 95.

discovered the previous term how poorly she had fared when she allowed someone else to handle her affairs (letter 69). The court letters suggest that she sometimes tired of revising her direct statements into the indirect, submissive court rhetoric. Occasionally her annoyance at being forced into the deferential role slips through, as when, for example, she points out that she is sending King Christian her lutenist even though it would be easier for him to obtain another fine musician than it will be for her to do so (letter 66); or her style becomes so fulsome in submission to and glorification of a patron like King Christian that one wonders if Stuart did not, by calling attention to the artifice of the hierarchy, undercut the sense of her submission and thus reduce the letter's effectiveness.

Both the annoyance and the fulsomeness reflect Stuart's discomfort with the role she was playing, and the latter suggests increasing anxiety. Stuart's inability to acquire funds from James was a denial of her value as a member of the royal family, a relegation to social insignificance,[1] and a dismissal to financial bedlam. Her anxiety seems particularly evident in the letters of 1606–1608 to the Danish court. As early as 1606, Stuart had written to Andrew Sinclair in letter 52 that "by the patronage of so worthy a Prince, so interested in them of whom my fortune depends, and so gratiously affected to me, I cannot doubt, but at last to comme to somme such stay, as shall give me perpetuall cause to pray for his Majesty." In that draft we see what Stuart first wrote: she hoped with Christian's patronage "to live safe."

On occasion, Stuart was able to leave court during these years. She went north to Hardwick Hall when her grandmother died in February 1608. The majority of Bess's estate was bequeathed to her sons, but Bess left Stuart a thousand pounds, a concession after having eliminated her from the will because of her attempt to escape Hardwick Hall.[2] In early 1609, Stuart joined the Talbots in Derbyshire while she convalesced from smallpox. In August 1609 she departed for the north country again, perhaps to avoid the plague, perhaps to leave London and its

---

1. Whigham, "The Rhetoric of Elizabethan Suitors' Letters," 875.
2. Durant, 161; Handover, 204, 236.

creditors behind. She pawned some of her jewels in order to meet expenses of over three hundred pounds, all of which are recorded in her gentleman usher Hugh Crompton's account book, from the purchase of cakes and ale at an alehouse beyond Nottingham to gifts to the poor women who presented Stuart a petition or a dish of warden pears, the musicians at Chatsworth, the officers who brought a present from the mayor and city officials of Chesterfield, and the poor who greeted her along the roads.[1] The trip was a royal progress of sorts, during which Stuart stayed with family and friends along her route and stopped at the spa at Buxton. While visiting her friend Lady Isabel Bowes, she asked Lady Bowes to have her brother locate a house Stuart could buy in the country, away from the court (see Bowes's response, Appendix B, letter 13).

By mid-December 1609, something had precipitated a crisis. Cecil had supported Stuart's successful petition to license the selling of wines and whiskey in Ireland, for which she had thanked him in August (letter 72), but by the middle of December, she offered to return the grant if Cecil would see her debts paid, although she avoided telling him what those debts amounted to. She asked that the king increase her pension and convert her allowance for diet into a yearly cash sum (letter 74), presumably because she hoped to receive permission to live in the country, where dishes from the king's table would be of little use.

By the end of December, Stuart was under guard, along with Hugh Crompton and one of her waiting-women. Rumors abounded: one ambassador heard that she planned to stir up a revolution against James; another heard that she had converted to Roman Catholicism; she was supposed to have sent money to the Prince of Moldavia, whom she hoped to marry.[2] Court observer John Chamberlain said he did not know what the business was, but by mid-January it was ended, "want beeing thought to be the chiefest cause of her discontentment." James, he said, had restored Stuart to favor and given her plate worth two

1. Seymour Papers 22; also described in Canon J. E. Jackson, "Longleat Papers, No. 5," *Wiltshire Archaeological Magazine* 19 (1880): 217–26.

2. The Florentine secretary's dispatch is cited in Eugenia Levi, "Lady Arabella Stuart," *The Athenaeum*, 11 September 1897, 353; *CSP, Venetian*, 11:410; Durant, 172–74.

hundred pounds as a New Year's gift, one thousand marks toward her debts, and an increase in her pension, which would seem more generous if he had not in 1609 casually given the Earl of Holderness over seven thousand pounds toward his debts.[1] The Venetian ambassador added that Stuart had answered her examiners well and asked to be matched in marriage or given leave to choose her own husband. By February 1610, he noted that she was seldom seen in public and had complained she had been mocked in a recent play.[2] Stuart was living quietly because sometime over the previous weeks she secretly had become engaged.

When Stuart came to court in 1603 as the second lady of England, she probably did not expect to live as the poor relation; from Hardwick Hall, she had written of the pain of living away from court in what she had called "exile with expectation" (letter 16), and she had envisioned herself as the exemplification of royalty. The least she could have anticipated was "to live safe." What she found was continual deference, dependence, and debt. It should not be a surprise that James's cousin chose a path offensive to him. Stuart was thirty-four. Marriage was supposed to be her profession in a political and religious sense, and no other was open to her. In a financial sense, marriage could be her salvation, if her husband or his family had means or if James would reconcile himself to the match and finally award her the patrimony long promised on her marriage. By marrying, she would force James's hand.

V. So Great a Blessing

> [I]f we be not able to live to it I for my part shall thinck my selfe a patterne of misfortune in enjoying so great a blessing as you so little a while.
>
>   Lady Arbella Stuart to William Seymour (letter 82)

---

1. John Chamberlain to Ralph Winwood, 13 January 1610, in Chamberlain, 1:294; Stone, 417.

2. *CSP, Venetian,* 11:410, 414, 427. Several critics have argued that the play was Ben Jonson's *Epicoene;* for a discussion of the issue, see *Ben Jonson,* vol. 5, ed. C. H. Herford and Percy Simpson (Oxford: Clarendon, 1937), 144–48. Marion A. Taylor has suggested that the play was *The Knight of the Burning Pestle* ("Lady Arabella Stuart and Beaumont and Fletcher," *Papers on Language and Literature* 8 [1972]: 252–60).

According to a statement William Seymour made to the Privy Council on 10 February 1610, he had eight days earlier "bouldlie intruded" himself into Stuart's chamber and announced that he desired to marry her. He had heard that Stuart had received King James's permission to make her choice of any subject in the land, and he had seen there an opportunity to make his fortune, "my selfe beinge but a younger brother, and sensible of myne owne goode, unknowne to the worlde, of meane estate, not borne to challenge any thinge by my birthright...and shee a Lady of great honor and vertue and as I thought of great means." They had met twice during the following week and agreed to wed; but there was no binding engagement between them, he emphasized, nor ever would be without James's permission.[1]

Stuart's actions, however, argue that the two had agreed to marry earlier and that for some months she had been making arrangements. Since the previous autumn, Stuart had searched for a country home and tried to have her debts paid and her allowance of diet converted into cash. If the couple had planned to wed, they would have needed money and a house to which they could retire from court. It was said to have been at a Seymour family home that Viscount Fenton located Stuart when he put her under guard in December,[2] and in January Stuart had insisted that James either choose a husband for her or allow her to choose. If Seymour did not broach matrimony until February, the number of coincidences is remarkable.

At the time, William Seymour was twenty-two, the younger brother of the Edward Seymour whom Stuart had hoped to marry in 1603.[3] William was well educated, an Oxford scholar who had presented Latin verses to King Christian IV in 1606[4] and taken his bachelor's degree in 1607. Stuart might have met him at Oxford; or, since the Seymours

---

1. BL Harley MS 7003, ff. 59–60.

2. "Article X [Lady Arabella Stuart and the Venetian Archives]," *Edinburgh Review*, October 1896, 497.

3. Seymour was born 1 September 1587. For a review of his life, see G. E. C[okayne], *The Complete Peerage*, rev. and enl. by Geoffrey H. White, vol. 12 (London: St. Catherine Press, 1953), 69–73.

4. The verses are extant, BL Royal MS 12 A.64, f. 17b.

owned at least one home in greater London, he might have been about the court for two years, although his name rarely is mentioned. In emphasizing his financial need as a younger brother who would not inherit the Hertford holdings, Seymour was pleading a case that Privy Council members doubtless understood. The problem, of course, was that as a claimant Seymour could challenge the throne. In emphasizing his "meane estate," Seymour either was being naive or, more likely, adopting a guileless role, the better to demonstrate his innocence.

According to the Venetian ambassador's reports, which are sometimes unreliable, but are an excellent source of court gossip, Seymour and Stuart—"a lady of high spirit and ability"—were called before James and the Privy Council and ordered to discontinue marriage negotiations. Stuart was required to beg the king's forgiveness, but did so only after arguing that she could not be blamed for seeking a husband of her degree. James promised she could marry anyone of whom he approved[1] and restored her to favor. In April 1610 Stuart was seated under the golden cloth canopy with the royal family as King James received the Prince of Wirtemburg.[2] In early June, when James's older son Henry was installed Prince of Wales, Stuart viewed the ceremony from the balcony of the Court of Requests with Princess Elizabeth and Prince Charles and danced in Samuel Daniel's *Masque of Tethys' Festival*. Dressed in a costume of silver, gold, and lace designed to wave like a river, she portrayed the nymph of the river Trent in Derbyshire.[3]

By then, Stuart and Seymour had decided to marry, and Stuart probably was the more decisive of the two. Seymour had written a message arguing that it was too dangerous for them to continue, that he had presumed beyond his rank (Appendix B, letter 14); but by late May 1610, according to Seymour's friend Edward Rodney, Seymour said that since Stuart had received the king's consent to choose her husband without

1. *CSP, Venetian*, 11:433, 439.

2. Hans Jacob Wurmsser von Vendenheym, "A Relation of the Journey," BL Add. MS 20001, in *England as Seen by Foreigners in the Days of Elizabeth and James the First,* ed. William Brenchley Rye (1865; rpt. New York: Benjamin Blom, 1967), 58, 66.

3. *Tethys Festival,* in *A Collection of Scarce and Valuable Tracts...of the Late Lord Somers,* 2nd ed., rev. and aug. by Walter Scott, vol. 2 (1809; rpt. New York: AMS Press, 1965), 196–97.

restriction and wanted to proceed and he had pledged her his faith, they would wed.[1] At midnight on 21 June 1610, Seymour, Rodney, and one of William's servants rowed a boat down the Thames to Greenwich Palace. Stuart and Seymour married clandestinely in Stuart's chambers there, at four in the morning of 22 June, with enough friends and servants in attendance to ensure that the legitimacy of the marriage could not be challenged, as had that of Seymour's grandparents early in Queen Elizabeth's reign.[2] Secrecy was maintained for a little over two weeks. On 8 and 9 July, Seymour and Stuart were examined and imprisoned; Seymour was placed in the Tower of London, just above Traitors' Gate, and Stuart in private custody at Sir Thomas Parry's residence in Lambeth.

The timing of the marriage was particularly unfortunate. In the summer of 1610, King James had been having trouble with Parliament and asserted that he would not be thwarted by his subjects. Since coming to England, he had encountered the Main and Bye Plots and the Gunpowder Treason, all involving Roman Catholics, without taking extreme measures against English Catholics; but he was said to have been shaken in May 1610 to learn that King Henry IV of France had been assassinated. In early June, James commanded priests and seminarians to leave England and English recusants to leave London; soon afterward, he demanded an oath of allegiance.[3] Even the previous February, when James had heard rumors of an alliance between Stuart and Seymour, London had been searched for strangers whose presence might suggest a Catholic plot against him.[4] After the French assassination, James was yet more fearful and determined to demonstrate his authority.

Stuart's letters indicate that she believed James had betrayed his responsibility to her and she had a right to marry (letters 91 and 93).

1. Rodney's examination, undated, BL Harley MS 7003, ff. 62–63.

2. The marriage, minister, and witnesses are recorded in Hugh Crompton's account book, Seymour Papers 22, f. 70, and in Seymour's examination before the Council, 8 July 1610, Bodleian MS Tanner 75, f. 353.

3. John Stow and Edmond Howes, *The Annales, or Generall Chronicle of England* (London: Thomas Adams, 1615), 906.

4. *CSP, Venetian*, 11:434.

When Seymour was accused of having violated his promise not to marry without consent, Stuart answered in his defense: Seymour, she said, had done nothing more than had Abraham and Isaac, who were also forced to disclaim their wives for a time.[1] Consistently, she argued that the couple's initial vows had morally bound them. According to the Venetian ambassador, James was annoyed when Stuart signed her married name to a petition,[2] and he passed the petition to Cecil, who after reading it declared that his own prose, "for all that he was first Secretary, could not rival that of a woman, for he thought it would tax all Parliament to draft an answer which should correspond to the arguments and eloquence of the petition."[3] King James, however, rejected Stuart's reasoning.

In January 1611, James officially informed Stuart that her husband was condemned to life imprisonment in the Tower of London and she to exile in the far north; she would be guarded by the Bishop of Durham,[4] much as Mary Queen of Scots had been guarded by Stuart's

---

1. Clement Edmonds to Thomas Edmondes, 16 July 1610, BL Stowe MS 171, f. 296.

2. After her marriage, Stuart signed her name *Arbella Seymour,* a usage that raises the question of whether she is more appropriately termed *Lady Arbella Stuart* or *Lady Arbella Seymour* (the form Ian McInnes used in the title of his 1968 biography). I have employed *Stuart* in this edition of her letters because *Stuart* was her identity for thirty-five of her forty years, the name under which she wrote the majority of her letters, and the name by which, even after her marriage, she was known among her contemporaries. For example, a posthumous engraving issued in 1619 by John Whittaker, Sr., is inscribed "Ladye Arbella Steuart, &c." (For discussion of a similar question in regard to Mary Sidney, Countess of Pembroke, see Katherine Duncan-Jones's comment in her review of Margaret P. Hannay's *Philip's Phoenix* [*Times Literary Supplement,* London, 1 June 1990, 587] and Hannay's letter in response [*Times Literary Supplement,* London, 29 June 1990, 695].) Among modern conventions for a shortened form of Lady Arbella Stuart's name, I have most often employed her surname, the convention commonly used with writers, rather than *Lady Arbella* or *Arbella,* forms that seem less respectful to some contemporary audiences.

3. *CSP, Venetian,* 12:49.

4. Historians have speculated that James removed Stuart because of rumors that she was pregnant. Stuart's attendant Anne Bradshaw testified in 1618 that Stuart's body had become distempered and swollen so that a gown had been enlarged, occasioning the rumors; but no midwife had been engaged, and the swelling subsided after a flow of blood (Examination of Mary of Shrewsbury, 26 June 1618, Univ. of London, Senate House, ULL MS 20, f. 146). James also may have been following through with his initial decision to sequester Stuart away from London; Dudley Carleton had written Thomas Edmondes the previous July about James's decision (13 July 1610, BL Stowe MS 171, f. 292).

step-grandfather. Instead of acquiescing, Stuart fought with her few available resources to stay near London, where she might have some access to her husband and to those who could mediate with James. First, she appealed to the courts for a writ of habeas corpus. Her plea was straightforward, but made too early in the history of English jurisprudence; the courts did not yet grant members of the royal family the rights of ordinary subjects under the law, as Stuart likely anticipated, since she closed her letter by saying that she hoped the justices would in any case become intercessors for her and judge her kindly until she was proven guilty of any offense deserving restraint (letter 93).

When law failed, Stuart became—whether by policy, from illness, or some combination of the two—too weak to travel. The journey north began in mid-March 1611.[1] Stuart was carried, bed and all, into a litter. Once under way, she protested she could not continue, and an unanticipated overnight stop at Highgate became six days. The Privy Council sent Sir James Croft with the king's orders to forcibly remove Stuart,[2] and she was compelled to travel six uncomfortable miles to Barnet, on the outskirts of London, where she remained until 1 April. At either Highgate or Barnet, she may have met with her husband: a document releasing Stuart's gentleman usher Hugh Crompton from accountability for his previous handling of their money was jointly signed and sealed in the presence of witnesses on 21 March, the day Stuart was moved.[3]

Her personal physician, Thomas Moundford, believed the source of Stuart's weakness was grief, but the poor condition of her body demanded that she recuperate before facing the rigors of travel. He wrote Gilbert Talbot that he feared for her life.[4] James, irritated by what he saw as unyielding contempt for his commands, sent another physician, Dr. Hammond, to examine Stuart's pulse and urine; Stuart showed no signs of fever or actual sickness, Hammond said, but was

---

1. King James's order to the Bishop of Durham, 13 March 1611, BL Harley MS 7003, f. 94; Thomas Parry's order to release the prisoner to the Bishop, 15 March 1611, BL Harley MS 7003, f. 98.
2. Privy Council to James Croft, 20 March 1611, BL Add. MS 34727, f. 12.
3. Seymour Papers 6, f. 5.
4. 28 March 1611, BL Harley MS 7003, f. 106.

weak and could not travel until strength of body and mind was restored.[1] Stuart had won a small battle; James granted her a month's rest at East Barnet. By mid-April Croft wrote the Privy Council that, to his knowledge, Stuart still had not been able to walk the length of her bedchamber. She said, he added, that Durham was so remote she despaired of returning or of being able to live out the year, whereas if she were placed elsewhere, she would be more hopeful.[2] James was adamant that Stuart conform to his commands. On 28 April, Sergeant Minors wrote Croft to prepare Stuart for travel because James had resolved that, if he were King of England, she would leave for Durham the following Monday.[3]

The extant text of this letter to Croft is in Stuart's handwriting. That she was allowed to read and copy Minors's letter suggests her keeper's sympathy and Stuart's full participation in the politics of these negotiations about her mind and body. She also had copied Croft's letter from the Privy Council ordering that she be enforced to travel, and someone with her had copied Croft's and Moundford's mid-April letter from the Bishop of Durham detailing King James's comments about her.[4] In her next appeal to the king, Stuart responded to the arguments put forward in these letters. In addition, she thanked James for the time he had graciously granted her, described her improvement, and asked for an additional month (letter 101). This much-drafted petition was successful, and Stuart was allowed from 11 May to 5 June to further convalesce.[5]

Having put together nearly three thousand pounds—most of it from Mary Talbot, to whom Stuart sold the needlework panels Mary of Scots had made during her imprisonment in the north—Stuart walked away from East Barnet on the Monday afternoon of 3 June 1611, cross-dressed like one of Shakespeare's heroines, in the company of a gentleman servant, William Markham. She had told Mrs. Adams, her chap-

---

1. Gilbert Talbot to Thomas Moundford, 29 March 1611, BL Harley MS 7003, ff. 116–17.

2. James Croft to the Privy Council, 17 April 1611, in Maria Theresa Lewis, *Lives of the Friends and Contemporaries of Lord Chancellor Clarendon* (London: John Murray, 1852), 3:154–55.

3. BL Harley MS 7003, ff. 118–19.

4. 20 March 1611, BL Add. MS 34727, f. 12; 17 April 1611, BL Harley MS 7003, ff. 120–21.

5. Thomas Moundford to William James, Bishop of Durham, [May 1611], BL Harley MS 7003, f. 107.

lain's wife, who watched Stuart disguise herself in man's hose, doublet, wig, black hat and cloak, russet boots, and rapier, that she was going to have "a private Visit" with her husband before the journey north. In the Tower, Seymour donned wig, beard, and a carter's clothing, and asked his barber Thomas Batten to keep visitors out by saying Seymour had a toothache; Batten was reported to have believed that Seymour "was gon but to lye a Night with his Wife, and would surely return thither of himself again."[1] Stuart and Seymour must have visited frequently for others to allow them to walk away so casually.

Stuart hiked the mile and a half to the inn where Hugh Crompton waited with horses—and the ostler noted the "Gentleman" looked too unsteady to make it to London—and then rode fourteen miles to join her attendants Anne Bradshaw, Edward Kirton, and Edward Reeves at Blackwall. Seymour, however, was late getting away. He had not arrived by the time the party had to leave or lose the tide. Stuart departed by hired boat, the Thames watermen forced to row all night to reach the port of Leigh and the French ship scheduled to take the group to Calais. Seymour, knowing he was late when he met his friend Edward Rodney outside the Tower, went straight to Leigh, but missed the French ship. He and Rodney, now dressed in elegant suits that marked them as gentlemen, paid the master of a hoy forty pounds for passage across the Channel, on the excuse that Rodney had to leave England because of a quarrel.[2]

The plan might have succeeded, but for a letter that alerted authorities to the escape within a day. Rodney had written Seymour's younger brother Francis, with whom he shared lodgings, a vaguely worded letter apologizing for not having shared the secret with him. Francis received the letter sooner than expected, at eight on Tuesday morning, about the time Stuart was boarding the French bark. In his alarm he raced to the Tower and insisted on seeing his brother, against Batten's excuses, whereupon Batten confessed Seymour was gone. The Lieutenant of the Tower entered and was shown the letter, and he and Francis hastened to

1. John More to Ralph Winwood, 8 June 1611, in Winwood, 3:279–81; Durant, 191–96.
2. John More to Ralph Winwood, 8 June 1611, in Winwood, 3:279–81; Durant, 192–96; William Sparrow and William Cage, Bailiffs of Ipswich, to Robert Cecil, 8 June 1611, BL Harley MS 7003, ff. 132–33.

the king at Greenwich Palace,[1] where Stuart and Seymour had married a year earlier and past which they had rowed during the night. Later that day the Privy Council issued a proclamation against giving Stuart or Seymour aid, and Admiral William Monson was searching the Channel.

In spite of storms and adverse winds, Stuart reached Calais ahead of her pursuers on 5 June. She lingered before landing, however, perhaps to await Seymour, and her boat's sails were sighted by the *Adventure*, under Captain Griffin Crockett. The *Adventure*, armed with shot and pikes, gave chase, overtook the slower, unarmed French bark, which had made for shore, and fired on it repeatedly, until the French bark was forced to yield. Stuart and all aboard were arrested. Questioned, Stuart was unable to say where Seymour was, except that she "hopeth that he is got over."[2]

Seymour and Rodney did land safely at Ostend on 7 June, but Stuart was returned to London and committed initially to the upper Bell Tower, a small, circular, stone room designated for dangerous prisoners, because there was no way to leave except through the living quarters of the Lieutenant of the Tower of London.[3] At her examination, Stuart was said to have answered "with good Judgment and Discretion" that she had wanted only liberty to live with her husband, while Mary Talbot, one of many arrested, demanded a public trial, implied Catholics would have supported Stuart, and reproached the Privy Council, from which her husband Gilbert was absenting himself.[4] By the end of the month, Stuart again was reported to be ill.[5]

The reactions of Stuart's contemporaries to her marriage and escape were diverse. Stuart was never formally charged with a crime, but

---

1. Francis Seymour to Edward Seymour, Earl of Hertford, 4 June 1611, BL Harley MS 7003, ff. 122–23.

2. John More to Ralph Winwood, 8 June 1611, in Winwood, 3:279–81; Captain Griffin Crockett to Admiral William Monson, 5 June 1611, BL Harley MS 7003, ff. 128–29.

3. For this information and a tour of the Bell Tower, I am indebted to Brigadier Kenneth Mears of the Tower of London.

4. John More to Ralph Winwood, 18 June 1611, in Winwood, 3:281–82; Levi, 353.

5. Levi, 353.

James's proclamation after her escape refers to her "divers great and hainous offences,"[1] defined later by prosecutor Francis Bacon in the trial of Mary Talbot as Stuart's having married "without acquainting his Majesty; which had been a neglect even to a mean parent," forgetting her position in choosing an inappropriate partner, and fleeing the sovereign's power.[2] James said Stuart should not "rule her life after her own caprice" and contended that she was his ward and had no right to dispose of herself in marriage.[3] Whatever James's public statements, however, in his view Stuart's greatest crime may have been her challenge to his patriarchal authority. James told the Bishop of Durham that her marriage was an "Indignitie" that had damaged his honor.[4] And he privately replied to her petition for mercy only that she "had etne of the forbidne trie" (see Appendix B, letter 15), righteously comparing himself to God the Father and her sin of disobedience to Eve's original sin in which evil was spawned and sexuality become shame.

A few people at court looked to law to define the crime—the Venetian ambassador wrote that Stuart's marriage could be considered "rebellion."[5] But most of those who criticized Stuart did so on the basis of social and moral codes: the marriage was "stolen," and the couple had lied by promising they would not marry without consent, then doing so.[6] A pamphlet writer branded Stuart a descendant of Eve, an unruly woman who had "touched pleasures in order to transgress,"[7] an

---

1. Beinecke Library Broadsides By6 1611.

2. Spedding, 4:297–98.

3. *CSP, Venetian*, 12:49, although the report is secondhand; Godfrey Goodman, *The Court of King James the First*, ed. John S. Brewer (London: Richard Bentley, 1839), 1:210. Handover points out that Stuart was not James's ward by law (287).

4. King James to William James, Bishop of Durham, 13 March 1611, BL Harley MS 7003, f. 94.

5. *CSP, Venetian*, 12:19.

6. Dudley Carleton to Ralph Winwood, 25 July 1610, in Winwood 3:201; Clement Edmonds to Thomas Edmondes, 16 July 1610, BL Stowe MS 171, f. 296.

7. *Epistola Viri Nobilis et Eruditi De Arbellae, Regii Anglici Sanguinis Faeminae Fuga & Reductione* (Hanover, 1611), a copy of which is held by the British Library. I am grateful to Clayton Miles Lehmann for translating this text into English, and it is his translation that is quoted here and below. A seventeenth-century English version and two later copies can be found in Alnwick Castle MS 93A/35.

accusation more revealing of misogynistic than royalist fears. The most blatantly sexist and sexual response to Stuart's marriage came from Dudley Carleton, writing to Thomas Edmondes, English ambassador at Paris: "I should tell you some newes of a secret mariage betwixt my Lord Beauchamps yonger sonne and the Lady Arbella, for which the poore gentleman doth pennance in the tower, and the Ladies hott bloud that could not live withowt a husband must be cooled in some remote place in ye countrie."[1] Carleton might have been less flippant had he foreseen Stuart would die in prison because of that marriage, but the very casualness of Carleton's remark in a letter between diplomats suggests his awareness of attitudes shared with his audience.

However, sympathy for Stuart was widespread even among those who would seem likely to have indicted her, such as members of the Privy Council. Before Stuart's escape, Prince Henry and Robert Cecil urged James to be lenient.[2] The council presented one of Stuart's petitions to King James, as did the queen (Appendix B, letter 15).[3] Sergeant Minors tried to postpone Stuart's trip north; Lady Frances Chandos told Dr. Moundford that she and her husband would provide for Stuart's needs;[4] Jane Drummond, waiting lady to Queen Anna, passed on Stuart's letters to the queen (Appendix B, letter 15). Even after the escape, the Earl of Nottingham advised James to let the pair go live together, and John More wrote Sir Ralph Winwood with some exasperation that the Scots were irrationally outraged and were inflaming James's fears: "[The Scots] aggravate the Offence in so straunge a manner, as that it might be compared to the [Gun]*Powder Treason*." James's English advisers, he said, saw little danger in the marriage.[5] Most signif-

---

1. 13 July 1610, BL Stowe MS 171, f. 292.

2. Handover, 266; Algernon Cecil, *A Life of Robert Cecil, First Earl of Salisbury* (London: John Murray, 1915), 332. According to John More in a letter to Ralph Winwood, Cecil also moderated the language of the proclamation issued after the escape (8 June 1611, in Winwood, 3:280).

3. *CSP, Venetian*, 12:49. The queen's unhappiness is described in Levi, 353.

4. Sergeant Minors to James Croft, 28 April 1611, BL Harley MS 7003, f. 118; Frances Chandos to Thomas Moundford, [March 1611], BL Harley MS 7003, f. 109.

5. 18 June 1611, in Winwood, 3:281.

icantly, the couple's jailors helped them to correspond and even to meet.

Equally revealing is the widespread expectation that James would relent. Stuart was not alone in her hopes. Stuart's uncle Gilbert Talbot was encouraged to believe that James's displeasure would be short. The Bishop of Durham assured himself and others that God would move the king's heart to compassion.[1] Even after Stuart had been recaptured, the Venetian ambassador met with James and reported that while Stuart faced execution if found to have allied herself with European Catholics, James would not be severe otherwise, "for all may be attributed to her great love for the person she had chosen to be her husband."[2]

Many people believed, as Stuart apparently did, that no one should be forbidden to marry; for them, love was a sufficient reason to defy authority. They saw the fault as James's for not having arranged a fitting match, and James knew of their censure; otherwise there would have been no need for him to justify himself to the Venetian ambassador, saying that he had known what was right and had decided to marry her suitably—she simply took matters into her own hands first.[3] An anonymous Latin treatise, published in Hanover in 1611, similarly defended James. The writer compared James's treatment of Stuart with Queen Elizabeth's, indicting Elizabeth, who had "a womanish fear" of seeing her power diminished if Stuart should marry and prove fertile. James, like a good father, merely wanted Stuart to reject this man whom she did not love and find another.[4] Whether Stuart loved Seymour cannot be known. The evidence suggests that if she did not love him when they were betrothed, she came to care: her surviving letter to him (letter 82) is warmly affectionate. But it is significant that the author of the pamphlet made this point about love explicitly, since he would have had no need to do so unless he thought his readers, if they saw Stuart's marriage as a love story, would support her.

---

1. Gilbert Talbot to Thomas Moundford, 29 March 1611, BL Harley MS 7003, ff. 116–17; William James to James Croft and Thomas Moundford, 17 April 1611, BL Harley MS 7003, ff. 120–21.

2. *CSP, Venetian*, 12:167.

3. *CSP, Venetian*, 12:174.

4. *Epistola Viri Nobilis et Eruditi De Arbellae*, BL copy.

Among the general public, many people did. Turning again to the diplomatic dispatches, we hear "there are many in this city of London who heartily deplore her unhappy case." The Florentine secretary's account of public response after Stuart's escape, when one would expect fears of a Catholic invasion to have been high, indicates that Stuart was praised for having disguised herself and managed the escapes, "for having deceived, under pretext of being ill, those men who were appointed to guard her person." Everyone, the secretary said, was cheering her on, hoping God would allow her both liberty and husband. One wonders whether those who praised Stuart's strength and resoluteness would have felt the same empathy had those qualities promoted anything other than love and marriage, woman's accepted role; the people did worry about whether Stuart had become Roman Catholic, but they were disappointed when she was retaken.[1] King James even investigated a Captain Flick's dinner-time recriminations against the crown, revealing James's uncertainty about the popular appeal of Stuart's cause, especially to those who already were disaffected with his policies.[2]

As Stuart wrote her letters and petitions from confinement, she knew that she was both supported and condemned. She had sympathetic friends who remained loyal, and at least one who allowed her to copy correspondence defining James's position. And Stuart had been at court long enough to have a good sense of her audience; in 1606 she had heard the responses to Elizabeth Southwell's escape to the continent, cross-dressed as Robert Dudley's page. Unlike 1603, when her lover had been fictional, Stuart did not try to cast her marriage as a romance, however she or the public interpreted it. In the one petition to James in which Stuart initially wrote of her "love to this gentleman that is my husband," she revised the phrase to read her "good likeinge" of him (letters 91A and B). Stuart's court letters from this period reflect her careful attention to the submissive rhetoric that would cast her in the most favorable light to the court, and especially King James.

---

1. 21 January 1611 dispatch, "Art. X," *Edinburgh Review,* 503; Levi, 353.

2. Documents related to the June 1611 investigation can be found in BL Harley MS 7003, ff. 134–37; according to William Gamble, secretary to the imprisoned Earl of Northumberland, Flick was committed to the Tower (Alnwick Castle MS 521:140).

In these letters, Stuart more frequently than in earlier letters alludes to the conventional images of womanhood. In contrast to the willful, carnal woman who is a daughter of Eve—the negative stereotype some people applied to her—Stuart portrays herself as a virtuous woman who has not transgressed the boundaries of appropriate female behavior; she is a humble "handmaide," a "poore afflicted gentlewoman," or an "unfortunat woman" (letters 86, 98, and 93). In an entreaty to Queen Anna she argues that she can address herself to no one more confidently than to another woman, in this case "the mirrour of our sexe" (letter 87). She creates a verbal picture of herself to be conveyed to the queen, along with a gift of gloves, evoking a vision of herself at her needlework and linking the hands that sewed with the hands that would wear the work, hands that Stuart gladly would kiss in homage (letter 84). She once even attempts to persuade James that her marriage was evidence of her womanly chastity and submission to her heavenly father; since her conscience told her that after a betrothal she was Seymour's wife in the eyes of God, to have done otherwise would have made her a "harlot." Surely, she says, a king of such wisdom would not want to see any woman so reduced in virtue, but especially not one who has the honor of being related to him (letter 88).

In keeping with this moral image, Stuart underscores her piety and willingness to obey God's laws. She relies on the Lord, who she hopes will move the king to compassion and who knows that she is loyal to James and his children (letters 84 and 86). At the same time, she entreats others to exercise their Christian virtues by relieving the suffering of one who has been brought low. She presents a petition to James at Christmas, the time of forgiveness, and in it appeals to James's godliness, assuring herself that he will never listen to the voice of malice and commit an evil against her, as King David did against Uriah—for which, she does not have to say, David suffered great remorse (letter 91). She is certain the queen will mediate because God would want so good a woman to have participated in so good a work as to reobtain the king's favor (letters 77 and 87). She prays that God will reward what Cecil does for her out of his love for God, allying the deity's cause with her own, and urges an unnamed aristocrat to intervene if for no other reason than because she is a Christian, a member of his spiritual community (letters 97 and 98).

In the undated appeals likely composed during the stressful spring of 1611, Stuart emphasizes her lowliness as one of God's unhappy creatures: she is "the most unfortunate and afflicted creature lyvinge," "the most penitent and sorrowfull creature that breathes," an "earthly creature" of whom no more can be required than confession and submission (letters 97, 99, and 94). The word "creature" elicits pity and decreases attention to Stuart's rank, since all who professed Christianity acknowledged themselves equally God's creatures; in Shakespeare's *King Lear*, it is only in the storm, when Lear's regal trappings have been taken, that he learns the lesson of empathy and understands what "a poor, bare, forked animal" a human being is (III.iv.106). Like other religious terms Stuart chose, then, it appeals to one's compassion, leveling writer and reader while acknowledging the reader's temporal superiority: "There but for the grace of God go I." The usage also implies Stuart's awareness of herself as a thing to others—less a friend than an object of charity. As Stuart modifies the term, however, her phrases seem at the same time to elevate her by suggesting her extraordinary suffering, even martyrdom.

In fact, Stuart's submissiveness is in part a conscious creation, to the extent that what she does can only be called fictionalizing, a strategy often adopted by the powerless. These important letters often exist in multiple drafts, and the drafts make clear that she frequently revised in order to add the proper flattery and convey a sense of hierarchy. In a letter to her cousin Drummond, written soon after her marriage, she asks that her cousin "present this letter to hir Majesty," then, rethinking, inserts "in all humility." She wants her cousin to thank the queen "for the gratious commiseration and respect" already shown, then crosses out "and respect," as though respect, something that hints of equality, is too much to suggest. Her hope to be restored to "hir Majesties favour" is modified to "hir Majesties service," and James's "gratious disposition" becomes "his *just and* gratious disposition" (italics mine), as she wants to emphasize the honesty of her cause (letter 77). Punishment that was "onely an effect of his Majesties displeasure," suggesting her guiltlessness and James's capriciousness, becomes "a signe of his Majesties displeasure"; Queen Anna's "compassi[on]" becomes "that gratious disposition which moveth your Royall minde to compassion" (letters 81A and 90A). Repeatedly, Stuart's revisions illustrate a genuine sensitivity to the nuances of language, and to the creation of an appropriately deferential tone.

The longer passages that she decided to omit are sometimes even more revelatory of the shift between her initial thinking and the submissive self she finally fashioned. In a letter to Queen Anna, likely written at Christmas in 1610 after her disgrace, Stuart first wrote that the season increased her hopes of pardon "because his Majesty I am sure forgiveth greater offences as freely as he desiret[h] to be forgiven by him whose Sacrament he is to receive." Her revised version is more demure and does not suggest that the king has committed offences for which he should ask pardon; she says only that she is presenting a petition "at this time when his Majesty forgiveth greatter offences" (letters 90A and B). In a letter to James, probably from 1610, Stuart initially wrote directly: "I have given your Majesty no true cause of displeasure when it shall please your Majesty throughly to consider of it," indicating his censure to be both unwarranted and ill-considered. She then inserted "*your just* displeasure" (italics mine), as though to flatter him, but the change only furthered the idea of his injustice, and she scratched out the passage entirely. The sense of it reappears later in the letter, more humbly phrased, as "But I assure my selfe if it please your Majesty in your owne wisdomme to consider throughly of my cause theare will no solide reason appeare to debarre me of justice and your princely favour which I will endevour to deserve whilest I breath" (letter 91A).

The revisions in another letter to the king, written in 1611 and asking for additional weeks to recover from her illness before being sent to the north, well illustrate Stuart's understanding of James. In an early draft she argued with some resentment that she had not been feigning illness, as her enemies had suggested, that she had tried to make her weakness known to James: but "not onely any protestation of my owne but the reiterated testimonies of such grave persons as advertised the like...seemed of lesse weight then the traducements of somme whisperers." In the following version she eliminates all criticism of James's judgment and advisors, saying only that she has tried to inform the king of her weakness, and goes on to praise James and acknowledge his status and virtue. She thanks him for the respite she has already had, without which she would have perished, and asks for more time: "if itt maie please your Majestie of your gratious goodnes to add 3 weekes more, M[r]. Doctor Moundford hopes I maie recover somuch strength as may enhable me to travell./ And I shall ever be willinge whilst I breathe to yeild your Majestie moste humble and dutifull obedience as to my Soveraigne for whose felicitie for ever in all things I cease not to praie" (letters 101B and C). According to Moundford, Stuart's submission won her time; he says, "This letter was penned by her in the best termes (as she cann doe righte well) and accompanied with matter best befytting his heighnes and her, it was often red without offence, nay, I maye treu-lye saye even commended by himselfe [James], with the applause of Prince and Counsell."[1] During the weeks that followed, Stuart prepared to escape to France.

One of the drafts of this successful letter is of particular interest because it was handwritten by someone else, perhaps because of Stuart's illness and likely at her dictation, and has angry marginal notes in a voice that sounds much like the Arbella Stuart of Hardwick Hall. King James had said he desired her obedience only as a point of honor. Beside her promise of obedience is a note indicating her disbelief: "that [promise] without the Jorney is inoughe yf the King desire but his honor salved." Next to her statement that she will after three weeks undergo the journey north without resistance is a bitter "as thoughe I had made resistans etc. and so the Jorney more perilous and painefull by my selfe whereuppon I must confess I bely my selfe extreemely in this." To the duty she owes James as her sovereign, she comments, "I take it to bee more then I owe by my allegiance to be separated from my husband duringe his pleasure." To the grace that someone in her posi-tion could hope for, she says, "what man of grace this is I cannot guess nor in what case I am." Beside her profession that James has "my

---

1. Thomas Moundford to William James, Bishop of Durham, [May 1611], BL Harley MS 7003, f. 107.

obedyent hart," she adds, "as thoughe none but this would serve" (letter 101D).

Occasionally, the anger and spirit of the letters from Hardwick Hall and the informal letters slip through in what appear to be final drafts of these much-revised court letters, such as when, during her illness, Stuart threatens the Privy Council (and indicates her awareness of herself as a political entity) with what the world would think if she were forced to travel and cause her own death (letter 95); or when within months after her wedding, she excuses her actions to James by pointing out his inconsistency and neglect:

> I humblie beseech your Majestie to consider howe impossible itt was for me to ymagine itt could be offensive unto your Majestie havinge fewe Dayes before geven me your Royall consent to bestowe my selfe on anie Subject of your Majesties (which likewise your Majestie had done longe since) Besides never havinge ben either prohibited any or spoken to for anie in this land by your Majestie these 7 yeares that I have lived in your Majesties house I could not conceive that your Majestie regarded my Mariage att all (letter 91B).

Despite the "I humblie beseech," her tone is hardly submissive here; instead, her indignation is only lightly veiled.

More often, however, Stuart increases the rhetoric of deference. Writing likely within a short time of her marriage, Stuart creates a picture of herself on her knees before James; her plea is that if she has displeased him, he will "lett itt be covered with the Shadowe of your gratious benignitie, and pardoned in that heroicall mynd of yours which is never closed to those who carrie A most Loyall hart to your Soveraintie, [and] A most sincere and Dutifull affeccion to your person" (letter 86). As the imprisonment stretched out and it became increasingly unlikely that, once exiled to the north, she would rejoin her husband, the degree of submission in her rhetoric well indicates the degree of her desperation. She writes, for example, to beg a lord's intercession with those close to the king: "my weaknesse not permitting me to write particulerly I have made choice of your Lordship humbly beseeching you to move as many as have any compassion of my affliction to joyne in humble mediation to his Majesty to forgive me the most penitent and sorrowfull creature that breathes" (letter 99). Despite her unhappiness and her illness, Stuart was still consciously revising to create the deferential tone; the "humbly beseeching you" was an addition.

A late petition drafted to King James is written on a torn, stained sheet of paper. It is undated, and probably also was composed during Stuart's illness, although it has traditionally been thought her last petition to James. For the only time in the extant letters, she clearly indicates regret for her marriage, whether she means it or not, and she does so in rhetoric that should have been humble enough to satisfy the most absolutist king, rhetoric that to a modern ear sounds an ironic note: "<In all humility> the most wretched and unfortunate creature that ever lived prostrates it selfe at the feet of the most mercifull King that ever was desiring nothing but mercy and favour, not being more afflicted for any thing then for the losse of that which hath binne this long time the onely comfort it had in the world, and which if it weare to do againe I would not adventure the losse of for any other worldly comfort, mercy it is I desire, and that for Gods sake" (letter 96). It is not certain that James received the petition; in any case, no mercy was forthcoming.

Throughout Stuart's years at court, those who received Stuart's formal letters were aware that she had not been reared to fulfill the traditional models of woman, but to rule. Certainly those who knew her at all well must have seen the contradiction between the rhetoric of her court letters and her speech and actions, which in her early years at James's court had been sometimes imperious; Thomas Cooke wrote to her aunt Mary Talbot with some alarm in 1604 that Stuart had "wrastled extraordenaryly" with James's advisors for access to the king "and rather extorted the same from them by feare, then obtained it by kyndness."[1] Surely there were times when her humble persona had provoked amusement from those who could well imagine the thoughts behind the words. And sometimes the contradiction between her words and her actions may have meant that her rhetoric was received with annoyance or resentment by those who realized they were being manipulated. The one time James accepted Stuart's statements of submission and

---

1. 12 February 1604, Lambeth Palace Library MS 3203, f. 182.

granted her an extension before her journey to exile in the north, she used the time to plan an escape to France. No matter how unjust were James's choices in relation to Stuart, it is understandable that he would not easily accept his cousin's words of humility or penitence at face value, any more than she accepted that he would do her good if she would only submit to his authority.

That Stuart felt little affinity for the submissive role and that her other forms of writing contain such strikingly different personas make it all the more significant that the personas of deferential woman and obedient subject so strongly inform these later court letters. Apparently she believed that her audience's expectations were entrenched enough that any other presentation of herself would have little success in achieving her liberty. Although Stuart may never have fully reconciled what Mary Beth Rose describes in women's autobiographies as "the felt conflict between self-effacement and self-assertion, between private and public life, and between individual personality and social role,"[1] cultural expectations did not altogether color what Stuart thought of herself. In the unrevised drafts and marginal notes of the court letters, even of these tumultuous years, we hear a voice that did not speak as humble woman or subject. Stuart chafed at the role. Her creation of a deferential self was an attempt to exploit the patriarchal models and use the language of flattery and obedience as an indirect means of achieving power when overt power was unavailable.

VI. *Subject to That Starre*

> I feare the destiny of your house and my owne both which have fared the worse for being subject to that starre.
> Lady Arbella Stuart to Francis Seymour (letter 89)

For most writers, the Stuart story ended straightforwardly: Lady Arbella Stuart lost her sanity and died in the Tower of London in 1615. The

---

1. "Gender, Genre, and History: Seventeenth-Century English Women and the Art of Autobiography," in *Women in the Middle Ages and the Renaissance: Literary and Historical Perspectives*, ed. Mary Beth Rose (Syracuse: Syracuse Univ. Press, 1986), 247.

primary source for the idea that Stuart became deranged was court observer and letter-writer John Chamberlain, who in 1613 and 1614 repeatedly commented on Stuart's distraction; in April 1613, for example, he wrote that she was said to be "crackt in her braine."[1] Some of Stuart's biographers, however, have disputed that view of Stuart as a lunatic prisoner and pointed to evidence that seems to contradict Chamberlain's rumors. Extant documents indicate that Stuart during those years supervised her personal affairs. After her gentleman usher Hugh Crompton was released from prison in July 1613, he resumed handling her accounts and recorded the occasions on which he sent money to William Seymour and others according to Stuart's written warrants; and in April 1614, the Privy Council directed the Lieutenant of the Tower to allow Stuart's servant Samuel Smith access to her so that he might receive her directions. Moreover, Stuart's friends and attendants attempted to free her, which they would have been unlikely to do had they believed her to be insane.[2]

The last years of Stuart's life are made only somewhat less confusing by an important collection of papers the British Library purchased in 1984, the contents of which both illuminate hitherto shadowy occurrences and introduce new mysteries. The collection, catalogued as Add. MS 63543, consists of thirty contemporary letters and documents related to Stuart's years in the Tower and to her husband's grandfather's marriage to Catherine Grey. That several documents and the dockets on others are written in the hand of Henry Howard, the Earl of Northampton, suggests that these manuscripts were gathered during the course of his work as a commissioner for King James.[3] The first half of the volume comprises papers directly connected to Stuart and having to do with Northampton's investigations into suspected escape plots. They include statements made by Stuart's physician, a minister, an

---

1. Chamberlain to Dudley Carleton, 29 April 1613, in Chamberlain, 1:443.

2. Bradley, 2:64; Handover, 290; Durant, 208. Hugh Crompton's account book is at Longleat, Seymour Papers 22; the Privy Council warrant of 29 April 1614 is reprinted in Lewis, 3:169–70.

3. For this idea about the collection's origin, I am indebted to W. H. Kelliher, curator of manuscripts at the British Library.

attendant, and the Lieutenant of the Tower, William Waad, in which conversations with Stuart are reported; the depositions and examinations of persons thought to have useful information about conspiracies and the sale of Stuart's pearls; and three letters written by William Seymour and his grandfather during the autumn of 1613, in which Seymour's actions on the continent are described.

Much of what follows about Stuart's last years draws on these rediscovered manuscripts. In combination with previously known documents, they suggest that Stuart indeed was distressed, perhaps even intermittently delusional, and yet remained active on her own behalf. As in 1603 and 1611, Stuart suffered illnesses that may have been physiological, strategic, or a combination of the two. As in 1603 and perhaps 1611, she could not or chose not to eat, which again made her body the site of controversy and gave her some measure of control over her situation. As in her earlier letters from captivity, she intrigued for release by trying to recast herself in James's eyes as a properly submissive subject; and on one of the two occasions for which evidence of distraction exists, what seems distraction may have been a conscious fiction. Stuart's death in 1615 was in part volitional, since she refused the care of her physicians.

During the first years of Stuart's confinement in the Tower, her husband lived largely in Paris, seemingly unsure whether to oppose or appease King James. In late 1611, the Archduke asked James to allow Stuart and Seymour to live together,[1] a request James refused. Seymour may have converted to Roman Catholicism at St. Omer that year,[2] presumably in hopes of acquiring Catholic support. According to the recently recovered letters written by the Earl of Hertford, the king ordered Hertford to send his grandson an allowance of four hundred pounds a year and instructions to stay away from Dunkirk and other known Catholic strongholds, indicating that James feared Seymour

---

1. In a letter dated 23 October 1611, HMC *De L'Isle Report*, 4:290, note.

2. B. Fitzgibbon, S.J., "The Conversion of William Seymour, Duke of Somerset (1588–1660)," *Biographical Studies 1534–1829* [now called *Recusant History*] 1 (1951–52): 117–19.

might be driven by destitution to ally himself with Catholics. By May 1613, Seymour, deeply in debt in Paris, had traveled to Dunkirk. That October, in a letter contained in Add. MS 63543, he wrote his angry grandfather that he had returned to Paris in all obedience to Hertford and King James, even though he had been weakened by fever and would be arrested for debt if he did not receive more money.[1] But an unknown correspondent gives a more inflammatory account of Seymour's behavior, saying that Seymour was to meet the Archduke's ambassador near Dunkirk, had complained that four hundred pounds was not enough to keep him, had been called openly a Prince of England, and was traveling with poet Henry Constable, a Catholic "who persuaded him to ill courses." Seymour was said to be resentful, determined as neither a beast nor a fool to take courageous action, and certain his wife would not live long.[2]

Whether Seymour was involved in a plot to rescue Stuart in 1613 is unknown, but by the time of his trip to Dunkirk he likely had heard that she had been ill and Mary Talbot had been accused of planning Stuart's second escape. From soon after Stuart's imprisonment in 1611 until early 1613, there are only glimpses of her: in 1612, Robert Cecil died of cancer, and Stuart's allowance was reduced; Mary Talbot's case for aiding Stuart was heard in the Star Chamber, after which the countess was fined and imprisoned; and Stuart was not allowed to attend Prince Henry's funeral.[3] In early 1613, Stuart became the subject of much speculation, because the court learned of a possible plot to deliver

---

1. Hertford's 5 November 1613 response to Seymour's letter, in which Hertford notes James's generosity, is BL Add. MS 63543, f. 19, and the allowance is confirmed in his 5 November 1613 letter to Thomas Edmondes, English ambassador in Paris, BL Add. MS 63543, f. 20; both of the Earl of Hertford's letters are secretary's copies. William Seymour's 8 October 1613 letter to the Earl of Hertford is BL Add. MS 63543, ff. 17–18. Seymour also wrote his brother Francis about his debts (14 May 1613, later copy, Alnwick Castle MS 93A/35, Part 4), and his 26 June 1613 letter to William Trumbull emphasizes his financial crisis and his loyalty to King James (BL uncatalogued Trumbull papers, Misc. 5, f. 94). I am indebted to Peter Beal for alerting me to the latter.

2. 26 May 1613, BL Cotton Cal. E. 11, ff. 335–36.

3. Handover, 286–89; Durant, 203–4. Durant mentions a letter Stuart wrote to King James expressing her sorrow for Prince Henry's death, but his citation refers to a letter Stuart had earlier written to Prince Henry.

Stuart to Roman Catholics—John Chamberlain was writing his friends in late January that Stuart had revealed something against her aunt the Countess of Shrewsbury.[1]

Until the recovery of the unpublished papers in Add. MS 63543, however, scholars have had few sources of evidence beyond contemporary rumor about what happened inside the Tower. According to Lieutenant Waad's statement in that volume, events had begun in the autumn of 1612, at about the time Mary Talbot was to be released into her husband Gilbert's custody. She and Stuart had conversed, Stuart in the gallery of the Lieutenant's lodgings and the Countess of Shrewsbury at her chamber window, after which Stuart had fallen dangerously ill and spoken bitterly against her aunt. Lieutenant Waad obtained the king's permission for Stuart's personal physician, Dr. Moundford, to visit, and Stuart improved. Before Christmas, Stuart conversed with her aunt and again fell into what Waad describes as "fyttes of distemper and convulsyons"; she sought to have her aunt denied access to her and used with "strange incivility" items Mary Talbot sent her.[2]

Stuart's remarks about her aunt, which Waad reported to King James, provoked the investigation. Dr. Moundford testified that Stuart seemed asleep when he again arrived on 12 January and asked her gentlewoman how Stuart was and why she had taken to her bed. The gentlewoman replied that Stuart did not eat or sleep, and Stuart told him her aunt was the cause. After Moundford offered a "*Cordiall* of *Pacience* and *Humilitie*" to ease her unquiet mind, Stuart refused to speak further; but the next morning she emphasized that she wanted her aunt removed. According to Moundford, Stuart revealed that Mary Talbot desired her to convert to Catholicism, which Stuart said was a truth that torture could not have procured, but which she was admitting because Waad kindly had obtained permission for Moundford to visit during her earlier illness.[3]

1. Chamberlain to Dudley Carleton and Ralph Winwood, 28 and 29 January 1613, in Chamberlain, 1:410, 413.

2. William Waad's statement, undated, BL Add. MS 63543, ff. 11–12. The statement is unsigned, but the contents identify the speaker as Waad.

3. Thomas Moundford's statement, January 1613, BL Add. MS 63543, ff. 5–6.

An unknown person, perhaps a waitingwoman, reported that in a private conversation Stuart had hinted of knowledge important to the realm: the secret was of "great Consequence," and Waad would not suffer for his part in discovering it, because "there is not the meanest Gentleman in England, if I bring him into a Busynes, he shall be cleared and suffer no wrong." According to the same statement, Stuart had said "[a]ll the world…will condemne me to undoe my *Aunt* that indured for me," but Stuart could not in conscience allow "a foolish woman" to "overthrowe a whole family," and she could not worry about reputation when the state was at issue. If this account can be trusted, Stuart's words are reminiscent of the rhetoric she had used a decade earlier when she had written of her fictional lover and envisioned herself as grandly heroic, avowing power and influence she lacked; her Aunt Mary will forswear all, Stuart is said to have asserted in early 1613, but surely "the meanest worde I speake, shall be of more credytt then all the oaths she can sweare."[1]

In the other of Dr. Moundford's two statements, he recounted what had occurred sometime in January when he and Dr. John Palmer, a minister, had visited Stuart in order that Stuart, who was no longer in bed, might repeat before witnesses what she had told Waad privately. In that meeting, Stuart explained that years earlier, when she was in custody at Lambeth after her marriage, Mary Talbot and others would have delivered her to Catholics, but Stuart had refused and vowed never to change her faith. Apparently surprised by the introduction of Lambeth, Waad pressed Stuart about whether the project had continued since then, and Stuart suddenly rose to close the conversation.[2] The evasion also argues that the plot was fictional, an attempt on Stuart's part to attract the court's attention, as she had in 1603, and to stimulate the

---

1. January 1613, BL Add. MS 63543, ff. 1–2. That this statement is in the same handwriting as Lieutenant Waad's statement (ff. 11–12) and the report of the Earl of Worcester's examination (ff. 7–8) suggests this testimony was taken by Waad or at his direction.

2. Thomas Moundford's statement, January 1613, BL Add. MS 63543, ff. 3–4. According to the docket, Moundford's declaration of what had been said was "also avowed by Doctor Palmer" to be true.

court to dispatch friends to visit her, by hinting of secrets while disclosing only old news that could harm no one.

But a record dated 1 February summarizing Stuart's examination by the Earl of Worcester indicates that Stuart then affirmed that Mary Talbot had a plot to deliver Stuart from the Tower into the hands of Catholics. Stuart is reported to have said that although she and her aunt had the same goal—Stuart would not deny she would go to "*Papists, Turkes, Jewes,* or *Infidels*" if it would get her out of the Tower—she would "not follow her *Aunts* courses" (as some historians have argued Stuart had in fleeing to France) or be at Mary Talbot's direction. Stuart refused to provide any details, and emphasized that she was revealing this plot only for Lieutenant Waad's sake. Waad, who composed the report, said Stuart even wanted someone, likely his daughter, to sleep in the same chamber with her to ensure that further contact with her aunt could be avoided.[1] The day before Princess Elizabeth's Valentine's Day wedding, Dr. Palmer reported that Stuart had told him on 9 February what Mary Talbot had said, and Waad had overheard, at the window: the Lieutenant's throat would have to be cut.[2]

Lieutenant Waad likely had not overheard. Had he done so, he would have recorded the exchange when he analyzed the evidence against Mary Talbot. Instead he concluded that the case rested on Stuart and would evaporate if she recanted or qualified her accusations, although he found the circumstantial evidence compelling. In arguing his position, he recounted Mary Talbot's anger over his conduct: the Countess of Shrewsbury, Waad said, had cursed and threatened him for not telling her that Stuart was sick and condemned him for reporting to the court what Stuart had uttered when she was in "some Melancholy humor" arising from grief over her husband's "deboshed cariage" and

---

1. Report of the Earl of Worcester's examination, BL Add. MS 63543, ff. 7–8. Because the manuscript is torn, a word beginning with what seems a *D* is largely missing: Stuart desired "to have my D[   ] to lye in her Chamber." Since Stuart was being held in a room either in Waad's quarters or accessible only through them, and his daughter later gave Stuart a key, it seems reasonable to suggest that the missing word is *Daughter.*

2. John Palmer's statement in a secretary's copy, 13 February 1613, BL Add. MS 63543, ff. 9–10.

would be sorry for what she had done when "she came to her selfe." The countess accused him of trying to force Stuart to flee and arranging events so that Mary would be blamed. Waad had no question that an escape had been plotted. Of course, he would have appeared foolish had he created so much furor over nothing, but his rationale was multifold: Stuart's sicknesses were "no fiction," and they occurred after conversations with an aunt she had loved until then; the countess never asked why Stuart wanted her removed or what Stuart had said of her, which suggested that she knew; and Mrs. Bradshaw left Stuart's service rather than participate in the plot (although it appears that Anne Bradshaw was ill).[1]

That Stuart was hyperbolic does not negate the possibility that Mary Talbot had tried to convert Stuart or engage her cooperation with Catholics; when Stuart had used similar language in 1603, Henry Cavendish arrived at Hardwick Hall with forty men. Mary Talbot was said to have become deeply committed to the Roman Catholic cause after having received in 1609 a piece of the Cross,[2] and something unusual had occurred, as Waad pointed out, if Stuart demanded her once-beloved aunt's removal. Many people believed in both Stuart's distraction and her aunt's guilt: by April, John Chamberlain said that Stuart was "crackt in her braine" and that the countess was under additional restraint "upon good cause as the voyce goes."[3] The court took matters sufficiently seriously that not long afterward Lord Grey was confined for what turned out to be a flirtation with one of Stuart's gentlewomen, and Thomas Bull was put in close confinement for twelve weeks after Stuart mentioned his name in some loose connection with Mary Talbot's.[4]

Whether or not Mary had proposed conversion or escape, it seems likely that Stuart was to some degree fictionalizing and using the fiction

---

1. William Waad's statement, undated, BL Add. MS 63543, ff. 11–12.

2. Handover, 252.

3. Chamberlain to Dudley Carleton, 29 April 1613, in Chamberlain, 1:443.

4. John Chamberlain to Dudley Carleton, 29 April 1613, in Chamberlain, 1:443; Henry Wotton to Edmund Bacon, 7 May 1613, *The Life and Letters of Sir Henry Wotton*, ed. Logan Pearsall Smith (Oxford: Clarendon, 1907), 2:23; Thomas Bull to Ralph Winwood, 20 July 1613, HMC *Buccleuch Report*, 1:139.

to try to achieve liberty. If the testimony is even reasonably accurate, her speeches were self-aggrandizing and excessive; by creating or embellishing and "reluctantly" revealing a plot that could not be proved, Stuart could demonstrate her loyalty and prompt James to free her to attend Princess Elizabeth's wedding. The plan resembles that of the fictional lover that Stuart had used in 1603 and that she later admitted had been a conscious ploy (letter 11). In 1613, Stuart could have expected the princess to request Stuart's presence; and at the time the investigation was being conducted, Stuart bought a chain of fifty-one pearls for fifteen hundred pounds and had pearls costing four hundred pounds embroidered on a gown,[1] indicating she hoped to attend the ceremony. (Her pearls would have been paltry next to the six hundred thousand pounds worth of jewels that King James wore,[2] but what she ordered was far beyond her means: the chain of pearls was divided and pawned within months, and the dress, its pearls never paid for, was given to the jeweler after Stuart's death.[3]) At the least, Stuart's seeming concern for the strict Lieutenant Waad might convince him to relax his guard or improve her treatment in the Tower.

My interpretation of the papers in Add. MS 63543 is supported by documents from other sources that imply Stuart tried a similar tactic with King James three months later. In May 1613, Waad was discharged as Lieutenant of the Tower and he and his daughter temporarily committed as prisoners. Contemporary accounts accuse Waad of embezzling Stuart's gold and jewels and of being too severe with her and casual with others.[4] By May, however, Stuart apparently had executed a plan to support her earlier assertion that she was refusing to participate in escape attempts, and thus establish her entire submission and

---

1. Abraham der Kinderen's examination, 1 March 1614, BL Add. MS 63543, ff. 13–14.

2. John Nichols, *The Progresses, Processions, and Magnificent Festivities, of King James the First* (London: J. B. Nichols, 1828), 2:546.

3. Abraham der Kinderen's examination, 1 March 1614, BL Add. MS 63543, ff. 13–14; Privy Council to the Lieutenant of the Tower, 28 September 1615, in Lewis, 3:170–71.

4. John Chamberlain to Dudley Carleton, 13 May 1613, in Chamberlain, 1:452; "A Narrative History of King James" (1651), *A Collection of Scarce and Valuable Tracts…of the Late Lord Somers*, 2:283–84.

obedience. According to Viscount Fenton, Stuart convinced Waad's daughter to give her a key, from which Stuart took a wax print and had a duplicate key made. Fenton himself presented the duplicate key to the king at Stuart's request,[1] presumably to demonstrate that James's prisoner could have escaped, but voluntarily chose instead to yield to his authority, perhaps what Stuart meant when she said she planned a different approach from her aunt's. Fenton's account is corroborated by Robert Carr, who said that Waad had been discharged for carelessness in letting Stuart have access to a key, and by William Gamble, secretary to the imprisoned Earl of Northumberland, who noted that Abigail Waad and a Mrs. Hoorde—likely the Bridget Horde who served the Talbots—were committed to the Tower over Stuart's key.[2] Although details are few, the episode suggests that Stuart was consciously trying to reshape James's impression of her, as she had in her letters; at the same time she initiated the removal of the jailor who, by taking Edward Rodney's letter to the king, had precipitated her recapture. The plan implies an uncharacteristic lack of concern on Stuart's part for Waad's daughter; and ironically, by demonstrating Stuart's superiority over James's guards and her ability to attract others to her cause, it more likely incited James to resentment than reward.

Documents in Add. MS 63543 also supplement references to a more direct attempt to free Stuart that may have been in the planning that summer Waad was removed, an attempt about which interested contemporaries ascertained so little detail that it seems likely the crown effectively suppressed information.[3] On 1 November 1613, a Mr. Ruthen, almost certainly Patrick Ruthven, was committed close prisoner in the Tower for what was said to be an escape route under his

1. Thomas Erskine, Viscount Fenton, to John Erskine, 20 May 1613, HMC *Mar and Kellie Report, Supplement, 1235–1708*, 51–52. Although Stuart was rumored to be distracted that spring, there is no indication in Fenton's letter that Stuart was at all distracted when he talked with her.

2. William McElwee, *The Murder of Sir Thomas Overbury* (London: Faber and Faber, 1952), 255; William Gamble's list of prisoners in the Tower, Alnwick Castle MS 521:140.

3. The Earl of Northampton wrote Somerset, saying that King James had decided the matter should remain secret (Cooper, 2:241).

study there; and although Gilbert Talbot was authorized later that month to take Mary Talbot home, the order was quickly reversed,[1] indicating that she was suspected of involvement. On the day Ruthven was more closely confined, his servant James Wade was examined. The report in Add. MS 63543, signed by Wade and by Gervase Helwys, the new Lieutenant of the Tower, reveals that Wade was questioned about who regularly visited Ruthven—two physicians, an astrologer, and an alchemist—and whether Wade had heard the noise of hammering in the study. Wade affirmed that he had, but thought his master and the alchemist were experimenting. Asked whether he had ever seen any results, all Wade could say was that he had been told to take an ounce of gold and silver to a goldsmith who had melted them together and beaten the metal into a long piece that was cut into pieces and returned, and then sent back to be done over again[2]—a statement that hardly clarifies the situation.

Ruthven's name recurs the following March[3] in connection with the disposition of pearls Stuart had bought from jeweler Abraham der Kinderen near the time of Princess Elizabeth's February 1613 wedding. Three papers in Add. MS 63543 relate to the inquiry. Although the examinates are vague on the chronology of events, ten of the fifty-one pearls had been pawned to goldsmith Fr[ancis?] Sanbourne within months of their purchase and later sold on the authority of John Falconer, who was employed in Stuart's affairs. Stuart or someone close to her had not fully trusted Falconer and rightly so; Sanbourne testified that Falconer had said a doctor—Dr. Palmer, Sanbourne thought—would have to be present if Sanbourne were to see the rest of the pearls and that Sanbourne should offer in the doctor's presence a lower price than he would actually pay Falconer later. William Hammond, likely

---

1. James Wade's examination, BL Add. MS 63543, ff. 21–22; Durant, 206.

2. BL Add. MS 63543, ff. 21–22.

3. Although one of these papers (jeweler Abraham der Kinderen's examination, ff. 13–14) was dated to 1 March 1613, the writer was using old-style dating, when the new year began on 25 March; another statement in the same investigation, the Earl of Northampton's examination of William Hammond, was taken on "the 26 of March 1614" (ff. 25–26).

the William Hammond who served the Talbots, first pawned and then sold the other forty-one pearls; he testified that he had not known they were Stuart's, because Mr. Ruthven gave them to him and received the money. Both Sanbourne and Hammond said Dr. Palmer had traced the pearls and sought their return, arguing that because they were Stuart's, they could be recovered.[1] Hammond added that after Palmer challenged the sale, Ruthven said he had warrant to act, which, if true, would indicate that he had the approval of Stuart or her agents.[2] It is unclear why Dr. Palmer would have sought the pearls or why the crown would have scrutinized the sales or why someone as prestigious as the Earl of Northampton, who had been responsible for the November probe, would have conducted the examinations, unless the sales were believed to have been connected to the escape, perhaps attempts to amass necessary monies. The ongoing investigation could explain why in early July Dr. Palmer and Hugh Crompton, Stuart's gentleman usher, were committed to the Tower. John Chamberlain could not determine a cause; he said only that it was about Stuart, who "is far out of frame this midsommer moone." Her servants Edward Reeves and Samuel Smith were said to have been involved as well in what most contemporaries believed was a rescue attempt. William Gamble, whose employer was inside the Tower, recorded that Palmer and Smith were committed "for my Lady Arabellays escape out of the Tower."[3]

The most puzzling of the rediscovered documents in Add. MS 63543 is a statement in Gervase Helwys's handwriting, headed 15 July. The manuscript also has been dated, in a different but closely contemporary hand, to 1613; the person who added the year may have had access to outside information about the events described, but the con-

---

1. Examination of Abraham der Kinderen, 1 March 1614, BL Add. MS 63543, ff. 13–14; examination of Fr. Sanbourne, undated, BL Add. MS 63543, ff. 23–24; examination of William Hammond, 26 March 1614, BL Add. MS 63543, ff. 25–26.

2. William Hammond's examination, 26 March 1614, BL Add. MS 63543, ff. 25–26.

3. John Chamberlain to Dudley Carleton, 7 July 1614, in Chamberlain, 1:546; Thomas Lorkin to Thomas Puckering, 6 August 1614, in Cooper, 2:241–42; Alnwick Castle MS 521:140.

tents of the statement seem equally consistent with the events of the summer of 1614.[1] According to the speaker, who may have been Helwys or one of his subordinates—perhaps the Tresham [?] whose name is recorded on the verso—Stuart approached him about an implausible plot to smuggle William Seymour into the Tower to live with her. If the report can be trusted, Stuart stopped the speaker in the gallery and asked if he—presumably the speaker was male—could maintain a confidence in order to prevent civil war. He defends himself from charges of abetting Stuart by arguing that he pretended to cooperate only in order to discover the particulars of her conspiracy. It would be rumored that Seymour had died, and he would be "buryed" and secreted into the Tower. Just a few people would know. To the objection that Seymour eventually would be seen, she said the windows on the side to the gardens would be boarded up. Told what would follow if Seymour were discovered, she said she had foreign and domestic supporters who would prevent it. Asked if her aunt Mary Talbot were involved, she said "by noe means." Stuart could have been mentally disturbed, amusing herself, or misleading authorities while an escape was being planned. If the document should be dated July 1614, it could explain Crompton's and Palmer's imprisonments, as well as John Chamberlain's report that Stuart was "far out of frame" then.[2]

On 8 September 1614, the Privy Council asked a divine, Dr. Fulton, to attend Stuart, who, the Council wrote, has "of late fallen into some indisposition of body and mind" and needs a "person of gravity and learning" to offer spiritual comfort and "visit her from time to time." The Privy Council's letter indicates that Stuart was ill again, as the members thought from grief, but does not suggest that Stuart had completely lost her reason. No one would ask a learned minister to discuss spiritual matters with and offer counsel to someone believed mentally

---

1. BL Add. MS 63543, ff. 15–16. Internal evidence indicates only that the statement was recorded between June 1613, almost two years after Stuart's escape, and September 1614, after which Stuart remained in bed. If Northampton alone was responsible for collecting the documents in BL Add. MS 63543, the year 1613 may be correct, since he died in June 1614.

2. John Chamberlain to Dudley Carleton, 7 July 1614, in Chamberlain, 1:546.

incapable. The Council also requested that Dr. Fulton make his first visit to the Tower "speedy and undelayed,"[1] which implies a need for haste. It is likely that Stuart either had become unusually ill or had taken charge by again refusing to eat or threatening to allow herself to die, which in early modern England well might have elicited a call for a divine. According to a report after her death, it was at this time that Stuart took to her bed and refused to allow her physicians even to feel her pulse.[2]

Outside the Tower, interest in Stuart was high during these years. For most of her imprisonment, Stuart was strictly kept from visitors; even her servant Samuel Smith was not allowed to speak to her except in the presence and hearing of the Lieutenant of the Tower.[3] That vigilance about her person, combined with James's alacrity in confining or more closely confining anyone about whom there was a whisper of suspicion, kept rumors fueled and thus creates what may be a false impression of near-constant activity by Stuart's friends on her behalf. In letter after letter, courtiers speculate about each new flurry in the Tower. Those with personal information, like Viscount Fenton, who had handled the duplicate key, passed on to friends what they knew and hypothesized about what they did not.[4]

Stuart's case also prompted literature that in turn influenced public opinion of her case. Not surprisingly, many contemporary plays drew on secret marriages and escapes in order to capitalize on the curiosity aroused by the clandestine marriage and subsequent flight of a ranking member of the royal family. The play most directly analogous to Stuart's case is John Webster's popular *Duchess of Malfi*. In Webster's tragedy, the young Duchess ignores her brothers' wishes and secretly marries her steward Antonio Bologna. After her brothers discover the truth, the

1. Lewis, 2:339.

2. HMC Appendix to Eighth Report, *MSS of the College of Physicians*, 229.

3. Privy Council warrant to the Lieutenant of the Tower, 29 April 1614, in Lewis, 3:169–70.

4. Thomas Erskine, Viscount Fenton, to John Erskine, 20 May 1613, HMC *Mar and Kellie Report, Supplement, 1235–1708*, 51–52.

Duchess tries to escape by feigning a pilgrimage, but she is apprehended by her brother Ferdinand's men and committed to prison, where Ferdinand tries to drive her to despair and madness and finally has her executed. Like Stuart, Webster's Duchess was a woman of rank with public responsibilities, a woman generally perceived as virtuous, who married clandestinely against the declared edict of her ranking male relative, lied and deceived others, attempted to flee, and was captured and imprisoned without trial for her crime. The play was begun in 1612, soon after Stuart's name had been heard by much of adult London; and it was performed at Blackfriars theater, in the neighborhood where Stuart had had her private home, in 1614, when rumors were circulating in London that Stuart was being driven mad by her incarceration. Given the parallels between Stuart and the Duchess, the timing of the play, and the Renaissance habit of analogical reading, surely many members of Webster's audience would have been reminded of Stuart as they watched his tragedy.[1]

Anne Lancashire discusses how in *The Second Maiden's Tragedy* (1611), probably by Thomas Middleton, the parallels to Stuart and Seymour were made through the addition-slips, small pieces of paper with additional text that were pasted onto the original manuscript. That the allusions appear on these slips suggests that they either were written separately in order to avoid having them read when the manuscript was submitted to the licenser or that they were inserted later in order to increase audience appeal. In the play, the character representing James is named the Tyrant, and the couple representing Lady Arbella Stuart and William Seymour are named the Lady and Govianus ("the rightful king"). In one addition, the couple, who are wrongfully and separately imprisoned by the Tyrant, meet through the kindness of their jailors; another addition refers to Govianus's leaving the land. As Lancashire

---

1. Stuart's case previously has been discussed as a contemporary parallel to *The Duchess of Malfi;* see, for example, Charles R. Forker, *Skull Beneath the Skin: The Achievement of John Webster* (Edwardsville: Southern Illinois Univ. Press, 1986), 299–300. See also my "The Crime of Marriage: Arbella Stuart and *The Duchess of Malfi,*" *Sixteenth Century Journal 22* (1991): 61–76.

notes, the similarity "could hardly have failed to occur to a Jacobean audience in late 1611."[1] Lines in the subplot of John Fletcher's *The Noble Gentleman* (performed in 1626 in what probably was a revival) allude so directly to Stuart that Baldwin Maxwell concluded the play could not have been originally presented between 1610 and 1615, as some had argued, because it would have touched King James too closely.[2] *Cymbeline* (1610–11) has been read as a Shakespearean plea for forgiveness, with Stuart symbolized by the virtuous, cross-dressed princess Imogen, whose marriage infuriates her father Cymbeline, King of Britain, and whose husband is banished to the continent.[3]

Whatever public sympathy for Stuart may have been generated by contemporary literature had no discernible effect on King James or on Stuart, who spent the last year of her life in bed. On 25 September 1615, Lady Arbella Stuart died. She was nearly forty. The poisoning of Sir Thomas Overbury in the Tower had proved that some of James's favorites could go as far as murder, and James rightly feared that some of his subjects would assume that he, like Ferdinand in *The Duchess of Malfi*, had had his disobedient female relative killed. Dr. Moundford and five of his fellow physicians were ordered to conduct a post-mortem. According to their post-mortem report, Stuart's death was caused by

> a chronic and long sickness; the species of disease was *illam jamdiu producem in cachexiam* [one that after a time resulted in ill-health and malnutrition], which, increasing as well by her negligence as by refusal of remedies (for a year she would not allow doctors to feel her pulse or inspect her urine). By long lying in bed she got bedsores, and a confirmed unhealthiness of liver, and extreme leanness, and so died.[4]

1. *The Second Maiden's Tragedy*, The Revels Plays (Manchester: Manchester Univ. Press; Baltimore: Johns Hopkins Univ. Press, 1978), 279. The additions also are discussed by Eric Rasmussen ("Shakespeare's Hand in *The Second Maiden's Tragedy*," *Shakespeare Quarterly* 40 [1989]: 1–26), who argues that Shakespeare may have been their author.

2. *Studies in Beaumont, Fletcher, and Massinger* (Chapel Hill: Univ. of North Carolina Press, 1939), 149–54.

3. Miss Winstanley, as discussed in Eleanor Grace Clark, *Ralegh and Marlowe: A Study in Elizabethan Fustian* (New York: Fordham Univ. Press, 1941), 191; Clark has a brief section on plays about Stuart, 188–92.

4. HMC, Appendix to Eighth Report, *MSS of the College of Physicians*, 229.

By modern standards, the physicians' report is vague. Acting in accordance with her earlier pattern of behavior, Stuart may have slowly starved herself to death, as David N. Durant believed.[1] The notes about malnutrition, leanness, and liver abnormality are consistent with that position, and Stuart's physicians were careful to note that they believed Stuart contributed to her own death through negligence and deliberate refusal of remedy. Their comments argue that Stuart made decisions about what would happen to her body, decisions that were understood to be conscious choices and that she was capable of enforcing. Refusing to act as her physicians advised would not necessarily have been seen as suicide and thus a violation of her religious beliefs; ignoring remedy could even be associated with martyrdom and mortification of the flesh, a turning to God. Stuart had written in a letter to Viscount Fenton that if there were no hope of restoration to favor she was ready to die, as long as she did not ensure eternal damnation by committing suicide: "I dare dy so I be not guilty of my owne death" (letter 94).

To many people then and now, refusal of remedy automatically signals insanity. But Stuart could not have been consistently distracted during her last years; as biographers Durant and Handover have pointed out, Stuart's friends would not have risked any rescue had they thought Stuart irrecoverably deranged;[2] and it would have been equally senseless for the Privy Council to send Samuel Smith to receive Stuart's directions about her financial affairs. The phrase "went insane" conveniently labels Stuart a female hysteric, a woman exhibiting the mental instability and melancholia often attributed to learned women, thus allowing observers such as John Chamberlain to dismiss her transgressions of the code of appropriate female behavior as "madness," without calling the system into question. Those who were acquainted with and attended Stuart consistently characterized her illnesses either as intentionally deceitful and obstinate or as psychosomatic in origin—in seventeenth-century terminology, as arising from her grief or her unquiet mind.

---

1. Durant, 207.

2. Durant, 208; Handover, 292.

While Stuart had much to grieve, both her family history and symptoms indicate that she also may have had an underlying disease. The documents from the Tower contained in Add. MS 63543 describe two previously unknown episodes of convulsions and include at least one statement that implies delusion. In combination with the post-mortem report and other texts delineating Stuart's symptoms over years, these documents suggest that Stuart's recurrent illnesses were attacks of porphyria, a disease unrecognized in the early seventeenth century.[1] Acute intermittent porphyria is a hereditary disease characterized by abdominal pain, difficulty in swallowing, muscle weakness, stomach and liver distention, mental shifts ranging from depression and excitement to delusions, convulsions, emaciation, and, if sufficiently severe, death. The disease is biochemical in nature, a genetic enzyme deficiency; symptoms appear after puberty and more commonly in women. Attacks range from mild to intense, with sudden onset and quick recovery, and may be provoked by stress, malnutrition, or medication.[2] Although no one has discovered evidence of the disease among Stuart's direct ancestors, porphyria did exist in the Stuart line. Many of King James's descendants had documented cases, and descriptions of James's health and urine (sometimes wine-red) argue that he had a milder version of the disease that likely killed his son, Prince Henry, at age eighteen. Medical historians have argued that Mary Queen of Scots, too, had porphyria.[3] If Stuart had the disease, it would have come to her through her father, and the common genetic source of

---

1. For discussions of and information about porphyria, I am grateful to Robert J. Flaherty, M.D., and John M. Opitz, M.D., chairman of the Department of Medical Genetics at Shodair Hospital.

2. For the symptoms of acute intermittent porphyria, see A. Kappas, S. Sassa, R. A. Galbraith, and Y. Woodman, "The Porphyrias," *The Metabolic Basis of Inherited Disease*, ed. Charles R. Scriver et al., 6th ed. (New York: McGraw-Hill, 1989), 1320–29.

3. Ida Macalpine, Richard Hunter, and C. Rimington, "Porphyria in the Royal Houses of Stuart, Hanover, and Prussia: A Follow-up Study of George III's Illness," *Porphyria—A Royal Malady: Articles Published in or Commissioned by the British Medical Journal* (London: British Medical Association, 1968), 18–21, 26–38. That King James had the disease is not merely surmise: his physician Sir Theodore Turquet de Mayerne kept such detailed notes on James's symptoms that, according to Dr. John M. Opitz, the diagnosis of porphyria appears quite sound. Antonia Fraser suggests that Mary Queen of Scots inherited the disease from her father, James V of Scotland, whose "hysterical" death puzzled historians (445).

the disease in both Stuart and King James would be Margaret Tudor.

In terms of modern medical knowledge, Stuart's illnesses fit the diagnosis. In mid-February 1603, Stuart was described as having abdominal pains and being forced to take medication. No letters survive from those two weeks, but afterwards Stuart vowed not to eat or drink at Hardwick Hall, which, if her illness had elicited a useful reaction, would have been good strategy, even though she risked another onset by refusing nutrition. In 1611, when Stuart said she was too weak to travel north to Durham, she may have experienced muscle weakness that rendered her unable to walk, especially if her physician, who insisted on cordials to calm her,[1] was prescribing cordials that provoked or prolonged the attack, such as the common combination of red wine with laudanum, or even red wine that was stored or served in leaden vessels.[2] In an undated letter to Viscount Fenton, probably from that period, Stuart described herself as so weak that she could write only with extreme pain (letter 94). She said later that in implying to King James that she had delayed the journey north, she had belied herself (letter 101D), although that illness, too, was useful in giving her time to plan an escape. In late 1612, Stuart was considered dangerously ill in the Tower, when Dr. Moundford was called to treat her convulsions; in saying that Stuart would come to herself again, Mary Talbot might have been relying on experience. Attacks of porphyria could explain a belief that Seymour was coming to live in the Tower, as well as the emaciation and unhealthy liver noted after Stuart's death.[3] If Stuart recognized in 1614 that her doctors' cordials aggravated her pain, she wisely rejected them; and by denying her physicians even the latitude to examine her urine or take her pulse, she may have been carrying out a decision not to continue a life with recurrent pain so intense it has been described as worse than childbirth.[4] If Stuart had porphyria, her death resulted from a complex set of interactions that

1. Thomas Moundford to Gilbert Talbot, 28 March 1611, BL Harley MS 7003, f. 106.

2. For information on the cordials that could provoke an attack of porphyria, I am indebted to Dr. John M. Opitz.

3. The Venetian ambassador heard that Stuart's death was sudden and accompanied by a tremor and weakness of the lower limbs ("Art. X," *Edinburgh Review,* 511–12).

4. According to Dr. John M. Opitz, a sufferer of porphyria can learn to understand the disease well enough to use it actively or passively to implement such a decision.

may have included her inability or refusal to eat, with porphyria as the underlying disease that brought about her natural death. Many sufferers of porphyria have been wrongly labeled as hysterics.[1] In that way, too, Stuart may have been misunderstood by those who denigrated her for weakness of mind and character.

That Stuart had porphyria cannot be proved at this distance—there are too many difficulties in interpreting medical terminology across four centuries—and it is possible that if Mary Queen of Scots had porphyria and Stuart lived with her aunt's attacks, she could have realized the response they provoked and consciously or unconsciously imitated them at times of great stress. But even if Stuart had the disease, as seems probable, that diagnosis should not be understood to imply that Stuart was not in control of her actions or striving to rule her own life. Until porphyria is advanced, the higher functions of reasoning remain intact between and sometimes during episodes.[2] Moreover, porphyria's attacks are intermittent, and Stuart had attempted to contract a secret marriage in 1603 long before her abdominal pains began and after months or years of unhappiness. Her letters describing her fictional lover were written before the pains were mentioned, although the subsequent exhaustion and malnutrition might account in part for Stuart's lack of caution in the letters that followed. She married William Seymour when there is not the slightest evidence of infirmity, and she appears to have been equally healthy, other than a general weakness from lack of exercise, when she attempted to escape to France. In the Tower, Stuart intrigued for freedom, and if her description of a plot to deliver her to Catholics seems in part delusion, she handled the issue with an intelligence that suggests otherwise. The letters in which Stuart attempted to work within the patronage network and to achieve liberty demonstrate careful control of rhetoric, and the anger that slips through in the court letters or in the marginal notes cannot be neatly correlated with times of physical pain. If Stuart had porphyria, her strength in the face of continual skepticism about the source of her pain is the more impressive.

---

1. For a discussion of the misdiagnosis of Mary of Scots, see Macalpine, et al., 35–38.

2. For an explanation of this point, I am grateful to Dr. John M. Opitz.

Extant sources record no outpourings of public affection after Stuart's death. Had anyone felt inclined to open display, acting on the inclination would have been both risky and pointless, since James's power was firmly established. Nonetheless James took the precaution of omitting a royal funeral when he had Stuart's body placed with those of Prince Henry and Mary Queen of Scots in the vault at Westminster Abbey. As Bishop Goodman admitted, according honor to one so out of favor would have reflected poorly on James's actions.[1] According to the Venetian ambassador, the court did not go into mourning, although Queen Anna wished it, because Stuart had died "contumacious," or rebellious. Even in death she was considered disobedient and insubordinate. King James inherited what was left of her goods. Within five months he allowed William Seymour to return to England and soon afterward restored him to favor.[2] Stuart's servants Hugh Crompton and Edward Kirton joined Seymour's household; both served as members of Parliament in the 1620s. Seymour married Frances Devereux, the daughter of Stuart's friend, the Earl of Essex; became a member of Parliament; fought for the royalists in the Civil War; was one of four peers at the funeral of Charles I; and became a physician and respected literary patron who twice served as Chancellor of Oxford University. He named his oldest daughter Arbella.[3]

The Venetian ambassador also recorded, however, that Stuart's death was "much regretted by many of the chief persons here," and Stuart's aunt Mary Talbot wrote of her deep grief and her hope that Stuart "died a Saint." Richard Corbet, Bishop of Norwich, echoed the Countess of Shrewsbury with confidence in an epitaph he privately composed for Stuart; he described Stuart's soul as "Enlarg'd at last, secur'd from hope and fear," finally freed to be "amongst Saints."[4] In another vein, Stuart

1. Goodman, 1:212–13.

2. "Art. X," *Edinburgh Review,* 512; William Seymour to King James, undated, in Lewis, 2:354–55; [Richard] H[arold] St. Maur, *Annals of the Seymours* (London: Kegan Paul et al., 1902), 194.

3. Durant, 209; Cokayne, 12:69–73.

4. "Art. X," *Edinburgh Review,* 512; Mary Talbot to Margaret Clifford, 8 December 1615, HMC, 11th Report, Appendix, Part 7, *Manuscripts of Lord Hothfield,* 83; Bradley, 2:274.

became the subject of a popular ballad, "The True Lovers' Knot Untied," which reflects the ambiguity of the era. On the one hand, the ballad is a patriarchal lesson; it is subtitled "the right Path whereby to advise Princely Virgins how to Behave themselves, by the Example of the Renowned Princess, the Lady ARABELLA." On the other hand, Stuart is portrayed as a victim of rank, "born unhappily," unable to love as "meanest people" might, and hoping death will "end the strife."[1]

The direction in which sentiment was moving, however, was clear. Increasing celebration of marital love and rising antagonism towards the monarchy soon made James's treatment of Stuart seem to anti-royalists a classic example of tyranny. An anonymous description of Stuart's death that Robert Nalson hand-copied into his miscellany sometime between 1650 and 1685 is particularly interesting in this regard. Because the narration's date of composition is unknown—it may have been composed soon after Stuart's death or decades later—it cannot be used to demonstrate a contemporary reaction to Stuart; but the work does reflect a sentiment current when Nalson recorded the piece, the seeds of which were present in Corbet's epitaph. In Nalson's piece, Stuart sees Christ himself at the foot of her bed, come to take her to heaven, and with "inward joy" she embraces him. Despite the cold, she refuses to have her bedclothes around her, preferring to mortify her body. And just as the Duchess of Malfi echoes Christ's "Father, forgive them" on Calgary, so too does the "charytable" Stuart forgive, saying, "I hate the sinne but I love the person" before committing herself to God's mercy.[2] By the mid-seventeenth century, some people viewed Lady Arbella Stuart as a Protestant martyr and saint.

By the late eighteenth century, Stuart was further transformed into a domestic heroine, with an emphasis on the woman rather than the princess. In an art ballad attributed to William Mickle, Stuart is an

---

1. J. Woodfall Ebsworth, ed., *The Roxburghe Ballads, Illustrating the Last Years of the Stuarts*, vol. 7 (1893; rpt. New York: AMS Press, 1966), 599–603.

2. Bodleian MS Top. Cheshire c. 6, f. 389, which also describes Stuart, in Latin, as having been "learned above her sex." Bettie Anne Doebler similarly points out the degree to which the language of the Duchess of Malfi's death evokes the language of the *ars moriendi* and leads the audience to admire the Duchess's Christian heroism in "Continuity in the Art of Dying: *The Duchess of Malfi*," *Comparative Drama* 14 (1980): 203–15.

innocent victim and a stereotypical young wife; she listens for her husband's firm footsteps or the sound of his "dear voice" and, consistently fearful, is carried away to France trembling in his arms, a languid combination of sighs and tears.[1] In 1828, Romantic poet Felicia Dorothea Hemans also wrote of Stuart as a devoted wife denied "that domestic happiness which her heart appears to have so fervently desired." To Hemans, however, to be womanly was to be strong and pure of soul; Stuart's womanly spirit enables her to withstand suffering and maintain her faith in God. Seymour is a friend and lover of "earnest tenderness" with whom Stuart shares a fervent, holy love; and although she might be crushed on earth, she knows she and Seymour will triumph beyond the grave.[2] Of the novels and drama written about Stuart in the 1800s, the most embellished was a romance (1844) by the popular George Payne Rainsford James. His novel, which he said he hoped would demonstrate the excellence of such virtuous womanhood, ends with a tearful reunion between Stuart and Seymour as last rites are administered to her; she dies in the arms of her loving husband.[3]

Stuart was an equally attractive subject for nineteenth-century historians. Louisa Stuart Costello provided a biography in her *Memoirs of Eminent Englishwomen* (1844); Maria Theresa (Villiers) Lewis included another in her "Life of the Marquis of Hertford" (1852);[4] Agnes Strickland discussed Stuart in her *Lives of the Tudor Princesses* (1868);[5] and two Victorian women interested in women's history, Elizabeth Cooper and Emily Tennyson Bradley (later Smith), located as many letters as they could, and published two-volume biographies in 1866 and 1889. To Cooper, Seymour was the weaker vessel and Stuart the stronger and

---

1. Cooper, 2:254–59.

2. *Records of Woman*, 3–20.

3. *Arabella Stuart: A Romance from English History*. The play was *Arabella Stuart* by the Reverend William Greenwall, described by Ebsworth as "little-known but meritorious" (600). Another novel was published in 1898 by Charles-Claude-Marie-Hector Artaud de la Ferrière in *Deux romans d'aventure au XVIe siècle: Arabella Stuart, Anne de Caumont* (Paris: Paul Ollendorff, 1898); Count Ferrière's novel, however, reads more like a researched biography than many a popular biography.

4. In her *Lives of the Friends and Contemporaries of Lord Chancellor Clarendon*.

5. London: Longmans, Green, 329–92.

more passionate; Cooper's Stuart was a woman who, by refusing to submit to King James, made a powerful plea for justice and human rights
in an era too corrupt and cowardly to respond.[1] Bradley emphasized
Stuart's wit and the "brilliancy of her humour"; like Cooper, Bradley
indicted early modern England: "let us leave a pure life and tragic fate,
to stand for ever at the judgment-bar of history, as a silent witness
against James Stuart and his servile ministers."[2] Blanche Christabel
Hardy in 1913 described Stuart as a woman ambitious for "aught but
love and a sheltered home," deeply in love with a man unworthy of
her.[3]

Interest in Stuart faded by the 1920s, but revived in mid-century,
with biographies by historians such as Phyllis Margaret Handover
(1957), who saw Stuart as a talented, tragic woman who would have
made a good scholar's wife, but lacked the toughness for politics; Ian
McInnes (1968), who emphasized Stuart's spirit and the flavor of the
era; and David N. Durant (1978), who sought in Stuart's childhood the
source of what he saw as eccentric and self-destructive behavior. In
1949, novelist Doris Leslie portrayed Stuart as willful, but charming;
and Molly Costain Haycraft, in a 1959 juvenile novel, emphasized Stuart's intelligence and concurrent lack of ambition: her Stuart is a woman
who has seen too much of the price to want a crown. In 1981, Jane
Bridgman portrayed Stuart as a romantic, but somewhat more sexually
active heroine.[4]

The outlines of Stuart's life are thus relatively well known. Since Stuart's death, the greatest number of publications about her have appeared
during the Victorian period, when women's nature and suffrage were at
issue, and the mid- to late-twentieth century, when feminism has
become one of the western world's dominant movements. As Karen
Newman recently noted, Arbella Stuart's story is a particularly appro-

---

1. Cooper, 2:224–25, on Seymour.

2. Bradley, 1:14; 2:81.

3. Hardy, 1.

4. *Wreath for Arabella* (New York: Roy Publishers, 1949); *Too Near the Throne: A Novel Based on the Life of Lady Arbella Stuart* (Philadelphia and New York: J. B. Lippincott, 1959); *Arbella* (Bognor Regis: New Horizon, 1981).

priate ground from which to analyze the position and rights and voices of women in early modern England.[1]

Raised to rule and always aware of her rank, Lady Arbella Stuart was not silent or obedient, nor was she passive in response to the forces arrayed against her. Articulate in her anger, she struggled to command her destiny through whatever means were available, from ruse to overt defiance.[2] She understood that she was a political commodity and used both her mind and body in her attempts to achieve control of her life. She demanded that she be justly evaluated by the court. Even though she did not attain her goals, Stuart pushed the social and political system to its limits, delineating for us what those limits were for a royal woman of her era. King James remained so compulsively fearful of Stuart, the unruly female within his own family, that nearly three years after her death he had his Privy Council investigate whether she had given birth to a child that had been secretly conveyed across the seas.[3] To her contemporaries, whether they praised or blamed her, Arbella Stuart was an example of female resistance to authority. And because Stuart's oppositional drama was performed on such a public stage, her story highlights the complex interactions of life and text. Stuart's reading informs her writing and the fictions she enacts, which others transform into texts that affect opinions of Stuart held by yet others who write texts that influence readers, and so on, echoing through generations. The process begins with her words, the words that allow us access to the mind of an unapologetically bright and learned aristocratic woman who laughed, cried, sewed, hawked, and was willing to oppose even the crown.

1. "City Talk: Women and Commodification in Jonson's *Epicoene*," *ELH* 56 (1989): 515, and in her *Fashioning Femininity and English Renaissance Drama* (Chicago: Univ. of Chicago Press, 1991), 143.

2. Lewalski also emphasizes this aspect of Stuart's life and letters in her recent "Writing Resistance in Letters."

3. Star-Chamber proceedings against Mary Talbot, 26 June 1618, Univ. of London, Senate House, ULL MS 20, ff. 145–50. The person who brought the government's case against Mary Talbot for refusing to reply to questions about her niece was Henry Yelverton, the man Stuart in 1609 had helped restore to favor; in 1618, he was King James's attorney general.

DESCENDANTS OF HENRY VII AND ELIZABETH OF YORK

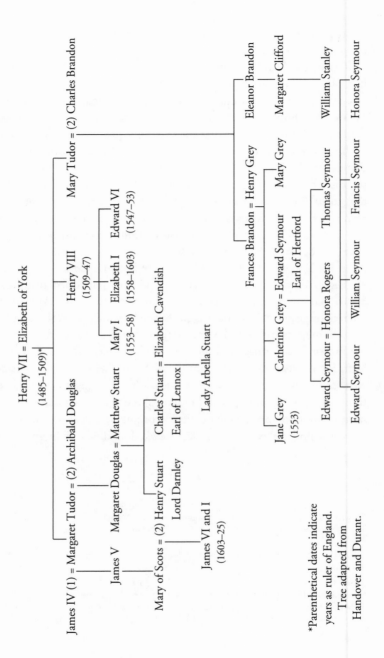

*Parenthetical dates indicate
years as ruler of England.
Tree adapted from
Handover and Durant.

TEXTUAL INTRODUCTION

Most of Lady Arbella Stuart's letters in this edition have been transcribed and edited from original manuscripts in Stuart's own handwriting. In her familiar letters and in rough drafts of her court letters, Stuart uses an informal italic hand, her characters slanted slightly to the right and formed with few extraneous strokes, her words written with frequent pen lifts. The italic hand, which allowed for speed as well as legibility, was becoming the most popular style of handwriting in England and, perhaps because it was considered easier to learn than the secretary hand, was the style taught to most seventeenth-century women regardless of class.[1] A sample of Stuart's informal italic hand may be seen in Figure 2. In presentation copies of her letters, Stuart uses an elegant and fashionable formal italic hand, the characters slightly more upright and angular than those of her informal hand and distinguished by graceful looped upper hooks and by clubbed ascenders and descenders, the clubs created by exerting additional pressure on and barely turning the pen point, as shown in the sample in Figure 3.

Like most aristocratic women, Stuart also had attendants who might write at her dictation or prepare fair copies of her drafts; and a few of the texts in this edition have been transcribed from copies in a secretary's hand or in a combination of hands, as one of Stuart's various secretaries finished a letter Stuart had begun or as Stuart further revised or signed a secretary's copy. Stuart's nine Latin letters to the Danish court are almost entirely in secretaries' hands; in these letters, Stuart appears to have structured her ideas in English, then dictated her Latin translation to a secretary and revised from that point.

Only four of Stuart's letters are transcribed from texts other than original manuscripts in Stuart's or her secretaries' hands: a letter of 2 August 1604 to Sir George Manners (letter 44) is taken from a text published in 1888 by the Historical Manuscripts Commission, because

---

1. See Martin Billingsley's comments in *The Pens Excellencie*, as cited in Giles E. Dawson and Laetitia Kennedy-Skipton, *Elizabethan Handwriting 1500–1650: A Manual* (New York: W. W. Norton, 1966), 10.

the original, held at Belvoir Castle, is not available to researchers; a letter of 7 August 1606 to Sir John Holles (letter 50) is extant only in a copy made by Holles's son; and two letters to Francis Seymour (letters 89 and 92) are drawn from eighteenth- and nineteenth-century transcripts, because the originals, sold in the nineteenth century, are currently unlocated. In 1603, Sir Robert Cecil had some of Stuart's letters copied, and these extant contemporary copies are listed in my headnotes to the letters; for each of these letters, however, there also exists a text in Stuart's hand, which is the version that appears in this edition.

Of the Stuart letters in this edition, ten (letters 54, 55, 57, 58, 59B, 60, 63, 64, 89, and 92) have never been printed in full in previous collections of her correspondence. One of those ten, a letter to King Christian (letter 64), will be entirely new to Stuart scholars, and the text of another, a letter to Francis Seymour (letter 89), has been recovered after being lost for a century. I have included three examples of Stuart's writing that are not letters in the strictest sense: her instructions to John Dodderidge (letter 3), her answers to Sir Henry Brounker's questions (letter 10), and her formal declaration to Brounker that she was not contracted to marry (letter 11).

Stuart's letters are presented with her original spelling, punctuation, capitalization, and word division ("with all" for our "withal").[1] Modern readers should be aware, however, that early seventeenth-century writers frequently used commas where we would use periods, and vice versa, and that the virgule, a medieval form that persisted into the Renaissance, was a common mark of punctuation, often employed by Stuart

---

1. In making these choices, my guiding principle has been to interfere as little as possible with the sound of Stuart's voice. In early modern England, an oral culture was in the process of becoming a print culture, and because spelling and punctuation were not yet fully fixed, they were especially reflective of the writer's internal voice. Spelling suggests pronunciation, and punctuation indicates pace and tone, and thus emotion. Luckily for modern readers, Stuart's spelling and punctuation are surprisingly consistent with our standards (although her secretaries' sometimes are less so). For a more complete discussion of rationale, see my "Behind the Arras: Editing Renaissance Women's Letters," *Voices of Silence: Editing the Letters of Renaissance Women*, ed. Josephine A. Roberts, Renaissance English Text Society Proceedings, 1991; rpt. *New Ways of Looking at Old Texts: Papers of the Renaissance English Text Society, 1985–91*, ed. W. Speed Hill, Medieval and Renaissance Texts and Studies, in conjunction with the Renaissance English Text Society (Binghamton, N.Y.: 1993), 229–38.

in combination with a period, as "./". (As in the previous example, original manuscript punctuation appears within quotation marks throughout the textual headnotes and footnotes, with editorially imposed punctuation outside them.) I have regularized the use of i/j, u/v, and long s and silently expanded most abbreviations, which were largely a matter of saving space in an era when paper was hand-made, imported, and expensive;[1] in the expansions, Stuart's usual spellings are maintained. Only three abbreviations—Mr., Mrs., and St.—never appear in expanded form in her extant letters and these have been left unexpanded according to her consistent usage, as have the initials she sometimes used in lieu of a full signature. Occasionally, where the manuscript clearly indicates the beginning of a new grammatical unit, I have added a comma or period within square brackets. For example, in the manuscript, a large space may precede a sentence beginning with the pronoun "I." In a printed book, readers overlook small discrepancies in spacing between words, and since "I" would always be capitalized, readers of the printed text might not notice that a new sentence had begun if a mark of punctuation were not added. As is usual with prose texts, the lineation does not reproduce the lineation of the manuscripts except in the closings, where the lines, although reproduced in a standardized format (flush left and right), retain the original lineation. Latin letters present a special problem, since few readers comfortably translate seventeenth-century court Latin; these letters appear in their proper chronological order in modern translation, with no attempt to reproduce Stuart's spelling or punctuation. The letters appear in Latin in Appendix A, edited according to the same principles as the English letters.

That some of Stuart's letters exist in multiple drafts is both a joy and an editorial puzzle, a joy because the various drafts and the revisions within them allow us to trace the evolution of Stuart's thinking. To unlock the puzzle, the editor must carefully evaluate which of the undated texts are drafts of a single letter, rather than separate letters with a similar goal, establish their order, and determine how to present

---

1. Dawson and Kennedy-Skipton, 6.

the drafts so that the revisions are clear in print. Providing only what appears to be the final copy would deny the reader access to Stuart's mind as she shaped her prose; thus, in this edition the letters are presented with their additions and deletions marked, and in some cases more than one version is supplied, each with attendant additions and deletions. The textual symbols are as follows:

[as]	Roman print within square brackets indicates letters or words provided by the editor.
<as>	Roman print within angle brackets indicates letters or words that were added or that replaced deletions in the manuscript.
[*as*]	Italic print within square brackets indicates letters or words that were deleted or written over in the manuscript.
[<*as*>]	Italic print enclosed in angle brackets and square brackets indicates letters or words first added and then deleted in the manuscript.

Large sections of prose containing many additions and deletions that Stuart then deleted in their entirety appear set apart by asterisks. Ink-blots and illegible deletions are not shown, although, if they are numerous or lengthy, they are mentioned in the notes. In trying to conserve space, Stuart sometimes tried to fit a word on the end of a line, saw it would not fit, and so deleted the word and rewrote it on the beginning of the next line; because such deletions are not revisions, they have been silently omitted.

If only one version of a letter is presented here, the first manuscript listed in the headnote is my source, and the locations of other contemporary copies are then provided. For letters printed here in several versions, those versions are listed in their order of composition, which is the same order in which they are presented in their edited forms. Unless otherwise noted, transcripts made after Stuart's death and printed versions of Stuart's letters are not listed: although later copies are interesting texts in their own right, the letters often were radically altered by modernization, which means these copies add less to our knowledge of

Lady Arbella Stuart's voice than to our understanding of shifts in cultural perspective and in the editorial principles of succeeding centuries.

The majority of Stuart's letters are dated, either in the texts or in the dockets, brief statements of contents often placed on Renaissance papers; her numerous undated texts, however, offer intriguing mysteries. Some of the undated texts can be loosely dated by reference to external events. In other cases, letters can be dated by an examination of the folios: in whatever manner the paper may have been folded and bound since the seventeenth century, drafts that appear on the same sheet of paper are likely to have been written at approximately the same time. In the present edition of Stuart's letters, dates appear as they were written in her manuscripts, that is, in old style, when the new year began not on 1 January, but on 25 March. To avoid the confusion created when, for example, a letter of 22 December 1603 is followed by one dated 2 January 1603, potentially puzzling dates appear in combined old and new style (2 January 1603/4) in my headnotes preceding the letters.

The same editorial principles have been applied to the letters written to Lady Arbella Stuart that appear in Appendix B. Of these letters, eight (letters B1, B3, B5, B10, B11, B12, B13, and B16) have not appeared in full in previous collections of Stuart's correspondence; and four (letters B10, B11, B12, and B16) are printed here for the first time. The letters to Stuart appear separately because, although they offer valuable context for some of Stuart's letters and useful contrast to her prose, they are so few that it seemed best not to interrupt Stuart's voice or, by incorporating them between Stuart's letters, to pretend to hear conversations that cannot exist without more voices.

Overleaf

FIGURE 2. Lady Arbella Stuart's informal italic hand, in an autograph letter to Gilbert Talbot, Earl of Shrewsbury, 17 June 1609 (Arundel Castle MSS, Autograph Letters 1585–1617, no. 167). By permission of His Grace The Duke of Norfolk.

FIGURE 3. Lady Arbella Stuart's formal presentation hand, in an autograph letter to Sir Robert Cecil, 22 June 1603 (Bodleian MS Ashmole 1729, f. 150). By permission of the Bodleian Library.

167

Because I know not that your Lo. hath forsaken one recreation
that you have liked heretofore, I presume to send you a
few idle lines to reade in your chamber, after you have tired
your selfe either w affaires, or any sport that bringeth wearines
And knowing you well advertised of all occurrents in serious
manner, I make it my end onely to make you merry, and
show my desire to please you even in playing the foole.
for no folly is greater (I trow) then to laugh when one
smarteth. But that my Aunty divinity can tell you S.t
Laurence deriding his Tormentors, bad them turne him
even upon the gridiron
on the other side for that he lay on was sufficiently
broiled, I should not know how to excuse my selfe from
either insensiblenesse or contempt of injuries. I grid it one
rob a house and build a Church w the money, the
wronged party may go pipe in an Ivy leafe for any
redresse. For money so well bestowed must not be taken from
that holy worke though the right owner go a begging
Unto you it is given to understand parables, or to com̄nd
the com̄ent. But if you be of this opinion of the Scribes
and Pharises I condemne your Lo. (by your leave) for an
Heretike by the Authority of Pope Ione. For theare is
a text saith you must not do euill that good may
come theareof. But now from doctrine to miracles
I assure you w in these few dayes I saw a paire of
Virginalles make good musick w.out helpe of any hand
but of one that did nothing but warme (not moue)
a glasse some 5. or 6. foote from them. And if I thought
thus great folkes inuisibly, and farre off worke in
matters to tune them as they please, I pray your Lo. forgiue
me, and I hope God will. To whose holy protection
I humbly recom̄end your Lo. From Broadstreet the 17. of Iune
1609.

My good Lord / it hath pleased his Maiesty to alter his
purpose concerning the pension whearof your Lo: writt to me; It
may please you to moue his Ma: that my present want may
be supplied by his Highnesse w. some sume of money which
needeth not be annuall if it shall so seeme good to his Ma:
But I would rather make hard shifte for the present then be too
troublesome to his Highnesse, who I doubt not will allow me
maintenance in such liberall sorte as shall be for his Maiesties
honour, and a testimony to the world, no lesse of his Highnesse
Princely bounty, then naturall affection to me. Which good
intention of his Ma:ts I doubt not but your Lo: will further, as
you shall see occasion, wheareby your Lo: shall make me greatly
bounden to you as I already acknowledge my selfe to be. And so
with humble thanckes for your honorable letter I recomend
your Lo:p to the protection of the Almighty, who send you all
honour and contentment. From Sheene the 22. of Iune

Your Lo:ps poore frend

Arbella Stuart

SELECTED BIBLIOGRAPHY

"Art. X [Lady Arabella Stuart and the Venetian Archives]." *Edinburgh Review,* October 1896, 483–513.

Bradley (later Smith), E[mily] T[ennyson]. *Life of the Lady Arabella Stuart.* 2 vols. London: Richard Bentley and Son, 1889.

Cooper, Elizabeth. *The Life and Letters of Lady Arabella Stuart, Including Numerous Original and Unpublished Documents.* 2 vols. London: Hurst and Blackett, 1866.

Costello, Louisa Stuart. *Memoirs of Eminent Englishwomen.* Vol. 1. London: Richard Bentley, 1844.

Durant, David N. *Arbella Stuart: A Rival to the Queen.* London: Weidenfeld and Nicolson, 1978.

Handover, P[hyllis] M[argaret]. *Arbella Stuart: Royal Lady of Hardwick and Cousin to King James.* London: Eyre and Spottiswoode, 1957.

Hardy, B[lanche] C[hristabel]. *Arbella Stuart: A Biography.* London: Constable, 1913.

Inderwick, F[rederick] A[ndrew]. "Arabella Stuart." *Side-Lights on the Stuarts.* 2nd ed. London: Sampson Low, et al., 1891, 22–122.

Lefuse, M. *The Life and Times of Arabella Stuart.* London: Mills and Boon, 1913.

Levi, Eugenia. "Lady Arabella Stuart." *The Athenaeum,* 11 September 1897, 352–53.

Lewalski, Barbara Kiefer. "Writing Resistance in Letters: Arbella Stuart and the Rhetoric of Disguise and Defiance." *Writing Women in Jacobean England.* Cambridge: Harvard University Press, 1993, 66–92.

Lewis, Maria Theresa (Villiers). *Lives of the Friends and Contemporaries of Lord Chancellor Clarendon.* Vols. 2 and 3. London: John Murray, 1852.

McInnes, Ian. *Arabella: The Life and Times of Lady Arabella Seymour, 1575–1615.* London: W. H. Allen, 1968.

Steen, Sara Jayne. "The Crime of Marriage: Arbella Stuart and *The Duchess of Malfi.*" *Sixteenth Century Journal* 22 (1991): 61–76.

_____. "Fashioning an Acceptable Self: Arbella Stuart." *English Literary Renaissance* 18 (1988): 78–95. Rpt. *Women in the Renaissance: Selections from "English Literary Renaissance,"* ed. Kirby Farrell, Elizabeth H. Hageman, and Arthur F. Kinney. Amherst: University of Massachusetts Press, 1990, 136–53.

Strickland, Agnes. *Lives of the Tudor Princesses Including Lady Jane Gray and Her Sisters.* London: Longmans, Green, 1868, 329–92.

LIST OF ABBREVIATIONS

Batho   Batho, G. R. *Talbot Papers in the College of Arms.* Vol. 2 of *A Calendar of the Shrewsbury and Talbot Papers in Lambeth Palace Library and the College of Arms.* London: Her Majesty's Stationery Office, 1971.

BL   British Library.

Chamberlain   Chamberlain, John. *The Letters of John Chamberlain.* Edited by Norman Egbert McClure. 2 vols. Philadelphia: The American Philosophical Society, 1939.

CSP   *Calendar of State Papers.*

DNB   *Dictionary of National Biography.*

Emerson   Emerson, Kathy Lynn. *Wives and Daughters: The Women of Sixteenth Century England.* Troy, N.Y.: Whitston, 1984.

HMC   Historical Manuscripts Commission (The Royal Commission on Historical Manuscripts).

Jamison   Jamison, Catherine, revised by E. G. W. Bill. *Shrewsbury MSS in Lambeth Palace Library (MSS 694–710).* Vol. 1 of *A Calendar of the Shrewsbury and Talbot Papers in Lambeth Palace Library and the College of Arms.* London: Her Majesty's Stationery Office, 1966.

OED   *Oxford English Dictionary.*

SPD   State Papers Domestic (Public Record Office).

Tilley   Tilley, Morris Palmer. *A Dictionary of the Proverbs in the Sixteenth and Seventeenth Centuries.* Ann Arbor: University of Michigan Press, 1950.

Winwood   Winwood, Ralph. *Memorials of the Affairs of State in the Reigns of Queen Elizabeth and King James the First.* 3 vols. London, 1725.

THE LETTERS
OF
Lady Arbella Stuart

1

TO ELIZABETH TALBOT, COUNTESS OF SHREWSBURY

Autograph, Stuart's presentation hand, Huntington Library MS HM 803. Addressed "To the right honorable my very good Lady and Grandmother the Countesse of Shrewsbury". Written 8 February 1587/8.

Stuart, aged twelve, wrote her grandmother one year to the day after the execution of her aunt Mary Queen of Scots, presumably from one of the houses of Mary and Gilbert Talbot, with whom she was then living.

❦

Good Lady Grandmother, I have sent your Ladyship, the endes of my heare which were cutt the sixt day of the moone, on saturday laste; and with them, a pott of Gelly, which my Servante made; I pray God you finde it good. My Aunte Cavendishe was heere on Monday laste, she certified me, of your Ladyships good health, and dispositione, which I pray God longe to continue. I am in good health, my Cousin Mary hath had three little fittes of an agew, butt now she is well, and mery. Thus with my humble duty unto your Ladyship and humble thanckes for the token, you sent me laste, and craveinge your dayly blessinge, I humbly Cease. Frome Fims, the .viii. of February. 1587   10

Your Ladyships humble, and obbediente

childe

Arbella Steward

Lines 1–2. **endes...moone:** It was a country custom to send hair trimmings to a loved one. Many activities were loosely timed according to the waxing and waning of the moon; even a century later, hair-cutting and nail-paring were believed best done while the moon was on the increase (Keith Thomas, *Religion and the Decline of Magic* [New York: Charles Scribner's Sons, 1971], 297).

Line 4. **Aunte Cavendishe:** Stuart's aunt Anne Cavendish, wife of William, who lived with Bess when the couple was not in London; or Stuart's aunt Grace Cavendish, wife of Henry, who was Bess's step-daughter and daughter-in-law.

Line 6. **Cousin Mary:** daughter of Mary and Gilbert Talbot, then aged eight.

Line 7. **agew:** ague; fever and chills.

Line 9. **token:** a personal gift, symbolizing a close relationship.

Line 10. **Fims:** The placename is uncertain. The word also has been transcribed as *Fines,* though the -ims seems clear enough, and as *Pims;* but none of the three indicates a known Talbot residence.

Line 13. **Steward:** After she became an adult, Stuart consistently spelled her name *Stuart.*

2

TO WILLIAM CECIL, LORD BURGHLEY

Autograph, Stuart's presentation hand, BL Lansdowne MS 34, ff. 145–46. Written 13 July 1588, from the Talbots' Coleman Street residence in London.

Stuart added this postscript to Gilbert and Mary Talbot's letter of leave-taking from court. Although the events of that Armada summer are unclear, Stuart and her family may have departed because Stuart was in disgrace or because Queen Elizabeth thought Stuart should be returned to the north for political reasons. Burghley, a family friend as well as Elizabeth's counselor, had been suffering acutely from gout and thus was not available for personal fare-wells.

❦

Je prieray Dieu Monsieur vous donner en parfaicte, et entiere santè, tout heureux, et bon succes, et seray tousjours preste a vous faire tout honneur, et service.

Arbella Steward

3

INSTRUCTIONS GIVEN TO JOHN DODDERIDGE FOR EDWARD
SEYMOUR, EARL OF HERTFORD

Autograph, Stuart's informal hand, Cecil Papers 135, f. 107. On the verso appears Dodderidge's statement: "This is the note which my Lady Arbella writ and gave me, for my instruccion to deale in this busines in witnesse wherof I have set to my hande./ John Daudridge". Cecil's copy in his secretary's hand, Cecil Papers 213, f. a90. Undated; written before Christmas Day 1602.

On Christmas Day, John Dodderidge (who also used the name John Good), one of Stuart's grandmother's servants, was riding in Stuart's service to the Earl of Hertford's Tottenham house. These instructions, if followed successfully, Stuart thought might lead to her marriage with Hertford's grandson Edward Seymour, another claimant to the throne, and thus to freedom from Hardwick Hall. (For Dodderidge's subsequent letter to Stuart, see Appendix B, letter 3.)

❦

If they comm like themselves they shall be shutt out at the gates, I locked up, my Grandmother [wi]ll be the first shall advertise and com-

---

Letter 2. Lines 1–3. **Je...service:** I will pray God to give you, Sir, perfect and entire health, all happiness, and good success, and will be always ready to do you all honor and service.

Letter 3. Line 2. **[wi]ll:** The paper is torn.　**advertise:** inform.

plaine to the Queene. If disguised they must fully prove themselves to be no sycophants to me. For the first lett them make somm offer to sell land, and m.ʳ Hancock and m.ʳ Proctor are good patternes to follow. so that they may have whom they will to tarry in the house and be wellcomm for a longer time then shall neede. I desire this may be somm ancient grave man. The yonger may comm as his sonne or nephew and tarry or go away as we shall then thinck good. For the second I protest your witnesse either by word or writing shall fully satisfy me But it will   10
be counted discretion in you, and confirme theyr good opinion of me if, you require them to bring all the testimonies they can. as somm picture or handwriting of the Lady Jane Gray whose hand I know. and she sent hir sister a booke at hir death which weare the very best they could bring, or of the Lady Catherin, or Queene Jane Seimer, or any of that family which we know they and none but they have. And let somm of the company be of my Uncle Henries aquaintance. who yet must not comm to the house because of my Aunt Grace and his servants but shall meet him at somm other place. Theyr care is no more but to comm spedily and secretly to Mansfeld or som place neare, and after you and   20
such intelligence as you have in the house will provide for the rest, you know none can better advise then John Good, whom I pray you aquaint with no more, but that it greatly concernes me, and he will without any inquisitivenesse do his best, and perchance take them for Northerne rather then Westerne men, and that weare theare best way both to him

---

Line 5. **m.ʳ Hancock…Proctor:** unidentified.

Line 13. **Lady Jane Gray:** Lady Jane Grey, the claimant who briefly had succeeded Edward VI to the English throne in 1553 and had been executed in 1554.

Line 14. **a booke:** Lady Jane Grey's Greek New Testament, in which, on the Sunday before she was executed, Lady Jane had written a letter to her sister Catherine, who later clandestinely married Edward Seymour, Earl of Hertford.

Line 15. **Lady Catherin:** Lady Catherine Grey, the Earl of Hertford's first wife.

Line 15. **Queene Jane Seimer:** Queen Jane Seymour, third wife of Henry VIII.

Line 17. **Uncle Henries:** Stuart's maternal uncle, Henry Cavendish, had come to Hardwick Hall for the holidays and supported Stuart's plan.

Line 18. **Aunt Grace:** wife of Henry Cavendish; she was not privy to Stuart's plans and might recognize men who were acquainted with her husband.

Line 20. **Mansfeld:** Mansfield, a town southeast of Hardwick Hall.

or any body else. No mention of the Earle of Hartford in any case nor of that countrey if they can[.] Cornish and Devonshire men and generally out of all parts of England resort to Sir John Birons thearfore let them be wary, the shortnesse of time will helpe to keepe counsell.

4

TO QUEEN ELIZABETH

Autograph, Stuart's presentation hand, Cecil Papers 135, f. 146. Addressed "To the Queenes most Excellent Majesty." Undated; written before 9 January 1602/3, when Henry Brounker left Hardwick Hall.

Stuart's initial apology for her attempt to escape Hardwick Hall was plain and straightforward.

❧

May it please your most Excellent Majesty./ Sir Henry Brunker hath charged me with many thinges in your Majesties [name] the most whearof I aknowledge to be true. and am hartily sory that I have given your Majesty the least cause of offence. The particulers and the manner of handling I have to avoide your Majesties trouble delivered to Sir Henry Brunker. I humbly prostrate my selfe at your Majesties feete craving pardon for what is passed and of your Princely clemency to signify your Majesties most gratious remission to me by your Highnesse letter to my Lady my Grandmother whose discomfort I shall be till then. The Almighty encrease and for ever continue your Majesties divine vertues and prosperity whearwith you blessed blesse us all.

> Your Majesties most
> humble and dutifull handmai[de]
> Arbella Stuart.

10

Letter 3. Line 28. **Sir John Birons:** Sir John Byron's Nottinghamshire residence was also near Mansfield.

Letter 4. Line 1. **Sir Henry Brunker:** Sir Henry Brounker, sent by Sir Robert Cecil as a representative of the crown to investigate the recent events at Hardwick Hall.

Line 13. **handmai[de]:** The text runs off the page.

5

TO MR. JOHN HACKER

Autograph, Stuart's informal hand, Cecil Papers 135, f. 123. Addressed "To m.ʳ· Hacker." and noted as "readde" by Robert Cecil. Undated; likely written mid-January 1602/3, since Bridget Sherland made a similar request to Hacker on Stuart's behalf on 15 January.

John Hacker of Nottinghamshire served Mary Talbot, Countess of Shrewsbury, with whom Stuart often had lived during her youth. He was one of the men from nearby counties whom Sir Henry Brounker had noticed were gathered in the Hardwick area in support of Stuart (Cecil Papers 91, f. 22). This letter of appeal, like those Stuart's lady-in-waiting Bridget Sherland wrote to Stuart's friends on her behalf, was intercepted and sent to Cecil at court.

❧

M.ʳ· Hacker. I pray you advertise my Aunt of Shrouesbury that my Lady my Grandmother and all heare are as well in health or better then when she was heare and this I assure hir on my faith to be true and no excuse. but if she will make me more bound to hir then ever I have binne in my life or ever shall or can be hearafter to hir or any living how great so ever they be or how well so ever they love me. I beseech hir to comm downe with the like speed she would do if my Lady my Grandmother weare in extremity, for the matters I would impart to hir and will neither for love nor feare impart to any other till I have talked with hir import us all and specially hir and me, more then the death of any one of us, and yet she 10 hath no cause to doubt much lesse to feare that any harme how little so ever should happen to any of us so she comm in time that I be not constrained to take the counsell and helpe of others who would make theyr owne advantage without that respect of any but themselves that I know she would have. It is not for feare of a chiding but somm other reason which she will allow of that I beseech hir not to take notice of my sending for hir, and she shall be bound by promise to keepe my counsell no longer then it please hir after she knowes it, and it concernes hir to know it, for else it is such as I dare and meane to trust a meere stranger with all, and will winne hir Majesties good opinion of whom so ever is 20

Lines 7–8. **in extremity:** dying.

emploied in it. I pray you advertise my Aunt hearof with all speede, and if it please you send hir this which I beseech hir to bring with hir and so forgetting all ceremonies fare you well.

Arbella Stuart.

6

TO QUEEN ELIZABETH

Autograph, begun in Stuart's presentation hand and finished in her informal hand, Cecil Papers 135, ff. 144–45. Docketed "the Lady [Arbella]s letter". Undated; written after her grandmother had received the court's response from Cecil and Stanhope in mid-January 1602/3. Perhaps intended to be sent to Brounker to deliver to Queen Elizabeth.

Sir Robert Cecil and Sir John Stanhope had written that Queen Elizabeth, although annoyed by what she had learned of Stuart's attempted marriage, believed Stuart had been abused by those who had suggested the Earl of Hertford would be interested in a match. The queen, they said, wished Stuart to remain with her grandmother (Cecil Papers 135, f. 128).

✣

I yeld your Majesty most humble and dutifull thanckes for your Highnesse most gratious interpretation of this accident most humbly craving the continuance of your Majesties good opinion which ever hath binne my greatest comfort. and after this Royall and singuler testimony when it pleaseth your Majesty notwithstanding all presumptions of the contrary to esteeme me not unworthy of your Princely care and love, I shall never hearafter doubt of and consequently not willingly yeld to griefe as I have donne heartofore and that very lately to almost my utter overthrow both of body and minde. But I see the Lords miraculous goodnesse shine in your Majesty his best resembling image and admire to see any so neere imitate his infinite goodnesse love and wisdomme to all his creatures and make that the happy cause of my never ending felicity which if your Majesty had censured according to the apparence might have made me <the> most unhappy of all living by continuing my exile out of your Majesties presence, which hath binne the onely motifue

10

Letter 6. Line 13. **apparence:** By this point the handwriting is shifting to an informal and faster hand.

both of this and many other occurents which as hitherto they have lien rather <by me> untold then unknowne to your Majesty so I have with all sincerity signified unto your Majesty by this worthy gentleman your Majesties most wellcomm messenger. and protest I have not swerved [*one bit*] at all from the plaine and direct truth neither in one respect   20 nor other as I shall answeare it to the Almighty when the thoughts of all heartes shall be revealed, and upon my allegiance to [*hir M*] your Majesty whose displeasure and not any punishment whatsoever is the onely thing I feare and the feare of God makes me most secure and confident that I shall not onely avoide that but for ever winne or rather confirme that most evident and natifue affection which your Majesty hath ever from my cradle showed unto me above all other of your Highnesse most Royall linage. I have not dealt rashly in so important a matter but takeing the advise of all the frends I have how I might attaine your Majesties presence and trying all the meanes I could possibly make or they devise   30 and none succeeding I resolved to crave my Grandmothers leave to present <my service> my selfe unto your Majesty and if [*that*] I could not obtaine that (for even that small and ordinary liberty I despaired to obtaine of hir otherwise my most kinde and [*gratiou*] naturall parent) I determined that should be the first and I protest last disobedience that I would willingly offend hir with for though I have donne very many thinges without hir knowledge yet I call the Judge of all hearts to witnesse they have binne such as (if she had not binne stricter then any childe how good <discreet and> dutyfull so ever would willingly [*have*] obey) she [*never had cause*] <should have had> more reason to winck at   40 then to punish so severely as she hath donne. And as I have forborne <till now> to impart thus much unto your most Excellent Majesty least it might diminish your Majesties good opinion of me and increase hir severity so I have all the <other> wayes I could devise <not> by way of complaint but mone disclosed my most distressed state to your Majesty

---

Line 19. **messenger:** Sir Henry Brounker.

Line 22. [*hir M*]: a significant revision because it suggests that in what follows Stuart was writing with a second audience in mind: Bess of Hardwick, whom she knew would also read her letter.

Line 45. **mone:** moan.

of whom onely I have expected and with silent and stolne teares implored and expected reliefe. and have utterly <neglected or> rejected all other meanes, how well liked of others soever. and whatsoever I have pretended so may my soule finde favour with the Almighty and my selfe
50   with your Majesty as this hath binne the principall ende of all my desires with out which I can thinck no state happy and with which all adversitye will seeme small in comparison. And if it please your Majesty to examine the whole course of my life your Majesty shall finde Gods grace hath mightily wrought in me poore silly infant and wretch that how soever others have taken wiser wayes, I have had as great care and have with more <and in truth> meere innocence preserved your Majesties most royall linage from any blott as any whosoever. and as I should have adjudged my selfe unworthy of life if I had degenerated from the most renowned stocke whearof it is my greatest honour to be a branch,
60   so for truth and not ostentation sake I protest I have endeavoured to contribut my myte to the treasure of honour long heaped up by the most worthy and with out comparison of all Europe most worthy Princes whose great measure of worthinesse, renowne, and felicity your Majesty with out comparison exceedes. and that you long and ever may do so is and at all times hath binne my dayly and fervent prayer to the Almighty and ever shall be to my lifes ende.

7

TO ELIZABETH TALBOT, DOWAGER COUNTESS OF SHREWSBURY

Autograph, Stuart's informal hand, Cecil Papers 135, ff. 139–41. An attendant at Hardwick docketed the letter "My Lady Arbells Declaration to my Lady hir Graundmother", and Cecil marked it "A" as "The Lady Arbellas first letter", noting "This the old Lady sent up". The pages contain more words illegibly deleted than usual. Cecil's copy in his secretary's hand, Cecil Papers 213, f. a88. Undated; written between 29 January, when Bess wrote the court without mentioning its contents (Cecil Papers 135, f. 127), and 2 February 1602/3, when she forwarded the letter to court (with Cecil Papers 135, f. 129).

Responding to her grandmother's demand that she write out the details of what had occurred when she sent Dodderidge to Hertford, Stuart instead cre-

---

Letter 6. Line 54. **silly:** defenseless; simple; deserving of compassion (*OED*).

ated a fictional lover that she hoped would lead to her removal from her grandmother's custody. By now Stuart knew her letters were being forwarded to
court: although she ostensibly writes to her grandmother, the revisions later in
the letter suggest she also had Queen Elizabeth in mind as audience.

�

I aknowledge my selfe most bound to hir Majesty for hir <most> gratious pardon of my offence, which appeareth more disgracefull in hir
Majesties eyes your Ladyships and those .2. grave and honorable counsellers by whose letter it pleaseth hir Majesty to reproove my offence
then [<*pardoninge*>] <it yet> doth in the opinion of [*the world*] many
others upon whose opinion I have laid the foundation of all the rest of
my life. Pardon me thearfore I beseech your [*yo*] Ladyship if with out
those ceremonies which either through ignorance, or anxiety of <a>
minde yet distracted between feare and hope, I sett downe the true reasons of this my proceeding. To imploy any, much more such base and   10
unworthy persons in such a matter, had binne a blott to my reputation
never to be washed away with floods of repentant teares, if my intent
had not binne to have it knowne <to hir Majesty> that such a matter
was propounded seriously, and by somm desired, by others not misliked. but utterly neglected, or rejected by my selfe from the first howre
I heard of it, till the last and not <more> now [*more*] <then at the first>
for all my Lord of Hartfords discourteous dealing with me who have
deserved better at his hands. and thearfore restraining my frends I
respected, I sent such as I thought [*fittest*] likeliest to displease his Lordship though I instructed them not to give his Lordship just cause of   20
offence, and adventured no more, then I was desirous they should
divulge so it weare with out my consent, for in truth I cannot finde in
my hart to disclose the counsell of any stranger or enimy that either by
theyr consent or chanceably commeth to my knowledge if it may be <or
I do but doubt it may be> prejudiciall to them. And I thanck God it fell
out better then I and my dearest and besttrusted whatsoever he be could

Lines 3–4. **those…counsellers:** Sir John Stanhope and Sir Robert Cecil.

Lines 10–11. **base…matter:** such as John Dodderidge (alias Good), a servant, or James
Starkey, a chaplain, who had agreed to carry a message. Marriage negotiations usually were
conducted by family members, not servants.

have devised or imagined though we have bett our braines about it these
.3. yeares. The ridiculous and contemptuous stile I beseech you excuse
with the reasons which this gentleman who taught it me alledged before
30 he could perswade me to play the foole in good earnest. It was convenient hir Majesty should see and beleeve, what busy bodies, untrue
rumors, unjust practises, coulorable [*de*] and cunning devises, are in
remote partes [*amonge*] <against> those whom the world understand to
be in a sort exiled hir Majesties presence undeservedly, though them
selves be never so wary or unwilling any should so much as speake of
them. and as hearin your Ladyships wisdom [*is*] <and fidelity hath
binne at least> comparable with my Lord of Hartfords, so I have many
good wittnesses and more then for theyr owne sakes I would I had had
that I have binne as precise and circumspect in avoiding all occasions
40 either of alluring, or encouraging any to reveile theyr affection how
<great> so ever how respectively so ever, how well so ever loved or liked
by my selfe, and whosoever hath made triall what would either perswade the most vertuous Lady, or the greatest Lady for so by theyr commaundment I must needes tell your Ladyship they will needes say and
sweare I am the one of theyr knowledge and they could wish me in the
highest degree of hir Majesties favour, and put me in hope if ever I may
attaine hir Majesties presence I shall receive the like gratious countenance for all this that I have ever donne. They I say who have made
most triall what promises, othes, vowes, threatnings, unkindnesse kind-
50 nesse faire meanes and fowle, neglect of others, withdrawing of comfort, counsell, hope of redresse or any thing in the world could
constraine or entice one of my sex, yeares, and <hitherto> unhappy fortune Can beare me witnesse that I am too stout to request a favour till I
be sure I may command it and they will take it as a favour donne to
them and not to me of whom they crave not so much as thanckes I

Line 32. **coulorable:** colorable; covert or feigned, with an appearance of virtue.

Line 32. **devises:** devices; contrivances or plots.   Line 39. **precise:** scrupulous.

Lines 44–46. **they will…favour:** i.e., they swear they know she is a most virtuous lady, and
they wish to see her a greater one, in highest favor with the queen.

Line 53. **stout:** proud and resolute.

assure your Ladyship nor any thing in the world but love in such honorable and Christian sort, as I weare to be condemned by your Ladyship
especially, if for your Ladyships comfort and my owne advancement, I
should still have rejected or like a deafe Aspe stopped my eares against
his voice, who never requested any thing but was more for my good and   60
honour then his owne. All the injuries he could he hath donne me, and
his creditt being as he right well deserves great with hir Majesty and his
frends many I impute even all my wrongs to him and freely forgive
them [*and*] all who have binne his (unwitting I am sure) perchance
unwilling instruments and if they had knowne by whom, to what end
they weare imploied as I thinck very few did if any, for secrecy is one of
his vertues and he hath as many as I beleeve any subject or forrein
Prince in all Europe or more.

The onely request that ever I made to him (many other things I
have in rude and uncivill manner bid him do, and he can take nothing   70
ill at my hand but one as he protesteth and I am <as> sure as one can be
of any mortall creature that he knoweth <the valew of an oth> and
esteemeth it the pawne of his soule) that he would procure my remove
from out of [*my*] your Ladyships custody, not that I would not thinck
my selfe most happy to spend all my life under your Ladyships governe-
ment, but that I cannot rule love and ambition in others as I thanck
God I can do both very well in my selfe, and in truth am not infected at
all with the latter, nor so apt to beleeve and soudainely to resolve in so
important a matter as I was content it should seeme to my Lord of
Hartford. of purpose and not by error I protest. As I may compare the   80
love of this worthy Gentleman (which I have already unrevocably
accepted and confirmed, and will never deny nor cannot nor will repent
whatsoever befall) to gold which hath binne so often purified that I
cannot finde one fault <to me> Jelousy onely excepted, so I have dealt
unkindely shrowdly proudely with him, and if any living have cause to

---

Lines 59–60. **like…voice:** a paraphrase of Ps. 58:4–5.

Line 61. **All…me:** i.e., that he has spoken against her, to disguise their relationship, and thus harmed her at court.

Line 85. **shrowdly:** shrewdly; hurtfully or even maliciously.

thinck me proud or shrowd it is he, whom I have loved too well (even
since I could love) to hide any thought word or deede of mine from him
unless it weare, to aw him a little when I thought his love converted into
hate for I did him the wrong to thinck so a great while, or to make him
90   weary of his Jelousy by letting him see it was the onely way to make me
fall out with him and anger him in the highest degree I could imagine.
with my Lord of Hartford I have dealt so precisely that it hath neither
binne in his powre to do me more hurt then reveale all he knew by me
nor <should have cause or coulour to> take [*it*] any thing so kindely to
keepe my counsell. When I writt I wept and I marvell it was not perceived, for I could neither forbeare weeping at meale times nor in truth
day [*and*] nor night till I had performed my promise and sett downe in
good and orderly sort <somm of> the severall devises and shiftes which
more then one had devised and practised with out either my knowledge
100   till it was past, or allowance either for what was past or to comm and
this [*gentleman*] <party> who trusts me with more then I would have
him even the secretest thoughts of his heart hath not <nor ever had> so
much as a promise that I would keep his counsell. He taught me by the
example of Samuell that one might pretend on errand and deliver an
other with a safe conscience. By the example of Sampson that one
might and (if they be not too foolish to live in this world) must speake
riddles to theyr frends [*which*] and try the truth of offred love and
unsuspected frends in somm matter whearin if they deale unfaithfully it
shall but make theyr ridiculous mallice appeare to theyr owne discreditt
110   and no manner of hurt to others. He assured me hir Majesties offense
would be converted into laughter when hir Majesty should see the
<honest> cunning of the contriver, to such an end as will be highly to

Line 88. **aw:** awe; inspire with fear.

Line 98. **shiftes:** shifts; stratagems.

Lines 103–5. **by...conscience:** At God's bidding, Samuel left King Saul under pretense of
making a sacrifice to God, and anointed David, who would become the new King of the
Israelites (1 Sam. 16).   Line 104. **on:** one.

Lines 105–7. **By...frends:** Samson set a riddle for the Philistines and was betrayed by his wife,
to whom he had revealed the answer; later, he disclosed the source of his strength to Delilah,
who also betrayed him, this time into torture and imprisonment (Judg. 14, 16).

hir Majesties likeing and [*my Lady my Grandmo*] your Ladyships and my good many waies. He told me he would have me enter into somm great action to winne my selfe reputation, try hir Majesties love to me though neither of us doubted of it, try what my frends would do for me, and how I could imploy my frends and servants, and make strangers to me effect my desires without being beholden to them. and building my hopes upon the rock lett the windes and billowes and tempests show that though my building be low yet it is not builded upon the sand for then had I binne ruined. but like the wise Architect who first draweth his platt and after makes an estimate of the charges giving somm allowance more then he thinckes will be needfull, and then finding him selfe able to go through cheerfully setteth his workmen to theyr severall workes. So we first did deliberately consult, and after speedely execute, that which we knew for a short time would be offensive to hir Majesty your Ladyship the Earle of Hartford, and div[ers] others, and worke an effect which I am most assured will be most acceptable to hir Majesty and it is even the best service that ever Lady did hir Souveraigne and Mistresse. I am more desirous hir Majesty should understand every part and parcell of the devise, every Acctor, every action, every word and sillable of that hir Majesty hath under <my> hand or John Goods then your Ladyship is, because I know more then your Ladyship doth or shall (because it is most for your Ladyships honour and good it should be so) till hir Majesty be aquainted and fully satisfied that I have donne nothing foolishly, rashly, or falsely, or unworthy of my selfe. Thearfore I humbly thanck hir Majesty for that liberty it pleaseth hir Highness to allow me by the which I may conferre with my frends without which I could not discover the trueth so soone and so well to hir Majesty as I trust to do, if it please hir Majesty to allow me the space of one moneth to cleare my selfe in, and liberty to send to any privy counseller, I will be accountable to hir Majesty but not to your Ladyship for all that ever I did in my life or ever will do. And I will reveile somm secrettes of love concerning my selfe and somm others which will be delightfull to hir Majesty to understand. I will send somm

---

Line 122. **platt:** plat; building plan.   Line 127. **div[ers]:** The paper is torn.

to complaine of them selves, I will informe hir Majesty of somm matters whearof hir Majesty hath yet no manner of suspition. I will offend none but my uncle of Shrouesbury, my Aunt and my uncle Charles, and them I will anger as much as ever they angred me and make my selfe as merry at them as the last lent they did at theyr owne pleasant device <for so I take it> of the gentleman with the red eyes, and if they will as they ought in duty reconcile them selves to your Ladyship your Ladyship shall commaund me to forgett all injuries they have donne me one onely excepted and that is the wronges they have donne this most worthy gentleman for whom I have already forsaken parents, kinne, and all the world hir Majesty onely excepted. For I vow as I shall be saved he telles me plainely he will not offend hir Majesty for my sake, and will rather forsake me for ever then incurre hir Majesties displeasure though the time be never so short. and thearfore though I have kept his counsell these many yeares and will do whilest I live, if it may be the least hurtfull to him or any of his, (for I never aquainted any <of mine> one or other I take God to witnesse) so I thinck it long till I may lett hir Majesty know his name who so farre exceedeth <all> the examples of hir Highnesse best favored, that he dare not see nor but by stealth send to hir that he loves as well as ever they did any. And if it please hir Majesty so to accept of him I shall thinck my selfe most happy if hir Majesty will grace him with hir favor and winne his heart from me if it be possible, and I will dayly pray for hir Majesty and him that he may dayly deserve hir Majesties favour more and more as I know he will indeavour, and if it please hir Majesty to give me but liberty to send to him, and heare from him (which in truth (I must do and he will do though it offend your Ladyship and can do whosoever oversee us) I will show your Lady- ship every letter of his I shall hearafter receave and be content your Ladyship shall reveale [*it*] all that to your [*Ma*] Ladyships knowledge passeth betwixt us not onely to hir Majesty, but to all the world, for I

Line 146. **complaine...selves:** bring charges against themselves, confess.

Line 151. **pleasant...eyes:** The incident is unknown, but Stuart is employing a ruse to cast blame on the family members—Gilbert Talbot, Mary Talbot, and Charles Cavendish—with whom she was close, but with whom her grandmother was at odds.

Line 171. **(which...(I:** There are two initial parentheses in the manuscript.

am so farre from being ashamed of my choise, that even for my owne
honour sake I could finde in my heart to reveale him but that in truth I
dare not with out his consent and he dare not till he have his pardon for
him selfe and his frends signified unto me by hir Majesties letter which
after I am to send to him and heare from him againe, and then he shall   180
either him selfe by what meanes it pleaseth him aquaint hir Majesty
with his fearfull presumption, or I will tell your Ladyship upon condition it may please your Ladyship to joine with me in begging hir Majesties gratious pardon to certein offendours, whose penance shall be to
make confession first to [*your*] hir Majesty and after to your Ladyship
how gladly they would have offended your Ladyship and how farre they
have offended hir Majesty for my sake and if they receive the sentence
of death out of hir Majesties mouth I dare answer for them they shall dy
content, but I trust hir Highnesse will with a smile deride theyr follies,
and at one of theyr handes accept a poore present I am in hand with for   190
hir Majesty [*at anot*] give another leave to deliver a message or letter to
hir sacred Majesty from me hir then fully absolved handmaide, and give
us all leave to impart our joy of hir Majesties pardon to us all one to
another, and devise the [*west*] best manner how to represent to hir Majesty the joy we conceive thearof and make our selves merry with makeing our selves perfect in our partes, which for want of conference we
have partly forgotten, and partly understand not, and hir Majesty more
merry if it please hir highnesse but to keepe our counsell, and I will
instruct them and send them to hir Majesty one after another and none
living shall understand <my> drift but hir Majesty the noble Gentle-   200
man whose name I conceale and whom it pleaseth them two to aquaint
with out limitation. One onely suite will I make to hir Majesty whearin
I most humbly crave your Ladyship to assist and further me that is that
it may please hir Majesty to suspend hir highnesse judgement of me till
hir Majesty see the end which cannot be so soone as I could wish for I
thinck every minute long but shall be hastened as much as may be I
assure your Ladyship on my faith. and surcease hir displeasure to my
selfe and all those with whom for my sake I doubt hir Highnesse is

---

Line 196. **perfect in our partes:** as in memorizing the lines of their roles in a play.

offended. and suffer none of them whose names hir Majesty hath under
210   my hand to comm or send to me unlesse I send for them and whosoever
comm to me at my request or unsent for either I will aquaint your
Ladyship or send them up poste or cause them to advertise som privy
counseller what they do at my request to what end[.] I trust I have fully
satisfied your Ladyship that I am neither so disobedient nor inconsid-
erat as your Ladyship might thinck me, and because [*the*] I report many
things which to your Ladyship seeme impossible your Ladyship next
under hir Majesty shall censure all my proceedings, when your Ladyship by hir Majestyes gratious letter or messenger unfoldeth these darke
speeches which let others do as please them I will never reveale but to
220   hir Majesty neither will I presume to present my unworthy service to
hir Majesty till it shall please hir Highnesse to commaund it, for somm
reasons whearwith I will with all speed advertise hir Majesty Whom the
Lord blesse and prosper for ever every way.

Arbella Stuart.

8

TO SIR JOHN STANHOPE AND SIR ROBERT CECIL

Autograph, begun and closed in Stuart's presentation hand but largely in her
informal hand, Cecil Papers 135, ff. 147–49. Addressed, in presentation hand,
"To the right honorable Sir John Stanhope knight Vicechamberlein, and Sir
Robert Cycell knight principal Secretary to hir Majesty". Docketed by Cecil
"The Lady Arbella to m^r ViceChamberlain Stanhope and me/". Written 6 Feb-
ruary 1602/3.
     Stanhope's and Cecil's letter had urged Bess to allow Stuart her former lib-
erty, but also to keep her from bad company and have her watched by discreet
gentlefolk, without "any extraordinarye restraynt" (Cecil Papers 135, f. 128).
Not surprisingly, Stuart and her grandmother differed on what Stanhope and
Cecil had meant.

✻

May it please you./ for as much as my Lady my Grandmother doth
interprett the letter which by hir most Excellent Majesties commande-
ment hir Ladyship received from your Honors. concerning hir Majesties

---

Letter 7. Lines 209–10. **hath…hand:** would have in a letter in Stuart's handwriting.
Lines 218–19. **unfoldeth…speeches:** explains these obscure words.

gratious acceptance of hir Ladyships faithfull discharging the trust reposed in hir by hir Highnesse; together with hir Majesties pardon of my offence, and interpretation of the originall ground thearof, and direction for my traictement hearafter, in other sence then I to whom it was hir Majesties pleasure it should be imparted do understand it: And during that variety of opinions hir Ladyship may suppose hir selfe charged [*with*] to looke to me with more strictnesse then I assure my   10
selfe it is hir Majesties <pleasure> I should be as heartofore I have found, and with most dutifull thanckes acknowledge; And on the other side, I supposing the limittes prescribed me larger then perhappes they are may unwilling[ly] transgresse hir Majesties commaundment when I meane nothing lesse; It may please your honors for avoiding all errors both on the right hand and on the left to expound your owne meanings in these pointes which now comm in question or any other which hearafter may./ Whither it be hir Majesties pleasure I shall have free choise of my owne servants to take keepe and putt away whom I thinck good either telling or not telling the reason. And whither I may send for whom I   20
thinck good or talke with any that shall voluntarily or upon businesse comm to me, in private if they or I shall so desire with out yeilding account to any but hir Majesty if hir Highnesse require it. And whither it be not hir Majesties pleasure I should as well have the company of somm yong Lady or gentlewoman for my recreation, and Schollers, Musick, hunting, hauking, variety of any lawfull disport, I can procure or my frends will afford me as well as the attendance of grave overseers; for which I thinck my selfe most bound to hir Majesty for it is the best way to avoide all Jelousies. Whither if the running on of yeares be not discerned in me onely, yet it be not hir Highnesse pleasure to allow me   30
that liberty being the .6. of this February .27. yeares olde, which many Infants have to chuse theyr owne Gardian, as I desire to do my place of abode. Finally whither it pleaseth hir Majesty I should be bound within straiter bonds then the duties of a most dutifull subject and servant to a

---

Line 11. **<pleasure>:** By this point, Stuart is using her informal hand.
Line 14. **unwilling[ly]:** The sheet is torn.
Line 29. **Jelousies:** jealousies; doubts and suspicions.

most gratious Souveraigne and Mistresse, of an obedient childe, faithfull frend. etc. according to the lawes of God and man in the strictest sort, without claiming at all to infringe or abuse Christian liberty. And then if it please hir Majesty to impose an extraordinary yoke of bondage upon me, I protest it will be more grievous to me because hir Majesty
40 imposeth it, then that I am not very well able, and inured to endure the heaviest crosses whearwith God maketh his knowne. But my humble suite is, it may please hir Majesty for Gods sake to lett me know the true causes whearfore; because the misjudging of them may be very prejudiciall to my selfe and others: And to sett downe the time how long, and without ambiguity to prescribe me the rules wheareby it pleaseth hir Majesty to try my obedience./ And forasmuch as by my Lady my Grandmothers commaundment I did sett downe somm thinges which it seemed good to hir Ladyship to send to your Honors, before I could either point, or correct any error thearin; great or little; in such <slight>
50 sort as may onely be a wittnesse how merry secure innocence can be even in the presence of a reverenced, and yet unappeased parent; and rather give an inckling that there is yet somm farther matter for which if I durst or could tell how I would humbly crave hir Majesties pardon, and hir Ladyships and the intercession of somme for theyr worth gratious in hir Majesties eyes. then [*give*] any certeine light of truth given. I humbly crave of your Honors to whose handes by Gods direction the first fruites of my scribled follies weare presented that you will vouchsafe to excuse the errors of youth all together./ And to the end hir Majesty may with that speed that I desire be fully satisfied that this action had no
60 corrupt beginning (which it is no small griefe to me hir Majesty should beleeve of any action of mine) it may please hir Highnesse to hasten the conclusion by sending downe somm faithfull servant of hir Majesties to see whither it will prove so fonde as your Honors write, or so ridiculous, as by my trifling manner of handling, it yet seemes, or so serious and

Line 49. **point:** punctuate.

Line 60. **corrupt beginning:** a phrase Stanhope and Cecil had used in their letter to Stuart's grandmother (Cecil Papers 135, f. 128).

Line 63. **fonde:** fond; foolish. *Fond* was a word Stanhope and Cecil had used to describe the attempted marriage.

many wayes acceptable to hir Majesty as I dare (with the adventure of my life if it otherwise prove) assure hir Majesty it will be./ And as at the first I presented an humble suite to hir Majesties faithfull servant Sir Henry Brouncker, which hir Highnesse most gratious foredeviner of the thoughts of my heart before I craved it had graunted; even at that time when hir Majesty had <reason> for to thinck I full little deserved that or any other favour. So I humbly reiterate the same suite to your Honors, that few may be aquainted with this matter till it be fully determined and judged by hir Majesty who yet may rather doubt a relapse or greater faultinesse, then hope of my innocence heartofore, or better government hearafter. Thearfore my most humble suite to hir Majesty is (and I humbly crave your Honors effectuall mediation thearin, that it may please hir Majesty once more to send downe that worthy gentleman Sir Henry Brouncker, who partly (and but partly) understanding the matter already, will sooner conceive and consequently advertise the rest; and will with fidelity deliver the names of the beloved parties, which especially my dearest I dare not trust paper with all, nor any living but whom it shall please hir Majesty to chuse and binde him with all the strictest commaundements that may be, whearof any one weare sufficient but that it concernes my soule and allmost all for whose sake I love my life more then for my owne, and if the least hayre of any one of theyr heads should perish, or hir Majesties displeasure continue for my sake it would ever after be more discomfortable to me, then if I endured a great adversity for theyrs, To deliver onely to hir Majesty whatsoever I shall deliver to him with out either omitting any part thearof how displeasant so ever to him selfe, or any frend of his, or ever revealing it to any with out my consent. And if I might receive hir Majesties promise under .2. lines of hir Highnesse owne hand, that it would please hir Majesty to keepe my counsell, I should with greater alacrity deliver my minde in what sorte it should please hir Majesty to commaund; and thinck my selfe happier of those .2. lines then of a Patent of greater valew then ever

70

80

90

Line 73. **relapse:** early modern Protestants' conventional term for conversion to Roman Catholicism.

Line 76. **thearin,:** The comma marks the end of the parenthetical comment.

Prince graunted under the great seale of England; and with as great confidence venture all I have to adventure as others would do a small matter with all manner of warranties. How much I shall thinck my selfe bound to them by whom I shall obtaine this high favour or treasure, I
100   know not what title worthy enough to give it, I hope your Honors see by the inestimable rate whearwith I would buy it or begg it and thearfore I humbly beseech you make me for ever bound to you by becomming humble and importunat sutors to hir Majesty in my behalfe to graunt me this greatest suite I ever made or will make to hir Majesty And it obtained vouchsafe I beseech you with all speed to satisfy my expectation who cannot but assuredly hope of good successe considering so just a suite is craved of so gratious a Queene, by so worthy intercessors as your Honors, to so good an end as hir Majesties service. And I beseech you let Sir Henry Brouncker, be the happy and swift messenger. The
110   almighty protect and direct your Honors and all your counselles, and actions and continue to prosper them as he doth, to his owne glory hir Majesties honour and safety, and consequently of the whole commonwealth. Vouchsafe to remember hir Majesty somtime I beseech you of

from Hardwick   Hir Majesties
the sixt of February./   most humble and dutifull
                                                             handmaide
                                                       Arbella Stuart./

9

TO MR. EDWARD TALBOT

Autograph, Stuart's informal hand, Bodleian MS Ashmole 1729, ff. 154–55. Addressed "To my honorable and assured good frend m.ʳ⁻ Edward Talbott". Cecil's copy in his secretary's hand, Cecil Papers 135, f. 170. Dated in the docket on the autograph copy 16 February 1602/3.
    Edward Talbot was Stuart's maternal step-uncle, a son of George Talbot's first marriage. Talbot himself forwarded this letter to Cecil and argued his innocence of any complicity in the affair.

꙳

Noble gentleman, I am as unjustly accused of contriving a Comedy as you (in my conscience) a tragedy counsellers are aquainted with both our badd handes, but whilest we may wash our handes in innocence, lett the grand accuser and all his ministers do theyr worst God will be on our side, and reveale the truth to our most gratious Soveraine maugre all wicked and indirect practises whearwith somm seeke to misinforme hir Majesty but I thancke the Almighty it pleaseth hir Highnesse to deale most gratiously with me, and by hir Majesties com-maundement have liberty to chuse my [*owne*] frends by whom I may better informe hir Majesty of somm matters nearely concerning my selfe and diverse of the very best frends you and I have, thearfore I request you most earnestly to deliver a message from me [*th*] to hir sacred Majesty which shall be greatly to hir Majesties contentment, your honour and behoofe, and is of great importance. it requireth great hast, and I have advertised a most honorable privy counseller that I have sent for you to imploy you in hir Majesties service so that you may not excuse your selfe or loose time in your owne respect whom it concernes more wayes then this. and of your owne honorable disposi-tion I doubt not but you would bestow a journey hither and so to the Court for my sake

> Your fathers love and your
> faithfull frend.
> Arbella Stuart

I pray you in kindest manner commend me to my Lady Ogle, and sweet m.ʳˢ· Talbott whom I am very desirous to see, and intreat hir to hasten you hither for the sooner you comm the better for us all.

Line 2. **you...tragedy:** In 1595, Edward had been accused of having conspired to kill his older brother, Stuart's uncle Gilbert Talbot. After the matter was examined in the Star Chamber, only Gilbert Talbot's physician, one Mr. Wood, was punished (*DNB*).

Line 3. **badd handes:** poor handwriting.   Line 6. **maugre:** despite.

Line 24. **Lady Ogle:** Catherine, Lady Ogle, wife of Stuart's uncle Charles Cavendish.

Line 25. **m.ʳˢ· Talbott:** Edward Talbot's wife, Jane Talbot, who was Lady Ogle's sister.

IO

ANSWERS TO SIR HENRY BROUNKER'S QUESTIONS

Autograph, largely in Brounker's hand, but with comments and signature in Stuart's informal hand, Cecil Papers 135, ff. 153–55; Cecil's copies in his secretary's hand, Cecil Papers 135, ff. 156–58, and Cecil Papers 213, f. a87. Cecil marked the original "B" and noted "Sir Henry Bronkerd being sent to lern the particulers of the writing which is marked A. broght this from her". In the docket of the second of the copies, Cecil crossed out his secretary's wording about this being the "Examination" of the Lady Arbella and substituted "The Exposition". Written 2 March 1602/3.

When Brounker returned, Stuart was interrogated. The questions repeat her phraseology in her letter to her grandmother (letter 7), and the written answers are close transcriptions of her responses, which Stuart then corrected.

The examination of the Ladye Arbella the seconde of march 1602

Beinge demaunded why she was distracted betweene fere and hope she aunsuered that she fered her majesties displeasure by reason of the letters she receaved from her, and by her Inocencye she hoped to recover her highnes favour:

Beinge demaunded by whome the practize with the Earle of Hartforde was propounded, desired [*and desired*] and well liked of her Ladyship sayde it was propounded by m^r Owen, and to her understanding desired and well liked of by my Lord of Hartforde:

10   Beinge demaunded why she restrayned her friendes and employed such as were likeliest to offende the Earle of Hartforde she sayde because she desired to bringe it to lighte and woulde not use those that beinge of creditt might have bounde her by theyre acte.

Beinge demaunded who [*so was*] persuaded her to play the foole in ernest she sayde that that was but a poeticall fiction.

Beinge demaunded what thes untrew rumours unjust practizes and colourable devises were and what is mente by <the> remote partes mentioned she aunsuered that the rumours etc concerned <the report of>

Line 8. **m^r Owen:** Hugh Owen, brother-in-law of the eighth Earl of Northumberland (who was related by marriage to Hertford). He had broached the subject a few years earlier with David Owen Tudor, one of Bess's former servants, whose son Richard was Stuart's page (Cecil Papers 135, f. 122).

my Lord of Hartfordes <people in the cuntrey> and that she accounted
the remote partes to be thes which are farr from the courte.   20

Beinge demaunded who [*the gene*] the gentleman was that had tryed
her by all meanes and knew she was to stoute to request a favour since
she mighte commaunde it she sayd that she ment by that the Kinge of
Scottes. <the word commaund was an error of the pen for hast.>

Beinge demaunded who it was agaynst whose love she had <longe>
stopped her eares though he never requested any thinge but was more
for her goode and honour then his owne she sayd that it was the King of
Scottes whose messenger <Thomas Nelson> had bene shutt out of the
gates, and yet was returned agayne in that tyme when all the worlde had
forsaken her with a very kinde message and token to be delivered by   30
Nelson from Roger Aston but yet not sent for.

This Nelson dwelleth at Elsor hall upon my Lady Arbellas lande and
served sometym the Kinge of Scottes laste deade.

Beinge demaunded what the gentleman was that was so worthely
favoured by her majestie and had don her so much wrong and wherin
she aunsuered that it was the Kinge of Scottes whome her highnes
favoured so much as for fere of offendinge him she mighte not be
allowed the libertye of the lawe to sew, nor to sende into Scotlande to
clayme an Earledome or the [lands] or recompense for them.

Line 23. **by that:** emended from "that by".   Line 24. **<the word...hast.>:** This sentence in
Stuart's handwriting modifies the previous statement in which *command* could suggest that
Stuart saw herself as queen. *Hast* is her usual spelling for *haste*.

Line 28. **<Thomas Nelson>:** perhaps the servant Nelson who survived the blast the night
Henry Stuart, Lord Darnley was murdered; Nelson called for help from the top of the town
wall. His name was added by Stuart.   Line 29. **worlde:** emended from "woordle".

Lines 30–31. **message...for:** King James had initiated correspondence with Stuart; see
Appendix B, letters 1 and 2.

Line 31. **Roger Aston:** Sir Roger Aston, an English agent serving King James in Scotland.

Line 33. **Kinge...deade:** Henry Stuart, Lord Darnley, Stuart's paternal uncle and King James's
father. He had been proclaimed King Henry of Scotland upon his marriage to Mary Queen of
Scots.   Line 38. **sew:** sue.

Line 39. **Earledome...[lands]:** the Lennox title and Scottish estates which James had seized
after Stuart's father's death and which Stuart had been unable to reclaim. I hypothesize that the
omitted word was *lands* or a word of similar meaning. Although she had lost both her jewels
and her estates, Stuart earlier had appealed for restoration of her lands.

40   beinge demaunded who he was that was so famous for his secrecye, and had more vertewes then any subjecte or forreyne prince she playnely aunsuered that it was the Kinge of Scottes.

Beinge demaunded who it was that had don many thinges at her commaundement and promised to procure her remove from the Countesse of Shreusburyes custodye she aunsuered that nelson promised in the Kinge <of Scottes> name to endevour my remove by her majesties favour.

beinge demaunded who they were that were so unruly in theyr love and ambition

50   Beinge demaunded what this gentleman was with whome she hath delte so unkyndly, shreudly and proudly, whome she hath tryed as goulde in the fire and hath alredye accepted him and confirmed it, and will never repent nor deny him whatsoever befall her she aunsuered that it [was] the Kinge of Scottes with whome [*I*] <she> appeale to nelson whether [*I*] <she> have delte proudly or no.

Beinge demaunded who it was that she had loved so well ever sohens she could love as she coulde never hyde any thoughte from him unles it were to awe him a little and to make him werye of his Jelousye she sayde the Kinge of Scottes

60   Beinge demaunded what the noble gentleman was that taught her to [*deliver*] <pretende> one arrande, and to deliver an other with a safe conscience, to speake riddles to her friends and to try the truth of offered love she sayde that she lerned these lessons [*my*] out of the Bible <and> by the King of Scotlandes example who proveth all things by Scripture.

Beinge demaunded who assured her that her majesties offence woulde be turned into laughter when she should see the honest cunning of the contriver to such an ende as will please her majestie <and> her Grandmother and be <for> her goode many wayes she aunsuered that
70   she must confess that it was one of her sole conceytes.

Line 46. **my:** Brounker appears to be transcribing Stuart's words directly.

Lines 48–49. **beinge...ambition:** No answer is given.   Line 56. **sohens:** since.

Lines 64–65. **who...Scripture:** James indeed was fond of Scriptural proofs. By 1603 James's publications included poetry and tracts on the Bible, witchcraft, and politics; his works were widely available and studied in England.   Line 70. **conceytes:** conceits; imaginative fictions.

Beinge demaunded who persuaded her to enter into some greate action, to wynne reputation to her self, to try her majesties love to try her friendes, and prove howe she coulde make straungers to effect her desires, and not be beholdinge to them she sayde that it was the desire of some in this countrye to see some of oure family by a quite contrary example recover the reputation which others had lost by not defendinge the veer men whome <them> selves sett on.

Beinge demaunded what it was that the noble gentleman and she did ferst deliberatly consulte, and after spedely execuut which they knew woulde for a short tyme offende her majestie, the oulde Lady and the   80 Earle of Hartforde, and but in the end woulde be a most acceptable service to her majestie and the best that ever ladye did to her soveraygne and mystres she sayde that this greate matter was [*the sendinge*] Jhon Goodes dispatch which though recalled afterwarde by my self tooke effecte which I trust in the ende wilbe acceptable to her majestie

Beinge demaunded what it is [*where*] which she so much desireth that her majestie shoulde be persuaded was not don foolishly, rashly, falsly, or unworthy her self, she sayde it was this practize of the Earle of Hartforde for which she perceavth that her majestie condemeth her.

Beinge demaunded what her meaninge is by requiringe a months   90 space to cleere her self in she aunsuereth that she desired that tyme to infourme her self better of that practize to the ende her majestie may be better persuade[d] of her.

Beinge demaunded what those secretes of love ar which she promiseth to reveile of her self and others, whome she will sende to complayne of them selves, and what the thinges ar wherof she will infourme her majestie having alredye no suspition of them she aunsuereth that she can not perfourme this promis till her friendes have free accesse unto her agayne which yet they dare not take.

Beinge demaunded wherin she can offende my Lord of Shrousburye   100 my Lady and her uncle Charles: she sayde she coulde do that by discovereinge theyre dishonorable dealinge towardes her self many wayes

---

Line 75. **oure:** i.e., Stuart's. Brounker has taken down her exact words, as he has in the next sentence as well.   Lines 76–77. **which...on:** It is unclear to what episode Stuart is alluding.
Line 77. **veer:** very.

Beinge demaunded what the injuryes were which were offred to this worthy gentleman by the Earle of Shrousburye my Lady and Sir Charles and what the gentleman was she sayde that the party was the Kinge of Scottes and the wronges ar the contemptuous woordes and skornes which they ofte do utter agaynst [*them*] him for whome she hath forsaken all the worlde her majestie only excepted.

Beinge demaunded who the gentleman is that woulde forsake her 110   rather then offende her majestie never so little she constantly affermeth that it is the Kinge of Scottes.

Beinge demaunded whose councell she hath kepte thes many yeres and will do whilst she live if the disclosing therof wilbe hurtfull to him or his and what he is whose name she longeth to discover to her majestie, and who dareth not see her <nor sende> but by stelth. she sayeth that it is the Kinge of Scottes.

Beinge demaunded who it is that she desireth her majestie to grace and to wynne his hart from her she sayth that it is the Kinge of Scottes.

Beinge demaunded who it is that she desireth libertye to sende to and 120   then she wilbe content that her Grandmother shall see all his letters and revele them to all the worlde she sayeth it is the Kinge of Scottes.

Beinge demaunded who that gentleman is by whose love she is so much honoured as she can not be ashamed of her choyce nor woulde sticke to revele him if she durst without his consent she sayth it is the Kinge of Scottes.

Beinge demaunded whether the Kinge of Scottes dare not geve his consent till he have pardon for him selfe and his friendes she aunsuered she thinks not.

Beinge demaunded who those friendes ar which wolbe contented to 130   dye for her <Majestyes> sake after they have made confession to her majestie how farr they have offended her. she sayeth that many ar

---

Line 108. **worlde:** emended from "wordle".   Line 121. **worlde:** emended from "woordle".

Line 130. **for...sake:** By adding "Majestyes" here in her own hand, Stuart has reversed the question. Her original letter described friends who would die for her sake, not Queen Elizabeth's. The rephrased question allows Stuart to answer by praising her uncle Henry Cavendish's loyalty to the queen, a loyalty in question at the moment, since he had supported Stuart's attempt to marry.

signefyed by one meaninge only her unkle henrye who she is persuaded beinge commaunded woulde thinke his life best bestowed in her majesties service.

Beinge demaunded whether she thought that her highnes woulde smyle at theyr follyes and accept a present from her standinge in no better termes with her she sayth that she shall never thinke her self fully pardoned till it please her majestie to accept a present from her.

Beinge demaunded what those partes ar, and who be the players that must impart theyre mutuall joyes and make them selves mery with makinge them selves parfect in theyre partes partly forgotten for lacke of conference and partly not understood she aunsuered [*one that*] those ar the inocentes who have bene abused in this practize of the Earle of hartfordes as she is.

Beinge demaunded whome she will sende to her majestie one after an other withoute acquaynting any creature living but her majestie the noble gentleman and whome it pleaseth them ii to acquaynte, she aunsuereth that she can not determyne that till she speake with her friendes.

Beinge demaunded who that noble gentleman is she sayde the King of Scottes.

Beinge demaunded what those darke speches ar which her majestie by her letter or messenger must unfolde before she would revele them she aunsuereth all this above written.

Arbella Stuart./

140

150

Line 138. **accept…from her:** Gift-giving was part of the system of patronage. Queen Elizabeth's acceptance of a gift would indicate her good will and friendship, even alliance.

Line 139. **players:** actors, extending the image of playing their *parts*.

Line 147. **ii:** two.

II

DECLARATION GIVEN TO SIR HENRY BROUNKER

Autograph, Stuart's informal hand, Cecil Papers 135, ff. 142–43. The handwriting begins neatly, but soon becomes hasty and heavily blotted; Brounker dated the sheet, and Cecil marked it "C", noting "This she also gave him." Cecil's copy in his secretary's hand, Cecil Papers 213, f. a89. Written 2 March 1602/3.

This declaration was written on the same day Stuart was examined by Brounker.

I take Almighty God to wittnesse, I am free from promise contract, marriage, or intention to marry, and so meane to be whilest I live, and nothing whatsoever shall make me alter my long settled determination, but the continuance of these disgraces and miseries, and the perill of the King of Scots his life, and if hir Majesty continue hir hard opinion of me, and I continue in my Lady my Grandmothers hands, then whatso ever befall I have determined of a course which if it please hir Majesty to like of will be for hir Majesties honour and best to my likeing, but yet so farre from my likeing is it to marry at all that I take God to witnesse I

10   should thinck my selfe a great deale happier of the sentence of death, then of hir Majesties choise, or allowance of my choise, suppose I might (as I am farre unworthy and am not so vaine to thinck) have my choise of all Europe and loved and liked them better then ever I did or shall do any. The reasons whearof I have delivered to Sir Henry Brounker. And take it upon my soule I do not dissemble at all hearin, but speake from the bottomm of my heart, as I shall answeare it to God and hir Majesty

I presumed to draw Sir Henry Brounker hither with an Allegory which I have moralized to him, and howsoever it please hir Majesty to interpret it, I protest I thought the matters I have declared worthy hir

20   Majesties knowledge, and durst not reveile them in plainer sort to any but hir Majesty or one whom it should please hir Majesty so strictly to commaund; it may be my scrupulous feare made the matters seeme greater to me then to the wiser, and thearfore I may be thought presumptuous in that earnest begging so great a favour, but I protest I yet

Line 24. **I yet:** emended from "I I yet"; in the manuscript, the "I" from the bottom of one page is repeated at the top of the next.

take them to be so important that I shall thinck my selfe happier if it please hir Majesty to pardon and passe them over in silence then of any thing whatsoever happened or could happen to me and my life shall be discomfortable to me while it lasteth if either it be reveiled to any but the unnamed party till I see how it will please hir Majesty to deale with me and if it please hir Majesty to consider that I am debarred hir pres-   30
ence not suffred to conferre with my frends nor advertise hir Majesty with out aquainting my Lady my Grandmother which I neither have nor dare do, and that I have reason to doubt all my actions shall receave the hardest interpretation especially if I do not with speed and sincerity deliver them to hir Majesties care of whose most gratious goodnesse I with most dutifull thanckes aknowledge all the favour I receive in this or any other matter. and that this <is> a matter which heartofore would have binne offensive to hir Majesty, and even the greatest and onely matter whearin for all the space of my life I have offended hir Majesty voluntarily and that being in my opinion forsaken of all the world I   40
have resolutely and with a settled determination grounded all my weake hopes and comfort upon this I confesse doubtfull foundation but the best I had left now hir Majesties favour which might wishes and indev-ors have prevailed should have binne my onely rock and defence was wonne and withheld from me, which shaken, dispaire may drive me for meere feare to misliked courses and that I am resolved to end my life in teares and solitarinesse or else to possesse hir Majesties gratious opinion of my innocence and upright dealing as I have deserved. or else to do worse in my owne opinion and that experience had taught me theare was no other way to draw down a messenger of such worth from hir   50
Majesty but by incurring somm suspition and having no ground whearupon to work but this, and this being love, and being bound in duty and conscience to make all the meanes I could to defend my selfe from perishing, for if hir Majesties favour be withdrawne I contemne death torment or whatsoever can be inflicted upon the most greevous offender I adventured and Oh if hir Majesty do not more gratiously

---

Lines 48–49. **do...opinion:** perhaps to commit suicide.
Line 56. **adventured:** have risked.

conceave of it have incurred hir Highnesse indignation. but yet lesse greevous shall it be to me now then at any time of my life heartofore it hath binne because I could never accuse my selfe before of giving hir
60   Majesty the least colour of just offence, and I protest my conscience doth not accuse me of any fault hearin but a small, honest necessary and consequently most pardonable presumption for which I doubt not but to obtaine pardon in regard of the satisfaction and expiation I offer to make thearfore which I know will be acceptable to hir Majesty and weare sufficient pennance for the greatest offence as I take this is the smallest that ever was made. First I will never trouble hir Majesty with any suite hearafter but forgett my long desired land, and confine my selfe to close prison [*f*]or as little liberty as it shall please hir Majesty in the severest rules of wisdom and pollicy to allott me. and thinck it the
70   highest favour I can possibly obtaine for I perceave dayly more and more to my increasing griefe I am and ever hearafter shall be more infortunat tha[*t*]n I lately thought I could possibly have binne. Secondely I will make a vow if it shall so please hir Highnesse to commaund upon condition I may reobtaine hir Majesties favour and have my deare and due liberty I will never marry whilest I live nor interteine thought nor conceale any such or other matter whatsoever from hir Majesty which I shall thinck worthy for hir Majesty to incline hir Princely eare unto And if this be not sufficient reason to prove my dealing faultlesse or at least pardonable or this be not <amends> sufficient I
80   must confesse my selfe void of sence and carelesse of any thing in this world can happen to me, for my case cannot be made worse any manner of way. in hir Majesties hand it is to mend it and make me thinck my selfe as happy as I can be, (and that will never be absolutely I perceive) such trecherous dealing have I found in this matter, and in Gods to end my sorrows with death which onely can make me absolutely and eternally happy.

Line 67. **land:** the English Lennox lands confiscated by Queen Elizabeth when Stuart's paternal grandmother died.

12
TO SIR HENRY BROUNKER

Autograph, Stuart's informal hand, Cecil Papers 135, ff. 159–60; Cecil's copies in his secretary's hand, Cecil Papers 135, ff. 161–63, and Cecil Papers 213, f. a86. Cecil marked the secretary's first copy "D", adding "This was written since Sir Henry came up with her Exposition marked B./ so as by this Time you see I think that she hath some strange vapours to her braine". Written 4 March 1602/3, dated in the docket on Cecil's first copy.

Sir Henry I cannot but wonder at your light beleefe when great ones tell you incredible tales, and incredulity when you have the word and oth of a Puritan, for a certeine truth. if your commission be not to examine such great ones as I presume to accuse in matters of truth, alas what a dwarfe am I thought at Court[.] if your commission stretch not beyond the Albion cliffes, and the Chiviot hilles, I would I weare with that most noble gentleman who I constantly affirme (but will not sweare) to be the King of Scots, and then we should agree in our tales, and make true English. wheras now I thinck (even you) are doubtfull what will becomm of us. Truly I can tell, and I will tell you truly, even as I told you; even as I would have it; for if I do not or rather have not since I saw you broken somm of your good frends of theyr will I am greatly deceived For wheras if the Noble gentleman you would needes suspect had binne transported by somm Archimedes to Newstead as miraculously especially to him selfe as certaine Romanes (those Romanes weare full of unsuspitious magnanimity) weare hoised over the walles of the besieged Siracus

10

Line 6. **Albion cliffes:** southern cliffs of England. Albion was a literary name for England, believed to derive from the Latin word for *white* and to allude to the white, southern cliffs.

Line 6. **Chiviot hilles:** the Cheviot Hills, along the English-Scottish border.

Line 8. **we:** Stuart and the King of Scots.   **make true English:** speak openly and virtuously.

Line 14. **Archimedes:** Greek mathematician and inventor (c. 287–212 B.C.). **Newstead:** Newstead Abbey in Nottinghamshire, a former monastery south of Mansfield; or the nearby town of Newstead.

Line 16. **Siracus:** Syracuse, a Greek town besieged by the Roman forces of Marcellus. Marcellus's battle plans so repeatedly were foiled by Syracusans employing Archimedes's inventions that the Romans began to think they were fighting gods. When Marcellus's soldiers finally and seemingly miraculously managed to hoist themselves over a lightly guarded section of wall and entered the town, they killed Archimedes, for which Marcellus wept. The story is from "The Life of Marcellus" in Plutarch's *Lives of the Noble Grecians and Romans.*

and drawne by one poore Scholler (who lightly are not the wisest nor
strongest faction) through the towne, which feate I thinck unlesse you
will beleeve for the Author my disgraced frend Plutarkes sake, you are like
20   never to see executed by any Architect, Mathematicien, or Ingenier
living, I will not sweare but I tell you as I thinck. now suppose he should
land at Bludworth haven and comm attended with .500. as I thincke that
is the smallest number that he is answerable for and that dare answer for
his good behaviour even at this present time I will not, no I [*dare*] assure
you I will not, no I will be sworne (if you minister the oth) I will not if I
can chuse see him, nor speak to him I vow I will not (for I can rule my
tongue howsoever I be overruled otherwise) till he have binne at Court,
and upon his othe and allegiance, and but that you Courtyers are wonder-
fully hardharted and slow of beleefe his word might be sufficient in a
30   greater matter. That he never had such a thought as you God forgive you
would impute unto him so highely to offend hir Majesty for an imaginary
devise of them who would shrowd theyr owne practise under his honored
name This is but the devise I say of somm great ones who would make you
beleeve miracles (for if you do not they are halfe undonne) or else of my
little little love that you knew not how to understand though I thinck you
meditated of my last words all night, till you called me to a rehersall in the
morning and I thought scarse worth the <little little> labour of reiterating
to your eares stopped with the inchantments of deluders. in such a
crooked dumpe (for theare is altum silentium betwixt us) that I would
40   not be intreated (nor could not be constrained, to speake one word more

---

Line 17. **lightly:** often.

Line 19. **Plutarkes:** Plutarch was the Greek biographer and philosopher (c. A.D. 46–120) who
described the siege of Syracuse (see note to line 16 above).

Line 22. **Bludworth haven:** unidentified haven in the Blidworth area southeast of Mansfield,
in Sherwood Forest; perhaps Stuart refers to the area's reputation as the haven for Robin Hood
and his band.

Line 39. **crooked dumpe:** Stuart's meaning is uncertain. *Crooked* meant the opposite of
straightforward and good, and a *dump* was a state of perplexity or dejection, or a melancholy
song (*OED*). Perhaps Stuart is suggesting that Brounker was in a bad humor or that his ears
were so filled with misleading songs (like those of the evil but enchanting Sirens in Homer's
Odyssey) that there was no point in talking to him.   **altum silentium:** a profound silence.

Line 40. **constrained,:** The comma marks the end of the parenthetical comment.

then was very necessary till this morning. and now because I am accou[n]table even for idle wordes, which is much, and idle conceits which is more, and cannot intreat you to stay so long, as to satisfy your owne eyes and eares with the <visible> truth which is most unkindely donne of you I pray you understand that after my Cousin Mary and I had spent a little breath in evaporating certeine court smoke which converted into sighes made somm eies besides ours runne or water, we walkd in the great chamber, for feare of wearing the mattes in the Gallery (reserved for you Courtyers) as sullenly as if our hearts had binne too great to give one an other a good word and so to dinner. after dinner I went in reverent sort to crave my Lady my Grandmothers blessing which donne hir Ladyship proved me a true prophet, and you either a deceived, or a deceiving Courtyer. for after I had with the armor of patience borne of a voley of most bitter and injurious words at last wounded to the hart with .2. false epithets and an unlookt for word. onely defending my selfe with a negative (which was all the words I said but not that I could have said in my just defence) I made a retraite to my chamber which I hoped by your charter [*had*] <should have> binne a Sanctuary[.] you came with authority as you said and I saw it under .2. hands that might have made any but me beleeve your word should have gonne <as> currant as the word of a Prince, or the great seale of England by which I might have recovered a little land, which a most noble great great uncle of mine gave his neece when he bestowed hir of a noble exiled gentleman. but I knew by what was past what would be and provided thearafter. I stand greatly upon my reputation, and thearfore resolutely leaving my wery standing I went away (but did not runne away nor ever ment it I assure you) a good sober pace, and

50

60

Line 45. **Cousin Mary:** the daughter of Mary and Gilbert Talbot.

Lines 46–47. **court...water:** court talk, which obscures and, like the smoke of a fire, can make people cry.

Line 48. **mattes...Gallery:** the rush mats carpeting the gallery, which were to be saved for special occasions, not walked on routinely.   Line 49. **sullenly:** dismally.

Line 59. **under .2. hands:** in a commission signed by Sir Robert Cecil and Sir John Stanhope.

Line 60. **gonne <as> currant as:** gone as current as; carried the authority of.

Lines 62–63. **land...gentleman:** the land Henry VIII had given Margaret Douglas, Stuart's paternal grandmother, on her marriage to Matthew Stuart, Earl of Lennox and a descendant of James II of Scotland.   Line 65. **wery:** weary.

though my eares weare battred on one side with a contemned, and in
truth contemptible storme of threatnings with which my Lady my
Grandmother thought to have wonne my resolved heart (as my little love

70   hath donne) and in the other summoned to a parley by my uncle William
I rather doubting to comm <to> the losse by being undermined (for the
west, and Darbyshire, and Wales are full of rich mines and consequently
passing cunning miners, else why should Courtyers [*thincke*] <take the
paines> to oversee them and the office of the Stanneries is both honorable
and profitable) then that (deafe Aspe as I am) I feared to be wonne to my
losse, to a dishonorable composition, for I stand upon points of honour,
went my way with out so much as lookeing behinde me (for feare of
Euridices relapse) and vowing I would never answear to those names by
which I was called, and recalled, and cried out upon (for if I should my

80   love might be ashamed of me as now he may well be of him selfe) I tooke
my way downe with a heavy heart and being followed by them whom it
might better have becomme us both I should have followed, I was faine to
sett a good face on bad fortune and theare we had another skirmish
wheare you and I satt scribling till .12. of the clock at night. but I finding
my selfe scarse able to stand <on my feete> what for my side and what for
my head, yet with a commaunding voice called a troupe of such viragoes
as Virgilles Camilla that stood at the receit in the next chamber and never
intreat[ing] them to give nor take blowes for my sake, was content to send

Line 70. **uncle William:** William Cavendish, whose family resided at Hardwick Hall much of
the year.   Line 73. **passing:** exceedingly.

Line 74. **office of the Stanneries:** the office of warden supervising the Stannaries, or mining
districts of England. Part of the Earl of Shrewsbury's wealth came from profitable Derbyshire
mines.   Line 76. **composition:** settlement.

Line 78. **Euridices relapse:** In Greek mythology, Orpheus entered the underworld in search of
his wife Euridyce and received permission to leave with her, but as she followed him, he
violated Pluto's instructions and turned to look at her, thus condemning her again to the
underworld.   Lines 81–82. **them...followed:** Stuart's grandmother and uncle.

Line 85. **my side:** A physician had been called earlier about Stuart's pains in the side, which her
grandmother believed proceeded from Stuart's unsettled mind (Cecil Papers 135, f. 150).

Lines 86–87. **troupe...Camilla:** Stuart's waiting-women, described as viragos, or heroic
women. Camilla was a courageous fighter who disdained marriage, loved freedom, and led a
troop of warrior men and women. See Virgil's *Aeneid*, Books 7 and, especially, 11.

Line 87. **at the receit:** at the receipt; ready to receive orders.   Line 88. **intreat[ing]:** The paper
is torn and the ends of several words lost over the next few lines.

you the first newes of this conflict; but though he weare my owne man I
sent for yet he being not so forward as certein voluntaries you know to go   90
on my errand, I satt me downe in patience, and fell a scribling my Lady
my Grandmother and my uncle little knew what or to whom though[t]
they looked on, till haveing written what I thought good whilest they
talked what they thoug[ht] good, I was not onely content to lett them
know it was to you but to read it to them, and immediately leaving the
disavantageous chamber wheare nobody could heare me [*or*] <that> durst
comm at me, I went downe a little lower not pressed down with one
abject thought of yeelding, but because I thoug[ht] theare to have found
somm of my regiment and so I did for theare was Key talkeing with a gentlewoman (what they said I never examined) and heare I made a stand   100
bethincking my selfe whom to send because they receive such rude entertainment, that it weare enough to make me destitute of messengers, if it
stood upon the losse of my life to send to my lov[e] but raising my spiritts
with the assured faire wordes of certeine hopefull yong men who do just
as I bid them without either other reason or warrant then my pleasure and
service, I went up to the great chamber and theare I found a troupe of (for
my sake) malcontents takeing the advantage of the fire to warme them by
till the sunne shining on our world with hotter and farther distant beames
make it needelesse, and amongst them one that I little thought had binne
theare who was that Sir Henry? my soudaine aparition comming alone,   110
through the hall, and comming in at that dore when they least lookt I
should made a soudaine alteration and wonderment among them for
they that stood shrunck backe as if they had binne afraide of me and
certeine Auxiliaries which I both left and found walkeing joined with
theyr shrincking fellowes, and with a generall putting off of hattes to the
end I should not doubt they would stopp theyr eares against me perchance expected I should have yielded them a reason, of my going out at
one dore and comming in at an other. but I with out cerimony directing
my speech to the unnamed yong man who stood with his hat in his hand
and my glove in his hatt said as this bearer can witnesse and so for brevity   120

Line 89. **my owne man:** her manservant.

Lines 96–97. **durst comm at me:** would dare come to help her.

Line 99. **Key:** one of Stuart's attendants.   Line 116. **doubt:** suspect.

sake leaving that to this bearers report my undaunted and most trusty servant. What happened after weare tedious to write for you care not what
becommes of me nor I neither greatly for I am resolved and knowing my
owne invincible power of uncorruptible assistants (even the host of
heaven least you should thinck I have changed my minde since I told you
theare was no trust in man) stand upon my gard and setting my hart at
rest and a watch before my lippes, have fortified my weake body as well as
I can, and getting all the munition of comfort and patience that the countrey will afford me, or my little circuite is capable of resolve rather to
130 indure a .10. yeares siege and even loose my Hector then you shall get my
love into your danger that deale thus with [*you*] <me> Are you not
ashamed to see your word thus broken before you be at your lodging?
truly by your letter me thinckes not, for it seemes you are no sooner gonne
hence but you forgett or mistake all you heare or see concerning me. but
the Noble George Earl of Shrouesbury presuming on his Godsonnes love
to him that he would not suffer his word to be broken though he had no
commission to promise [*even*] a rebell pardon, yet as you did assured a
somtime noble gentleman and till he was a traitor frend of his to putt his
life in his hands, as you would have me my love and did so and as it proved
140 with him, so may it prove with my love for he is at your discretion and not
mine if he have deserved it as I trow not but I will not sweare for him. but
for my selfe I will

Lines 121–22. **my...servant:** the young man bearing the letter, George Chaworth.

Line 130. **indure...Hector:** Stuart is comparing herself to the city of Troy, which endured a
siege and lost its hero Hector, rather than deliver Helen or submit to the wily Greeks.

Lines 135–40. **Noble...with him:** The allusion is to George Talbot, fourth Earl of Shrewsbury.
In the 1536–37 northern rebellion against Henry VIII, Shrewsbury offered pardon to his
former friend Lord Thomas Darcy, who was nonetheless convicted of treason and beheaded in
1537. (For his leadership in fighting the rebels, Shrewsbury was credited by some later
historians with having saved Henry VIII's crown.)

13

TO SIR HENRY BROUNKER

Autograph, Stuart's informal hand, Cecil Papers 135, f. 164. Addressed "To Sir Henry Bronker at Lambeth Marsh"; Cecil marked this "D", as in letter 12, and added "This was sent after m^r Bronkerd came". Cecil's two copies in his secretary's hand, Cecil Papers 213, f. a85. Written Friday, 4 March 1602/3, dated in dockets on the copies.

🜚

Sir Henry this gentleman m.^r· Chaworth can witnesse my many great and incresed wrongs which if you will not beleeve I cannot helpe[.] if you do and helpe not to redresse to your powre I thinck you do not discharge the charge imposed on you by hir Majesty to see my traictement according to my condition and desert, nor the trust I have reposed in your sincerity and faire promises[.] unregarded menaces <I> assure you shall neither daunt me, nor the worst that any mortall creature can do unto an other shall not extort a thought out of my mouth, fairer meanes might have laden you home with that treasure you camme for without aquittance but now I have no more to say to you but I will say no more   10
thinck, say, or do what you list.

Hardwick this Friday.   Damnata iam luce ferox
                                                   Arbella Stuart.

I deale better with you then you with me for I doe not torture you with expectation nor promise better then I will performe

14

TO SIR HENRY BROUNKER

Autograph, Stuart's informal hand, Cecil Papers 135, f. 165. Addressed "To Sir Henry Brouncker at Lambeth Marsh." Undated; likely written Sunday, 6 March 1602/3.

Letter 13. Line 6. **unregarded menaces:** disregarded threats.   Line 12. **Damnata...ferox:** furious by daylight, having been condemned; a quotation from Lucan's *Pharsalia* 4.534. In the passage from which this phrase is taken, trapped warriors battle the enemy that surrounds them until nightfall enforces a temporary truce; at dawn they reject dishonorable submission and again fight furiously, then boldly kill themselves, thus through suicide defeating their conquerors.

⚘

Sir Henry, this day of rest doth not priviledge my travelling minde from imploying my restless penne in performing part of my promise in send-ing up certeine innocents to play theyr parts like Adams regenerat chil-dren. If it please you to examine this long since offered and newly intertained servant of mine what matters of profitt and love his yong yeares have binne crossed in, And he [*re*] make as good a rehearsall as he did loverlike and gentleman like <partly> deliver, <partly> forgett, and <partly> excuse his first imploiment hither it will neither be imperti-nent nor unpleasant for you to heare. his errand to you is no more at this time but to know if you will admitt him for an actor his part is in penning, and if it please you to lett me know any thing concerning my selfe it shall be wellcomm whatsoever comming from you. You shall shortly have a resident with in few miles of you [*of*] <by> whom you may satisfy your inquisitivenesse and still new springing cavilles. In the meane time Almighty God be with you most worthy knight. Hardwick. this Sonday.

Your pore frend
Arbella Stuart

15

TO SIR HENRY BROUNKER

Autograph, Stuart's informal hand, Cecil Papers 135, f. 166. Addressed "To Sir Henry Brounker at Lambeth Marshe". Undated; likely written Monday, 7 March 1602/3.

⚘

Sir Henry, I sent my Page <this afternoon> for somm bookes into my quondam study chamber, which he might not be suffred to enter, much lesse I to receive the comfort and good counsell, of my dead

---

Letter 14. Line 3. **regenerat:** regenerate; reformed or spiritually reborn; such persons would confess their sins.   Line 5. **servant of mine:** a young man named Bassett.

Line 13. **resident:** unidentified; perhaps a veiled allusion to her own projected escape, which was planned for later in the week.   Line 14. **cavilles:** cavils; frivolous objections.

Letter 15. Line 2. **quondam:** former.

counsellers and comforters, if you thinck to make me weary of my life and so conclude it [*to*] <according> m.ʳ Starkeys tragicall example you are deceived. if you meane to shorten the time for your frends sake, you are deceived in that too, for such meanes prevaile not with me. if you thinck it hir Majesties pleasure hir commaundment should either be unjustly pretended, or covertly and cunningly infringed I hope it is not hir Majesties meaning nor your delusive dealing, and sure I am it is 10 neither for hir Majesties honour, nor your creditt I should be thus dealt with all. Your will be donne[.] I recommend my innocent cause and wrongfully wronged and wronging frende to your consideration, and Gods holy protection, to whom onely be ascribed all honour praise and glory for now and for ever Amen. for all men are liers. Theare is no trust in man whose breath is in his nosthrilles. And the day will comm when they thatt judge shall be judged, and he that now keepeth theyr counsell and seemeth to winke at iniquity, and suffer it to prosper like the greene bay tree, will roote out deeprooted pride and mallice, and make his righteousnesse shine like the noone day. I was halfe a Puritan 20 before and m.ʳ Holford who is one whatsoever I be, hath shorthned your letter and will shorten the time more then you all. as he hath already driven me my Lady my Grandmothers presence with laughter, which upon just cause you are my good wittnesse I cannot forbeare. Farewell good Knight

Monday

Your pore frend

Arbella Stuart

Line 5. **m.ʳ...example:** James Starkey, formerly resident chaplain at Hardwick Hall, had committed suicide in early February; see the Introduction, page 41.

Lines 15–16. **Theare...nosthrilles:** a paraphrase of Isa. 2:22.

Lines 16–20. **And...day:** This sentence, with its references to the noonday light and the green bay tree (the *cedar* in modern translations of the Bible), summarizes Ps. 37.

Line 21. **m.ʳ Holford:** a gentleman of whom little is known beyond that he was a Puritan acquaintance of the family and that he was later called to London to be examined about Stuart. See George Chaworth's comments in his letter to Stuart, Appendix B, letter 4.

Line 22. **he:** emended from "he he"; the word occurs at the end of one line and again at the beginning of the next.

16

TO SIR HENRY BROUNKER

Autograph, Stuart's informal hand, Cecil Papers 135, ff. 130–38. No address.
Written Ash Wednesday, 9 March 1602/3.
    Stuart was writing on the second anniversary of the Earl of Essex's execution
for treason.

꙼

Sir as you weare a private person I found all humanity and courtesy
from you and whilest I live will thanckfully acknowledge it, and with
all humility and duty yeild hir Majesty more due thanckes for <first>
choosing and after upon my humble suite reemploying you then for
any o[*f alle*]<r> all the favours I have received from hir Majesty since
my birth to this day and if they weare all sett together it farre exceedeth
them all. But your commission was as it seemed so strangely streight
that it was not possible hir Majesties expectation should be better satisfied. which as I know it proceeded not of hir Majesties gratious disposi-
10   tion so was it not <altogether> long of me but others I dealt as I did and
you perceived somm truthes which I confessed not. as you promised
somm favours I found not. When it shall please hir Majesty to afford
me those ordinary rightes which other subjectes cannot be debarred of
justly, I shall endevour to receive them as thanckfully now as if they had
binne in due time offred, though the best part of my time be past
whearin (my hart being not so seasoned with sorrow as it is) comfort
should have binne wellcomm and better bestowed becaus[e] my hart
was not then so over-worne with just unkindnesse and sorrow hath
binne capable <of joy> and thanckfully gladd of any small kindnesse or
20   favour. They are dead whom I loved, they have forsaken me in whom I
trusted, I am dangerous to my guiltlesse frends <in all respects> if it
weare not because they are my frends <as> worthy hir Highnesse
favourable countenance, as theyr unjustly (to my disgrace and theyr
hurt) favoured enimies. So that I must conclude as a privat person I

Line 7. **streight:** straight; specific.
Line 17. **becaus[e]:** The paper is worn.   Line 18. **just:** complete.

would trust you as soone as any Gentleman I know upon so small aquaintance, but whilest hir Majesty referreth the managing of my matter to those .2. counsellers hir Majesty shall be abused for I am able to prove hir Majesty is highely abused in this matter. and I dare [*to*] say no more then I have and will rather loose my life then utter one word more then I have donne Nay I will rather dishonour my selfe so much   30 to deny what I have affirmed then committ my cause to theyr partiall examination and relation. You delivered <me at your first comming> a most gratious message wherain I apparently discerned the long diswonted beames of hir Majesties gratious inclination to me, I sincerely delivered the truth, and was rewarded with a most hard censure, and frustration of my most earnest and reasonable suites that I might attend on hir Majesty <or> be from my Grandmother at least. but my woodden yoake was made of iron, and I can beare it as long as I thinck Good to convince them that impose it of hardnesse of hart, and shake it off when I thinck good to take my Christian liberty, which either   40 shall be apparently denied me and the whole world made judge upon what cause, or colour, or how justly given or taken and by whom. or must [*p*] be prevented by a reflux of hir Majesties favour to me in greater measure then I have hitherto found. which I do not doubt of if it would please hir Majesty to take that course, which hir Royall inclination would take with those of hir owne bloud, if it weare not <to my great astonishment> diverted from them, to those 2. counsellers kinred. they favour theyr kinred against hir Majesties[,] hir Majesty defendeth not hir innocent, unstained bloud against theyr mallice. doth hir Majesty favour the Lady Catherines husband more then the   50 Earle of Essex frend? are the Stanhopes and Cecilles able to hinder or diminish the <good> reputation of a Stuart hir Majesty being judge?

Line 27. **those .2. counsellers:** Sir John Stanhope and Sir Robert Cecil.

Line 31. **partiall:** partial; biased.   Line 34. **diswonted:** unaccustomed.

Line 41. **apparently:** publicly, openly.   Line 42. **colour:** color; excuse.

Lines 50–51. **doth…frend:** i.e., does the queen favor the Earl of Hertford, husband of Lady Catherine Grey, more than Stuart herself, friend of Robert Devereux, second Earl of Essex?

have I stained hir Majesties bloud with unworthy or doubtfull marriage? have I claimed my land <these .ii. yeares> though I had hir
Majesties promise I should have it and hath my Lord of Hartford
regarded hir Majesties expresse commaundment <and [been] threatned
and felt indignation> so much? have I forborne so long to send to the
King of Scots to expostulat his unkindnesse and declare my minde to
him in many matters and have no more thanckes for my labour? Doth
60   it please hir Majesty to commaund me by hir letter <in m.ʳ· Secretaryes
hand> to my Grandmother, to be soudainely examined for avoiding
excuses and will it not please hir, by a letter of hir owne hand to
commaund that which hir Majesty cannot commaund as my
Souverain[e] but as my most honoured, loved and trusted kinswoman?
Shall I many weekes expect what I most earnestly begged and longed
for and must I reveale the secrettes of my heart importing my soule, my
life, all I hold deare in this world in a shorter time then at your <now>
first comming I told you I could when it seemes hir Majesty careth not
for knowing any thing concerning me, but to breake my just desires?
70   Shall m.ʳ· Holford be sent for by commission and I not have commission to send for whom I will and I not protest I have hard mesure? Who
can graunt out the Commission which can even in good nature, good
manners, or equity require such a confession? Have I conceiled this
matter thus long from frends, servants, kinsfolkes, all the world, to
reveale it now Jhon Good was so extreamely [*and*] cunningly and partially handled, and I so injuriously intreated that they who have either
occasioned executed furthered or suffred such vigour to light on me

---

Line 54. **land:** the English Lennox lands confiscated by Queen Elizabeth when Stuart's
paternal grandmother died.

Line 57. **forborne:** emended from "borborne".

Line 60. **m.ʳ· Secretaryes:** Sir Robert Cecil was Principal Secretary to Queen Elizabeth.

Lines 61–62. **soudainely...excuses:** quickly examined so there would be no time to develop
excuses.

Line 64. **Souverain[e]:** The paper is worn.

Line 70. **Shall...commission:** Holford, who had been mentioned by James Starkey in loose
connection with Stuart's attempt to escape Hardwick Hall (Cecil Papers 135, f. 175/2), had
been called to London for examination.

Lines 75–76. **partially:** unfairly.

and so long to continue may thanck them selves if they have lost all <the> interest of voluntary obedience they had in me? do you thinck I say that I will reveale that to my servants or frends now which shall be prejudiciall for them to be suspected to ghesse at, much more to know, much more to conceale? I can assure you all that are of my Counsell are out of all possibility of danger and out of your reach neither doth hir Majesties commaundment prevaile so farre, though hir fame and intreaty be every wheare glorious and powerfull and for my selfe I will rather spitt my tongue in my Examiner or Torturers face, then it shall be said to the dishonour of hir Majesties abused authority and bloud an extorted truth came out of my lippes. I [*w*] would have binne an <eternall> honour to hir Majesty that she whom neither the Privy Signet nor the Great Seale of England had availed in great matters and ordinary courses, durst trust [*.2*] <the .2. first> lines of hir Souveraines hand after such a retrograde course as hathe binne held against me these many yeares, with that infinitely deare adventure. If hir Majesty have regarded my contentment or most bitter teares of discontent heartofore I may hope hir Highnesse may do so hearafter and so hir Highnesse hath when a noble unintreated mediatour who now holdeth his peace hath delivered his opinion of my traictement. But I am growne a woman and thearfore by hir Majesties owne saying am not allowed the liberty of graunting lawfull favors to Princely sutors how then dare subjects justify theyr most justifiable affection? It is a sufficient reason for a Counseller <and Judge> to alledge to hir Majesty in excuse of staying and crossing the due course of law in suites of great importance that the wronged gentleman is my deserved frend. and I take God to record I have deserved a great deale more frendship of him then I finde. How dare others visit me in distresse when the Earle of Essex then in highest

80

90

100

Line 89. **Privy Signet:** the small seal used by the queen or with her approval.

Line 96. **noble…peace:** Stuart may refer to the Earl of Essex, who had defended her at court, or to William Cecil, Lord Burghley, also dead, who had been kind to her when she was young and had tried to regain her Scottish lands.

Line 103. **wronged gentleman:** unidentified. Perhaps Stuart refers to Essex or to King James. Some of Queen Elizabeth's advisors had argued that Stuart could not reclaim the English Lennox lands, but should look to Scotland for redress.

favour durst scarse steale a salutation in the Privy chamber wheare
howsoever it pleased hir Majesty I should be disgraced in the Presence
<at Greenwich>, and discouraged in the Lobby at Whithall it pleased
hir Majesty to give me leave to gaze on hir and by triall pronounce me
110 an Eglett of hir owne kinde <as> worthy [*to*] even yet (but for my [   ])
to carry hir [*thunderbolt*] Thunderbolt and prostrat my selfe at hir feete
(the Earle of Essex fatall ill-sought [*desire*] unobtained desire) as <any>
Hebe whose disgraces may be blushingly concealed but not unseene. or
Ganimed though he may minister Nectar in more acceptable manner.
But whether do my thoughts transport me now? Let me live like an
Owle in the wildernesse since my Pallas will not protect me with hir
shield. You saw what a dispaire the greatnesse of my enimies and the
hard measure I have received (and my fortune is not yet bettered) drave
innocent discreet <learned> and godly m.ʳ Starkey into. will you be
120 guilty of more bloud? you saw what misconceits you bredd in him after

---

Line 106. **salutation:** greeting.   Lines 106–10. **wheare…kinde:** a reference to events of
1588, when Stuart had been called to court because a marriage/alliance was being negotiated
for her and England. Queen Elizabeth had examined Stuart, praised her, and implied that she
would be named heir; but Stuart had been publicly humiliated at Greenwich and Whitehall
palaces and dismissed from court, because, according to a much later report, she had assumed
the privileges of a princess. There were, however, also rumors of a romance between Stuart and
Essex, which either emerged from or would explain the queen's anger when her favorite paid
attention to the young woman whom Elizabeth herself had found it expedient to suggest was
his future queen. See the Introduction, pages 20–21; Durant, 51–55; and Handover, 75–81.

Line 110. **Eglett:** eaglet.   [   ]: The word Stuart deleted is unreadable.

Line 111. **Thunderbolt:** in classical mythology, the weapon wielded by Zeus, Lord of the Sky
and supreme ruler, and sometimes carried by Pallas Athena, his favorite child.

Line 113. **Hebe:** the goddess of Youth, daughter of Zeus and Hera, cupbearer to the gods.

Line 114. **Ganimed:** Ganymede, cupbearer to Zeus.

Lines 115–16. **Let…wildernesse:** an allusion to Ps. 102, in which the distressed speaker
describes himself as suffering like a pelican of the wilderness or an owl of the desert.

Line 116. **my Pallas:** Queen Elizabeth, figured as Pallas Athena, the warrior goddess who
protected the State and its people. Pallas was often portrayed as armed with a shield and with
an owl, her special bird, beside her.

Line 119. **m.ʳ Starkey:** Depressed because William Cavendish had not awarded him a living
and because he had been examined in January in relation to Stuart's attempted marriage, James
Starkey, former resident chaplain at Hardwick Hall, had hanged himself in February. In his
suicide letter, he confessed the small part he had played in helping Stuart, explained he was
innocent of what he had been told Stuart had accused him of, and begged her forgiveness
(Cecil Papers 135, f. 175/2). Stuart's comments here suggest she had either read Starkey's letter
or been informed of his feelings.

.12. yeares experience of me in such sort that he did not beleeve my true griefe whearof he was an eywittnesse and suspected me of a monstrous fault which by his owne testimony he had no reason for but that sombody told him somm untruth of me. and shall I thinck the examined and wrong incensed Nobility, will not impute theyr wrongs to me who[*m*] am so unjustly under .2. counsellers hands by hir Majesties silent assent intituled the Author of this Action? For the passion of God lett me comm to my triall in this my prison instantly and I doubt not but my messenger pathetically declared my wofull plight which others without intreaty or commission offred and will redresse and yet they know but a small part of what you know and yet enough for me I thanck God and no more then .100. more do, who are like to corrupt (if that be corruption) somm that yet weare never corrupted to somm of my idle conceits Thearfore lay the Axe to the roote of the tree in time, and let me loose my head [*for*] which for lesse cause and upon no ground but my frends faults hir Majesty hath threatned to take as I told you, whilest nobody will hinder it, and I shall joyfully and thanckfully receive as God receive my soule, and long to heare you have made that most earnest and humble suite of mine, but it must be in your owne name for else it will not be graunted, and if my Lord of Herford will lend his helping hand and the .2. Counsellers for his sake or what other privat or publick respect so ever makes them deale thus sinisterly with me who [*p*] would presume to <have and> take the upper hand of the best of them but for hir Majesties knowne pleasure of derogating <from> my due many wayes, to write [*downe*] theyr bloudy pleasure in hir Majesties name my messenger shall diligently attend, or I doubt not but they may finde enough ready enough to go of theyr errand specially to such an end. Hir Majesty I know would be highly offended to have such a matter effected without hir Highnesse likeing but what will not or cannot one of them do and guild over with somm coulourable rule of pollicy, or officious pretence of superabundant love, to the best

130

140

150

Lines 134–35. **lay...time:** a paraphrase of Matt. 3:10 and Luke 3:9.

Lines 148–51. **Hir Majesty...love:** In this section on her execution, Stuart may be alluding again to the Earl of Essex, or to Mary Queen of Scots. In both cases, Elizabeth was said to have been reluctant to sign the death warrants and convinced to do so.

Line 150. **coulourable:** colorable; plausible, having the appearance of good.

deserver of love [*in*] and duty in farre more respective sort then it is performed by them who cannot keepe theyr owne counsell how would
they mine if they knew it? I know hir Majesty would be highly
offended at them and conceive a more gratious opinion of me when, I
have declared and compared somm of theyr dealings and somm of
mine which I will prepare to send to you by m.ʳ Chaworth when he is
able to fetch them, and what dealing I am like to receive from you I
shall judge by that he brings me from you whatsoever it be. let it not be
160 Ambiguous and it shall be unfeinedly wellcomm comming from you
fully as much as it deserves. you will [*d*] needes deceive your selfe contrary to your owne knowledge, why do you thinck I will not graunt that
in your absence which you could not obtaine whilest you weare heere,
admitt I had binne in love and would have declared his name I assure
you on my faith I would have delivered it you in writing and by my
good will have seene you no more after till I had binne out of feare of
blushing which though I did not as I thinck whilest you weare heere I
should have donne or at least did with in few dayes after you weare
gonne but theare was somm cause though very little but it was true and
170 no suposition or false accusation, or authorised examination which
wrought that with me very unusuall effect. which I am lother to be
accused by though it be a very fallible conjecture even with me or I
thinck any body, then by the false tonges of as many as list to conspire
with my enemies in uttering soothing and augmenting theyr authorised
lies. and thearfore what so ever an other would do I know and assure
you I would rather write then speake my minde in a love matter espetially of my owne but I say this to convince your obstinat and I thinck
invincible incredulity, who judge of love, charity, words, othes, mod-
esty, truth, vowes, obedience, patience, silence, according to certeine
180 prodigious examples and erronious rules which the Prince of darknesse
settes more usually and authentically before your eyes which I doubt
not but grieve your generous hart to see and perchance your sinne of
silence is now and then punished with a blush though you be not guilty
of the offence. But do not deceive your selfe so much to thinck I either

---

Line 173. **list:** choose.   Line 174. **soothing:** corroborating.

have or will confesse my [*sel*] <pure and> innocent selfe guilty of love
till you deserve that extraordinary trust (which they who for the saving
of theyr soule submitt them selves to Auriculer confession, have all the
assurance one mortall man can give or an other possibly require) many
waies whearby I may both try your love to me and your credit with hir
Majesty and my credit with you, for why should I speake unlesse you   190
will beleeve? how shall I beleeve any good till I see it? nay you are
beholden to me, if your creditt and perswasions and reasons will in
seven yeares make me forgett these injuries and beleeve any word writing or assurance hir Majesty can make so confidently as you who never
saw them without effect would have perswaded me to do who could
have showed you visible signes and reasons of my just incredulity and
hardnesse of [*health*] hart, who might be condemned by all the world
for a credulous foole if I could beleeve any thing but what I finde and
that is unkindenesse and rigour, or a faintharted foole which weare farre
worse if I should yeild to power which hath already spent it selfe against   200
my unyeilding hart, which will rather burst then utter one thought by
constraint of any <and> the greater <the threatnings> and the more
violently it is assaulted the greater will the Victory be. I have conquered
my affection. I have cast away my hopes, I have forsaken all comfort, I
have submitted my body and fortune to more [*then*] subjection then
could be commaunded, I have disposed of my liberty, I have cutt off all
meanes of your attaineing what you seeke till you seeke it of me by such
meanes as I tell you. What harme can all the world do me now. Even as
much as it would do me good to follow your counsell that is none[.]
My servants shall be taken from me, then shall I be no more troubled   210
with theyr troublesomme importunity, and inquisitivesse[.] I shall but
heare of my frends trouble as m.^r. Holfords and by comparison of my
owne thinck it nothing. but you will say I occasion it, but my
conscience will not accuse me nor they in the end will not thinck so but
we shall agree that it is <they> who abuse hir Majesty and wrong me
whose mallice extends so farre every way as theyr base-bredd suspicions

Lines 186–87. **they...confession:** those who believe in auricular confession, i.e., Roman
Catholics.   Line 213. **occasion:** cause.

can reach for paiching every idle [*w*] worde to every foolish imagination
and gathering every unlikely possible conceite with a deale of trash of
theyr owne invention and lining it with secret whisprings, and shaping
220   it as best pleaseth theyr fancy <who> have made you present hir Majesty with a mishapen discouloured peece of stuffe fitting none nor fitt
for hir Majesty to looke upon which if either I might be suffered or not
hindered I will not say helped but why should I not be help[*e*]t I pray
you in such a peece of worke? should have binne presented to hir Majesty in a forme well beseeming hir Majesty whearas now it is so tossed
up and downe that it hath almost lost the glosse, and even by the best
slubbred up in such hast that many wrong stitches of unkindnesse must
be picked out which nedd not have binne so bestowed and many wrong
placed conceits ript out whearof somm may be cast away but most
230   being right placed will do very well, the more you thinck to make the
more you marre when all is donne I must take it hand, and [*sp*] shape
my owne cote according to my cloth, but it shall not be after the fashion of this world god willing but fitt for me, and [*becomm*] every way
becomming of that virtu in me whither it be a native property of that
bloud I comm of, or an infective virtu of the Earle of Essex who could
go neither frend nor foe knew whither till he arrived amongst his
unwitting enimies from whom he ever returned with honour and was
received home with joy till all ingratefull not to be bound more strictly
by a letter of hir Majesties hand then all the bonds and commaund-
240   ments of any or all other mortall creatures, he stole from his charge as if
he had longed for the most gratious wellcomm he received and was
punished for his unmannerly [*pre*] (but I thinck in any lovers opinion)
<pardonable> presumption of kissing that brest in his offensively wett
riding clothes with makeing those milde kinde wordes of reprehension
the last that ever his eare received out of his deare Mistresse mouth. of
whose favour (not in respect she was his Souveraine as I protest he ever

---

Line 217. **paiching:** patching.

Line 227. **slubbred up:** slubbered up; put together carelessly.   Line 232. **cote:** coat.

Lines 240–44. **he stole...clothes:** When Essex returned from the 1599 Irish campaign
without permission, he rushed directly into Elizabeth's privy chamber at Nonsuch; for his
actions in Ireland he was tried for misconduct and denied his court offices.

said to me) how greedy <he was> even in the Earle of Leiceters time before he so fully possessed it by many degrees as after to hir Majesties eternall honour he did, I and I doubt not many more better beleeved at Court are good wittnesses. and how over violently hasty (after .2. yeares 250 silent meditation) to recover it he was this fatall day Ashwensday and <the> newdropping teares of somm might make you remember if it weare possible you could forgett. Quis talia fando Temperet a lachrimis? Myrmidonum Dolopumue aut duri miles Ulissei? and weare not I unthanckfully forgettfull, if I should not remember my noble frend who graced me by hir Majesties commaundment disgraced orphant, unfound ward, unproved prisoner, undeserved exile in his greatest and happy fortunes [*to*] <with> the adventure of eclipsing part of hir Majesties favours from him which weare so deare so wellcomm to him? Shall not I, I say now I have lost all I can loose or allmost care to loose, now I 260 am constrained to renew these malincholy thoughts, by the smarting feeling of my great losse who may well say I never had nor shall have the like frend nor the like time to this to need a frend in Court spend thus much or rather thus little time inck and labour, without [*y*] incurring the opinion of writing much to little purpose? I do it not to be requited with your applause, for then I might utter more wellcomm matter in .2. wordes, nor that my troubled wittes cannot discerne how unlookt for, how subject to interpretation, how offensive almost every word will be even to you. But for somm reasons which I will tell you least, you returne to that opinion I tooke so very unkindely at your 270 hands That the more I writt to the lesse purpose it was. First as I voluntaryly confine my selfe to teares silence, and solitarinesse and submitt and desirously expect somm yet more apparent token of hir Majesties causlesly conceived displeasure towards me, so I determined to spend this day in sending you the ill favoured picture of my griefe who went away so desirous to see the Picture of that most Noble gentleman the

---

Line 247. **Earle...time:** when Sir Robert Dudley, first Earl of Leicester and Essex's stepfather, was alive and in high favor with Queen Elizabeth.

Lines 253–54. **Quis...Ulissei:** Virgil's *Aeneid* 2.6–8: What Myrmidon or Dolopian or soldier of harsh Odysseus could refrain from tears at the telling of such things?

Line 258. **<with>...of:** at the risk of.   Line 270. **least:** lest.

King of Scots whom because you know not the power of Divine and
Christian love at Court so generally well as for hir Majesties honour
and of the place, I would you did cannot beleeve one can comm so
280   neere Gods precept who commandeth us to love our neighbour like our
selfe, as to love an unkinde but otherwise worthy kinsman so well as
nobody else (it seemes to your knowledge) doth any but theyr
paramours, which if you can make him beleeve will be an excellent
requitall for his [*unlikely*] <unprincely> and unchristian giving eare, to
the slaunderou[s] and unlikely surmise of the Earle of Essex and me.
But he hath studied too much divinity to thinck either the word misap-
lied or the matter impossible to be most true and lawfully allowable, of
any married man, which made you so captious and inquisitive, because
you are more conversant in Court and in the Arcadian phrase which
290   ned no comment to you, then in the Church or our Churches translation of the Testament which commaundeth holy love and holy kisses, I
am in good hope you will take exceptions to St. Paules wordes now you
have them under my hand, and then I have made you partly amends
for the labour you have bestowed in reading so long and peevishly
tedious <a> letter. Secondly being allowed no company to my likeing
and finding this the best excuse to avoid the tedious conversation I am
bound to, I thinck the time best spent in tiring you with the idle conceits of my travelling minde till it make you ashamed to see into what a
scribling melancholy (which is a kinde of madnesse and theare are sev-
300   erall kindes of it) you have brought me and leave me, if you leave me
till I be my owne woman and then your trouble and mine too will
cease. or make you condempned of idlenesse and discourtesy if you

---

Line 283. **him:** the King of Scots, who had believed rumors of an affair between Stuart and
Essex.   Line 288. **which…inquisitive:** Brounker had been unwilling to believe the King of
Scots was Stuart's lover, because King James was a married man.

Line 289. **Arcadian phrase:** the language of pastoral romance.

Line 292. **take exceptions to:** take acceptions to; accept or receive. *Exception* and *acception*
often were confounded in the seventeenth century (*OED*).

Line 292. **St. Paules wordes:** Paul several times repeated Jesus' injunction to *love thy neighbor
as thyself;* he also advised the faithful to love one another and closed his letters by reminding
them to greet one another with a *holy kiss* (Rom. 16:16; 1 Cor. 16:20; 2 Cor. 13:12; 1 Thess.
5:26; 1 Pet. 5:14).

requite my long letters with such short and Courtyerlike peremptory letters as all I have received from you have binne, whearby I perceive you content your selfe with the highe and by you right well deserved style of hir Majesties faithfull servant, and forgett you professe your selfe both by word and writing to be my frend and now I have it under your hand that your hand is the paune of your creditt and you would have me trust you, before I be sure you will beleeve what I say or have tried or at least found your frendship in somm pointes before I may in discretion trust you any farther, I pray you first let me know, what you have delivered of me, to whom, how it is taken, or mistaken with the freedomm of a frends penne, who have no cause to trust you any more till I see you dare trust me and my messenger with all you know in this matter which must needes be infinitly more then it hath pleased you yet to deliver. but hitherto you have dealt like a commissioner your words have binne Questions and objections and promises and threatnings but none of your owne and consequently neither possible for you to keepe nor me to trust how well so ever you wish me or I trust you. but now I thanck God your Commission is at an end lett me see what you will or can do either to perswade me by good and solide reason to alter my minde and committ my counsell to somm frends eare or hand to deliver it to hir Majesty or what you can do for me by your creditt with hir Majesty if I should follow your counsell and put my life my soule and all that I hold deare into your hands, or hir Majesties by your perswasion? if it would be as I know it would be so much for your satisfaction and creditt to finde and understand this concealed truth which seeke and examine and torture whom you list you shall never finde but in my hart and oh that you would seeke it theare wheare it is as deeply printed and in the same Characters of undeserved redresselesse unkindnes as Calais in Queene Maries. till your greater and more regarded imploiments give you as much time as I shall require with out

310

320

330

Lines 329–31. **as deeply...Maries:** After desperate pleas for reinforcements and supplies, which were not forthcoming, English Calais surrendered to French forces in January 1558. Many people saw Queen Mary's failure to save the garrison as an irredeemable betrayal of loyal English subjects. Stuart's secret is deeply imprinted in her heart, as is the loss of Calais in the hearts of the English people.

limitation (for then I cannot) or wearisomnesse to you (for when I am werisomm my counsell will be burdensomm [*to*] for you to keepe) to convert my feare, dispaire, greefe, mistrust and other deepe rooted conceits which long time and wofull experience have grafted in my hart and I have watered in teares full oft and now they bring forth the to me bitter to others misliked leaves which hide the desired fruite of your labour from your knowledge till time have brought it to maturity, and
340 then an other is like to steale the thanckes but not of hir Majesty which I should have thought my selfe happy you might have received of hir Highnesse by my meanes. But I perceive you thinck it not worth the labour howsoever you pretend, for then your owne discretion would have made you beleeve that which I thinck I nor an Angell from heaven I thinck cannot make you beleeve that is the truth when I speake it or write it, else you would have bestowed the labour to comm back from Nottingham upon the soudain, apparently true and greevous accident happened to me before you weare theare But you weare in Commission and had not <the Christian> liberty to visitt one in sorrow, sicknesse
350 prison and many wayes distressed for which God will call all the world to account one day. and particulerly you to whom I do and then misjudge me as you list, the paine is past already. Will you not use me as well as Traitours are used who am not guilty of though[t] word or deede which rightly interpreted can[*not*] be the least offensive to hir Majesty and can be racked to no greater then a sinne of silence? Had the Earle of Essex the favour to dy unbound because he was a Prince, and shall my hands be bound from helping my selfe in this distresse[?] before I confesse somm fault (like the innocent I told you of) which I never committed and renew my suite to you to convert these unwellcomm
360 Counsellers letters to a Commission to take my head? But remember if I endure these greevous wounds with <out> striving or speaking it is because I have recommended my selfe to the Lord of Hostes whose

---

Line 347. **apparently:** obviously. **accident:** incident.

Line 348. **happened...theare:** Stuart describes the episode in letter 12, which she wrote to Brounker the day after he left Hardwick Hall for London. Nottingham was the town on his route where her messenger probably found him.

Line 353. **though[t]:** The paper is worn. Line 355. **racked:** tortured on the rack.

Angelles have lifted my soule from my afflicted body higher then they are able to reach that exceede hir Majesties commission and torture the condemned to exile with expectation. If I have deserved the land should spue me out, I will feed my selfe with the idle and windy conceite of an Ostracisme, and my unregarded poore selfe shall be all the richesse and commpany I crave to transport and if a Princes word (who for ought <I> have heard never brake promise be so much to be relied upon for so small a matter, as you would have perswaded me in a greater) be sufficient assurance I assure you if you can [g] begg the licence of <any> transportation it will requite your as you count it lost labour and great paines (which otherwise I thinck I must dy indebted to you for. for gold and silver have I none neither would you generous and rarely faithfull Courtyer take it) [*whi*] with profitt which from hir Majesties hand must needes seeme worthy the begging and taking and honour[.] It may be this hope may prove vaine so vaine is the trust reposed in man, and I confesse I have binne deceived by them I have best trusted, and I would they had all binne forreners, and strangers that have deceived and wronged me. Then had not I hoped for land, liberty, and extraordinary favour from hir Majesty nor looked my parent, kinne, and pretended frends should amend or comfort my bad fortune, but as happy as any (by all likelyhood) have lived like my selfe, with such honourable and Princely traictement, as absolute and great Princes have thought hir Majesties [*cou*] kinswoman worthy of and <as> desirously as Princes desire any thing (or seeme to desire) what is in anothers power to graunt or deny, have sought at hir Majesties hands and perchance may receive but not from hir Majesty more then you will beleeve possible and yet no more then is in pore me to grant in one word which will make you beleeve me ever after, and if you will needes urge me to it they will be gladd of it, and yet not be a jott beholden to any that with hardmesure plead for them whom if they knew they would hinder. I speake unbeleeved truth and ill understood and worse

370

380

390

Lines 366–67. **idle and windy conceite:** useless and empty idea.

Lines 374–75. **neither…it:** Brounker had refused the money Bess tried to give him the first time he left Hardwick Hall.   Line 386. **desirously:** earnestly.

construed riddles, but it is to you whom I am bolde to trouble, and as if
it please you to examine <me> as a frend I am content as a frend to
answer you upon such security as frends require and take one of
another in matters of this nature. <so> if as one whose commission is
expired to do me good it is lesse in your power to helpe me now, then
when you went or I last writt to you and I have dayly (by m.ʳ Holfords
400   speedy and rough sending for) lesse and lesse cause to looke either for
favour or justice and consequently to trust or looke for any. But I take
God to witnesse for my servant m.ʳ George Chaworths sake I have
donne (but now it is dasht) [more] <then ever I will do againe> for all
the commandements and threatnings and wrongs and torments all the
Counsell, Rackmasters and all the ministers of hir Majesties indignation, can poure upon me. or at his entreaty or all the worlds till I be
used like my selfe, with as great honour and respect and kindenesse, as
is every way due to me. who am not ignorant either of my birth or
desert, nor sencelesse of wrong, nor hopelesse of redresse, which as it is
410   my duty <first> to begg as I have donne, and after a while to expect
from hir Majesty so it is my duty to God to procure by all the lawfull
meanes with speed because my weake body and travelling mind must
be disburdned soone or I shall offend my God and I weare better
offend my Prince, and I shall be guilty of my owne misfortune wheras
now others are altogether answerable to God and the world, and the
world will give theyr verdict when and wheare they dare, and God his
sentence on my side I do doubt not for such is his promise and written
word, sealed with the bloud of his ownely deare sonne, confirmed by
the manyfold testimonies of comfortably concurring scriptures, and the
420   examples of his deare Saintes, and yet he is content our wavering faith
should receive the further assurance of his sacraments, and requiteth
our imperfect obedience with thanckes and honour and an immortall
crowne of glory To him be glory onely and for ever Amen and lett the
Elders and Princes say Amen at least to the Hosanna which children
and yong men so cheerefully and successfully beginne least the stones of

---

Line 406. **his:** George Chaworth's.
Line 413. **I...God:** perhaps by taking her own life, an act widely condemned as a sin.

the trampled streetes condemne those that have tongs and tread upon them, of ill imploying or which is worse not imploying them to his praise. How many vaine wordes are spoken and who dare speake for me? How many wanton favours are earnestly and importunatly begged, and who dare <humbly> and even once and no more, remember hir Majesty to cast hir gratious eye upon me at least with no lesse favour then I deserve? How many inquisitive questions are asked of me and how little inquisitive are my frends and aquaintance [*to*] what becommes of me? What faire words have I had of Courtyers and Counsellers and lo they are vanished into smoke[.] who is he amongst you all dare be sworne in his conscience I have wrong? and dare tell the Earle of Hartford he hath donne it? and the .2. counsellers they wrong theyr estate to shew such respect to kinred, greatnesse, and wisdomm, and richesse to lett innocence [*and*] be thus oppressed, and truth suppressed? And yet theare yet are somm amongst you have pawned theyr creditt and theyr soule too to do more for me upon a lesse occasion unintreated at theyr perill, I will pray Almighty God not to take the forfett, but I will see them hangd as high as ever favorit was (and that was according to his owne ambitious direction <meaning to have> bestowed that high, and ayry death of an innocent that spent his time in giving attendance at the Kings gate whose Queene [*who*] was his neece but that was more then even the King knew) before I will claime promise though promise be debt of the proudest of them. I will rather break a penall law and though hir Highnesse countenance be with drawne from me so that like Hester I cannot hope of pardon for hir Majesties golden scepter is turned to a scourge upon me yet I shall be as well able to pay [*my Lord of He*] the uttermost farthing hir Majesty shall

430

440

450

Lines 423–28. **lett…praise:** an allusion to Christ's entry into Jerusalem (Matt. 21).

Line 428. **vaine:** vain; foolish or worthless.   Line 429. **wanton:** trifling.

Lines 443–47. **hangd…knew:** In the biblical book of Esther, Haman, the king's favorite, was hanged on the gallows he had built in hopes of hanging Mordecai, Queen Esther's uncle, who attended at the palace gates (Esther 2–7).   Line 445. **of:** on.   Line 448. **debt of:** owed by.

Lines 450–51. **like…scepter:** In the book of Esther, those who spoke to the king without invitation were executed, unless the king pardoned them by holding out his golden scepter; Queen Esther was pardoned (Esther 5:2).   Line 451. **scourge:** whip.

impose upon me, as my Lord of Hartford neither will I first fly and
then indure my punishment, but first endure my punishment, and
then I trust hir Majesty will give me leave to leave all my troubles
behinde me and go into a better place then hir Majesty hath provided
for me these .27. yeares whearin I have had experience what it would
please hir Majesty all my frends yea all England to do for me, that did
nothing for my selfe. no not so much as utter one word which had
460   binne better uttered for me many a yeare ago and shall never be spoken
to English man nor woman, whatsoever it is. For declaring my minde
to hir Majesty more then I have donne I dare not, my words have binne
already too offensively taken and too unjustly wrested by them that had
least cause so to do[.] I am deafe to commaundment and dumbe to
Authority. I know hir Majesty excelleth hir sexe and all gods creatures
in many <Princely> vertues whearof secresy is one and in hir brest durst
I repose my life my honour what not if I had hir favour and promise.
And hir Majesty shall see somm resemblance one of my sexe, yeares,
and condition very well with all correspondencies and with out all
470   incongruities as plaine with out ambiguities <as> I could for hir Majesties honour wish theyr words and actions weare, for these pleites and
foldes and slight devises do but glitter in the ey and theyr small value is
discerned who soever make them worne for fashion shake. wheares
mine shall be strange, and new and richly worth more then I am worth
or any Lady of a subject in this land. but you shall not know the devise
at Court least you prevent me, or the foreknowledge take away the
grace of the soudain and gorgeous change of my suite which how little
so ever my mourning weede be respected will make <me> envied who
am not pittied, but hard it will be for any of them all to follow me it
480   will be so costly and yet to me so easy that they will at least for civility
confesse them selves lesse worthy of that which theyr betters have had
much a do to perswade me to take in free guift aknowledging me (in
theyr partiall opinion) worthy of more then they can give which is
more then incredulous you can beleeve should be offred much more so

---

Line 467. **what not:** what not? i.e., everything else.   Line 468. **resemblance:** resembling.
Line 471. **pleites:** pleats.   Line 477. **suite:** suit, in the sense of clothing, as well as a petition.

long unreceived by pore me. and in truth I thanck God for your hardnesse of heart and willfull blindenesse, for else, I might relent if you
could see to follow my directions who faine would enjoy meaner fortunes at home but Gods will be donne onely in his powre it is to dispose of all his creatures without respect of persons. Now I have spent
this day in pourtraying my malincholy innocence in the undeceiving   490
black and white you see after my rude manner, I must tell you true I
thinck it will not yet be your fortune to understand my meaning for it
is not my meaning you should; nor your pleasure to confesse all you
ghesse much lesse all you beleeve though you beleeve not all you should
much lesse as you should of me, if the Pompe of this world had not
bewitched your Court-dazled eyes. But I have said enough to make you
inexcusable every way if you will not or cannot either go the way I tell
you, or lett me without your hard hardly removed prejudicate miscon-
ceites take my good and Godly course which howsoever it be to hir
Majesties if I be not made incapable of any comfort will be highly to   500
my honour and contentment and happy shall I be. and I doubt not but
they that <now> condole my misfortunes will fill your eares when you
thinck all my words but bragges and idle conceits impossible to take
effect with congratulation and applause of my dehorted and admirable
Silence. Almighty God be with you I will not excuse my prolixity neither is your wiser brevity so commendable now you are your selfe and
are so many lines behinde to me who I thinck must outgo you all in
kindenesse and desert and you may do very well and yet not comm
neare me in that point God forgive my excesse and your defects in love
and charity. From Hardwicke this Ashwensday.   510

Your pore frend.
Arbella Stuart.

Line 487. **faine:** fain; gladly.

Lines 504–5. **dehorted...Silence:** silence courageously maintained despite others' exhorta-
tions that she speak.

17
TO SIR HENRY BROUNKER

Autograph, Stuart's informal hand, Cecil Papers 135, f. 152. No address, but a note on the verso indicates Brounker received the letter. Undated; likely written 17 March 1602/3.

This letter probably was written the day Brounker again arrived at Hardwick Hall, this time because Stuart had attempted to leave with her uncle Henry Cavendish.

🜲

Sir I see both the cause, and the end of your comming thearfore I pray you spare your owne trouble, and mine in seekeing that which by these meanes will not be gott. if you comme as a commissioner, consider what powre one mortall creature how great soever hath over an other how miserable soever. if as a frend deserve that holy name before you take it upon you. I would neither deceive nor be deceived, grieve you with my untowardnesse, nor be grieved with your cunning and importunat inquisitivenesse. Thearfore pardon me if with out cerimony I shutt you out of dores, if you will not at my most earnest entreaty, for-
10   beare to comm to me selfe-confined with in this chamber, till I be absolutely cleared and free every way and have my just desires granted and allowed.

                                        Satis et sine nomine nota
                                              Arbella Stuart

18
TO SIR ROBERT CECIL

Autograph, beginning and ending in Stuart's presentation hand, but largely in her informal hand, Cecil Papers 135, f. 176/3. Addressed, Stuart's presentation hand, "To the right honorable my very good Lord the Lord Cecill./" Secretary's copy sent to Gilbert and Mary Talbot, Talbot Papers 2, ff. 186–87. Written 14 June 1603.

On Queen Elizabeth's death, Stuart's small pension of two hundred pounds had ceased. As she had little personal income, a retinue to maintain, and increased expenses because she was no longer living in her grandmother's home, she hoped Cecil would remind King James to award her a new pension.

Letter 17. Line 13. **Satis...nota:** known well enough even without name. This closing may be a literary reference, like the closing to letter 13, but I have been unable to locate the source.

⚘

My good Lord./ I presume to trouble your Lordship in renewing that request, which when I last spake with you it would not please you to graunt; or at least to lett me know you would make me bound to you in that kinde; that is that it will please your Lordship to remember the Kings Majesty of my maintenance, which if it be not a matter fitt for you (as which your Lordship hath already dealt in) my uncle of Shrouesbury is greatly deceived or hath deceived me, but I suppose neither, and thearfore presume so much of your honorable disposition that you will indeavour to obtaine me that which it will be for his Majesties honour to graunt, and thearfore your Lordship in that respect (if   10 thear[e] weare no other) I doubt not will performe more the[n] it was your pleasure to promise me, I thinck because you would have the benifitt greater comming unpromised. And so wishing your Lordship increase of honour and happinesse I cease. From Sheene the .14. of June.

Your Lordships poore frend
Arbella Stuart./

19

TO SIR ROBERT CECIL

Autograph, Stuart's presentation hand, Bodleian MS Ashmole 1729, ff. 150–51. Addressed "To the right honorable my very good Lord the Lord Cecill./" Written 22 June 1603.

⚘

My good Lord./ it hath pleased his Majesty to alter his purpose concerning the pension whearof your Lordship writt to me; It may please you to move his Majesty that my present want may be supplied by his Highnesse with somme summe of money which needeth not be annuall if it shall so seeme good to his Majesty But I would rather make hard shifte for the present then be too troublesomme to his Highnesse, who I

Letter 18. Line 11. **thear[e]:** The sheet is torn, here and below.   Line 14. **Sheene:** Sheen Park, Surrey, where Stuart was staying with the Marchioness of Northampton, Helena Parr.

Letter 19. Line 4. **summe...annuall:** i.e., cash to cover current debts, with the issue of an annual pension to be determined whenever King James chose.

Lines 5–6. **make hard shifte:** make hard shift; manage with difficulty.

doubt not will allow me maintenance in such liberall sorte as shall be
for his Majesties honour, and a testimony to the world, no lesse of his
Highnesse Princely bounty, then naturall affection to me. Which good
10 intention of his Majesties I doubt not but your Lordship will further, as
you shall see occasion, wheareby your Lordship shall make me greatly
bounden to you as I already acknowledge my selfe to be. And so with
humble thanckes for your honorable letter I recommend your Lordship
to the protection of the Almighty who send you all honour and
contentment. From Sheene the .22. of June

Your Lordships poore frend
Arbella Stuart./

20

TO SIR ROBERT CECIL

Autograph, Stuart's presentation hand, Bodleian MS Ashmole 1729, ff. 152–
53. Addressed "To the right honorable my very good Lord the Lord Cecyll./"
Written 23 June 1603.

꧁

My good Lord./ I humbly thanck your Lordship that it will please you
amongst your great affaires to remember my suites to his Majesty[.] For
the alteration of my pension I hope I shall shortly have the meanes to
aquaint your Lordship with it my selfe. If I should name two thousand
poundes for my present occasions it would not exceed my necessity,
but I dare not presume to crave any certein summe, but referre my selfe
wholly to his Majesties consideration, and assure my selfe I shall finde
your Lordship my honorable good frend, both in procuring it as soone,
and makeing the summe as great as may be. So with humble thanckes to
10 your Lordship for your continuall favours, I recommend your Lordship
to the protection of the Almighty. From Sheene. the .23. of June. 1603

Your Lordships poore frend
Arbella Stuart./

21

TO SIR ROBERT CECIL

Autograph, Stuart's presentation hand, Cecil Papers 100, f. 134. Addressed "To
the right honorable my very good Lord the Lord Cecyll./" Written 26 June
1603.

Cecil had spoken to King James, who had agreed to a stop-gap gift of six hundred and sixty-six pounds until the issue of Stuart's pension was decided.

🌿

My good Lord./ I humbly thanck your Lordship for procuring and hastening the Kings liberality towards me. I acknowledge my selfe greatly bounde to your Lordship and have sent this bearer my servant to attend your pleasure, whose important affaires I am constrained to interrupt with this necessary importunity. And so wishing your Lordship all honour and contentment I recommend you to the protection of the Almighty. From Sheene the .26. of June. <u>1603</u>

Your Lordships poore frend./
Arbella Stuart./

22

TO SIR ROBERT CECIL

Autograph, Stuart's presentation hand, Cecil Papers 134, f. 39. Addressed "To the right honorable my very good Lord, the Lord Cecill./" Written 30 June 1603.

By 30 June, Stuart had received the funds.

🌿

My good Lord./ I have received his Majesties liberality by your Lordships meanes; for which I aknowledge my selfe greatly bounden to your Lordship of whose patience I presume in reading these needlesse lines, rather then I would by omitting your due thanckes a short time, leave your Lordship in the least suspence of my thanckfulnesse to you, whose good opinion and favour I highly esteeme. And so wishing your Lordship all honour and happinesse I recommend you to the tuition of the Almighty and cease. From Sheene the .30. of June .<u>1603</u>.

Your Lordships assured frend.
Arbella Stuart./   10

Letter 22. Line 7. **tuition:** care.

23

TO GILBERT TALBOT, EARL OF SHREWSBURY

Autograph, Stuart's informal hand, Talbot Papers 2, ff. 188–89. Addressed "To the right honorable my very good uncle the Earle of Shrouesbury". Written 14 August 1603.

🜨

I humbly thancke you for your letter to my Lord Chamberlein Sidney in my behalfe which I have not yet delivered; and for letting me understand your course which though it bend directly northward will not hinder you from thincking and lookeing to the South, wheare you leave me to take my fortune in an unknowne Climat with out either art or instruction but what I have from you whose skilfull directions I will observe as farre forth as they are Puritanlike and though I be very fraile I must confesse yet I trust you shall see in me the good effects of your prayer, to your great glory for reforming my untowardly resolutions and
10 mirth (for great shall the melancholy be that shall appeare in my letters to you) which as the best preservatifue of health I recommend to you to whom I wish long life, honour, and all happinesse. From Farnham the .14. of August <u>1603</u>

Your disciple
Arbella Stuart.

24

TO MARY TALBOT, COUNTESS OF SHREWSBURY

Autograph, Stuart's informal hand, Talbot Papers 2, ff. 190–91. Addressed "To the right honorable my very good Aunt the Countesse of Shrouesbury". Written 23 August 1603.

🜨

Madame./ I have written to my uncle how the world goes with me, I beseech you gett him to write to m[r]y Lord [*Cel*] Cecill in my behalfe

---

Letter 23. Line 1. **Lord Chamberlein Sidney:** Sir Robert Sidney, Chamberlain to Queen Anna.   Line 3. **northward:** i.e., back to Derbyshire, after having served as Commissioner of Claims for the king's coronation in July.

Line 12. **Farnham:** Farnham Castle, Surrey; Stuart was traveling with the court, which was moving continually during the summer to avoid the plague.

and to take notice of his <and my Lord Henry Howards> crossing the Kings intention for my allowance of diett[.] I thinck that makes [*them*] <others> deny me that the King graunted, and makes even himselfe thinck any thing enough when so wise counsellers thinck it too much. You know his inclination to be kinde to all his kinne and liberall to all he loves and you know his protestations of extraordinary affection to me thearfore I am sure it is evill counsell that withholdes him so long from doing [*from*] for me in as liberall sort or more as he hath donne for any. The Queene was very desirous to have accompanied the King. when she speakes of you she speakes very kindely and honorably of you. Our great and gratious Ladies leave no gesture nor fault of the late Queene unremembred as they say who are partakers of theyr talke as I thanck God I am not. m.ʳ Elfinston is my very good frend and yours much devoted. I pray you let me heare of my faults from you when you will have me mend them for I am sure you shall heare of them theare. and I neither [think] those faultes which are thought so heare nor those qualities good that are most gratious heare now you are a by stander you may judge and direct better then ever. I humbly take my leave. praying the Almighty to send you all happinesse. From Basing the .23. of August

10

20

Your Ladyships neece to commaund
Arbella Stuart./

I beseech you commend me to my uncle Charles and my Aunt and all my Cousins with you. Sir William Stuart remembreth his service to you and my uncle./

Line 3. **Lord Henry Howards:** Henry Howard, Earl of Northampton, had corresponded with James before James's accession to the English throne and wielded considerable power in the new government.

Line 4. **diett:** board in the form of a specified number of dishes from King James's tables.

Line 15. **m.ʳ Elfinston:** likely John Elphinstone, Gentleman Usher to Queen Anna and brother of King James's Scottish counselor Sir James Elphinstone.

Line 21. **Basing:** Basing House, near Basingstoke.   Lines 25–26. **uncle...you:** Charles and Catherine Cavendish, who, with their family, apparently were visiting the Talbots.

Line 26. **Sir William Stuart:** Sir William Stewart, who occasionally handled business matters for the Talbots.

25

TO GILBERT TALBOT, EARL OF SHREWSBURY

Autograph, Stuart's informal hand, Lambeth Palace Library MS 3201, ff. 124–25. No address. Written 16 September 1603.

At my returne from Oxford wheare I have spent this day whilest my Lord Cecill amongst many more weighty affaires was dispatching somm of mine I found my Cousin Lacy had disburdened him selfe at my chamber of the charge he had from you, and streight fell to prepare his fraught back for hindering his back returne to morrow morning. as he intendeth. I writt to you [*of*] the reason of the delaye of Taxis audience it remaineth to tell how Jovially he behaveth him selfe in the Interim. he hath brought great store of Spanish gloves, Haukes hoods, Leather for Jerkins and moreover a perfumer These delicacies he bestoweth
10   amongst our Ladies and Lordes I will not say with a hope to effeminat the one sex but certeinly with a hope to grow gratious with the other as he already is. The Curiosity of our sex drew many Ladies and gentle-women to gaze at him betwixt his landing place and Oxford his abiding place, which he desirous to satisfy (I will not say nourish that vice) made his Coche stay, and tooke occasion with petty guiftes and courte-sies, to winne soone wonne affections who, comparing this manner with monsieur de Ronées, hold him theyr farre wellcommer guest. At Oxford he tooke somm distast about his lodging and would needes
20   lodge at an Inne, because he had not all Christs colledge to him selfe and was not received into the towne by the Vizchancellour in Pontificalibus which they never use to do but to the King or Queene, or Chancellour of the University as they say, but those scruples weare soon

---

Line 3. **Cousin Lacy:** perhaps John Lacy of Derbyshire, who was in London in 1603 because of a suit in Chancery (Batho, K71, K171).

Line 5. **fraught:** cargo, load.   Line 6. **Taxis:** Juan de Taxis, Count de Villamediana, the Spanish ambassador.   Line 9. **Jerkins:** vests or jackets.

Line 17. **monsieur de Ronées:** Maximilien de Béthune, of Rosny, the French ambassador.

Lines 20–21. **in Pontificalibus:** pontifically, with the pomp of processions and speeches.

disgested, and he vouchsafeth to lodge in a peece of the Colledge till his repaire to the King at Winchester. Count Arimburg was heere within these few dayes and presented to the Queene, The Archduke and the Infantas pictures most excellently drawne. Yeasterday the King and Queene dined at a Lodge of Sir H Leas .3. miles hence. and weare accompanied by the French Imbassadour, and a Dutch Duke, I will not say we weare merry at the Dutchkin least you complaine of me for telling tales out of the Queenes coche, but I could finde in my heart to write unto you somm of our yeasterdayes adventures but that it groweth late, and by the shortnesse of your letter I conjecture you would not have this honest gentleman overladen with such superfluous relations. My Lord Admirall is returned from the Prince and Princesse and either is or will be my Cousin before incredulous you will beleeve such incongruities in a Counsellour as love maketh no miracles in his subjectes, of what degree or age whatsoever. His daughter of Kildare is discharged of hir office and as neere a free woman as may be and have a bad husband. The Dutch Lady my Lord Wotton spoke of at Basing proved a Lady sent by the Dutchesse of Holstein to learne the English fashion[,] she lodgeth at Oxford and hath binne heere twice and thincketh every day

30

40

Line 23. **disgested:** digested; dispersed.

Line 24. **Count Arimburg:** Charles de Ligne, Count d'Aremburg, the Spanish ambassador in the Netherlands; he served the Infanta and her husband Albert, Archduke of Austria, rulers of the Spanish Netherlands.

Line 27. **Sir H Leas:** Sir Henry Lee was a family friend who had been Queen Elizabeth's Master of Ceremonies, and who had a house in nearby Ditchley.

Line 28. **Dutch Duke:** likely Count Maurice of Nassau, who used the title Duke of Guildres.

Line 34. **Lord Admirall:** Charles Howard, the Earl of Nottingham and hero of the victory over the Spanish Armada, who married Lady Margaret Stuart, forty-some years his junior (Emerson, 167), soon after this letter.

Line 37. **His...Kildare:** Nottingham's daughter Frances, Countess of Kildare, who recently had stepped down as state governess to Princess Elizabeth. Her "bad husband" was Henry Brooke, Lord Cobham, then in the Tower of London on charges of having conspired to depose James and put Arbella on the throne.

Line 39. **Lord Wotton:** Edward Wotton, recently made a baron.

Line 40. **Dutchesse of Holstein:** Queen Anna's sister Augusta, who had married Duke John Adolphus of Holstein-Gottorp in 1596.

[long] till she be at home so well she liketh hir entertainment or loveth hir owne countrey[,] in truth she is civill and thearfore cannot but looke for the like which she brings out of a ruder countrey. But if ever theare weare such a Vertu as courtesy at the Court I marvell what is becomm of it? for I protest I see little or none of it but in the Queen who ever since hir comming to Newbury hath spoken to the people as she passeth and receiveth theyr prayers with thanckes and thanckfull countenance barefaced to the great contentment of natifue and forrein people for I
50   would not have you thinck the French Imbassador would leave that attractive vertu of our Late Queene Elizabeth unremembred or uncommended when he saw it imitated by our most gratious Queene, least you should thinck we infect even our neighbours with incivility. But what a Theame have rude I gotten unwares[,] it is your owne vertu I commend by the foile of the contrary vice and so thincking on you my penne accused my selfe before I was aware thearfore I will put it to silence for this time onely adding a short but most hearty prayer for your prosperity in all kindes and so humbly take my leave. From Woodstocke the .16. of September.
60   Your Lordships neece
                                            Arbella Stuart./

26

TO MARY TALBOT, COUNTESS OF SHREWSBURY

Autograph, Stuart's informal hand, Talbot Papers 2, ff. 192–93. Addressed "To the right honorable my very good Aunt the Countesse of Shrouesbury". Dated by Mary Talbot's secretary 16 September 1603.

Stuart's aunt evidently suggested in a postscript that, since the government was investigating a conspiracy to depose King James and place Stuart on the throne, Stuart should be more circumspect in what she wrote.

🌿

Madame./ if you receive the letters I write I am sure you see I faile not to write often how the world goeth heere both in particuler with me

---

Letter 25. Line 49. **barefaced:** without the mask that upper-class women often wore to protect their skin while traveling.   Line 59. **Woodstocke:** Woodstock Palace, Oxfordshire.

and otherwise as farre as my intelligence stretcheth wherfore I rather interpret your postscript to be a Caveat to me to write no more then How I do, and my desire to understand of your health[,] that is no more then is necessary, then a new commaundemente to do that which I already do; but least in pleasing you I offend my uncle I have adventured to write to him one superfluous letter more, and that I may include no serious matter in his I send you all I have of that kinde which is that the King hath under his hand graunted me the aforesaid messe of   10 meate and .800. pounds per Annum. and my Lord Cecill will dispatch it, I trust with all speede for so his Lordship promiseth. Your long expected messenger by whom I should have understood your minde is not yet comm and t[he] Queene is going hence to morrow; but the change of place will not cease my expectation till I understand from you you have changed your minde in that matter, which if you do, I shall hope it is with a minde to comm up shortly and let me know it your selfe according to a bruite [*of*] we have heere which I would faine beleeve. you shall not faile to receive weekly letters God willing unlesse lack of health, or meanes or somm very great occasion hinder me. M.ʳ·   20 Elfingston who you may see is with me late as well as early remembers his service to you. And so, I humbly take my leave praying the Almighty to send you all honour happinesse contentment etc.

Your Ladyships neece to commaund
Arbella Stuart./

27

TO MARY TALBOT, COUNTESS OF SHREWSBURY

Autograph, Stuart's informal hand, Talbot Papers 2, ff. 257–58. Addressed "To the right honorable my very good Aunt the Countesse of Shrouesbury". Undated; likely written summer or autumn 1603, soon after Queen Anna's arrival in England.

Letter 26. Lines 10–11. **messe of meate:** mess of meat; diet from the king's table.

Line 11. **.800. pounds per Annum:** as a pension.

Line 14. **t[he]:** There is a hole in the paper.

Line 18. **bruite:** bruit; rumor.

※

Madame./ this eve[r]lasting hunting the [to]oth ache, and the continuall meanes (by my Lord Ceci[ll]) to send to you makes me onely write
these few lines to show I am not unmindefull of your commaundements and reserve the rest I have to write both to you and my uncle
somme few howres longer till my paine asswage and I have given my
never intermitted attendance on the Queene who dayly extendeth hir
favours more and more towards me. The Almighty send you and my
uncle all prosperity and keepe me still I beseech you in your good
opinion who will ever remaine

10

Your Ladyships neece to
commaund
Arbella Stuart./

28

TO MARY TALBOT, COUNTESS OF SHREWSBURY

Autograph, Stuart's informal hand, Talbot Papers 2, ff. 194–95. Addressed "To
the right honorable my very good Aunt the Countes of Shrouesbury". Written
6 October 1603.

※

Madam./ according to your commaundment I send your Ladyship a
few scribled lines, though I be now going in great hast to give my attendance with somm company that is comm to fetch me. I am as diligently
expected, and as soone missed as they that performe the most acceptable service. And because I must returne at an appointed time to go to
my booke I must make the more hast thither. So praying [*foy*] for your
happinesse I humbly take my leave. from Winchester the .6. of October
<u>1603</u>

Your Ladyships neece to
commaund
Arbella Stuart

10

Letter 27. Line 1. **eve[r]lasting:** There are holes in the paper, here and below.
Letter 28. Line 7. **Winchester:** Winchester Castle, Hampshire.

29
TO GILBERT TALBOT, EARL OF SHREWSBURY

Autograph, Stuart's informal hand, Talbot Papers 2, ff. 196–97. Addressed "To the right honorable my very good uncle the Earle of Shrouesbury". Written 27 October 1603.

꙳

I humbly thanck your Lordship for the (as to me it seemed I assure you) short letter of .2. sheets of paper, which I received from you by this bearer m.ʳˢ· Nelson[,] the letters to my Lord Cecill and [*the other*] <Sir Thomas Edmonds> weare delivered though not so soone, as I wished, [*m*] they being both absent from hence so that Sir Thomas his was delivered to the doore keeper of the Counsell chamber and Sir Thomas, not comming hither so soone as was expected m.ʳ· Hersey thought good to fetch it from him and how he hath since disposed of it I know not nor doubt not but he hath donne with it as you would have him, for he seemes to me very well instructed in your minde[,] my Lord Cecill had his as soone as he camme. my bad eyes crave truce till they may without theyr manifest danger write a letter of a larger volume and so praying for your Lordships honour and happinesse in the highest degree that ever subject possessed I humbly take my leave. From Fulston the .27. of October <u>1603</u>

10

Your Lordships neece
Arbella Stuart

Line 3. **m.ʳˢ· Nelson:** perhaps the Mrs. Nelson who had served Stuart's paternal grandmother, Margaret, Dowager Countess of Lennox, and Stuart's mother, Elizabeth, Countess of Lennox (Batho, G195). Nelson had remained with the family.

Lines 3–4. **Sir Thomas Edmonds:** Sir Thomas Edmondes, a Privy Counselor with whom Gilbert Talbot regularly corresponded.

Line 7. **m.ʳ· Hersey:** John Hercy, a Talbot retainer.

Line 14. **Fulston:** the manor at Faulston, southwest of Salisbury, in Wiltshire.

30

TO MARY TALBOT, COUNTESS OF SHREWSBURY

Autograph, Stuart's informal hand, Talbot Papers 2, ff. 198–99. Addressed "To the right honorable my very good Aunt the Countesse of Shrewsbury". Written 4 November 1603.

In November, the trials of those who had been arrested in July and accused of plotting to put Stuart on the throne were about to begin.

꙳

Madame./ I humbly thank you for your good advise against New-yearestide, I thinck theare will be no remedy but I must provide my selfe from London though I be very loth to do so./ I understand by Sir William Stuart how much I am bound to you and my uncle./ I will bethinck my selfe against your long expected trusty messenger comme whatsoever he be, and that expectation shall keepe me from troubling you with so plaine and tedious a discourse as I could finde in my hart to disburden my minde withall to you. I humbly thanck you for my ser-vant George Chaworth. And so praying for your happinesse I humbly
10 cease. From Fulston the .4. of November <u>1603</u>

Your Ladyships neece to
commaund
Arbella Stuart

31

TO MARY TALBOT, COUNTESS OF SHREWSBURY

Autograph, Stuart's informal hand, Talbot Papers 2, ff. 200–201. Addressed "To the right honorable my very good Aunt the Countesse of Shrouesbury". Dated in the docket 6 November 1603.

꙳

Madame./ because I received a letter from you by this gentlewoman, I dare not for incurring [*the*] hir opinion of my relapse into somm

---

Letter 30. Lines 1–2. **Newyearestide:** when Stuart would need to send New Year's gifts appropriate to her rank to the royal family and influential people at court.

Line 9. **George Chaworth:** the gentleman servant who had helped Stuart when she was at Hardwick Hall. What Mary Talbot had done for him is unknown; perhaps she or her husband had promoted Chaworth for office, since shortly after this time he entered King James's service. Letter 31. Line 2. **relapse:** having fallen.

unkindenesse towards you but send you a few lines. I will keepe a note of the dates of my letters[,] that letter of yours which I received since by m.$^{r.}$ Hersey I have answered by him, my eyes are extreemely swolne and yet I have not spared them [*for your sake*] when [*I may have had meanes to d*] I have had occasion to imploy them for your sake thearfore now they may boldly crave a cessation for this time onely performing [*to b*] theyr office whilest I subscribe my selfe such as I am and ever will con-tinue that is   10

Your Ladyships neece to commaund
Arbella Stuart./

32

TO GILBERT TALBOT, EARL OF SHREWSBURY

Autograph, Stuart's informal hand, Talbot Papers 2, ff. 202–3. Addressed "To the right honorable my very good uncle the Earle of Shrouesbury". Written 28 November 1603.

⚹

I must onely returne your Lordship humble thanckes for the letters I have received from you and reserve the answer till I trust a few dayes make me able to write with out extreame paine of my head. m.$^{r.}$ Cooke can tell your Lordship all the newes that is heere And so praying for your Lordships happinesse I humbly take my leave. From Fulston the 28. of November. <u>1603</u>

Your Lordships neece
Arbella Stuart

Letter 31. Line 4. **dates...letters:** Mary Talbot likely had worried that some of Stuart's letters had not reached the Talbots, which might seem especially alarming as the treason trials approached. The confessions of some of the conspirators in the Bye Plot had implicated Stuart's uncle Henry Cavendish, who had been called to court for examination in late October.

Letter 32. Line 3. **extreame...head:** from the cold Stuart mentions in the accompanying letter to Mary Talbot (letter 33).

Line 3. **m.$^{r.}$ Cooke:** Thomas Cooke, secretary to Gilbert Talbot (Jamison, MS 702, f. 47).

33
TO MARY TALBOT, COUNTESS OF SHREWSBURY

Autograph, Stuart's informal hand, Talbot Papers 2, ff. 204–5. Addressed "To the right honorable my very good Aunt the Countesse of Shrouesbury". Written 28 November 1603.

🜬

Madame./ I humbly thancke you for your letters, pill, and hartshorne, I have taken continued, and encreased an extreame colde, [*and*] <I> meane to sweate to day for it. m.ʳ· Cooke can tell you how the world goes heere And so praying for your happinesse I humbly take my leave From Fulston the .28. of November. 1603

Your Ladyships neece to commaund
Arbella Stuart/

34
TO GILBERT TALBOT, EARL OF SHREWSBURY

Autograph, Stuart's informal hand, Talbot Papers 2, ff. 208–9. No address. Written 8 December 1603.

🜬

It may please your Lordship to pardon me if writing now in hast with a minde distracted with the severall cares of a householder, and those that this remove, and newyearstide adde thearto, I omitt somm times that which weare perchance more materiall to write then that I write and forgett many things which according to the manner of us that have onely after-wittes comme not to minde till your letters be gonne and then are too ancient newes to be sent by the next[.] I received your Lordships letter safe by m.ʳˢ· Nelson. and that YOUR in my Aunts letter

---

Letter 33. Line 1. **hartshorne:** the horn or antler of a hart, a source of ammonia, used as medicine and in foods; Mary Talbot's daughter, Elizabeth Grey, included a recipe for hartshorn jelly in her *Choice Manuall, or Rare and Select Secrets in Physick and Chyrurgery* (13th ed., London: Gartrude Dawson, 1661), 14. Or an herb shaped like antlers, used for treatment of excessive discharges and intestinal obstructions, as well as in salads (William Bullein, *Bulleins Bulwarke of Defence Againste All Sicknes, Sornes, and Woundes* [1562; facsimile reprint, Amsterdam and New York: Da Capo Press, 1971], sig. H4).

Letter 34. Line 3. **remove:** The court was moving to Hampton Court Palace for the holidays.

was plurall so that I ment I had received your Lordships and hirs, how
ill so ever I expressed it: I will amend my obscurity God willing. Your   10
Lordship taxeth my obscurity in the comment upon a part of somm letter of mine you desired to have explained, but whatsoever you tooke for
the explanation of it, I am sure I sent you none, for I knew not what it
was you desired to have expounded[.] I pray you take not that Pro concesso in generall which is onely proper to somm monsters of our sex. I
cannot deny so apparant a truth as that wickednesse prevaileth with
somm of our sex because I dayly see somm even of the fairest amongst
us misled and willingly and wittingly ensnared by the Prince of darknesse. But yet ours shall still be the purer and more innocent kinde.
Theare went 10000 Virgins to heaven in one day, looke but in the   20
Almanack and you shall finde that glorious day. and if you thinck theare
are somm but not many of us that may prove Saints I hope you are
deceived, But not many rich, not many noble shall enter into the king-
domm of heaven. So that Richesse and Nobility are hinderances from
heaven as well as our native infirmity. You would thinck me very full of
divinity or desirous to shew that little I have <in both which you should
do me wrong> if you knew what businesse I have at Court [*whi*] and
yet preach to you. pardon me it is not my function. now a little more to
the purpose[.] I have delivered your 2. patents signed and sealed to m.ʳ·
Hercy, if it be not an unexcusable presumption in me to tell you my   30
mind unaskt as if I would advise you what to do pardon me if I tell you
I thinck your thanckes will comm very unseasonably so neare New-
yearestide. especially those with which you send any gratuity. thearfore
consider if it weare not better to give your Newyearsguift first <to the
Queene> and your thancks after, and keepe m.ʳ· Fowlers till after that

Line 11. **comment upon:** explanation of.

Lines 14–15. **Pro concesso:** concession, admission of guilt.

Line 20. **10000…day:** an allusion to St. Ursula, a legendary British princess who was martyred
with her 11,000 virgin handmaidens; her martyrdom was honored on 21 October.

Lines 23–24. **But…heaven:** an allusion to Matt. 19:23, "a rich man shall hardly enter into the
kingdom of heaven" (also Mark 10:23–24; Luke 18:24–25).

Line 35. **m.ʳ· Fowlers:** William Fowler was secretary to Queen Anna and, with Stuart, had
promoted the Talbots to the queen.

good time[.] Newyearstide will comm every yeare, and be a yearly trib-
ute to them you begine with. You may impute the slownesse of your
thanckfulnesse to m.ʳ˙ Hercy or me that acquainted you no sooner with
your owne matter[.] The spanish Imbassadour, invited Madame de
40   Beaumont the French Imbassadours Lady to dinner requesting hir to
bring somm English Ladies with hir[,] she brought my Lady Bedford.
Lady Rich, Lady Susan, Lady Dorothe with hir and great cheere they
had. a fortnight after he invited the Duke[,] the Earle of Mar, and
diverse of that nation requesting them to bring the Scottish Ladies, for
he was desirous to see somm naturall beauties[.] [*They*] <my Lady Anne
Hay, and my cousin Drummond> went and after the sumptuous dinner
weare presented first with .2. paire of Spanish gloves a peece, and after
my Cousin Drummond had a Diamond ring of <the valew of> .200.
crownes given hir, and my Lady Anne, a <gold> chaine of Spanish work
50   neare that valew. my Lady [*Cay*] Cary went with them, and had gloves
theare, and after a <gold> chaine of little linkes twise about hir neck
sent hir. Yeasterday the Spanish Imbassadour[,] the Florentine, and
madame de Beaumont tooke theyr leave of the Queene till she comm to
Hampton court. Theare is an Imbassadour comm from Polonia and
faine he would be gonne againe because of the freezing of theyr seas, but
he hath not yet had audience. The Venetians lately sent 2. Imbassadors
with letters both to the King and Queene[,] one of them is returned
with a very honorable dispatch but he staying but few dayes and the
Queene being not well, he saw hir not, the other stayes heare still it is
60   said the Turk hath sent a Chalice to the King. It is said the Pope will
send a knight to the King in Imbassage. The Duke of Savoyes Imbassage
is dayly expected But out of this confusion of Imbassages will you know

Lines 39–40. **Madame…Lady:** Anne de Rabot, wife of Christophe de Harlai, Count de
Beaumont, the French resident ambassador.

Lines 41–42. **Lady Bedford…Dorothe:** Lucy Russell, Countess of Bedford; Lady Penelope
Rich; Lady Susan de Vere; and Dorothy Percy, Countess of Northumberland.

Line 43. **Duke[,] the Earle of Mar:** Lodovic Stuart, Duke of Lennox; John Erskine, Earl of
Mar.   Line 46. **my cousin Drummond:** Lady Jane Drummond.

Line 50. **my Lady Cary:** likely Lady Elizabeth [Trevanion] Carey (see Emerson, 225–26).

Line 54. **Polonia:** Poland.

how we spend our time on the Queenes side[.] Whilest I was at Winchester theare weare certein childeplayes remembred by the fayre ladies. Viz. I pray my Lord give me a Course in your park. Rise pig and go. One peny follow me. etc. and when I camm to Court they weare <as> highly in request as ever cracking of nuts was. so I was by the mistresse of the Revelles not onely compelled to play at I knew not what for till that day I never heard of a play called Fier. but even perswaded by the princely example I saw to play the childe againe. This excercise is most used from .10. of the clocke at night till .2. or .3. in the morning but that day I made one it beganne at twilight and ended at suppertime. Thear was an enterlude but not so ridiculous (as ridiculous as it was) as my letter which heare I conclude with many prayers to the Almighty for your happinesse and so I humbly take my leave. From Fulston the .8. of December 1603.

70

Your Lordships neece
Arbella Stuart.

35

TO MARY TALBOT, COUNTESS OF SHREWSBURY

Autograph, Stuart's informal hand, Talbot Papers 2, ff. 206–7. Addressed "To the right honorable my very good Aunt the Countesse of Shrowsbury". One corner of the paper has been torn away and the words filled in on the sheet used for the repair. Written 8 December 1603.

Stuart opens with remarks on the trials of those who had conspired to put her on the throne.

❀

Madame./ I humbly thancke you for your kindnesses expressed many wayes and lately in the letter sent from you by my Cousin Lacies man, how defective soever my memory be <in> other wayes assure your selfe I cannot forget even small matters concerning that great party, much lesse [*sug*] such great ones as I thanck God, I was not aquainted with all.

Letter 34. Line 73. **enterlude:** interlude; a play, usually a comedy; perhaps Shakespeare's *As You Like It*, believed to have been played before the court on 2 December.

Letter 35. Line 4. **party:** affair, plot.

Thearfore when any great matter comes in question rest secure I
beseech you, that I am not interessed in it as an Actour, howsoever the
vanity of wicked mens vaine designes, have made my name passe
through a grosse and a suttle lawyers lippes of late, to the excercise [*of*]
10   and increase of my patience, and not theyr credite. I trust I have not lost
so much of your good opinion as your pleasant postscript would make
one that weare suspitious of theyr <assured> frends [*which*] <(as> I
never was) beleeve. for if I should not preferre the reading of your kinde
and most wellcomm letters before all Court delightes (admit I delighted
as much in them as others do) it weare a signe of extreame folly, and
likeing Court sportes no better then I do and then I thinck you thinck I
do I know you cannot thinck me so transformed as to esteeme any
thing lesse then them[,] as your love and judgement together makes me
hope you know I can like nor love nothing better, then the love and
20   kindnesse of so honorable frends as you and my uncle. whearfore I
beseech you lett me heare often <to> declare your love by the length
<and number> of your letters. My [*owne*] follies, ignorances will
minister you sufficient matter for as many and as long letters as you
please [*to take*] which I beseech you may be as many and as copious as
may be without your trouble. I have satisfied the honorable gentlewoman without raising any expectation in hir to receive letters from
you, which is a favour I desire onely <may be reserved still> for my selfe,
[*and*] my Lord Cecill, and your best esteemed frends; I asked hir advise
for a newyearesguifte for the Queene, both for my selfe who am alto-
30   gether unprovided, and a great Lady a frend of mine that was in my case
for that matter, and hir answer was the Queene regarded not the valew
but the devise[,] [*she*] <the gentlewoman> neither liked gowne, nor pet-
icoate so well, as somm little bunch of Rubies to hang in hir eare, or
somm such dafte toy. I meane to give hir Majesty 2. paire of silk stock-
ins lined with plush and 2. paire of gloves lined if London afford me not
somm daft toy I like better whearof I cannot bethinck me. If I knew the
valew you would bestow, I thinck it weare no hard matter to gett hir or

---

Lines 8–9. **my...late:** Sir Edward Coke had discussed Stuart during his prosecution of Sir
Walter Ralegh.   Line 21. **<to>:** An illegible, deleted line precedes this word.

Line 22. **[owne]:** The paper now is torn, and the word cannot be read; *own* is the word Bradley
transcribed (2:192) over a hundred years ago, when presumably the paper was intact.

m.^{rs.} Hartshide understand the Queenes minde with out knowing who asked it. The time is short and thearfore you had neede loose none of it. I am making the King a purse. And for all the world else I am unpro-   40
vided. This time will manifest my poverty more then all the rest of the yeare, but why should I be ashamed of it when it is others fault and not mine?/ my quarters allowance will not defray this one charge I beleeve./ Sir William Stuart continueth his charitable desire, but he cannot per-swade me to loose my labour how little so ever he esteeme his owne to so good an end, which I wish, but thinck not se[n]sible, at least by me. Thus praying for the increase of your happinesse every way I humbly take my leave. From Fulston the .8. of December. <u>1603</u>

Your Ladyships most affectionat
neece to commaund   50
Arbella Stuart

36

TO GILBERT TALBOT, EARL OF SHREWSBURY

Autograph, Stuart's informal hand, Talbot Papers 2, ff. 210–11. Addressed "To the right honorable my very good uncle the Earle of Shrewsbury./" Written 18 December 1603.

That night the Queene camme hither which was on friday the .16. of December I received your Lordships packett to me by one of my Lord Cecilles men. m.^{r.} Hercies letter I keepe till I see him, which will be very shortly as he lately told me. I humbly thank you for your thanckes to my Lord Cecill for me. I am a witnesse not onely of the rare guifte of speach which God hath given him, but of his excellent judgement in chusing most plausible and honorable Theames as The defending a wronged Lady The clearing of an innocent knight. etc. I humbly thanck you for

---

Letter 35. Line 38. **m.^{rs.} Hartshide:** Margaret Hartside, one of Queen Anna's attendants.

Line 40. **purse:** a money-bag, which generally would be filled with gold sovereigns for presentation.   Line 43. **quarters allowance:** two hundred pounds.

Letter 36. Line 7. **plausible:** commendable.

Lines 7–8. **defending...knight:** When Sir Edward Coke, in prosecuting Sir Walter Ralegh, "was in danger of trying Arbella instead" (Handover, 185), Cecil spoke up to defend Stuart as innocent of complicity in the plot to overthrow King James. Cecil also exonerated her uncle Henry Cavendish, a knight of Derbyshire.

your letter to my Lord Bishop of Winchester which if it be written (as I
10   doubt not but it is) in that sort as may availe the recomended is worth
.10. favours of greater valew that you had binne willing to graunt, but if
as being written Invita Minerva they be unto him like Urias sealed letter,
alas what have I donne? Well I suspect you not thearfore now you may
deceive me. and you deceive me (who am better perswaded of your
judgement) if you do not perceive I cast that doubt onely to make you
merry with looking into the infinitnesse of suspition if one will nourish it
<not> that I have the least doubt of your honourable dealing with [*me*]
<any> and especially my selfe. The invitation is very colde if the
Christmas guests you write of accept it not, for they knew theyr
20   wellcomme and entertainment in a worse place and yet were so bold to
invite themselves [*to th*] thither. I humbly thanck you that for my sake
they shall be the wellcommer to you who in regard of theyr nearenesse of
bloud to your selfe and my Aunt must needes be so very wellcomm that
(if you had not written it) I should not have thought they could have
binne more wellcomm to you in any respect then that. Your venison shall
be right wellcomm to Hampton court and merrily eaten. I dare not write
unto you how I do, for if I should say well I weare greatly to blame, if ill I
trust you would not beleeve me I am so merry. It is enough to change
Heraclitus into Democritus to live in this most ridiculous world, and
30   enough to change Democritus into Heraclitus to live in this most wicked

---

Line 9. **Lord Bishop of Winchester:** Thomas Bilson, to whom Stuart is through her uncle
making suit, presumably for an ecclesiastical office; she also mentions the issue in letter 39.

Line 12. **Invita Minerva:** like Minerva's invitation. When the peasant Arachne declared her
weaving to be superior to the goddess Minerva's, Minerva challenged her to a contest;
Arachne's work was perfect, and Minerva struck her until Arachne hanged herself (Ovid's
Metamorphoses, Book 6).

Line 12. **Urias sealed letter:** the sealed letter Uriah carried, in which David instructed Joab to
put Uriah into the heaviest fighting and let him be slain (2 Sam. 14).

Line 19. **Christmas guests:** Stuart's uncle Henry and aunt Grace Cavendish, whom Stuart in
letter 42 asks Gilbert to bring to London.

Lines 22–23. **nearenesse…Aunt:** Henry was Mary's brother, and Grace was Gilbert's sister.

Line 25. **venison:** an important aristocratic gift, indicating that the recipient was especially
valued.

Line 29. **Heraclitus:** the sad philosopher, who urged people to put aside their desires (Greek,
fifth century B.C.). **Democritus:** the laughing philosopher, who advocated cheerfulness
(Greek, fifth century B.C.).

world; if you will not allow reading of riddles for a Christmas sport, I know not whether you will take this Philosoficall folly of mine in good part this good time. I writt to your Lordship <by a messenger of m.ʳ· Hercies in answer of yours I received by> my Cousin Lacies man of such newes as then weare newes as I thinck in the north. and now have I none to send but that the King will be heare to morrow. The Polonian Imbassador shall have audience on Thursday next. The Queene intendeth to make a mask this Christmas to which end my Lady of Suffolk and my Lady Walsingham have warrants to take of the late Queenes best apparell out of the Tower at theyr discretion[.] Certein Noblemen (whom I may not yet name to you because somm of them have made me of theyr counsell) intend another. Certein gentlemen of good sort an other. It is said theare shall be .30. playes[.] The King will feast all the Imbassadours this Christmas. Sir John Hollies <yeasterday> convoyed somm <new-comm> Imbassadour to Richmond and it was said <(but uncerteinly)> to be a Muscovian. I have reserved the best newes for the last, and that is the Kings pardon of <life to> the not-executed traitours. I dare not beginne to tell of the Royall and wise manner of the Kings proceeding thearin, least I should finde no ende of extolling him for it till I had written out a payre of badd eyes And thearfore praying for your Lordships happinesse I humbly and abruptely take my leave. From Hampton court the .18. of December <u>1603</u>./

40

50

> Your Lordships neece
> Arbella Stuart

Line 38. **mask:** Samuel Daniel's masque *The Vision of the Twelve Goddesses*.

Lines 38–39. **Lady of...Walsingham:** Katherine Howard, Countess of Suffolk, and Lady Audrey Walsingham, Keeper of Queen Anna's Wardrobe.   Lines 41–42. **made...counsell:** taken me into their confidence.

Line 43. **.30. playes:** including several performed by the King's Men, one of which likely was Ben Jonson's *Sejanus His Fall,* in which Shakespeare made his last known appearance as an actor (Yoshiko Kawachi, *Calendar of English Renaissance Drama 1558–1642* [New York and London: Garland, 1986], 128).

Line 44. **Sir John Hollies:** Sir John Holles, a family friend.   Line 46. **Muscovian:** from the principality of Muscovy; Russian.

Line 47. **pardon...traitours:** George Brooke, William Clarke, and William Watson had been executed; but on 10 December, Lord Cobham, Lord Grey, and Sir Griffin Markham had been led to the scaffold and there told that King James had reprieved the remaining parties.

Line 51. **Hampton court:** Hampton Court Palace, to the west of London.

37

TO MARY TALBOT, COUNTESS OF SHREWSBURY

Autograph, Stuart's informal hand, Talbot Papers 2, ff. 212–13. Addressed "To the right honorable my very good Aunt the Countesse of Shrewsbury./" Written 22 December 1603.

🦋

Madame./ I received your Ladyships letter by your old servant David 3 dayes ago, and his desire being I should speake to somm of the counsell in his behalfe and he knowing he had brought a letter of recommendation to me least he should thincke me disobedient to you who willed me to <do> what I could for him, I offered to speake to the Duke of Lennox in his behalfe who is the onely counseller now my uncle is away that I will move in any <such> suite, but I told him it would be to so little purpose, that though <at that present> he seemed to desire his furtherance, I have not seene him since and so upon better consideration I
10 thincke he takes the right way and will spare that needelesse labour of mine to speake to one for him that can do him little good. but whether I shall see David any more before his returne to you or not I know not and thearfore m.^r. Hercy having left this packett of his with me to be sent by the first sure messenger I could heare of I have rather made bolde with this bearer as he can tell you [*rather*] then either stay it (for [*he*] <m.^r. Hercy> saith it requireth hast) or rely on the uncerteinty of your servant. The Polonian Imbassadour had audience to day. other newes heare is none <that I know> and thearfore I beseech you make my excuse to my uncle that I write not to him in this busy time and
20 scarcity of occurrents. And so praying the Almighty to send you both all happinesse I humbly take my leave. From Hampton court the .22. of December.

> Your Ladyships most affectionat neece
> to commaund
> Arbella Stuart./

Line 1. **David:** perhaps the Rowland David who wrote the earl for instructions in 1607 (Jamison, MS 702, f. 65).

Mr. Hercy sent a packett [*of*] <by post> whearin I writt to my uncle
and you in answer of those I received from you by my Cousin Lacies
man[.] I beseech you let us know if you received them safe if I had
thought they would have binn sent by post I would have written more
reservedly   30

38

TO GILBERT TALBOT, EARL OF SHREWSBURY

Autograph, Stuart's informal hand, Talbot Papers 2, ff. 214–15. Addressed "To
the right honorable my very good uncle the Earle of Shrouesbury". Written 2
January 1603/4.

𝕭

This bearer comming to me in such hast as he can tell your Lordship I
onely observe your commaundement in scribling never so little never so
ill and reserve all I have to write of to your Lordship that is somm Hardwick newes and such vanities as this place and holy time afford me till
Emeryes returne by whom I have received a large essay of your Lordships good cheere at Sheffield I humbly thanck you and my Aunt for it.
One m.^{r.} Tunsted expecteth letters from your Lordship and camme
once him selfe and said he would send to my chamber often in adventure you should send them to me. And thus praying to the Almighty to
send your Lordship so much increase of honour and happinesse that   10
you may confesse your selfe to be the K[ings] happiest subject I humbly
take my leave From Hampton court. the .2. of January. 1603

Your Lordships neece

Arbella Stuart

I beseech you obtaine my pardon of my Aunt for not writing to hir at
this time.

Letter 37. Lines 26–28. **whearin…man:** likely letters 34 and 35.

Letter 38. Line 5. **Emeryes:** William Emerey, a Talbot retainer (Jamison, MS 694, f. 15).

Line 5. **essay:** sample for trial.

Line 6. **Sheffield:** either Sheffield Castle or Sheffield Manor in Yorkshire, where the Talbots
were spending the holidays. Sheffield Castle was the seat of the Earls of Shrewsbury.

Line 7. **m.^{r.} Tunsted:** Robert Tunsted, servant of the Earl of Shrewsbury, who had written the
earl in December for an advance on his wages because he was in need (Batho, M154).

Line 11. **K[ings]:** The sheet is torn.

39
TO GILBERT TALBOT, EARL OF SHREWSBURY

Autograph, Stuart's informal hand, Talbot Papers 2, ff. 216–17. Addressed, presentation hand, "To the right honorable my very good uncle the Earle of Shrewsbury". Written 10 January 1603/4.

🜚

This bearer having leave for a short time to visit the north, and not giv-ing me time sufficient to write the description of the .3. maskes besides 2 playes plaid before the prince since my last advertisment of these serious affaires, I must beseech your Lordship to pardon the shortnesse of my letter proceeding partly of the short warning I had of his going downe, partly of the shortnesse of my witt who at this instant remember no newes but is either too great to be conteined in <my> weake paper or vulgar, or such as with out detriment but of your Lordships expectation, may tarry the next messenger. I have heere inclosed sent your Lordship

10   the Bishop of Winchesters letter in answer of yours, I beseech you lett me know what you writt, and what he answers concerning the party in whose favour I craved your letter, that I may lett the good warden know [*as*] as soone as may be. my Lady of Worceter commendeth hir as kindely to your Lordship and not to my Aunt as you did your selfe to hir in [*yo*] hir Lordships letter, and is as desirous to raise jelousy betwixt you <two>, as you are like to do betwixt them. Thus praying to the Almighty to send your Lordship infinit and perpetuall honour and hap-pinesse I humbly take my leave. From Hampton court. the .10. of January

20   Your Lordships neece
                                              Arbella Stuart./

I had almost tried whither your Lordship would have performed a good

---

Lines 2–3. **3...prince:** On 1 January Prince Henry had seen *Robin Goodfellow,* perhaps a revival or adaptation of *A Midsummer Night's Dream,* and *A Mask of the Knights of India and China,* now lost (Kawachi, 129). The majority of the plays and masques performed at court during this theatrically active season are unknown.

Line 10. **Bishop...yours:** an issue first mentioned in letter 36.

Line 13. **my Lady of Worceter:** Elizabeth, Countess of Worcester, married to Edward Somerset, the fourth Earl. They were said to be happily married, although economically drained by the large number of their children (Emerson, 105).

office betwixt two frends undesired for I had forgotten to beseech you to excuse me to my Aunt for not writing to hir at this time.

I thinck I am asked every day of this new yeare .7. times a day at least when you comm up, and I have nothing to say but I cannot tell, which it is not theyr pleasure to beleeve, and thearfore if you will not resolve them nor me of the truth, yet teach me what to answer them

40
TO GILBERT TALBOT, EARL OF SHREWSBURY

Autograph, Stuart's informal hand, Talbot Papers 2, ff. 218–19. Addressed "To the right honorable my very good uncle the Earle of Shrewsbury". Written 11 January 1603/4.

My Lord Cecill sent me a faire paire of bracelets this morning in requitall of a trifle I presented him at Newyearstide which it pleased him to take as I meant it. I finde him my very honorable frende, both in word and deede, I pray you give him such thancks for me as he many wayes deserves. and especially for this extraordinary and unexpected favour, whearby I perceive his Lordship reckneth me in the nomber of his frends for whom onely [*they*] <such great persons as he> reserve such favours. Thus praying for your Lordships happinesse I humbly take my leave From Hampton court the .11. of January

Your Lordships neece   10
Arbella Stuart.

41
TO MARY TALBOT, COUNTESS OF SHREWSBURY

Autograph, Stuart's informal hand, Talbot Papers 2, ff. 220–21. Addressed, presentation hand, "To the right honorable my very good Aunt the Countesse of Shrewsbury". Written 21 January 1603/4.

Madame./ I have sent my uncle and you, all the newes that I had to write, so that for your lesse trouble and the sparing of my eyes till somm other time I beseech you lett these few lines serve to testify <to you bothe> my obedience in writing by every messenger though never so little. Thus praying for your encrease of honour, comfort and happinesse I humbly take my leave From Hampton court the .21. of January. 1603

> Your Ladyships most affectionate
> neece to commaund
> Arbella Stuart./

42

TO GILBERT TALBOT, EARL OF SHREWSBURY

Autograph, Stuart's informal hand, Talbot Papers 2, ff. 222–23. Addressed "To my uncle of Shrouesbury". Written 3 February 1603/4.

Having sent away this bearer with a letter to my Aunt and not your Lordship with an intention to write to you at length by m.ʳ Cooke, I found so good hope of my Grandmothers good inclination to a good and reasonable reconciliation betwixt hir selfe and hir devided family, that I could not forbeare to impart to your Lordship with all speede. Thearfore I beseech you putt on such a Christian and honorable minde, as best becommeth you to beare to a Lady so neere to you and yours, as my Grandmother is. And thinck you cannot devise to do me a greater honour, and contentment then to let me be the \<onely\> mediatour
10   [*and*] moderator and peacemaker betwixt you and hir. you know I have cause onely to be partiall on your side so many kindenesses and favours have I receaved from you and so many unkindenesses and disgraces have I receaved from the other party; yet will I not be restrained from chiding you (as great a Lord as you are), if I finde you either not willing to harken to this good motion, or to procede in it as I shall thinck reasonable. Consider what power you will give me over you in this and take as great over me as you give me over you in this, in all matters but one, and in that your authority \<and perswasion\> shall as farre exceede

---

Letter 42. Line 4. **hir selfe…family:** Bess and Gilbert, Bess's stepson and son-in-law, had been at odds for years over the Shrewsbury estates. In her 1601 will, Bess had left Gilbert and Mary, as well as Charles Cavendish, only her prayers; and after Stuart's attempt to marry, in March 1603 Bess before witnesses had eliminated Stuart and Henry Cavendish as well (Handover, 135–36, 204). The reconciliation was partially successful.   Line 18. **one:** her marriage.

theyrs as your kindenesse to me did in my trouble. If you thinck I have
either discretion or good nature, you may be sure you may referre much   20
to me, if I be not sufficient for this treaty, never thinck me such as can
adde strength, or honour to your family. But m.ᵣ· Cooke perswades me
you thinck otherwise then so abjectly of me. And so praying to the
Almighty you may such a course both in this and all your other honorable designes, as may with your most honour and contentment, bring
you to those good endes you wish whatsoever [*I b*] they be. I humbly
take my leave. From Hampton court the .3. of February. <u>1603</u>

Your Lordships neece

Arbella Stuart./

I beseech you bring my uncle Henry and my Aunt Grace up with you to   30
London they shall not long be troublesomm to you God willing but
because I know my uncle hath somm very great occasion to be about
London for a little while and is not well able to beare his owne charges,
nor I for him as I would very willingly if I weare able to so good an end
as I know he commes to now and thearfore I beseech you, take that
paines and trouble of bringing them up and keeping them a while with
you, for my sake, and our families good. I have hearinclosed sent you a
letter to him, which if you will graunt him this favour I require of you,
I beseech you send him, [*but first reade,*] if you will not returne it to me,
and let him not be so much discomforted to see I am not able to   40
obtaine so much of you for him. In truth I am ashamed to trouble you
with so many rude, and (but for my sake as you say) unwellcomm
requests but if you be weary of me, you may soone be dispatched of me
for ever (as I am tolde) in more honorable sort then you may deny this
my very earnest request.

Lines 30–31. **up…London:** when the Earl of Shrewsbury came for King James's official state
entry, which had been postponed until March because of plague in the city.

Line 41. **obtaine…him:** It is unclear whether Henry and Grace Cavendish came to London
with the Talbots.

Line 44. **in…sort:** i.e., in marriage. Which rumor Stuart refers to is unknown. There was talk
of a marriage to Count Maurice of Nassau, of the United Provinces. Or it might already have
been rumored that the King of Poland, Sigismund III, whose ambassador had been received by
James in late December 1603 and thought well of Stuart, would ask for her hand. Within
months, the Polish king sent a marshal with the marriage proposal.

43

TO GILBERT TALBOT, EARL OF SHREWSBURY

Autograph, Stuart's informal hand, Talbot Papers 2, ff. 232–33. Addressed, presentation hand, "To my uncle of Shrowesbury." One corner of the manuscript is missing. Undated; likely written late February 1603/4, after Stuart was made carver to Queen Anna and well before mid-March, when the Talbots were in London for King James's state entry.

🙥

I humbly thanck your Lordship for sparing me never so few words in the time of your taking Physick, which I would not should have binne more, for doing you harme in holding downe your head at such a time but when you are well I hope to receive somm Hardwick newes which untill your Lordship be a great deale briefer then that plentifull argument requireth will cost you a long letter./ my Aunt findeth fault with my brevity as I thinck by your Lordships commaundment for I know she in hir wisdomm respecteth cerimony so little that she would not care in time of health for hearing from me every weeke that I am well
10 and nothing else. and I know hir likewise too wise to <make> that <the> cause of <hir> offence, suppose in pollicy she should thinck good to seeme or be offended with me whom perchance you now thinck good to shake off as weary of the alliance. But I conclude your Lordship hath a quarrell to me and maketh my Aunt take it upon hir, and that is (for other can you justly have none) that you have never a letter of mine since your going downe to make you merry at your few spare houres which if it be so your Lordship may commaund me in plaine termes and deserve it by doing the like. And I shall as willingly play the foole for your recreation as ever. I assure my selfe my Lord Cecill, my Lord of
20 Pembrok, your honorable new ally, and divers of y[our] old acquaintance write your Lordship all the newes of [Court] that is stirring, so that I will onely impart s[omm] trifles to your Lordship at this time as

---

Lines 19–20. **Lord of...ally:** William Herbert, third Earl of Pembroke and son of Mary Sidney, who was to marry the Talbots' eldest daughter, Mary, in November.

Line 20. **y[our]:** The sheet is torn, here and below.

concerne m[y] selfe. After I had once carved the Queene neve[r] dined
out of hir bed chamber nor was attended by any but hir chamberers, till
my Lady of Bedfords returne. I doubted my unhandsomm carving had
binne the cause thearof, but hir Majesty tooke my indevour in good
part and with better words then that beginning deserved put me out of
that errour. At length (for now I am called to the Sermon I must hasten
to an end) it fell out that the importunity of certeine great Ladies in [*so*]
that or somm other suite of the like kinde had donne me this disgrace,   30
and whom should I heare named for one but my Aunt of Shrouesbury
who they say at the same time stood to be the Queenes cupbearer. If I
could have binne perswaded to beleeve or seeme to beleeve that whearof
I knew the contrary, I might have binne threatned downe to my face
that I was of hir counsell thearin, that I deeply dissembled with my
frends when I protested the contrary for I was heard to confer with hir
(they say) to that purpose. But these people do little know how circumspect my Aunt and your Lordship are with me, I humbly thanck you for
the example. I heare the mariage betwixt my Lord of Pembrok and my
Cousin is broken, whearat somtime I laugh other whiles am angry som-   40
times answer soberly as though I thought it possible, according as it is
spoken in simple earnest, scorne, pollicy or howsoever, at the least as I
conceive it to be spoken. And your Lordships secrecy is the cause of this
variety (whearby somme conjecture I know sommthing) because I have
no certein direction what to say in that case. I was asked within these 3.
dayes whither [*he*] your Lordship would be heere within .10. dayes,
unto which (to me) strange question, I made so strange an answer as I
am sure either your Lordship [or] I are counted great dissemblers. I am
none, quit your selfe as you may. But I would be very glad you weare

---

Line 23. **carved:** Stuart had been awarded the office of meat carver to Queen Anna.

Line 25. **Lady of Bedfords:** Lucy Russell, Countess of Bedford, one of the queen's most trusted ladies-in-waiting. **doubted:** suspected.

Lines 39–43. **I heare...be spoken:** In 1601 Pembroke had refused to marry Queen Elizabeth's attendant Mary Fitton, who was pregnant. That refusal may account in part for the gossip concerning his intentions.

Line 48. **[or]:** The paper is torn.

50 heere that I need not chide you by letter as I must needes do if I be chid-
den either for the shortnesse, rarenesse, or precisenesse of my letters
which by <your former> rules I might <thinck> a fault, by your late
example a wisdomme, I pray you reconcile your deedes and words
together, and I shall follow that course hearin which your Lordship best
allowes of. in the meane time I have applied my selfe to your Lordships
former likeing and the plainesse of my owne disposition. And so praying for your Lordships health honour and happinesse I humbly take my
leave. From Whitehall

Your Lordships neece

60
Arbella Stuart./

44
TO SIR GEORGE MANNERS

HMC, Rutland I (24), *The Manuscripts of His Grace the Duke of Rutland*, 395.
(Stuart's autograph manuscript is preserved at Belvoir Castle, which is closed to
researchers.) Gaps in the manuscript apparently were filled in by the transcriber.
Written 2 August 1604, from Whitehall; dated in HMC volume.

Sir George Manners was married to Stuart's first cousin Grace Pierrepont.
His mother's family seat was Haddon Hall, fifteen miles from Hardwick Hall.
Manners had been imprisoned for his part in the Earl of Essex's plot of Febru-
ary 1601, and in 1603 he had been suspected of aiding Stuart.

❦

Good Cousin, I thinck very long since I heard fro[m you]. I shall be
very glad to heare you [are a]s well as I wish, or as you desire. H[ow]ever
you of more experience and discr[etion] content yourselves w[ith]
hoping yo[ur fri]ends are well, I cannot satisfy m[ysel]fe without sending to see how you [are]. And so with kindest salutations to you and
yours I take my leave.

Letter 43. Line 51. **precisenesse:** seriousness.
Line 52. **<thinck> a:** emended from "a <thinck>".
Line 58. **Whitehall:** Whitehall Palace, principal London residence of the sovereign.

45

TO MARY TALBOT, COUNTESS OF SHREWSBURY

Autograph, Stuart's informal hand, Talbot Papers 2, ff. 226–27. Addressed "To the right honorable my very good Aunt the Countesse of Shrowsbury". Dated by Mary Talbot's secretary 3 October 1604.

꧁

Madame./ I was very glad to receive your letter and my uncles from that party which delivered them to me, with somme newes which I am very glad of and pray God to send your Ladyship and my uncle as much joy thearof as your selves desire. m.ʳ· Cooke and your Ladyships redde deare shall be very wellcomme, or any messenger or token whearby I may understand of your well being and the continuance of your affection to one who [*wl*] will remaine

Your Ladyships neece to commaund
Arbella Stuart./

46

TO GILBERT TALBOT, EARL OF SHREWSBURY

Autograph, Stuart's informal hand, Talbot Papers 2, ff. 228–29. Addressed "To the Earle of Shrowesbury." Written 18 October 1604.

꧁

I humbly thancke your Lordship and my Aunt for the sixe very good red deare pies I have received from your Lordship by m.ʳ· Hercy. [*your*] my Aunts thanckes which I received for my plaine dealing with m.ʳ· Booth, and the few lines I received <last> from your Lordship and my Aunt by m.ʳ· Hercy have relation to certein conditions and promises as well on your Lordships part as mine, and thearfore your Lordships

---

Letter 45. Line 2. **newes:** probably that the protracted financial negotiations for the Talbot-Pembroke marriage had been concluded, and King James had approved the union (Batho, K217). By October 1604, word was spreading among the Herbert family that the match was set (Margaret P. Hannay, *Philip's Phoenix: Mary Sidney, Countess of Pembroke* [New York and Oxford: Oxford Univ. Press, 1990], 189).

Line 4. **redde deare:** red deer; a highly valued species of deer, of a reddish-brown color.

Letter 46. Lines 3–4. **m.ʳ· Booth:** likely one of the two Mr. Booths, John and Robert, employed by Gilbert Talbot. John Booth was the earl's steward (Jamison, 206).

confidence of my conditionall promise, resteth <not in me onely>. I
assure my selfe you are so honorable and I so deere unto you, that you
will respect as well what is convenient for me as [*whay*] what you earnestly desire. especially my estate being so uncerteine and subject to
injury as it is. your Lordship shall finde me constantly persever in a
desire to do that which may be acceptable to you and my Aunt, not
altogether neglecting my selfe. And so I humbly take my leave, praying
for your happinesse. From Whitehall, the .18. of October. <u>1604</u>

> Your Lordships neece
> Arbella Stuart./

47

TO GILBERT TALBOT, EARL OF SHREWSBURY

Autograph, Stuart's informal hand, Talbot Papers 2, ff. 230–31. Addressed "To
the Earle of Shrowsbury." Written 24 December 1604.

I have sent sooner then I had time to write to your Lordship of any
thing heere, and yet not so soone but I am sure I am already
condempned by your Lordship and My Aunt <either> for slothfull, or
proud, or both, because I writ not by the very first went downe after I
received your letters, so have I fully satisfyed neither your Lordship nor
my selfe, and yet performed a due respect to a very honorable frend,
whose honour and happinesse I shall ever rejoyce at and thinck my
owne misfortunes the lesse, if I may see my wishes, for your Lordships
and my Aunts, permanent, happy, and great fortune take effect And so I
humbly take my leave. From Whitehall the .24. of December. <u>1604</u>.

> Your Lordships neece
> Arbella Stuart./

Though I have written your Lordship no newes, I have sent you hearinclosed very good store from m.^{r.} Secretary Fowler. My olde good spy
m.^{r.} James Mourray desireth his service may be remembred to your

---

Letter 47. Line 6. **frend:** likely her cousin Mary, the Talbots' daughter, who had come to court
as the new Countess of Pembroke.

Line 14. **good store:** i.e., a goodly amount of news in a letter.

Line 15. **James Mourray:** unidentified; perhaps the James Murray who once served King
James as messenger to Queen Elizabeth.

Lordship and my Aunt, but if I should write every tenth word of his whearin he wisheth you more good then is to be expressed at Court on a Christmas Eve, you would rather thinck this scribled paper, a short Text with a long Comment underwritten, then a letter with a Postscript.

48

TO PRINCE HENRY

Autograph, Stuart's presentation hand, BL Harley MS 6986, ff. 71–72. Addressed "To the Prince./" Written 18 October 1605.

🦋

Sir./

My intention to attend your Highnesse to morrow (God willing) cannot stay me from acknowledging by these few lines how infinitely I am bound to your Highnesse for that your gratious disposition towards me which faileth not to show it selfe upon every occasion whither accidentall or begged by me, as this late high favour and grace it hath pleased your Highnesse to do my kinsman at my humble suite./ I trust to morrow to let your Highnesse understand such motives of that my presumption as shall make it excusable. For your Highnesse shall perceive I both understand with what extraordinary respectes suites are to be pre-   10 sented to your Highnesse; and withall that your goodnesse doth so temper your greatnesse as it encourageth both me and many others to hope that we may taste the fruites of the one by meanes of the other. The Almighty make your Highnesse every way such as I, m.^{r} Newton, and Sir David Murray (the onely intercessours I have used in my suites or will in any I shall present to your Highnesse) wish you, and then shall you be even such as you are, and your growth in vertu and grace with God and men shall be the onely alteration we will pray for. And so in all humility I Cease. From London the .18. of October 1605

Your Highnesse   20
most humble and dutifull
Arbella Stuart./

Letter 48. Lines 14–15. **m.^{r}...Murray:** the Prince's tutors. Mr. Newton was Adam Newton.

49
TO ROBERT CECIL, EARL OF SALISBURY

Autograph, Stuart's presentation hand, Cecil Papers 134, f. 94. Addressed "To my honorable good Lord the Earle of Salisbury./" Written 2 May 1606.

   By 1606, Stuart was in need of additional funds; this suit, however, was not granted.

꙼

My good Lord./ I lately moved his Majesty to graunt to me such fees as may arise out of his seale which the Bishops are by the law to use as I am informed./ I am inforced to make somme suite for my better support and maintenance; as heartofore I have found you my good Lord, so I must earnestly entreate your Lordship to further this my suite; and thearin I shall rest much bound to you./ Sir Walter Cope hath binne requested to recommend this my suite to your Lordship for that I thought his mediation would be lesse troublesomme to you, then if I sollicited your Lordship my selfe, or by somme other my frends. I pray
10 God graunt your Lordship long and happy life.

<u>ii</u>. of May.   Your Lordships much bound
<u>1606</u>.   Arbella Stuart./

50
TO SIR JOHN HOLLES

Copy by Holles's son, BL Add. MS 70505, f. 135. Docketed by Holles's son "From my Lady Arbella to Sir Jhon Holles in excuse of her not cumming to my sisters Arbellaes christning 1606." Addressed "To my very good frend Sir Jhon Holles." Written 7 August 1606.

   Sir John Holles was a family friend from Nottinghamshire. Because King Christian IV of Denmark, Queen Anna's brother, had arrived at court and Stuart was expected to participate in the festivities, she was unable to attend the christening of Holles's daughter Arbella.

꙼

Good Sir Jhon Hollis I must request you to excuse my not cumming to you this day, with those necessities wherunto I am subject, and advyse what satisfaction you will have me make my Lady and you for this

---

Letter 49. Line 6. **Sir Walter Cope:** Chamberlain of the Exchequer.

disappointment. I have sent you a Ladies answere whom I requ<e>sted
to supply my place in that good office I owe you, as soone as I knew I
could not come today my selfe. So that I must desyre you either to
direct my man, to some who will do me this kyndnes or stay till I may
performe it my selfe and so with my beste wishes to my Lady, your selfe,
and yours I take my leave from Hampton Court the .7. of August <u>1606</u>.
Your very loving frend Arbella Stuart.   10

51

TO SIR ANDREW SINCLAIR

Autograph draft, Stuart's informal hand, BL Harley MS 7003, ff. 42–43.
Addressed "To my Honorable good frend Sir Andrew Sinclar." Undated; written August 1606.

While King Christian of Denmark was visiting England, he apparently
joked that the Earl of Nottingham, who had married the much younger Margaret Stuart, risked becoming a cuckold; when the remark was reported to Lady
Nottingham, she angrily protested by letter, embarrassing the king. Chamberlain Andrew Sinclair, although he did not explain the exact nature of the controversy, told Stuart that the king felt unjustly accused and hoped she would
defend him. (For Sinclair's letter to Stuart, see Appendix B, letter 6.) Christian's
behavior, however, had not been as blameless as Stuart suggests; the vigorous
and popular king had become drunken and scandalized some observers of the
court.

My honorable good frend./ I yeild his Majesty most humble thanckes
that it pleaseth him to adde that advertisment I received from you
<yeasternight> to the rest of the favours whearwith it hath pleased his
Majesty to honour me, and I pray you assure his Majesty that next unto
that I shall spend in prayers for his Majesties prosperity, I shall thincke
that breath of mine best bestowed which may adde if it be but a drop to
the sea of his honour./ I have observed his Majesties behaviour [*with*] as
[*great d*] <diligently> as any and I may truly protest I [*s*] never saw <nor
heard> that deede or word of his, which did not deserve high prayse,
whearof I shall beare wittnesse I doubt not with many more, for I assure   10

Letter 50. Line 5. **supply…you:** stand as godmother for her by proxy, which the lady could
not do.

you it is not possible for a Prince to leave a more honorable memory
then his Majesty hath donne heere. And if any speak or understand it
otherwise it must proceede [*either*] of theyr unworthinesse, [*or*] <and>
be esteemed [*that*] <as a> shadow of Envy which infallibly accompanies
the brightnesse of vertu. I spent yeasterday at London, and have not yet
seene [*the Queenes*] <hir> Majesty since hir sorrowfull returning hither
but I <am> assure<d> [*my selfe*] hir Majesty will performe all the offices
of a kinde sister to hir most deare and worthy brother, in which cause I
thinck my selfe happy to have a part[.] I beseech his Majesty this indis-
20   cretion of my Lady of Nottingha[m] may not empaire his good opinion
of our sexe or climat but that it will please him to retaine the innocent
in his wonted favour, and especially my selfe who will not faile to pray
for his <Majesties> safe and happy returne with all other [*felicities*] dayly
increasing felicities and remaine

Your assured thanckfull frend
A.S.

52

TO SIR ANDREW SINCLAIR

Autograph draft, Stuart's informal hand, BL Harley MS 7003, f. 48. No
address. Undated; perhaps written October 1606.

Sir Andrew Sinclair responded to Stuart's letter quickly, saying that he had
been commanded to assure Stuart that King Christian thought highly of her
and would willingly advance her fortunes. (For Sinclair's letter, see Appendix B,
letter 7.) As a further honor, King Christian and Queen Anna Cathrine sent
personal letters to Stuart, thanking her for presents she had proffered. This
draft of a letter to Sinclair, designed to accompany letters to the royal couple,
may have been revised into the more subdued letter to Sinclair that follows,
which was translated into Latin and copied for Stuart's files, or it may have been
written later in the correspondence.

ℵ

My honorable good frend./ I yeild both theyr Majesties most humble
thanckes for theyr gratious favours, and have presumed so to do by
letters to themselves, which I must account one of theyr speciall graces,
that it pleaseth them to licence me to do, for by the patronage of so

---

Letter 51. Line 20. **Nottingha[m]:** The writing runs off the page.

worthy a Prince, so interested in them of whom my fortune depends, and so gratiously affected to me, I cannot doubt, but [*to live safe, and*] at last to comme to somme such stay, as shall [*both*] give me perpetuall cause to pray for his Majesty whose gratious favour so many wayes expressed is of it selfe an especiall comfort and honour to me. And for you my honorable frend, by whose good meanes I enjoy this happi-   10
nesse, I can but acknowledge my selfe your debtor till God make me able better to expresse my thanckfulnesse, [*which I*] <as I> doubt not [*of*] by Gods grace but I shall be made, by your [*good meanes*] good indevors, and the mediation of your most gratious master. Whose favour of it selfe is so highly and duly esteemed by me [*as*] <that> I hold my selfe so throughly appaied thearwith, as I should desire no more but the preservation of it; but that I perceiv [*by your letter*] vertu is of it selfe delighted to do good; and the neglect of offred bounty, would deprive them of the honour and contentment they receive in well doing. [*Thearfore*] Thearfore when the first opportunity is offered that I may   20
request your paine to comme hither, accompanied with his Majesties gratious letters, upon any good and hopefull occasion of mine, I will rely so much on your frendship, that you will do so, and till the season serve, I will consult with my frends of somme suites that I have pro-pounded to me, whearof one hath a very great good appearance. But his Majesties favour is so precious to me, and I am so loth to trouble you with out almost assurance to make you amends by partaking the fruite of your paines, and frendship, that I will rather loose time then not be in very assured hope to prevaile by these meanes when I imploy them. [*which*] And so requesting you to present these inclosed to theyr Majes-   30
ties and to maintaine me in theyr favour I take my leave.

Line 6. [**to live safe, and**]: Stuart's initial hope that with Christian's support she would "live safe" reflects anxiety about her situation, and her deletion of the phrase may suggest her belief that such anxiety should not be so openly revealed.

Line 16. **appaied:** apayed; contented.

53
TO SIR ANDREW SINCLAIR

Translated from secretary's copy, BL Harley MS 7003, f. 52. (For the Latin text, see Appendix A, letter 1.) Addressed to "His Eminence, the Christian and Frisian Lord, of Borreby, Chancellor to the King of Denmark." Written 24 October 1606.

This Latin letter to Sinclair is, like Stuart's Latin prose in general, more formal than her usual English letters.

♄

Most illustrious Lord, I have taken care that most humble and deserved thanks for their boundless kindness toward me be sent to the most august King and Queen by means of these letters, which if your Excellency will deign to deliver into the royal hands of each, and will yourself profess my devotion and respect to their Majesties, a very welcome and friendly service for me, it will have made you clearly worthy, and confirmed what all say of you, that you are indeed the greatest patron of noble honors (especially for our people) next to the King. Moreover, the singular favor you have shown in gracing me with so honorable a salutation before the fleet was the reason for my requesting this of you so readily and confidently. May Almighty God keep your Excellency safe. Hampton, 24 October 1606.

One who wishes
your Excellency well
A.S.

54
TO KING CHRISTIAN OF DENMARK

Translated from secretary's copy, BL Harley MS 7003, f. 53. (For the Latin text, see Appendix A, letter 2.) No address. Undated; perhaps written October 1606.

By writing to Stuart, King Christian and Queen Anna Cathrine opened the door to personal contact between Stuart and themselves. This Latin letter to King Christian may be a draft of the one that follows, since in both Stuart

---

Letter 53. Headnote. **Borreby:** in Latin *Borebiu,* a puzzling Latinization; according to the Royal Danish Embassy Information Office, the word probably refers to Borreby, the manor built in 1556 for Johan Friis, then a high-ranking Danish official.   **Chancellor:** term used in the Renaissance to refer to a chamberlain or official secretary to a monarch.

Lines 9–10. **salutation...fleet:** presumably compliments paid at the ceremonial review of the fleet on 10 August, the day before King Christian sailed for Denmark.

acknowledges the honor conferred upon her and expresses her hope that she may be permitted to continue the correspondence.

※

Among all the things transpiring fortunately for me with the aid of the divine will, I confess it especially hoped for and pleasant that your Majesty wishes me received and enrolled into the number of those whom your Majesty deigns to remember and to favor. Which kindness of yours I shall indeed actively strive (as far as it is in me) both to deserve and to preserve. I therefore humbly ask your Majesty that your Majesty deign to render me blessed more often by joyful letters of whatever sort about your Majesty's own and your Majesty's family's happiness, for which if I show myself to be grateful in no other kind of duty, I shall at least pray with most frequent petitions to Almighty God, that the same matter 10 always may be given for your writing and, in truth, for my humble heart-felt rejoicing. Moreover, since I am unaware whether your Majesty is being assured regularly about the safety of our most serene princes, your Majesty's dear blood relations, let it be permitted me to convey this information by letter; in which regard just as nothing is more pleasant than happy reading and writing, so nothing is more proper and fitting for me, because of my most fortunate bond of affinity to your Majesty. Therefore humbly relying on your well-disposed kindness, I shall make an effort that no occasion for writing or for providing a well-deserved service to your Majesty fall from my hands, to the extent that I deter- 20 mine that these things will not be unpleasant to your Majesty. May Almighty God bless your Majesty forever and fulfill all your prayers public and private.

55
TO KING CHRISTIAN OF DENMARK

Translated from secretary's copy, BL Harley MS 7003, f. 51. (For the Latin text, see Appendix A, letter 3.) Addressed "To the most august prince Christian, by the grace of God King of Denmark, Norway, the Wends and Goths, Duke of Slesvig, Holstein, Stormarn, and Ditmarsken, Count of Oldenborg and Del- menhorst, for her patron most respectfully" and "To the most august prince Christian the Fourth, by the grace of God King of Denmark, Norway, the Wends and Goths, Duke of Slesvig, Holstein, Stormarn and Ditmarsken, Count of Oldenborg and Delmenhorst, for his Majesty, the most devoted Arbella Stuart prays perpetual and perfect felicity from Almighty God." Writ- ten 24 October 1606.

The two addresses on this letter suggest the importance Stuart attached to her correspondence with Christian: she was carefully drafting even the form of her address.

☿

Since your Majesty deigned to inform me, in your Majesty's own letter, of your fortunate return and present well-being, I offer my most great and humble thanks and confess that I am affected with a double joy, both because I have received the most hoped-for news and the reward which was long in my prayers (and this in your Majesty's own hand) and also because I see that I possess the same place in your royal heart where your kindness and grace had settled me not long ago. And also this your mindfulness of me has now been alienated neither by protracted absence nor by the multitude of very great affairs (in which your
10   Majesty must be buried so soon after your return to your homeland), but rather magnified by the reflection of the rays of the island and your Majesty's own kindness, a noble comfort, and at the same time a constant and most honorable testimony to all that no one who has offered your Majesty a rightly devoted heart (as it is permitted one destitute of merit) should despair, but know that he may receive grace from your Majesty (and this long before it is deserved), and firmly retain it, once acquired, as your Majesty attracts and enrolls by benevolence and grace into the number of your own people and worthily remembers and favors your own. Now let me be permitted, by your Majesty's order, to
20   present some sign of my very devoted spirit and obedience by letter, and also (should an affair require it) to request the power and aid of your famous name in advancing my affairs. Indeed, I hope that so reverent a task will not be irritating in any way, and I promise it will not be employed unsuitably, since your Majesty directs your kindness to a heart that is mindful and grateful. May Almighty God furnish your Majesty with every supreme happiness, and watch over your Majesty forever. Hampton, 24 October 1606.

Your Majesty's most devoted and dutiful

Ar. St.

56
TO QUEEN ANNA CATHRINE OF DENMARK

Autograph draft, Stuart's informal hand, BL Harley MS 7003, f. 49. Addressed "To Anna Cath. Etc." Latin copy in secretary's hand, BL Harley MS 7003, f. 51. (For the Latin text, see Appendix A, letter 4.) Written 24 October 1606, dated in Latin copy, from Hampton Court.

�֎

I yeild your Majesty most humble thanckes for your gratious accepta-
tion, of that trifle, which with blushing at the unworthinesse thearof I
presumed to present unto your Majesty onely out of the confidence of
the Sympathy of your gratious disposition, with that I found in the
most puissant and noble King your husband [*whea*] whearin as I finde
my selfe nothing deceived, having received so extraordinary [*and*] a
favour from you, so I am incouraged hearafter to continue the like sig-
nification of my dutifull respect and affection to your Majesty in hope it
will please you by wearing my handyworke, to continue me in your gratious favour and remembrance. And So Praying for your happinesse.   10

57
TO UNNAMED PERSON

Secretary's draft, BL Harley MS 7003, f. 49. No address. Undated; likely written October 1606, since it appears on the same sheet as the English draft of letter 56.

To maintain her ties with the Danish court, Stuart tried to ensure that she would have suitable messengers for her letters.

✖

efter the wretting of my letter Being credablie Informit that youe wuld
not be at court this winter bot remaine at home I thoght meit to Imploy
the chansler of denmark in your absence for the deliferie of my ansers
[*of*] <to> thos letters I resivit [*of*] <from> ther majesties/ and reserve
your paines [*tale me*] till <a> better occasione and letters of greter consequence whiche I hop youe my link for this next spring as youe [*may*]
may understand be elphinstones letter here Inclosit

Letter 56. Line 5. **puissant:** powerful.

Letter 57. Line 7. **elphinstones...Inclosit:** It is possible that the letter to which Stuart refers may be one to Sir John Elphinstone from Sir Andrew Sinclair (BL Harley MS 7003, f. 44). In it, Stuart is highly praised: Sinclair says that King Christian never ceases both privately and publicly to "exalt hir Laydyships rare vertus," which might mean that Christian would support her in a suit of importance by spring. More likely, the letter Stuart mentions has been lost.

58

TO UNNAMED LADY(?)

Secretary's draft, BL Harley MS 7003, f. 53. No address. Undated; perhaps written October 1606, since it appears on the same sheet as letter 54.

It is possible that Stuart received this letter and had it copied for her files. Had she been the letter's recipient, however, the original could have been filed; and since the handwriting appears again completing a letter begun in Stuart's hand (letter 94), this letter probably is one Stuart dictated or asked an attendant to write at her direction (as the crossed out "my Lady" might suggest).

❧

Madame./ [*my La: my Lady*] I thanck your Ladyship for your fine token and am very glad to hear of my prety servant who I know is growen a great scholler since I saw him if your Ladyship dare trust me with him towards the latter end of this christmas I have a peec of service to imploy him in that will very well beseem him and I assure you he shallbe as carefully looked to as if you wer present[.] Thus desiring present and certayne answer with many good wishes to S your self and the prety man I remayne

Your Ladyships loving
frend

10

59A AND 59B

TO SIR ANDREW SINCLAIR

Autograph draft, Stuart's informal hand, BL Harley MS 7003, f. 45. No address. Latin copy in secretary's hand, BL Harley MS 7003, f. 54. (For the Latin text, see Appendix A, letter 5.) Addressed to "His Eminence, the Christian and Frisian Lord, of Borreby, Chancellor to the King of Denmark." The autograph draft is undated, but likely written July 1607, since it is an English draft of the significantly revised Latin version that follows, dated 15 July 1607.

Because the opening of Stuart's English version of this letter, the first text presented here, is very close to that in the Latin version, I have incorporated her wording into the translation.

❧

Sir you having not onely performed the kindnesse I required of you in delivering my letters to theyr Majesties but returned me so great and

---

Letter 58. Line 7. **S:** unidentified.

unexpected a favour as his Majesties letters, have doubly bounde me to you, and I yeild you thearfore many great thanckes, beseeching you to continue in preserving theyr Majesties favour to me, for which [*of*] good office I most desire to becomme obliged to you so worthy and reverent a person. It may please you <now> with most humble thanckes to present [*these*] <this> letter to his Majesty for whose prosperity none doth more dayly and devoutly pray then I, and this [*trifle*] to the Queenes Majesty which is so very a trifle as I was ashamed to accompany it with a letter to hir Majesty and if a peece of worke of my owne which I was preparing had binne ready I had prevented his Majesties gratious and your kinde letter <in sending to you>, but I was desirous <not> to omitt hir Majesty in the aknowledgement of my duty to hir Royall husband, and thearfore loth to stay the finishing of a [*better*] greater have sent this little peece of worke in accepting whearof hir Majesties favour will be the greater. Thus am I bold to trouble you even with these womanish toyes whose serious minde must have somm relaxation and this may be one to vouchsafe to discend to these petty offices for one that will ever wish your happinesse [*and*] increase and continuance of honour. Etc.

10

20

🜨

Most illustrious Lord, you having not only performed a kindness in delivering my letters to their Majesties but returned me so great and unexpected a favor as his Majesty's letters, have doubly bound me to you, and I yield you therefore many great thanks, beseeching you to continue in preserving their Majesties' favor to me, for which office I most desire to become obliged to you so worthy and reverent a person. It may please you now with most humble thanks to present this letter to the most puissant King and this trifle to the most serene Queen, which I would ask your most generous worthiness to offer again to the most puissant princes in whatever way is appropriate in my case, which you are most expert at doing. Meanwhile, if during your most busy life you can find leisure to perform your kind services, how freely do I confess that I would rejoice to become indebted to no one more willingly when the occasion arises. Keep the most lofty princes informed of my affairs, you who know what is suitable, and have intelligence of the most

10

convenient access to royalty; these things that I send are little dependent on their own virtue and splendor; at least grace will adorn them, which is usually granted when gifts are offered with good faith, benevolence, and a convenient reason for presenting and conveying what is selected as a gift. May honor and glory increase for you (most glorious man) with life. From the royal court at Theobalds, 15 July 1607.

60

TO KING CHRISTIAN OF DENMARK

Translated from secretary's copy, BL Harley MS 7003, f. 54. (For the Latin text, see Appendix A, letter 6.) Addressed "To the most august prince Christian the Fourth, by the grace of God King of Denmark, Norway, the Wends and Goths, Duke of Slesvig, Holstein, Stormarn, and Ditmarsken, Count of Oldenborg and Delmenhorst, for her patron most respectfully." Written 15 July 1607.

Most august, serene, and powerful King, when I read the letters of your most august Majesty, I was prostrated by the greatest joy that I am regarded with honor by so great a king, whose constancy toward me, if it were permitted me to increase through my deserts, I would solicit with fervent prayers; but since it required nothing but an inclination of spirit, I shall fulfill with the faithful desire for obedience what I cannot fulfill with the duties I owe your Majesty. Nevertheless, in whatever state of fortune I be, your most august Majesty will discover that my will will always be inclined to and my soul fastened without pretense on loyalty to your Majesty; especially since your Majesty offers his immense kindness to my use and convenience; which kindness I embrace unhesitatingly, certain that it (if the opportunity arises) is neither useless for me nor lacking. I ask Almighty God on bended knee that he keep your most august Majesty flourishing and safe forever. From the royal court of Theobalds, 15 July 1607.

Your Majesty's
most devoted and dutiful
Ar. Stuart

Letter 59B. Line 21. **Theobalds:** Theobalds, in Middlesex, newly a royal palace, and a place Sinclair would remember well. King Christian had been lavishly entertained there in July 1606 when it had been owned by Robert Cecil; King James had so enjoyed Theobalds that Cecil had surrendered it in May 1607, in exchange for Hatfield.

61

TO SIR ROGER WILBRAHAM AND OTHER MASTERS OF THE COURT OF REQUESTS

Secretary's hand, with Stuart's signature, SPD, James, vol. 28, ff. 150–51. Addressed "To the Right Worshippfull and my very Lovinge Frend Sir Roger Wilbraham Knight, And the Rest of the masters, of his majesties court of Requestes be this letter." Written 3 November 1607.

༈

After my very harty commendations. Wher as this pore man Richard Alkorne hath a suit dependinge in his majesties court of Requestes, conserning a coppie Woulde wherin he hath an estate for tearme of his Life which as I am geven to understand is to receave a hearinge before you to morowe, I am moved in regard of his ancient and dilligent service in court to sollicitte your lawfull favor to be shewen unto hime on this behalfe./ wher in you maye do a very charitable deed, And geve me occacion to rest very thankfull unto you for the same./ Thuse referringe the pore mans whole estate to your grave consideracions I bid you hartelye farwell. Whithall this third of November 1607.   10

Your very lovinge frind
Arbella Stuart./

62

TO GILBERT TALBOT, EARL OF SHREWSBURY

Autograph, Stuart's informal hand, Talbot Papers 2, ff. 244–45. Addressed "To the right honorable my very good uncle the Earle of Shrowsbury". Written 2 December 1607.

༈

Good uncle./ I writ to you with in these .48. howres by m.ʳ Stanley, and am very glad of the occasion of so good a messenger, and so honorable

---

Letter 61. Line 2. **court of Requestes:** The Court of Requests, sometimes called the poor person's court, had been established to hear cases of people who could not afford to sue in courts of common law. Although that distinction had faded by 1607, Requests was still the least expensive branch of the system.

Line 3. **coppie Woulde:** coppice wood, or thicket of trees.

Letter 62. Line 1. **m.ʳ Stanley:** unidentified; perhaps Henry Stanley of Nottinghamshire.

and kinde a letter, as I received from your Lordship by m.^{r.} Parker to
scrible unto you againe, and that a great deale the rather because <this
short time and calme climat affording none> you have given me the
best theame to write of which is thanckes, for your not checking my
importunity [*but*] in begging venison, but endevouring to satisfy it in
better sort then I presumed of, for the worst hinde of many I am sure in
any one of your grounds should be very wellcomme hither, and then if
it be possible to have so good a one as your Lordship wishes you know
what a delicate it will be to them that shall have <it>; and how
wellcomme such a testimony of your love and favour shall be to me./
And beseeching your Lordship to remember me humbly to my Aunt for
honour and happinesse as for your Lordship I will pray, I take leave
From Whitehall the .2. of December. <u>1607</u>

Your Lordships neece
Arbella Stuart

63

TO SIR ANDREW SINCLAIR

Translated from secretary's draft, with autograph Latin address in Stuart's informal hand, BL Harley MS 7003, f. 50. (For the Latin text, see Appendix A, letter
7.) Addressed to "His Eminence, the Christian and Frisian Lord, the Chancellor of Denmark." Written February 1607/8, perhaps 28 February, the same
date as that of letter 64.

I have received the letter that your Eminence recently sent me, in which
you assured me that the letter I had sent not long ago to the most
august King, and the trifles I had sent to the most serene Queen, rendered to their Majesties by your means, were far from unwelcome,
which I confess I find very pleasing, and I readily acknowledge your
service, but since this is not the first act of courtesy that holds me
bound to you, you must claim from me such benefits (if ever chance

---

Letter 62. Line 3. **m.^{r.} Parker:** John Parker, who sometimes handled business affairs for the
Earl of Shrewsbury.

Letter 63. Line 1. **your:** In Latin, Stuart employs *vestrae*, the plural form of *your* that indicates
formality.

offer an opportunity) that your excellent favors to me demand, and which I freely acknowledge, nor am I able to conceal after this mutually affirmed exchange of favors, given to me unsought, that I was overcome   10
by your Eminence's kindness and benevolence. I shall always hope that all things turn out happily for your Eminence. Given: This Day: February 1607.

I shall pray for your Eminence's continuing good health and endless happiness, than which scarcely anything could more please me, as I trust your Eminence knows.

64
TO KING CHRISTIAN OF DENMARK

Translated from secretary's copy with revisions, the James Marshall and Marie-Louise Osborn Collection, the Beinecke Rare Book and Manuscript Library, Yale University, Osborn Files 37.88. (For the Latin text, see Appendix A, letter 8.) Docketed by Stuart's secretary "Copy of my Lady Arbellas letter to the King of Denmark." Written 28 February 1607/8, dated in the docket.

The section within asterisks has been lightly crossed out.

🐦

Most August and Powerful King

In your Majesty's last letters were two things for which I have especially prayed. First, that the grace in which I may boast of standing with your Majesty not only has not been withdrawn from me, but become (if this were possible) ever greater and that your Majesty's affairs have pro-ceeded so well and so happily that all your friends (among whom I count the entire Christian world) must justly rejoice at the knowledge. And with your Majesty's indulgence I shall add a third thing which offers me great pleasure, that your Majesty considers me not unworthy to be made a sharer in such immense joy, for which reasons I confess   10
myself so very happy that I believe letters can afford no more pleasure than I have taken from these. **And although I am justly irritated that my fortune, in these even greater mounds of my debtors [[   ] *at least*]

Letter 63. Line 12. **Given:** dictated. After this word, the secretary has left space for the location to be added; similarly, after *This Day* space has been provided for the day of the month to be inserted.   Letter 64. Line 13. [   ]: Two deleted words are illegible.

and when I seem not unworthy the patronage and grace of so great a king, should supply nothing clearly, nevertheless, I must not bear it unhappily, if, knowing that my devoted spirit has been rightly obedient to your Majesty, I yet have nothing else by which I might express my gratitude for your Majesty's supreme bounty toward me. For, to such generous rulers, generosity is its own reward, and I think it not
20   unseemly if your most august Majesty already has received any glory from this kindness and generosity of spirit, for which** I ask Almighty God on bended knee that he continue to bless your Majesty so that, all things falling fortunately in accordance with your Majesty's wishes, we may for as long as possible celebrate the reign and safety of such a king and such a patron.

The sentence that follows, written in the margin, may have been a postscript or a replacement for the section deleted above.

⚜

If at this time I shall seem not to have satisfied my duty unto you, I ask and implore that your most illustrious Majesty attribute this to my grandmother the Countess of Shrewsbury who, having very recently and sadly died, surrendering her wishes for her own property and for
30   me, has lost the opportunity to express her obedience and gratitude for your Majesty's supreme bounty toward me, which I am unable not to profess.

65

TO KING CHRISTIAN OF DENMARK

Translated from secretary's copy, BL Harley MS 7003, f. 37. (For the Latin text, see Appendix A, letter 9.) No address. Written 1607/8, likely 15 March, since it appears on the same sheet as the copy of letter 67.

There is no record that King Christian furthered any of Stuart's projects; however, he apparently made suit to her through his sister for the services of Stuart's lutenist, Thomas Cutting. For Queen Anna's, Prince Henry's, and Sir John Elphinstone's letters on this subject, see Appendix B, letters 8–10.

Letter 64. Lines 28–29. **recently...died:** on 13 February.

❧

Most August and Powerful King

Only a few days had passed after I had sent my previous letter to your most august Majesty when the letter of our most eminent and serene Queen was brought to me, from which I learned that your Majesty desires that my servant Thomas Cutting, who (God willing) now conveys this letter, be sent to your Majesty, so that your Majesty might be able to employ him among those most accomplished at the lute. And indeed although he pleases me because he stands out among the few accomplished in that art, and although I know that, in the royal good fortune to which all the most excellent studies, prayers, talents, and   10 services, in this as in other arts, are directed most readily, it is easier to add to the number of those who excel in any art than to achieve proper measure, yet since I have sought nothing more diligently or eagerly than an occasion that would offer me the opportunity of demonstrating my respect and unfeigned disposition to devote myself to your royal pleasure, I most willingly embraced this opportunity, however small, and him whom, entrusted to the most excellent teachers and instructed in this art to my pleasure, I accepted with not inconsequential commendations because of the quality of his art and uprightness of his character, this same man I send with no less commendation (now that it pleases   20 your Majesty), ready to send (had I that power) Orpheus or Apollo. I pray highest God that all your Majesty's affairs harmonize and accord with your desires, not only among the musicians and in the court, but also in your life and realm. Given: This Day: 1607.

66

TO QUEEN ANNA

Secretary's copy, BL Harley MS 7003, f. 37. No address. Undated; likely written 15 March 1607/8, since it appears on the same sheet as the copy of letter 67.

Letter 65. Line 21. **Orpheus:** the son of Calliope and Apollo, whose irresistible music gave him power over all living things.   **Apollo:** the god who played the lyre so beautifully that the other gods on Mount Olympus became lost in his music.

✣

May it Please your most Royall Majestie

I have receaved your Majesties most gratious and favorable toaken
which you have beene pleased to send me, as an assurance, both of your
Majesties pardon, and of my remayning in your Gratious good opinion,
the which, how greate contentment it hath brought unto me, I fynde no
wordes to expresse, And therefore most humbly addressing my selfe to
the awnsweare of your Majesties pleasure, signifyed in your letter,
touching my licenceing my servaunt Cotting, to depart from me for the
service of his Majestie of Denmark, I shall beseech your Majestie to
10   conceave, that although I know well, how farre more easy it is, for so
great a Prince, to command the best musiciens of the world, then for
me to recover one not inferior to this, yet do I most willingly imbrace
this occasion wherby I may in effectes give somme demonstration of my
unfeyned disposition to apply my selfe [*ever un*]to [*all*] your Royall
pleasure[*s*] And therefore most willingly referring my sayde servaunt to
your Majesties good pleasure, [*and most humbly beseeching that my selfe
may still remayne in your Gratious, and Princely favour and protection*] I
will in all humility kysse your Majesties Royall handes, And ever
beseech Almighty God to graunt unto your Majestie all honorable hap-
20   pynes that may be imagined.

67

TO PRINCE HENRY

Autograph, Stuart's presentation hand, BL Harley MS 6986, ff. 78–79.
Addressed "To the Prince his Highnesse". Secretary's copy, BL Harley MS
7003, f. 38. Written 15 March 1607/8.

✣

May it please your Highnesse

I have received your Highnesse letter, whearin I am lett to understand
that the Queenes Majesty is pleased to command Cuttinge my servant
for the King of Denmark, concerning the which your Highnesse
requireth my answer to hir Majesty the which I have accordingly

returned by this bearer, referring him to hir Majesties good pleasure, and disposition. And although I may have somme cause to be sorry, to have lost the contentment of a good Lute, yet must I confesse, that I am right glad to have found any occasion, whearby to expresse to hir Majesty and your Highnesse, the humble respect which I ow you, and the readinesse of my disposition to be conformed to your good pleasures; whearin I have placed a great parte of the satisfaction which my heart can receive./ I have according to your Highnesse direction, signified unto my uncle and aunt of Shrewsbury your Highnesse gratious vouchsafeing to remember them, who, with all duty, present theyr most humble thancks, and say, they will ever pray for your Highnesse most happy prosperity; And yet my uncle saith he carrieth the same splene in his heart towards your Highnesse that he hath ever done. And so praying to the Almighty for your Highnesse felicity I humbly cease. From Sheffeild the 15:^(th) of March. <u>1607</u>

Your Highnesse
most humble and dutifull
Arbella Stuart

68

TO MARY TALBOT, COUNTESS OF SHREWSBURY

Autograph, Stuart's informal hand, Talbot Papers 2, ff. 255–56. Addressed "To the right honorable my very good Aunt the Countes of Shrousbury". Undated; written late March 1607/8, at the end of Stuart's visit to Hardwick Hall.

    Stuart had gone north after her grandmother's death and stayed several weeks while her grandmother lay in state at Hardwick Hall. Although Stuart had visited the Talbots at Sheffield, she left for London from Hardwick.

❦

Madame./ I humbly thanck you for both your letters, I deferred to write to you till I had taken my leave heere and then I intended to have sent one to your Ladyship and my uncle to deliver my humble thanckes for so many kindnesses and favours as I have received at this time of my being heere from you both and to take a more mannerly farewell then I

Letter 67. Line 6. **bearer:** Cutting himself.   Line 14. **uncle…Shrewsbury:** the Talbots, whom Stuart was visiting.   Line 17. **splene:** spleen; grudge or ill-will.

could at our parting, but your Ladyship hath prevented my intention in
sending this bearer by whom in these few lines I will performe that duty
not complement of aknowledging my selfe much bound to you for
every <particuler> kindnesse and bounty of yours at this time which
10   reviveth the memory of many more former, and I assure you that none
of my Cousins your daughters shall be more ready to do you service
then I./ the money your Ladyship sends my Lady Pembroke shall be
safely and soone delivered hir. And so praying for your Ladyships happinesse honour and comfort in as great measure as your selfe can wish I
humbly take leave. From Hardwik this monday.

> Your Ladyships most affectionate neece
> to commaund
> Arbella Stuart

I pray your Ladyship commend me to my uncle Charles and my Aunt,
20   and my .2. prety cousins, I thinck I shall many times wish my selfe set
by my cousin Charles at meales.

69

TO GILBERT TALBOT, EARL OF SHREWSBURY

Autograph, Stuart's informal hand, Talbot Papers 2, f. 254. No address. Written
8 November 1608.

❦

I was much ashamed to be overtaken by your Lordships letter by m.^r
Fowler, before I had answered your former, but I presume of your pardon for such peccadillos. Good wishes cannever comme amisse,
whether from amongst cuppes, or beades and thearfore at all adventures
I humbly thank your Lordship[.] For want of a Nunnery I have for a
while retired my selfe <to> the Friers, wheare I have found by experi-

---

Letter 68. Line 10. **former:** perhaps especially those during her trials at Hardwick Hall in
1603.   Line 12. **Lady Pembroke:** Stuart's cousin Mary, the Talbots' daughter.

Lines 19–20. **uncle…cousins:** Charles and Catherine Cavendish and their sons William and
Charles.

Letter 69. Line 4. **cuppes, or beades:** wine-cups or prayer-beads; i.e., at drink or at prayer.

Line 6. **Friers:** Blackfriars precinct, just outside London, formerly the site of the Black Friars
monastery; Stuart had bought a house in the district.

ence this tearme how much worse they thrive that say Go ye to the plough, then Go we to the Plough, so that once more I am settling my selfe to follow the Lawyers most diligently./ I pray God the cheese I hearwith send your Lordship prove as good as great (which few of you great Lords are by your leave), and truly I hope well of it because the fellow of it which is tasted heare is so. And as I have sent your Lordship somm of the stoppingst meate that is, so I have sent you somm of the sharpest sallett that ever I eat, a great person loveth it well (as I told your Lordship at my being with you), and that is all I can say in the commendation of it./ If you have of it in the countrey I pray you let me know that I may laugh at my selfe for being so busy to gett this. God send you a good stomack and a good digestion shall be the Motto to these .2. bodies of sallet and cheese, I hope with the good allowance of all the Impresa-makers by north Trent And so beseeching the Almighty to send you all honour and happinesse I humbly Cease. From Blackfriers the .8. of November. 1608.

> Your Lordships neece
> Arbella Stuart./

70

TO CHARLES GOSLING

Secretary's hand with signature, postscript, and address in Stuart's informal hand, BL Stowe MS 142, ff. 30–31. Addressed "To my loving frend Charles Gosling". Written 28 March 1609.

Letter 69. Line 7. **tearme:** the Michaelmas legal term.   Lines 7–8. **Go ye...Plough:** an allusion to a popular proverb, "The Plow goes not well if the plowman holds it not" (see Tilley, P435 and 431); perhaps a pun on the Plough as a popular tavern name: people do not thrive if they say "You go work the plough" and then themselves go to the tavern.   Line 8. **Go we:** emended from "Go we go".

Line 10. **as good as great:** as tasty as it is large; with the lords, as virtuous as they are high ranking.

Line 13. **stoppingst:** most constipating.   Line 14. **sharpest sallett:** strongest or spiciest salad. Seventeenth-century salads were composed of a wider variety of root vegetables and herbs than is usual in modern salads, and were sometimes preserved with brine or vinegar.

Line 20. **Impresa-makers:** who made mottoes—such as "God send you a good stomack and a good digestion"—to accompany emblems.

Line 20. **by north Trent:** along the northern Trent river, which flows through Derbyshire.

Charles Gosling, of Derbyshire or Nottinghamshire, had been one of Bess's servants at South Wingfield manor (Durant, 164).

🜚

[*Father*] <Charles> Gosling. Uppon the good conceyt I have of you for a just wellmeaning man and wellwishing to me I have thought fitt to wryte you this letter desyring you to call to remembraunce all you can and take your sonnes <help> wherin he knoweth or both or eyther of you think you can learn owt anything of the Contract betwixt my cosen William Ca[ve]ndish and m^rs Margett Chaterton. That wryte to me so soon as you can and if you can beleave I have powr to do you or your sonne good expect my remembraunce of what you do herein And so I commytt you to god. From the Court at Whytehall this 28th of Marche
10   1609

Your loving frend
Arbella Stuart

Remember the old buck of sherland and the rosted tench I and other good company eat so savorly at your house, and if thou be still a good fellow and an honest man, show it now, or be hanged.

71

TO GILBERT TALBOT, EARL OF SHREWSBURY

Autograph, Stuart's informal hand, Arundel Castle MSS, Autograph Letters 1585–1617, no. 167. Addressed "To the right honorable my very good uncle the Earle of Shrowesbury./" Written 17 June 1609.

🜚

Because I know not that your Lordship hath forsaken one recreation that you have liked heartofore, I presume to send you a few idle lines to

---

Letter 70. Line 1. **<Charles>:** added in Stuart's hand. Perhaps she inserted the name *Charles* to eliminate the possibility that she was writing to a Roman Catholic priest; *Father* could also distinguish father from son if, as in this family, they had the same given name.

Line 6. **William Ca[ve]ndish:** Stuart's sixteen-year-old cousin William, son of Catherine and Charles Cavendish. He married Elizabeth Basset sometime after 1610 and the writer Margaret Lucas in 1645.   **m^rs Margett Chaterton:** Margaret Chatterton, formerly one of the ladies of Bess's household.

Line 13. **sherland:** Shirland, a region of Derbyshire.   **tench:** a freshwater fish, similar to carp.

reade in your chaire; after you have tired your selfe either with affaires, or any sport that bringeth wearinesse And knowing you well advertised of all occurrents in serious manner; I make <it> my end onely to make you merry, and show my desire to please you even in playing the foole. for no folly is greater (I trow) then to laugh when one smarteth. But that my Aunts divinity can tell you S.ᵗ· Laurence deriding his tormen-tors <even upon the grideiron> bad them turne him on the other side for that he lay on was sufficiently broiled, I should not know how to   10 excuse my selfe from either insensiblenesse or contempt of injuries. I finde if one rob a house and build a Church with the money, the wronged party may go pipe in an Ivy leafe for any redresse. For money so well bestowed must not be taken from that holy worke though the right owner go abegging[.] Unto you it is given to understand parables, or to command the comment. But if you be of this opinion of the Scribes and Pharises I condemne your Lordship (by your leave) for an Heretike by the Authority of Pope Jone. For theare is a text saith you must not do evill that good may comme thearof. But now from doctrine to miracles[.] I assure you with in these few dayes I saw a paire   20 of Virginalles make good musick without helpe of any hand but of one that did nothing but warme (not move) a glasse somme .5. or .6. foote from them. And if I thought thus great folkes invisibly, and farre off worke in matters to tune them as they please, I pray your Lordship for-give me, and I hope God will. To whose holy protection I humbly

---

Line 8. **S.ᵗ· Laurence:** one of the most famous Roman Catholic martyr/saints, whose emblem is the gridiron; Mary Talbot, unlike Gilbert, was Roman Catholic.

Line 13. **pipe...leafe:** console oneself for failure by a frivolous activity (proverbial, Tilley, I110).

Lines 13–15. **money...abegging:** perhaps a reference to a failed lawsuit to recover part of Stuart's inheritance.

Line 18. **Pope Jone:** Pope Joan. The story of the woman who became pope (and gave birth while in office) circulated widely in seventeenth-century England. It was the subject of a play, now lost, performed by Lord Strange's company in the early 1580s (Kawachi, 65).

Lines 18–19. **you...thearof:** a paraphrase of Rom. 3:8.

Line 21. **Virginalles:** virginals; boxed harpsichords without legs.

recommend your Lordship. From Broadstreet the .17. of June .1609.

Your Lordships neece

Arbella Stuart./

30 I humbly pray your Lordship to bestow two of the next good personages <of yours> shall fall, on me. not that I meane to convert them to my owne benifit, for (though I go rather for a good clerke [*rather*] then a worldly wise woman) I aspire to no degree of Pope Jone but somme good ends whearof this bearer will tell your Lordship one. My boldnesse showes how honorably I beleeve of your disposing such livings.

72

TO ROBERT CECIL, EARL OF SALISBURY

Autograph, Stuart's presentation hand, SPD, James, vol. 47, f. 254. Addressed "To the right honorable my very good Lord the Earle of Salisbury Lord high Tresorer of England." Dated in the docket August 1609.

Cecil had supported Stuart's successful petition to license the selling of wines and whiskey in Ireland.

❦

My honorable good Lord./ I yeild you humble thanckes for the honorable care it hath pleased you to have of me, both in the election and effecting of this suite; which shall ever binde me to humble thanckfulnesse towards your Lordship For whose long life, honour, and happinesse I pray to the Almighty and rest

Your Lordships much bounden and assured

frend

Arbella Stuart./

73

TO ROBERT CECIL, EARL OF SALISBURY

Autograph, Stuart's presentation hand, SPD, James, vol. 50, f. 136. Addressed "To the right honorable my very good Lord, the Earle of Salisbury Lord high Thresorer of England./" Written 17 December 1609.

Letter 71. Line 26. **Broadstreet:** the Talbots' London house in Broad Street.

Line 30. **personages:** parsonages; parsons' benefices or livings.

Having been warned that she might have trouble collecting the monies due her from her new license, Stuart wanted the royal seal to validate the patent.

❧

My honorable good Lord./ having binne a long suitor, as your Lordship knowes, whose honorable favour I humbly thanck you, I have founde from time to time, I am now advised by somme frends of mine, of good judgement and experience, to procure the great seale of England to my booke. Both because it will be a furtherance to a speedier dispatch of this suite in Ireland; and that this businesse must be donne and executed by deputation, which cannot be donne with out the great seale heere first obteined; with out which also the booke may receive alteration, and a check theare. Thearfore I humbly beseech your Lordship that by your favour, on which I onely rely, I may obteine the great seale   10 of England to the booke heerewith presented to your Lordship./ For whose honour and happinesse I pray; and so humbly take leave. From Puddle-wharfe the .17. of December .<u>1609</u>.

Your Lordships much bounden poore
frend
Arbella Stuart./

74
TO ROBERT CECIL, EARL OF SALISBURY

Autograph, Stuart's presentation hand, SPD, James, vol. 50, f. 137. Addressed "To the right honorable the Lord high Tresorer of England./" Undated; likely written later December 1609, after letter 73 in which Stuart makes no mention of returning the grant.

❧

Wheare your Lordship willed me to sett downe a note of those 3. things, whearin I lately moved you. They are theise. The first that I am willing to returne back his Majesties gratious graunt to me of the wines

---

Letter 73. Line 5. **booke:** the official book for the patent, in which rates and receipts would be recorded.

Line 13. **Puddle-wharfe:** Puddle Wharf, the area surrounding this landing place on the north bank of the Thames, near Blackfriars.

in Ireland; so as your Lordship will take order for the paying of my debts when I shall upon my honour informe you truly what they are. The next that his Majesty will be gratiously pleased to augment my allowance in such sorte, as I may be able to live in such honour and countenance hearafter, as may stande with his Majesties honour, and my owne comfort. And lastely that wheare his Majesty doth now allow
10 me a diett, that he will be pleased, in sted thearof to let me have one thousand pounds yearely./ Some other things I will presume to intreate your Lordships like favour in, that may stand me in sted; but for that they are such as I trust your Lordship will thinck his Majesty will easily graunt, I will now forbeare to set them downe./

Your Lordships poore frend
Arbella Stuart./

75
TO GILBERT TALBOT, EARL OF SHREWSBURY

Autograph, Stuart's informal hand, BL Harley MS 7003, f. 71. Docketed by her secretary "My Ladies letter to my lord of Shrewsbury". Written 16 July 1610.

After Stuart's 22 June marriage to William Seymour became public on 8 July, both were arrested.

If it please your Lordship theare are diverse of my servants with whom I [*never*] thought <never> to have parted whilest I lived; and none that I am willing to part with. But since I am taken from them, and know not how to maintaine either my selfe or them, being utterly ignorant how it will please his Majesty to deale with me I weare better to put them away now, then towards winter. Your Lordship knowes the greatnesse of my debts and <my> unablenesse to do for them either now or at

---

Letter 74. Lines 10–11. **in…yearely:** According to a letter from Lady Isabel Bowes (Appendix B, letter 13), Stuart was planning to obtain a house in the country, where an allowance of diet would be useless.

Letter 75. Line 1. **servants:** In January 1610, before her marriage, Stuart had twenty-three servants (Seymour Papers 22), some of whom had been with her for years; in the summer of 1611, after the marriage, Stuart and Seymour had thirty-two servants (BL Harley MS 7003, f. 72).

Michaelmasse. I beseech your Lordship let me know what hope you can give me of his Majesties favour with out which I and all mine must live in great discomfort. and make me so much bound to you as both of   10
your selfe and by meanes of any that you take to be my frends, or pitty me to labour the reobtaining of his Majesties favour to me. So humbly thancking your Lordship for the care it pleaseth you to have of me and mine, and for your honorable offer I humbly Cease. From Lambeth the .16. of July. 1610.

The poore prisoner your neece
Arbella Seymaure.

[*I pray your Lordship remember me humbly to my Aunt.*] The bay gelding and the rest are at your Lordships commaundement./

76

TO GILBERT TALBOT, EARL OF SHREWSBURY

Autograph, Stuart's informal hand, BL Harley MS 7003, f. 74. Docketed by her secretary "To my lord of Shrewsbury". Written 19 July 1610.

❦

I acknowledge my selfe much bound to your Lordship for your care of disposing of my servants. but I cannot ghesse what to do with any of them till I know how his Majesty is enclined towards me. Thearfore I againe very humbly and earnestly beseech your Lordship to move his Majesty at his returne to be gratious to me. That according to his Majesties answer and disposition towards me, I may take order for my servants or any thing else concerning me. So with humble thanckes I take leave From Lambeth the .19. of July.

I pray your Lordship remember me humbly to my Aunt./ [*and my Cousins./*]   10

Letter 75. Line 8. **Michaelmasse:** Michaelmas, the church holiday celebrating the archangel Michael on 29 September; Stuart would have received her quarterly allowance then, and her servants' wages would have been due.

Line 14. **Lambeth:** Sir Thomas Parry's house in the Lambeth district, where Stuart was confined.

Letter 76. Line 5. **me:** An illegible, deleted phrase follows.

77
TO LADY JANE DRUMMOND

Autograph draft, Stuart's informal hand, BL Harley MS 7003, f. 61. No address. Docketed ".i. letter", likely indicating it was placed in Robert Cecil's files. The system of numbering is like the one Cecil used in 1603; Cecil was still handling the investigation, as evidenced by the large number of related letters addressed to him; and the handwriting of the docket on letter 82 appears to be his. Undated; likely written July 1610.

One of two Scottish attendants whom Queen Anna had brought with her to England, Jane Drummond was Stuart's cousin and the queen's first lady of the bedchamber. Because this draft is unusually heavily revised and the text therefore difficult to read, a text incorporating Stuart's revisions appears in a footnote below.

☙

Good Cousin. I pray you do me the kindenesse to [*deliver*] <present> this letter <of mine in all humility> to hir Majesty and with all my most humb[le] and dutifull thanckes, for the gratious commiseration [*and respect*] it pleaseth hir Majesty to have of me [*in this time of <my> adversity*] as I heare to my great comfort. [*I doubt not And*] <I presume to [*trouble*] make suite to hir Majesty because> if it please hir Majesty to intercede for me [*to his Majesty I doubt not <I hope>*] I cannot but hope to be restored to hir Majesties [*favour*] <service> and his Majesties favour, [*the meanes I have hitherto tried succeeding not makes me*] <whose

10   <just and> gratious disposition I verily thinck would> have binne moved to compassion er this by the consideration [*both*] of the cause[*s which*] in it selfe honest and lamentable, and of [*the*] the honour I have to be so neare his Majesty and his in bloud, but that it is gods will hir Majesty should have a hand in so [*good*] honorable and charitable a

---

Headnote. **Revised Text:** Good Cousin. I pray you do me the kindenesse to present this letter of mine in all humility to hir Majesty and with all my most humble and dutifull thanckes, for the gratious commiseration it pleaseth hir Majesty to have of me as I heare to my great comfort. I presume to make suite to hir Majesty because if it please hir Majesty to intercede for me I cannot but hope to be restored to hir Majesties service and his Majesties favour, whose just and gratious disposition I verily thinck would have binne moved to compassion er this by the consideration of the cause in it selfe honest and lamentable, and of the honour I have to be so neare his Majesty and his in bloud, but that it is gods will hir Majesty should have a hand in so honorable and charitable a worke as to reobtaine his Majesties favour to one that esteemeth it hir greatest worldly comfort. So wishing you all honor and happinesse I take leave and remaine Your very loving Cousin A.S.

Line 2. **with all:** withal; in addition.   Line 3. **humb[le]:** The writing runs off the page.

worke as [*this will*] <to reobtaine> his Majesties favour to one that esteemeth it [*more then life, happ. and I that I*] <hir greatest worldly comfort>. So wishing you all honor and happinesse I take leave and [*res*] remaine

Your very loving Cousin

A.S.   20

78A AND 78B
TO LADY JANE DRUMMOND

Autograph draft, Stuart's informal hand, BL Harley MS 7003, f. 70. Secretary's copy, begun by Stuart, but largely in her secretary's hand, BL Harley MS 7003, also f. 70. Docketed by her secretary "To the Lady Drummond"; in another hand appears ".2. letter by Smith now", the notation for copies that probably reached Robert Cecil's files. Undated; likely written July 1610, soon after letter 77.

❦

Good Cousin./ I thincke my selfe as much beholden [*to you as if my man had brought me assurance of his Majesties favour by hir Majesties meanes, because I finde your kindnesse in remembring me and preventing suspitions*] But I cannot rest satisfied till I may [*learne*] <knowe> what disaster of mine hindreth his Majesties goodnesse towards me, having such a mediatrix to pleade so just and honest a cause [*as mine However*] Thearfore I pray you with all earnestnesse let me know freely what hath binne donne concerning me. So wishing you all honor and happinesse I take leave.

Your   10

❦

Good Cousin I thinck my selfe as much beholden to you as if my man had brought me the effect of my humble suite by her Majesties gratious meanes on whose favour I will still cheifely relye but if (having such A mediator) I shalbe refuced, in so honest wish, and lawfull A cause I may trulie esteeme my self the object of A most unfortunate creature, And if her Majesty would be pleased to lett me understand the true cause of

---

Letters 78A and 78B. Headnote. **Smith:** Samuel Smith, a servant who joined Stuart's household near the time of her marriage.   Letter 78B. Line 2. **me:** From this point, the letter is in Stuart's secretary's hand.   Line 5. **the object of:** the very image of.

this Disaster not given (I trust) but taken against me I shold hold itt for A greate and highe favour, And I earnestlie entreate you to be A meane to her Majesty for this favour. and that your self also will deale openly and freely in letting me knowe, what you understand or conceave thereof. And so I shall thinck my self exceedingly beholding unto you and remaine./

79
TO QUEEN ANNA

Autograph draft, Stuart's informal hand, BL Harley MS 7003, f. 75. Autograph, Stuart's presentation hand, incorporating her revisions, BL Lansdowne MS 1236, ff. 60–61; addressed "To the Queenes most Excellen[t] Majestie./" and docketed "Lady Arbella 3", the notation for materials probably placed in Robert Cecil's files. Autograph copy, differing only in accidentals, Stuart's informal hand, BL Lansdowne MS 1236, f. 62. Secretary's copy, BL Harley MS 7003, ff. 76–77. Written 23 July 1610.

❧

May it please your most Excellent Majesty since I am debarred the happinesse of attending your Majesty or so much as to kisse your Royall hands, to pardon my presumption in presenting your Majesty in this rude forme, <my> most humble thanckes for your Majesties gratious favour and mediation to his Majesty for me. Which your Majesties goodnesse (my greatest comfort and hope in this affliction) I most humbly beseech your Majesty to continue. So praying to the Almighty to reward your Majesty with all honour and felicity both in your Royall selfe and [*all*] yours, in all humility I cease. From Lambeth the .23. of July. 1610.

Your Majesties
most humble and dutifull
subject and servant
A. S.

Letter 78b. Lines 10–11. **letting…thereof:** For Lady Drummond's response, see Appendix B, letter 15.

Letter 79. Line 5. **for:** An illegible, deleted phrase follows.

Line 14. **A. S.:** In the copy in her presentation hand, Stuart signed her name *Arbella Seymaure*.

80

TO THE PRIVY COUNCIL

Autograph, Stuart's presentation hand, BL Harley MS 7003, ff. 92–93. Docketed "The Lady Arbella her petition to the Lords for the remove of her servants: to some better ayer. 4", probably for Robert Cecil's files. Undated; likely written July 1610.

☙

To the right honorable, the Lords of his
Majesties most honorable privy counsell./
Right honorable and my very good Lords./ I am constraind to trouble you, rather then be guilty of the danger of life whearin Hugh Crompton, and Edward Reeves, two of my servants lately committed to the Marshalsea for my cause, remaine. I am informed diverse neare that prison, and in it, are lately dead, and diverse others sicke of contagious and deadly diseases./ Whearfore I humbly beseech your Honors to commiserate theyr distresse, and consider that they are servants, and accoumptable for diverse debts and reckninges, which if they should dy   10
would be a great prejudice to me and others. And thearfore I humbly beseech you to move unto his Majesty my most humble suite and theyrs, that it will please his Majesty they may be removed to somme other healthfull Aire.

Arbella Seymaure.

81A AND 81B

TO THE PRIVY COUNCIL

Two autograph drafts, Stuart's informal hand, BL Harley MS 7003, f. 90. Third autograph draft, Stuart's presentation hand, BL Harley MS 7003, f. 91. Stuart's docket on f. 91 reads "Petition to the counsell before I writ one to the King." and the letter is further docketed "Lady Arabella Peticion to the Councell./ 5", which suggests that her draft went into Robert Cecil's files. Fourth autograph, Stuart's presentation hand, SPD, James, vol. 56, f. 154. The docket on f. 154 describes the letter as "Lady Arbella to the Lords that it will please them to be a meanes to his Majesty for hir". This last autograph was the copy sent to the Privy Council. Dated in the docket on the final copy July 1610.

Letter 80. Lines 4–5. **Hugh Crompton:** Stuart's gentleman usher, who had been with her since before 1591 (Durant, 180) and had handled her accounts.

Line 5. **Edward Reeves:** one of Stuart's servants who had served William Seymour prior to the marriage.

Two of the four versions are presented in full here: the initial draft in which the majority of revisions were made (f. 90) and the final presentation copy.

❧

[*May it please your Lordships*]
I humbly beseech your Lordships [*th*] now that by examinatio[n] of all parties, the errour for which we suffer his Majesties displeasure must needes appeare neither greater nor lesse then it is. to give me leave to becomme an humble suitor to your Lordships [*that*] with the relation thearof [*it will please your Lordships*] to testify unto his Majesty my hearty sorrow for his Majesties displeasu[re] **Restraint [*of*] <from> liberty, comfort, <and> counsell of frends <and all the effects of imprisonment> are in them selfes very grievous, and inflicted as due
10   punishments for greater offences then mine. but that which makes them most heavy to me is that [[*it*] <*that*> *is the* <*onely*> *portion his Majesty so gratious*] they proceede from his Majesties displeasure whose favor was <not onely> my stay and hope but greatest joy. [*The which if I weare restored and that*] If our punishment weare to do his Majesty service or honour <I should endure> Imprisonment and [*all*] <any> affliction [*whatsoever should be wellcome*] <with patience and alacrity>. But being [*onely an effect*] <inflicted <onely> as a signe> of his Majesties displeasure, it is [*most*] <very> grievous. [*but that the conscience of having committed* [*in*] *the least of all errors* [*that*] *upon which punishment is*
20   *inflicted*] [*Whearefore I humbly beseech your Lordships who delight not in lengthning sorrow to*]** <and to> be our [*honorable mediators*] <intercessors> to his [*most gratious*] Majesty [*to have compassion o[n]* <*ſ> us*] <for us> whose errour we hope his Majesty [*will*] in his owne gratious disposition, will rather pardon, then [*have*] any further expiate with [*any torment and*] affliction. [*The clearenesse of my conscience*] <And [*ou*] by Gods grace> the whole course of our life hearafter shall testify our dutifulnesse and humble thanckfulnesse

In her first draft above, Stuart often writes for the couple: "we suffer", "our punishment", "our intercessors", "for us whose errour we hope", and "our life

---

Line 2. **examinatio[n]:** The word runs off the page.
Line 7. **displeasu[re]:** The word runs off the page.

hearafter shall testify our dutifulnesse". In the second draft, which is close to the wording of the presentation copy below, she revises "for us" to "for me" (see second sentence) and then consistently uses the singular pronoun. In the third draft, written as a presentation copy and then revised in an informal hand, Stuart's only changes were to shift one "your Lordships" to "your Honors" and three "your Lordships" to "you", making the letter more personal in tone. The fourth and final copy, the presentation copy, reads as follows:

※

To the right honorable, the Lords of his
Majesties most honorable privy counsaile

Right honorable and my very good Lords./ I humbly beseech you give me leave to becomme an humble suitor to you, to let his Majesty understand my hearty sorrow for his Majesties displeasure. And that it will please your Honors to becomme intercessours to his Majesty for me. Whose errour I assuredly hope his Majesty of his owne gratious disposition, will (by your good meanes) rather pardon, then any further expiate with imprisonment or other affliction. Which and more if it weare to do his Majesty service or honour, I should endure with alacrity. But   10
this is very grievous, especially as a signe of his Majesties displeasure; on whose favour all my worldly joy, as well as fortune dependeth. Which if I may reobtaine, all the course of my life hearafter shall testify my dutifull and humble thanckfulnesse./

Arbella Seymaure./

82

TO MR. WILLIAM SEYMOUR

Autograph, Stuart's informal hand, BL Harley MS 7003, ff. 150–51. Docketed "Lady Arbella to m^r William Seymour 6", apparently in Cecil's hand, which suggests this copy was placed in his files. Whether Seymour received it is unknown. Undated; perhaps written summer 1610.

Stuart would have had reason to worry about her husband's health in the Tower of London, especially if he were still in close confinement there, which he was until some time after his petition to the Council (see letter 83) was granted.

※

Sir, I am exceeding sory to heare you have not binne well, I pray you let me know truly how you do, and what was the cause of it for I am not satisfied with the reason Smith gives for it. But if it be a colde I will impute it to somme Sympathy betwixt us having my selfe gotten a swolne cheeke at the same time with a colde. For Gods sake let not your griefe <of minde> worke upon your body. you may see by me what inconveniences it will bring one to. And no fortune I assure you daunts me so much as that weakenesse of body I finde in my selfe, for si nous vivons l'age d'un veau as Marot sayes we may by Gods grace be happier then we looke for in being suffered to enjoy our selves with his Majesties favour. but if we be not able to live to it I for my part shall thinck my selfe a patterne of misfortune in enjoying so great a blessing as you so little a while. No separation but that deprives me of the comfort of you. for whearsoever you be or in what state so ever you are it suffiseth me you are mine. Rachel wept and would not be comforted because hir children weare no more. and that indeed is the remedilesse sorrow and none else. and thearfore God blesse us from that, and I will hope well of the rest. though I see no apparent hope. but I am sure Gods booke mentioneth many of his children in as great distresse that have donne well after even in this world. I assure you nothing the State can do with me can trouble me so much, as this newes of your being ill doth. and you see when I am troubled I trouble you too with tedious kindnesse for so I thinck you will account so long a letter your selfe not having written to me this good while so much as how you do. but sweet Sir I speake not this to trouble you with writing but when you please. be well. and I shall account my self happy in being

your faithfull loving wife.
Arb. S.

83

LADY ARBELLA STUART OR MR. WILLIAM SEYMOUR TO THE
PRIVY COUNCIL

Autograph, Stuart's informal hand, BL Harley MS 7003, f. 113. Docketed by her secretary "A Copie of A letter to the Councell/". Undated; likely written summer 1610. Stuart's similar letter (letter 81) was sent to the Council in July.

This letter, usually attributed to Seymour, is in Stuart's handwriting. Since the manuscript is a file copy, not a draft with revisions, Stuart may simply have

---

Letter 82. Lines 8–9. **si…veau:** if we live to the age of a calf; an allusion to "De Jehan le Veau," a poem by Clément Marot (French, 1496–1544). Jehan died young, as a "calf," rather than being allowed to live and fulfill his potential.

Line 13. **that:** death.   Lines 15–16. **Rachel…more:** a paraphrase of Jer. 31:15.

copied Seymour's letter for her file, or she may have drafted the letter and kept a clean copy. In either case, Stuart and Seymour likely collaborated on their strategies: Stuart's similar letter to the Privy Council (letter 81) originally was written as "we" and later revised to "I", a change that suggests she knew the Council would be receiving this separate letter from Seymour.

❧

May it please your Lordships
Since his Majesty is so highly offended with me that I dare not as yet (fearing farther to encure his Majesties disfavour) offer any manner of petition to his Princely handes, before the way be made more easy, I onely addresse my selfe to your honorable Lordships being now bereft of my nearest frends, through his Majesties indignation, humbly beseeching you to be intercessors to his Majesty that it would please him of his gratious and accustomed bounty, to restore me to his most wisht-for favour and my former liberty, or if that may seeme too large a suite that it would please his Majesty in the meane time to graunt me   10
the liberty of this place, to the recovering of my former health, which throug[h] my long and close imprisonment is much decaide and will not easily I feare me be repaired, whearof the Lieutenant can well certefy your Lordships/ I must confesse I have offended his Majesty which is my greatest sorrow, yet I hope not in that mesure that i[t] should deserve my utter ruine and destruction, since I protest my offence was committed before I knew it to be an offence./ Whearfore I humbly beseech your Lordships since the bottome of this wound is searched, to be a meanes that it may be healed. Thus relying on your Lordships honorable dispositions I humbly take my leave resting all-   20
wayes

To be commaunded by your Lordships
W.S.

Line 13. **Lieutenant:** William Waad, Lieutenant of the Tower.

Line 15. **i[t]:** The sheet is torn.

Line 17. **before...offence:** Both Stuart and Seymour maintained that their engagement, entered into before the marriage had been forbidden, had bound them to each other (see letters 88 and 91). Early modern England recognized two forms of betrothal: an *in verbis de futuro* betrothal (one spoken in the future tense as "I shall") and an *in verbis de praesenti* betrothal (one spoken in the present tense as "I do"). Although both carried a certain moral force, the latter was a binding contract, a marriage in all but the name. See also Seymour's message to Stuart, Appendix B, letter 14.

84A, 84B, AND 84C

TO LADY JANE DRUMMOND

Autograph draft, Stuart's informal hand, BL Add. MS 32092, f. 221. Secretary's copy with Stuart's autograph addition, BL Harley MS 7003, ff. 68–69. Third autograph, Stuart's informal hand, BL Harley MS 7003, ff. 66–67; addressed "To my honorable good Cousin M.^rs. Drummond./" Undated; likely written summer 1610, after Stuart received Lady Drummond's response to letter 78.

The first and third versions of this letter are presented in full here; from the second—the secretary's copy—only Stuart's addition appears.

🜚

Good Cousin. I pray you present hir Majesty my most humble thanckes for the token of the continuance of hir Majesties favour towards me, that I received in your letter./ Which hath so cheered me as I hope I shall be the better able to passe over my sorrow (till it please God to move his Majesties hearte to compassion of me) whilest I may theareby assure my selfe I remaine in hir Majesties favour though all other worldly comforts be withdrawne from me. And I will never cease to pray to the Almighty to reward hir Majesty for hir gratious regard of me in this distresse with all happinesse to hir <Royall> selfe and hirs. I must
10   also render you my kindest thanckes for your so frendly and freely imparting your opinion of my suite. But wheras my good frends may doubt my said suite will be more long and difficult to obteine then they wish, by reason of the wisdomme of this state [*to others*] <in dealing with others> of my quality in the like cause. I say, that I never heard [*n*]or read of any bodyes [*estate*] <case> that might be truely and justly compared to this of mine which bei[ng] throughly considered will be found so farre differing as theare can be no true resemblance made thearof with any others, and so I am assured that both theyr Majesties (when it shall please them duely to examine it in theyr Princely wis-
20   dommes) will easily discerne. And I do earnestly intreate you to move hir Majesty to voutchsafe the continuance of hir so gratious a beginning on my behalfe, and to perswade his Majesty to weigh my cause aright, and then I shall not doubt but speedily to receive that Royall Justice and

Line 3. **your letter:** See Appendix B, letter 15.
Line 16. **bei[ng]:** The sheet is torn.

favour that my own soule witnesseth I have ever deserved at his Majesties hands and will ever endevour to deserve of him, and his, whilest I have breath. And so with many thanckes to your selfe for your kind offices I take leave and rest

Your very loving Cousin.
A. S.

The second draft, the secretary's copy, incorporates Stuart's revisions from the first draft, but has few other changes. Stuart then decided to send Queen Anna a gift of embroidered gloves and added the following comment below her second draft.

⚘

[*And if it please hir Majesty to*] I presume to send [*hearwith a peece of my worke*] [*a*] <this> peece of [*my*] <my> worke [*during*] [<*during my restraint*>] [*since my comming hither that* [*hir*] *if it please hir Majesty*] <I pray you likewise present hir Majesty this peece of my worke> <which> I humbly beseech hir Majesty to [*weare*] <accept> in remembrance of the poore prisoner hir Majesties most humble servant that wrought them [*with in a time of as great sorrow as may be*] [<*in great sorrow*>] [*during this time of my exile from hir Majesties presence*] in hope [*they*] those Royall handes will [*gratiously accept and*] voutchsafe to weare them which till I have the honour to kisse I shall live in a great deale of   10 sorrow

The third version, the autograph on ff. 66–67, reads as follows:

⚘

Good Cousin./ I pray you present hir Majesty my most humble thanckes for the token of the continuance of hir Majesties favour towards me that I received in your letter./ which hath so cheered me as I hope I shall be the better able to passe over my sorrow (till it please God to move his Majesties heart to compassion of me) whilest I may thearby assure my selfe I remaine in hir Majesties favour though all other worldly comforts be withdrawne from me./ and will not cease to pray to the Almighty to reward hir Majesty for hir gratious regard of me in this distresse with all happinesse to hir Royall selfe and hirs./ I pray you likewise present hir Majesty this peece of my worke which I humbly   10 beseech hir Majesty to accept in remembrance of the poore prisoner hir

Majesties most humble servant that wrought them in hope those Royall
handes will voutchsafe to weare them which till I have the honour to
kisse I shall live in a great deale of sorrow./ I must also render you my
kindest thanckes for your so frendly and freely imparting your opinion
of my suite./ But wheras my good frends may doubt my said suite will
be more long and difficult to obteine then they wish by reason of the
wisdomme of this State in dealing with others of my quality in the like
cause, I say that I never heard nor read of any bodies case that might be
20 truely and justly compared to this of mine which being truely considered will be found so farre differing as theare can be no true resemblance made thearof with any others; and so I am assured that both
theyr Majesties (when it shall please them duely to examine it in theyr
Princely wisdommes) will easily discerne. And I do earnestly intreate
you to move hir Majesty to voutchsafe the continuance of hir so gratious a beginning on my behalfe and to perswade his Majesty to weigh
my cause aright, and then I shall not doubt but speedily to receive that
Royall Justice and favour that my owne soule witnesseth I have ever
deserved at his Majesties hands, and will ever end[e]vour to deserve of
30 him and his whilest I have breath. And so with many thanckes to your
selfe for your kinde offices I take leave and rest

Your very loving Cousin.
Arbella Seymaure./

85

TO THE PRIVY COUNCIL

Secretary's copy, BL Harley MS 7003, ff. 85–86. Docketed by her secretary "A
Copie of A letter to the Lords of the Councell/". Undated; perhaps written
summer or autumn 1610.

May itt please your Lordships to give me leave to be an humble Suitour
to you, that whereas upon his Majesties direccion I was restrayned of
my libertie by your Lordships warrante, And that I have presumed to
preferre my most humble Peticion to his Majestie to be restored into his
gratious good favor againe, (which is my greattest comforte on earth)
your Lordships will be pleased, to preferre my said Peticion to his most

gratious Majesties handes, And if your Lordships will also vouchsafe
your favourable interpretacion of my offence, and be A meanes to his
Majestie on my behalf, I shalbe infinitelie bound to pray for your honorable and happie prosperities, and remayne humblie   10
                    Att your Lordships commaundementes./

86

TO KING JAMES

Secretary's copy, BL Harley MS 7003, f. 85. Undated; perhaps written summer
or autumn 1610, since it appears on the same sheet as letter 85.

May itt please your most excellent Majestie to regard with the Eies of
your Royall and gratious harte, the unfortunate estate of me your Majesties handmaide. Who knowinge your gratious favour to her, to be the
greattest Honour, comforte and felicitie that this World can afford her,
doth nowe feele any parte of the Contrarye, to be the most greevous
affliccion to her that can be ymagined, whereinsoever your Majestie will
saie I have offended I will not conteste, but in all humilitie prostrate my
selfe att your Majesties feete, onely I doe (most humbly [*beseech you*] on
my knees) beseech your Majestie to beleeve, that that thought [*did*]
never yett entered into my harte, to doe any thinge that might justlie   10
deserve any parte of your indignacion, but if the necessitie of my state
and fortune, together with my Weakenes, have caused me to doe somewhat not pleasinge to your Majestie (Most gratious Soveraigne) lett itt
be covered with the Shadowe of your gratious benignitie, and pardoned
in that heroicall mynd of yours which is never closed to those who carrie A most Loyall hart to your Soveraintie, A most sincere and Dutifull
affeccion to your person, And that prayeth for the most happie prosperitie of your Majesty our most gratious Queene, and your Royall yssue in
all things for ever, amongst which number Almightie God (who
knoweth the secretts of all harts,) knoweth me to be one, who am also   20
          Your Majesties most humble faithfull subject and servant./

87

TO QUEEN ANNA

Autograph, Stuart's presentation hand, SPD, James, vol. 57, f. 224. Addressed "To the Queenes most Excellent Majesty./"; docketed "Lady Arbella to the Quene with hir Petition to the Kinges Majesty enclosed." Dated in the docket October 1610.

❧

May it please your most Excellent Majesty
I presume to send herewith a copy of my humble petition to the Kinges Majesty wheareby your Majesty may perceave (with lesse trouble then any other relation of mine) as much (in effect) as I can say of the condition of my present estate and harde fortune. Now to whom may I so fittely addresse my selfe with confidence of helpe and mediation, as to your Royall person (the mirrour of our sexe) and being for me your Majesties humble and devoted servant, and in a cause of this nature, so full of piety and commiseration, I will wholy rely upon your Princely
10   goodnesse, whom I humbly beseech to vouchsafe to enter into a gratious consideration of the true estate of my case and fortune, and then I nothing doubte, but that in the true noblenesse of your Royall minde your Majesty will be pleased to mediate for me, in such sorte, as in your most Princely wisdomme and favour the same shall be moved. And I shall allwaies pray for the everlasting honour and felicity of your Majesty with all your Royall issue in all thinges and will remaine for ever

Your Majesties
most humble and dutifull subject and
20   servant,
Arbella Seymaure./

Headnote. The English words "the loss of thy late Sister hath honnered thee with the service of my fayre flower" appear hastily written on the verso, followed by related phrases in French, including, most completely, "J'ai perdu ta successeur / mais non pas tu", and "La perte de ta seur / te portait l'honneur / desire se[r]viteur / de ma belle fleur". Bradley believed the hand was probably Stuart's (2:247); I disagree because the formation of the characters and the spellings of "honnered" and "fayre" are unlike Stuart's usual hand and spelling. I think it likelier that Stuart's letter was presented to Queen Anna and the lines of poetry were added later by someone else.

88

TO KING JAMES

Autograph, largely Stuart's presentation hand, but finished and signed by a secretary, BL Add. MS 32092, f. 220. No address. Secretary's copy of the same, BL
Harley MS 7003, ff. 87–88. Undated; perhaps this was the petition enclosed
with letter 87.

❧

May it please your most Excellent Majesty./. the unfortunate estate
whearunto I am falne, by being deprived of your Majesties presence (the
greatest comfort to me upon earth;) together with the opinion is conceived of your Majesties displeasure towards me; hath brought as great
affliction to my minde, as can be imagined. Neverthelesse touching the
offence for which I am now punished, I most humbly beseech your
Majesty (in your most Princely wisdomme and judgement) to consider
in what a miserable state I had binne, if I had taken any other course
then I did; for my owne conscience witnessing before God that I was
then the wife of him that now I am, I could never have matched with   10
any other man; but to have lived all the dayes of my life as an harlot,
which your Majesty would have abhorred in any, espetially in one who
hath the honour (how otherwise unfortunate soever) to have any
droppe of your Majesties bloud in them. But I will trouble your Majesty
no longer, but in all humility attending [*that liberty*] your Majesties
good pleasure for that libertie (the want whereof depriveth me of health
and all other worldly comforts) I will never forgett to pray for your Majesties most happie prosperitie for ever in all things. And so remaine

Your Majesties
most humble and faithfull subject and servant: 20
Arbella Seymaure:/

Line 15. [**that liberty**]: After this error, the handwriting is that of Stuart's secretary, who
finished what had now become a copy, since the mistake rendered it unsuitable for
presentation.

89

TO MR. FRANCIS SEYMOUR

Eighteenth-century transcript, Alnwick Castle MS 93A/35, Part 2. Addressed
"To my honorable good brother Mr. Francis Seymaure./" The British Library
sold the original unpublished manuscript at Sotheby's, 16–17 March 1888, and
it is currently unlocated. Undated; likely written near 4 November 1610, when
her husband wrote a similar letter to Francis.

Francis Seymour was William's younger brother.

My honorable good brother./ I thanck you for your kinde letter and
willingnesse to take paines to comme hither./ I should be most glad to
see you, but since it is not convenient we should be otherwise aquainted
yet, I pray you let me heare from you sommtimes by letter. that howsoever higher powers crosse the greatest part of my happinesse in depriv-
ing me for a time of your deare brother my husband, I may not be
altogether a stranger to your family and your selfe in particuler, whose
extraordinary kindnesse in this time, shall be requited God willing on
my part with the redoubled love of so neare alliance and obligation. I
will endeavour to make my patience deserve excuse if not commendation at your hands, but it is the vertue I wish may be lest put to proofe
in my frends of all others. —And if your brothers fortune and mine be
likely to prove well except seeming frends prove false and voluntary
othes be turned to perjury, I must confesse I feare the destiny of your
house and my owne both which have fared the worse for being subject
to that starre./ Your brothers constancy notwithstanding I bring him
nothing yet but trouble I hope will make for your advantage when you
go a wooing in good houre be it I pray God to your own honour and

---

Line 11. **lest:** When Bradley saw the original letter, which she apparently was allowed to quote
only in part, she transcribed this word as *best* (1:268), which reverses the meaning of the *lest* in
this transcript.

Lines 15–16. **subject...starre:** an allusion to the astrological belief that the stars determine
people's ranks and destinies; both families have suffered for being of royal blood.

Lines 16–18. **Your brothers...wooing:** i.e., your brother's constancy to me in spite of my
having brought him nothing yet but trouble will, I hope, advantage you with a prospective wife
by suggesting that you will be equally constant in love.

Line 18. **good houre:** a fortunate time, when the stars are well aligned.

good and my Lord your Grandfathers comfort with whose good inclination towards his most dutyfull childe my husband and me I thanck   20
you for sweetning the latter end of your letter. I pray you writ[e]
[of]ten, and leave ceremonies. so shall we soonest be [a]cquainted and I
thinck my selfe most beholden to [y]ou. So wishing you all honour and
happinesse I rest

Your assured loving sister
Arbella Seymaure

90A AND 90B

TO QUEEN ANNA

Autograph draft, Stuart's informal hand, BL Harley MS 7003, f. 82. Secretary's
copy with revisions in Stuart's hand, BL Harley MS 7003, f. 78. No address.
Undated; likely written December 1610. Stuart might expect pardon over the
Christmas holidays (see below); and, although several of Stuart's biographers
have dated this letter, and the one to King James that follows, to Christmas of
1611, Stuart refers in James's letter only to her marriage, not to the escape to
which she logically would have alluded if the letter had been written in 1611.

🌿

May it please your most Excellent Majesty to consider how long I have
lived a spectacle of his Majesties displeasure to my unspeakeable griefe,
and out o[f] that [*Princely compassi*] <gratious> disposition which
moveth your Royall minde to compassion of the distresse[d] [*of and gr*]
please it your Majesty to move his Majesty [*to*] in my behalfe. I have
presumed to [*send*] present your Majesty hearwith the copy of [*an*]
<my> humble petition to his Majesty against this time when [*I <the
rather> hope the better of pardon because his Majesty*] I am sure [*pa*] <his
Majesty> forgiveth greater offences as freely as he desiret[h] to be forgiven [*by him whose Sacrament he is to receive*]. [*But*] <Though> your   10
Majesties intercession at any time I know weare sufficient. Thus hath
<my long experience of> your Majesties gratious favour to me and all
good causes incouraged me to presume to addresse my selfe unto your

---

Letter 89. Line 21. **writ[e]:** The paper is torn, here and below.

Letter 90A. Line 3. **o[f]:** The words run off the sheet at several points in this text.

Majesty and increased the obligation of my duty [*to*] in praying continually unto the Almighty for your Majesties felicity in all things. [*So I*]
<And> in all humility to [*rest*] remaine

Your Majesties

☙

May itt please your most Excellent Majesty to consider howe longe I
have lived A Spectacle of his Majesties displeasure to my unspeakeable
greif, and out of that gratious Disposition which moveth your Royall
mynd to Compassion of the distressed please itt your Majestie to move
his Majesty in my behalfe/ I have presumed to present your Majestie
hearewith the Copie of my [*humble*] <humble> Petition to his Majestie
[*against*] <at> this time when [*I am sure*] his Majesty forgiveth greatter
offences [*as freelie as he desireth to be forgiven*] Though your Majesties
intercession att any time I knowe were sufficient, Thus hath my longe
10   experience of your Majesties gratious favour to me and [*all*] good
Causes incouraged me to presume to addresse my self unto your Majestie and increased the obligation of my Duetie in prayinge continuallie
unto the Almightie for your Majesties felicitie in all thinges, [*And in all
humilitie remaine*] And to remaine./

Your Majesties./

9IA AND 9IB

TO KING JAMES

Autograph draft, Stuart's informal hand, BL Harley MS 7003, f. 82. Docketed
by her secretary "To the King". Secretary's copy, BL Harley MS 7003, f. 57.
Docketed by her secretary "A Copie of my Petition to the Kings Majestie".
Undated; likely written December 1610, since a draft appears on the same sheet
as a draft of letter 90, indicating the two were paired.

☙

May it please your most Excellent Majesty
I do most heartily lament my harde fortune that I should offend your
Majesty the least especially in that whearby I have long desired to merit
of your Majesty as appeared before your Majesty was my Souveraine
And though your Majesties neglect of me [*and*] my love to this

gentleman that is my husband and my fortune drew me to a contract
before I acquainted your Majesty I humbly beseech your Majesty to
consider how impossible it was for me to imagine it could be offensive
to your Majesty having few dayes before given me leave to bestow my
selfe on any subject of your Majesties (which likewise your Majesty had   10
donne long since) [*and*] <Besides> having never <binne> prohibited
[*me any these .7. yeares nor never*] <nor spoken <to [*me*]> of any in this
land by your Majesty> these .7. yeares that I have lived in your Majesties house [*whearby*] I could not conceive that your Majesty regarded
my marriage [*at all*] [*as a thing*] <at all [*w*]>. And I protest if your Majesty had vouchsafed to tell me your minde, and accept the free will
offring of my obedience I would not have offended your Majesty **<as I
have donne in this sort> though I verily hope I have given your Majesty
no true cause of <your just> displeasure when it shall please your Majesty throughly to consider [*of that*] <of it> if I have I account my selfe   20
the most unfortunate creature living but <for> my conscience bearing
me witnesse I most humbly beseech your Majesty thearfore to pardon
my <fault proceeding of> ignorance and necessity since your Majesty
and** Of whose gratious goodnesse I presume so much that if it weare
as convenient <in a worldly respect> as malice may make it seeme to
separate us whom God hath joyned, your Majesty would not do evill
that good might comme thearof, nor [*leave*] make me that have the
honor to be so neare your Majesty in bloud the first precedent that ever
was, though our Princes may have left somme [*which I assure my selfe
your Majesty will* [*re*] *holdeth*] [<*of theyr dealing with theyr kinne*>] as lit-   30
tle imitable for so good <and gratious> a Kinge as your Majesty as
Davids dealing with Uriah. But I assure my selfe if it please your
Majesty in your owne wisdomme to consider throughly of my cause

---

Line 6. **fortune:** financial state; also condition in life.

Line 26. **whom...joyned:** an allusion to the Anglican marriage service: "Those whom God hath joined together, let no man put asunder."

Lines 26–27. **not...thearof:** a paraphrase of Rom. 3:8.

Line 32. **Davids...Uriah:** Because David wanted to marry Uriah's wife Bathsheba, David ordered that Uriah be put in the front line of battle (2 Sam. 11).

[*but I shall*] theare will no solide reason appeare to debarre me of justice and your princely favour which I will endevour to deserve whilest I breath and never ceasing to pray for your Majesties felicity in all things [*but*] remaine

Your Majesties

most humble

The secretary's copy, with further revisions such as Stuart's shift from referring to her "love to" Seymour to her "good likeinge of" him, reads as follows:

꒰

May itt please your most Excellent Majestie

I doe most hartelie lament my hard fortune that I should offend your Majestie the least, especiallie in that wheareby I have longe desired to meritt of your Majestie as appeared before your Majestie was my Soveraigne And thoughe your Majesties neglect of me, my good likeinge of this gentleman that is my Husband, and my fortune, drove me to A Contracte before I acquainted your Majestie I humblie beseech your Majestie to consider howe impossible itt was for me to ymagine itt could be offensive unto your Majestie havinge fewe Dayes before geven

10   me your Royall consent to bestowe my selfe on anie Subject of your Majesties (which [*lykewise*] likewise your Majestie had done longe since) Besides never havinge ben either prohibited any or spoken to for anie in this land by your Majestie these 7 yeares that I have lived in your Majesties house I could not conceive that your Majestie regarded my Mariage att all, Whereas yf your Majestie had vouchsafed to tell me your mynde and accepte that free will offeringe of my obedience I would not have offended your Majestie Of whose gratious goodnes I presume so much that if itt weare as convenient in A worldlie respect as mallice may make itt seeme to seperate us whom God hath joyned, your

20   Majestie would not doe evill that good might come thereof, nor make me that have the honour to be so neare your Majesty in bloud the first presedent that ever was, thoughe our Princes maie have lefte some as litle imitable for so good and gratious A Kinge as your Majestie as Davids dealinge with Uriah But I assure my selfe if itt please your Majestie in your owne wisdome to consider throughlie of my cause there will noe solide reason appeare to Debarre me of Justice and your

Princelie favour, which I will endeavour to Deserve whilst I breathe And never ceasinge to praie for your Majesties felicitie in all thinges remaine

Your Majesties Etc.

92

TO MR. FRANCIS SEYMOUR

BL Add. MS 15970, f. 10, a copy made from the original, which was sold to W. Bindley on 25 October 1898 and is currently unlocated. Addressed "To my honorable good brother m^r Frannces Seymaur./" Undated; likely written January 1611, since, in an eighteenth-century transcript (Alnwick Castle MS 93A/35, Part 3), Gorges's letter accompanying the bill (Appendix B, letter 16) is dated 6 January 1610/11.

By the time that Stuart received a bill from an Italian creditor, Prospero Gorges, she probably had been told that she was to be dismissed to the far northern city of Durham in the custody of William James, Bishop of Durham.

🙼

Sweet brother these weare your brothers points that you and [*your*] others have donne us the honour to weare for our sake, thearfore I make bolder to entreate you to show this letter and bill to my Aunt or any frend you think will lay out so much for me at this time when it seemes every one forsakes me but those that cannot helpe me.

Your most unfortunate sister

Arbella Seymaure

93

TO SIR THOMAS FLEMING, LORD CHIEF JUSTICE OF ENGLAND, AND SIR EDWARD COKE, LORD CHIEF JUSTICE OF COMMON PLEAS

Autograph, Stuart's informal hand, BL Harley MS 7003, f. 152. Addressed "To the right honorable the Lord Chiefe Justice of England and the Lord Chiefe Justice of the Common Pleas". Undated; written early 1611, after Stuart had been told she would be removed from Lambeth to Durham.

Letter 92. Line 1. **points:** laces, usually metal-tipped, used to fasten clothing.

Line 3. **Aunt:** Mary Talbot, to whom Gorges refers in his letter.

Letter 93. Title. **Addressees:** Fleming was Chief Justice of the King's Bench, the higher common-law court, and Coke was Chief Justice of the Court of Common Pleas, the lower common-law court.

In February Stuart received formal notification to prepare for her journey to Durham. She had not been charged with an offence and here appealed to the justices to intervene.

❧

My Lords wheareas I have binne long restrained from my liberty which is as much to be regarded as my life and am appointed as I understand to be removed farre from these Courts of Justice wheare I ought to be examined tried, and then condemned or cleared to remote parts whose Courts I hold unfitter for the tryall of my offence, this is to beseech your Lordships to enquire by an *Habeas Corpus* or other usuall forme of Law what is my fault and if upon examination by your Lordships I shall thearof be justly convicted let me indure such punishment by your Lordships sentence as is due to such an offendor And if your Lordships may not or will not of your selves graunt unto me the ordinary reliefe of a distressed subject then I beseech you becomme humble intercessors to his Majesty that I may receive such benifitt of justice as both his Majesty by his oth <[*by his*] those of his bloud not excepted> hath promised and the Lawes of this Realmes afford to all [*subjects*] <others> And though unfortunat woman I should obteine neither yet I beseech your Lordships reteine me in your good opinion, and judge charitably till I be proved to have committed any offence. either against God or his Majesty deserving so long restraint or separation from my lawfull husband So, praying for your Lordships I rest

Your afflicted poore suppliant

.A.S.

94

TO THOMAS ERSKINE, VISCOUNT FENTON

Autograph draft, Stuart's informal hand, but finished by a secretary, BL Harley MS 7003, ff. 153–55. Addressed "To the right honorable the Viscount Fenton./" Undated; likely written the second half of March 1611.

Letter 93. Line 6. **Habeas Corpus:** writ issued by a judge to order that a person restrained of liberty be brought into court, where the lawfulness of the restraint could be evaluated.

In mid-March, Stuart's journey northward began, and she became so ill that even James's physician recommended that Stuart rest before continuing. Fenton, a relative by marriage and the Captain of the Guard, had been kind to her at various times.

This letter and several of those that follow sometimes have been dated to Stuart's second imprisonment in the Tower; but while there are many reports of Stuart's requests from and activities in the Tower, there are no letters by her that can be dated definitely to that period of her life. These letters more likely are the ones Stuart mentioned in letter 101B when she said that she had tried to make her weakness known to King James "by my Lord Fenton, and to the Lords of your Majesties most honorable privy counsell by writing"; if so, this letter was written in March 1611, perhaps after Stuart had been forcibly carried to Highgate or Barnet.

⚘

My Lord the long acquaintance betwixt us and the good experience of your honorable dealing heartofore, maketh me not onely hope, but be most assured that if you knew my most discomfortable and distressed estate, you would acquaint his Majesty with all, and consequently procure [*lett*] my reliefe and redresse as you have donne other times. I have binne sicke even to the death from which it hath pleased God miraculously to deliver me for this present danger, but finde my selfe so weake **by reason I have wanted those ordinary helpes whearby [*others*] <most> in my case be the[y] never so poore or unfortunat soever are preserved alive at least for Charity <I can neither get clothes nor posset   10 ale for example nor any thing but ordinary diett and complement fitt for a sicke body in my case when I call for it, not so much as a glister saving your reverence> [*that*] that unlesse I may be suffered to have those about me that I may trust, this sentence my Lord Tresorer pronounced after his Majesties refusing that trifle of my worke by your persuasion as I take it will prove the certaine and apparant cause of my

---

Lines 10–13. <**I...reverence**>: This insertion runs up the left margin of the page.

Line 10. **clothes:** likely bedclothes.   Lines 10–11. **posset ale:** a warm drink of milk and ale, often with other ingredients, used as a remedy for illness.

Line 11. **and:** The sense might be more clear if *and* were replaced by another *nor*.

Line 12. **glister:** enema.

death, whearof I thought good to advertise you that you both may be
the better prepared [*either*] in case you or either of you have possessed
the King with such opinions of me, as thearupon I shall be <suspected
20   and> restrained till helpe comme too late, and [*th*] be assured that neither phisition nor other <but whom I thinck good> shall comme about
me whilest I live till I have his Majesties favour with out which I desire
not to live, and if you remember of olde I dare dy so I be not guilty of
my owne death, and oppresse others with my ruine too if theare be no
other way. as God forbid to whom I committ you and rest as assuredly
as heartofore if you be the same to me.

Your Lordships faithfull frend.
A.S.**

that unles it please his Majesty to shew me mercy [*that*] and that I may
30   receive <from you> at least some hope of regayning his majesties favor
againe it will not be possible for me to undergoe the great burthen of his
princely displeasure good my lord consither the fault cannot be uncom-
mitted neyther can any more be required of an earthly creature but confession and <most> humble submission whitch if it would please your
lordship to present to his majesty [*I cannot dout of some remove*] <[*and
lett hi*]] whose favor I esteeme far above any> worldly comfort I cannot
dout but his majesty [*thus who*] would be pleased to mitigate his displeasure and lett me receave comfort./ [*I wish your lordship would in a
few lines understand my misery for my weaknes is sutch that* [*writing*] *<it>
40   is very paynfull to me to write and cannot be pleasant to any to read from
your hands my lord I received the* [*fa*] *first favor*] <whitch> *favor if I may
obtayne* [*this favor*] *from your lordship now in my greatest necessity I
shall ever acknowledg my self bound to you for it and the rest of my life
shall* [*be wholy framed*] shew how highly I esteem his majesties favor. [*I*

Line 17. **both:** presumably Fenton and Robert Cecil, Lord High Treasurer of England.

Lines 23–24. **if…death:** perhaps an allusion to the events of early 1603, when Stuart refused
to eat or drink until she was removed from Hardwick Hall; if the letter was written from the
Tower, this sentence may allude to the events at Barnet.

Line 29. **that unles:** From this point the letter is in a secretary's hand; *that* continues the
sentence preceding the deleted text within asterisks.

the almighty] the almighty send you[r] lordship health and [*putt it into*] make you his good [*to help*] means to help me out of this great grief./

Your lordships most
distressed frend

95
TO THE PRIVY COUNCIL

Autograph, Stuart's informal hand, SPD, James, vol. 62, f. 122. Addressed "To the right honorable my very good Lords the Lords of his Majesties most honorable privy counsell". Secretaries' copies, BL Harley MS 7003, ff. 147–48 and f. 58 (the latter of which is in the same hand as BL Harley MS 7003, ff. 83–84 and 104–5; see letters 97 and 101D). Undated; written the second half of March 1611.

⚘

May it please your Lordships / I protest I am in so weak case as I veryly thinck it would be the cause of my death to be removed any whither at this time though it weare to a place to my likeing. My late discomfortable journey (which I have not yet recovered,) had almost ended my dayes and I have never since gonne out of a few little and hott roomes, and am many waies unfitt to take the ayre. I trust your Lordships will not looke I should be so unchristian as to be a cause of my owne death, and I leave it to your Lordships wisdomme, to consider what the world would conceive if I should be violently inforced to do it Thearfore I beseech your Lordships to be humble suitors in my behalfe that I may   10 have somme time given me to recover my strength which I should the sooner do, if I weare not continually molested. And I will hope and pray that God will incline his Majesties heart every way to more <compassion> towards me who rest

Very humbly at your Lordships commaundment
Arbella Seymaure.

Letter 95. Line 1. **weak case:** poor physical condition.

96

TO KING JAMES

Autograph draft, Stuart's informal hand, BL Harley MS 7003, f. 146. No address. The sheet is cut in half and ends in mid-deletion, although bits of ascenders indicate that the text continued. Undated; perhaps written spring 1611.

Because its tone is so desperate, this letter has traditionally been considered Stuart's final plea to King James from the Tower, but it may have been written at any time during Stuart's imprisonments. There is no indication whether the letter was ever finished or delivered.

🜨

[*In most humble wise*] <In all humility> the most wretched and unfortunate creature that ever lived prostrates it selfe at the feet of the most mercifull King that ever was desiring nothing but mercy and favour, not being more afflicted for any thing then for the losse of that which hath binne this long time the onely comfort it had in the world, and which if it weare to do againe I would not adventure the losse of for any other worldly comfort, mercy it is I desire, and that for Gods sake. [*Let either Freake or*]

97

TO ROBERT CECIL, EARL OF SALISBURY (?)

Secretary's copy with Stuart's revisions, BL Harley MS 7003, ff. 104–5. Docketed "Draught of a letter./" Undated; likely written spring 1611, since it is in the same hand as BL Harley MS 7003, ff. 58 and 83–84 (see letters 95 and 101D), the latter of which was written then.

Although the intended recipient is not named, Stuart's references to his previous good opinion of her and to his excellent gifts of persuasion argue that she was writing to Cecil.

🜨

My Lord
The noblenes of your nature and the good opinion it hath pleased your Lordship to houlde of mee heeretofore embouldeneth mee to beseech your Lordship to enter into consitheracion of my distress and to be

---

Letter 96. Line 8. **Freake:** one of Stuart's embroiderers, who had been with Stuart since before 1603.

touched with the misery I am in for want of his Majesties favour whose
clemencye and mercye ys suche that if it would please you to make my
greefe knowne and howe neerely it toucheth [*mee*] my hart that it hath
bin my harde fortune to offend his Majestie I cannot doubt but itt
[*will*] <would> procure mee boath mittigation of the harde doome, and
mercye in some measure to yeild comfort to my sowle overwhelmed   10
with the extremytie of greefe which hath almost brought me to the
brinck of the grave[.] I beseech your Lordship deale so with mee as my
prayers may procure you gods rewarde for what you do for his sake
(which thoughe it be but a cuppe of coulde water[)] I meane anie small
hope of mittigation of his Majesties displeasure) shalbe most thanckfully receaved by mee: and I doubt not but if it please your Lordship to
trye your excellent gifts of perswation his Majestie will lend a gratious
eare to your Lordship and I shall rest ever bounde to pray for your Lord-
shipps happines who nowe my selfe rest the most unfortunate and
afflicted creature lyvinge   20

A:S:

98
TO UNNAMED KNIGHT

Autograph, Stuart's informal hand, BL Cotton Vespasian F. 3, f. 75. No
address. Copy, BL Add. MS 32092, ff. 222–23. Bradley notes she found a copy
docketed "to Cromwell" (2:262), presumably Sir Oliver Cromwell, and Lewis
also indicates Cromwell was the recipient (3:169); but neither of these BL
manuscripts bears an inscription. Undated; perhaps written spring 1611.

⚶

Sir though you be almost a stranger to me but onely by sight, yet the
good opinion I generally heare to be held of your worth together with
the great interest you have in my Lord of Northamptons favour makes
me thus farre presume of your willingnesse to do a poore <afflicted>
gentlewoman that good office (if in no other respect yet because I am a
Christian) as to further me with your best indevors to his Lordship that

---

Letter 97. Lines 11–12. **which...grave:** added in Stuart's hand.   Letter 98. Line 3. **Lord of
Northamptons:** Henry Howard, Earl of Northampton, was one of James's most influential
advisors.

it will please him to helpe me out of this great distresse and misery and regaine me his Majesties favor which is my chiefest desire. Whearin his Lordship may do a deede acceptable to God and honorable to himselfe
10   and I shall be infinitely bound to his Lordship and beholden to you, who now till I receive somme comfort from his Majesty rest

the most sorrowfull
creature living
Arbella Seymaure

99

TO UNNAMED LORD AND RELATION

Autograph draft, Stuart's informal hand, BL Harley MS 7003, f. 149. No address. Undated; the comment on her weakness suggests the letter was written spring 1611.

⚘

My Lord my extremity constraining me to labour to all my frends to becomme sutors to his Majesty for his pardon of my fault, and my weaknesse not permitting me to write particulerly I have made choice of your Lordship <humbly beseeching you> to move as many as <have> any [aw] compassion of my affliction to joyne in humble mediation to his Majesty to forgive me the most penitent and sorrowfull creature that breathes

Your distressed Cousin
A. S.

IOO

TO KING JAMES

Autograph, Stuart's informal hand, BL Harley MS 7003, f. 89. No address. Undated; written late March or early April 1611, after Stuart was granted a month's respite.

⚘

May it please your most Excellent Majesty gratiously to accept my most humble thancks for these Halcyon daies it hath pleased your Majesty to graunt me. And since it hath pleased your Majesty to give this testi-

---

Letter 99. Line 3. **particulerly:** particularly; to each individual.

mony of willingnesse to have me live a while, in all humility I begge the restitution of those comforts without which every houre of my life is discomfortable to me, the principall whearof is your Majesties favour, which none that breathes can more highely esteeme then I who whilest I live will not cease to pray to the Almighty for your Majesties prosperity and rest

Your Majesties   10
most humble and faithfull
almost ruined subject and
servant
Arbella S.

IOIA—D

TO KING JAMES

Two autograph drafts, Stuart's informal hand, BL Harley MS 7003, f. 79. No address. Secretary's copy, BL Harley MS 7003, ff. 80–81, marked "10", Cecil's normal notation, but without the descriptive comment usual with items in Cecil's files. Secretary's copy with marginal comments, BL Harley MS 7003, ff. 83–84; docketed by the secretary "Draught of a petition to his Majestie./" Undated; written late April or early May 1611.

According to Dr. Moundford (BL Harley MS 7003, f. 107), this letter was read aloud before the Privy Council to the great approval of King James and Prince Henry. For modern readers, this petition is of special interest because it is extant in so many drafts and because in ff. 83–84, Stuart comments on her text.

Stuart's first draft, quickly abandoned with heavy lines drawn through the text, reads as follows:

❧

May it please your most Excellent Majesty [*whearas*] <since> it hath pleased God to lay so many heavy crosses upon me as have made me I thincke one of the most miserable creatures living not to aggravate them with beleeving that imputation of my obstinacy which to my great griefe I heare your Majesty conceiveth

The second draft also contains sections deleted with heavy lines:

❧

May it please your most Excellent Majesty though it hath pleased God to lay so many heavy crosses upon me as I account my selfe the most miserable creature living yet none is so grievous to me as the losse of your Majesties favour, which [*to*] appeareth not so much to [*me*] <my unspeakeable

griefe> in any [*other effect*] <other effect of it> (though the least of many it
hath already brought forth is sufficient for my utter ruin) as <in> that
your Majesty giveth credence as (I heare) to those sinister reports which
impute that to obstinacy which proceeded <merelie out> of necessity
<not willing> that I might [*not*] be <thought> guilty of hastning my owne
death by any voluntary action <of myne> having first endevored <by all
good meanes> to make my <extreame> weakenesse knowne to your Majesty **by my Lord Fenton, and to the Lords of your Majesties most honorable privy counsell by writing. and many other waies <before my
remove fro> Whearby the But <In But> my misfortune being such [*as not
onely*] as not onely any protestation of my owne but the reiterated testimonies of such grave persons as advertised the like [*been*] [*weare*] seemed
of [*lesse*] <small> weight [*then the traducements of somme whisperers*]**
<But nothing availing me> Certeinely I had <sodenlie> perished if your
Majesty had not speedily had compassion of me in graunting me [*somme*]
<this time of> stay <for my recoverie to> which if it may please your Maj-
esty <of your gratious goodnesse> to adde .3. weekes more [<*in*> *which I
hope*] <M.ʳ· Doctor Mondford hopes> I [*shall*] <may> recover so much
strength, as may enable me to [*obey your Majesty*] [*give this testimony which
yet I have binne altogether unable to do that I shall during*] <travell> And I
shall [*never refuse <by> Gods willing <grace>*] <ever be willing> whilest I
breath to yeild your Majesty most humble and dutifull obedience as to
my Souveraign for whose felicity for ever in all thing I [*will not*] cease
<not> to pray, and [*re*] in all fortunes rest

Your Majesties

most humble and [*dutifull*] <faithfull>

subject and servant

Arb.S.

Line 8. **<merelie out>:** added in her secretary's hand.   Line 9. **<not willing>:** added in her
secretary's hand.   **<thought>:** added in her secretary's hand.   Line 10. **<of myne>:** added in
her secretary's hand.

Line 12. **Lord Fenton:** Thomas Erskine, Viscount Fenton; see letter 94.   Line 18. **<sodenlie>:**
added in her secretary's hand.   Line 20. **<for...to>:** added in her secretary's hand.

Line 22. **Doctor Mondford:** Dr. Thomas Moundford, Stuart's physician, later President of the
College of Physicians.

Line 30. **<faithfull>:** added in her secretary's hand.

Folios 80–81 contain a secretary's clean copy of the above text, incorporating Stuart's revisions:

❦

May itt please your most Excellent Majestie

Thoughe itt hath pleased God to laie so manie heavie crosses upon me as I account my self the most miserable creature livinge, yett none is so greevous to me as the losse of your Majesties favour, which appeareth not somuch to my unspeakeable greefe in anie other effect of itt (thoughe the least of manie itt hath alreadie brought forthe is sufficient for my utter ruyne) as in that your Majestie giveth credence (as I heare) to those sinister reports, which impute that to my obstinacie which proceeded meerelie out of necessitie, not willing that I might be thought guiltie of hastning my owne death by anie voluntarie action of myne, having first endeavored by all good meanes to make my extreame weakenesse knowne to your Majestie But nothing avaylinge me certenlie I had sodaynlie perished if your Majestie had not speedelie had compassion of me in graunting me this time of stay for my recoverie, to which if itt maie please your Majestie of your gratious goodnes to add 3 weekes more, M^r. Doctor Moundford hopes I maie recover somuch strength as may enhable me to travell./ And I shall ever be willinge whilst I breathe to yeild your Majestie moste humble and dutifull obedience as to my Soveraigne for whose felicitie for ever in all things I cease not to praie, and in all fortunes rest

10

20

Your Majesties
most humble and faithfull
subject and servant
A. S.

The text of ff. 83–84 is the same for much of the letter, although Stuart deletes the comment about causing her own death—"not willing that I might be thought guilty of hastning my owne death by any voluntary action of myne"— and increases her request from three weeks to a month or three weeks. At the last sentence, however—after "as may enable me to travell"—the conclusion differs completely. This version continues as follows:

❦

And for my owne part as an <u>arg[u]ment</u> that I had never anie other thought then to gaine your Majesties favoure by obedyence I do <u>promise</u>

to undergoe the Jorney after this time expired without anie <u>resistans or</u> <u>refusall to do such things as are fitt for mee to do to make my Jorney<s></u> <u>less painefull, or perillous</u>, beinge nowe so assured that your Majestie hath no purpos to make my correction my ruine in anie sort as I will hope Confidently when I have herein satisfied the <u>dutie I owe you as my</u> <u>Sovereigne that ys nowe displeased</u> to receive that grace and goodnes from you <u>which one in my case</u> may hope <for> from your most gratious Majestie <u>who hath profere of my obedyent hart</u> and votchesafes to acknowledge mee to bee of your bludd thoughe in all respects

Your Majesties
most humble and
faithfull subjecte and
servante.
A.S.

The underlined portions of this text are underlined in the manuscript, with Stuart's responses to the words recorded by a secretary in the margins. Next to the promise to undergo the journey is "that without the Jorney is inoughe yf the King desire but his honor salved./" Beside the commitment to offer no resis-tance is "as thoughe I had made resistans etc. and so the Jorney more perilous and painefull by my selfe whereuppon I must confess I bely my selfe extreemely in this." To the duty she owes James as her sovereign, she comments, "I take it to bee more then I owe by my allegiance to be separated from my husband duringe his pleasure". To the words about James's grace and her case, she says, "what man of grace this is I cannot guess nor in what case I am." To the clause about her obedient heart, she notes, "he hath hadd better profe[r]s [*of*] then this and as thoughe none but this would serve./"

Why she would have had her comments recorded is unclear; nor is it certain that this version was the one that so gratified King James, although Stuart was granted a second month's respite, as she requested here. During that time, Stu-art planned her escape.

Appendix A
LATIN LETTERS OF LADY ARBELLA STUART

AI
TO SIR ANDREW SINCLAIR

Secretary's copy, BL Harley MS 7003, f. 52. Addressed "Illustrissimo Domino, Christiano Fris[io], Domino de Borebiu, regni Daniae Cancellario./." (For a translation, see letter 53.) Written 24 October 1606.

✣

Illustrissime Domine, humillimas ac debitas gratias Augustissimo Regi ac Reginae propter immenso eorum erga me benignitate[m] per has literas referendas curavi, quas si in regias utriusque manus tua Excellentia dare voluerit, verbisque suis me devotissima[m] et observantissimam utriusque Majestatis profitebitur, pergratum et peramicum mihi officium, et te plane dignum fecerit, dum ea comprobaveris quae in ore omnium de te feruntur, te summum scilicet divinorum honorum (nostrae autem gentis praecipue) apud regem fautorem esse. Caeterum humanitas tua erga me singularis, qui me tam honorifica salutatione apud classem condecorasti, quod lubentius et confidentius hoc abs te 10 peterem in causa fuit. Deus Optimus Maximus Excellentiam tuam incolumem servet./. Hamptoniae .24. October 1606.

Tuae Excellentiae
quae bene precatur,
A. S.

A2
TO KING CHRISTIAN OF DENMARK

Secretary's copy, BL Harley MS 7003, f. 53. No address. (For a translation, see letter 54.) Undated; perhaps written October 1606.

✣

Inter omnia quae divini numinis auxilio mihi faeliciter contigerunt,

---

Letter A1. Line 2. **immenso:** a grammatical error for immens*am*.
Line 4. **devotissima[m]:** The sheet is torn.

267

illud imprimis optatum et gratum fuisse fateor, quod Majestas vestra me in eorum numerum ascitam et ascriptam vellet, quos in memoria habere et favere dignatur. Quam quidem benignitatem vestram tum promereri tum conservare (quantum in me erit) conabor *impigrè*. Majestatem igitur vestram quam possum submisse rogo, ut laetissimis huiusmodi de sua suorumque faelicitate literis me beatam reddere saepius dignetur, quae si nullo alio officii genere me gratam praebuero, frequentissimis saltem precibus Deo Optimo Maximo orabo, ut semper
10 eadem vobis scribendi, et mihi, lice[a]t humiliter, vere tamen et ex animo laetandi materia detur. Quamvis autem cum sum nescia Majestatem vestram de Incolumitate Serenissimorum principum nostrorum, charisi consanguin[ei] suorum, quotidie certiorem fieri, liceat mihi tamen illud hissce literis inferere, qua re sicut nihil utrinque scriptu lectuuè iucundius, ita mihi <sane> nihil [*sane*] aptius, quam ex illo faelicissimo affinitatis vestrae vinculo, Majestatis vestrae non omnino alienam me videri spero: Ideoque propensiori benignitate vestra non audacter freta, dabo operam ut nulla vel scribendi occasio, vel debitum officium praestandi ausa, (quam haec Majestati vestrae non
20 iniucunda futura existimam) mihi excidat e manu. Deus Optimus Maximus Majestatem vestram secundum supraque sua vota omnia tum publica tum domestica faelicitate beare velit.

A3
TO KING CHRISTIAN OF DENMARK

Secretary's copy, BL Harley MS 7003, f. 51. Addressed "Augustissimo Principi Christiano Dei gratia Daniae, Norvagiae, Vandalorum Gottorumque Regi, Duci Schlesvici, Holsatiae, Stormariae et Dittmarsiae, Comiti in Oldenburg et Delmenhort Patrono suo observandissime." and "Augustissimo Principi Christiano quarto Dei gratia Daniae, Norvagiae, Vandalorum Gottorumque Regi, Duci Schlesvici, Holsatiae, Stormariae et Dittmarsiae, Comiti in Oldenburg et Delmenhort, suae Majestatis devotissima Arbella Stuarta perpetuam et cumulatam faelicitatem a Deo Optimo Maximo precatur./." (For a translation, see letter 55.) Written 24 October 1606.

Letter A2. Line 5. **impigrè:** This word, unlike the rest of the text, is in an italic style of handwriting.

❧

Cum sui ipsius literis me de faelicissimo suo reditu ac praesenti incolumitati certiorem fieri dignata sit Majestas vestra, quam possum maximas et humillimas retribuo gratias ac duplici me fateor gaudio affici, cum et optatissimum nuntium, et quod mihi longe praemium in votis erat (idque a vestra manu) acceperim, tum quod eundem locum in animo vestro regio me possidere videam, quo benignitas et gratia vestra me dudum constituerat. Atque haec vestra modo memoria neque absentia dilata neque maximorum negotiorum multitudine (quibus vestram Majestatem tam breviter post reditum in patriam p[a]ene obrui necesse est) alienata, sed potius radiorum insulae ac propriae suae   10
benignitatis reflexu adaucta, rem mihi lautam solatio, sed et perpetuo ac honoratissimo simul testimonio quibuscunque fuerit, nemini qui Majestati vestrae animum rite devotum attulerit (licet meritis destituto) esse desperandum, quin et gratiae aliquid apud vestram Majestatam gradum (eumque longe praeter meritum) assequatur, et assequatum firmiter retineat: cum eadem quae attraxerit atque in suorum numerum ascripserit benignitas ac gratia, suos etiam in memoria habere ac fovere dignetur. Liceat autem deinceps ex Majestatis vestrae jussu devotissimi animi et obsequii mei aliquod per literas specimen praebere, adeoque (cum res postulaverit) clarissimi nominis vestri opem et auxilium in   20
rebus meis praemovendis petere. Quam quidem piam operam neque ullo modo irritam fore spero, neque male collocatam polliceor, cum in animum memorem ac gratum Majestatis vestrae suam benignitatem exerceat. Deus Optimus Maximus Majestatem vestram summa quaque faelicitate augeat, et quam diutissime tueatur./. Hampton. 24 October 1606

Majestati. vestrae devotissime ac devinctissime

Ar. St./.

A4

TO QUEEN ANNA CATHRINE OF DENMARK

Secretary's copy, BL Harley MS 7003, f. 51. Addressed twice, "Augustissimae Annae Catharinae dei gratia Daniae et Reginae, Electoralis Brandenburgensis Stirpis, Ducissae in Schlesvicia et Comitissae in Oldenburg et ut supra./." and, in left margin, "Augustissimae principi Annae Catharinae Dei gratia Daniae,

Norvagiae, Vandalorum Gottorumque Reginae Ducissae in Schlesvicia, Holsatia, Stormaria et Dittmarsia, Comitisse in Oldenburg et Delmenhort./." (For Stuart's English version, see letter 56.) Written 24 October 1606.

※

Augustissima Regina, humillimas Majestati vestrae gratias ago, cum tam serena fronte minusculum quod vestrae Majestati ausa sum in devoti animi testimonium offerre dignata sit accipere et me tam insigni favoris sui indicio honestare. Quod antehac erga Majestatem vestram ausa sum, id omne benignitati Augustissimi regis, coniugis vestri dilectissimi attribuendum, [*velim,*] cum eandem morum suavitatem qua ille est proditus, in vestra quoque Majestate sperarem inesse. Qua quidem in conjectura cum me non falsam animi benignissimae vestrae literae testantur, additum mihi animum sentio, ut posthac symbolo aliquo mea manu contexto, observantiam et singularem humillimamque animi propensionem erga Majestatem vestram saepius tester, atque simul ut eadem opera firmius in memoria ac gratia vestra haeream; quod ut mihi contingat, semper in summis mihi votis erit. Deus Optimus Maximus Majestatem vestram summa quoque faelicitate beet, et quam diutissime tueatur. Hampton. 24. October 1606.

Majestati vestrae devotissime ac devinctissime.

Ar. St./.

A5

TO SIR ANDREW SINCLAIR

Secretary's copy, BL Harley MS 7003, f. 54. Addressed "Illustrissimo Domino, Christiano Fris[io], Domino de Borebiu, regni Daniae Cancellario." (For a translation, see letter 59B.) Written 15 July 1607.

※

Illustrissime Domine, quam duplici officio mihi humanitatem tuam testatam volueris, dum non solum meas quas Regi Reginaeque dederam literas tradideris, sed et quas regi mihi vicissim dare visum est, ea plenas serenitate quam vix sperare quidem per meam mihi fortunam licuerit, eas mihi transmittendas curaveris, utroque nomine gratias tibi quam possum maximas ago, quaesoque (vir Amplissime) ut quemadmodum facis, gratiam meam apud Augustissimam Celsissimamque Regiam Regineamque Majestatem favere progas. Has ego nunc regi potentis-

simo literas, et haec reginae serenissimae exiqua munuscula mittenda
censui, quae ut tua opera potentissimis principibus cum iis quae me   10
decent, quaeque tu rectissime calles, humilitatis et observantiae indiciis
offerantur, tuam Amplissimam Dignitatem exoratam iterum atque
iterum velim. Praefata interim (si ea tibi per tuam occupatissimam vitae
rationem his officiis sine molestia perfungi vacaverit quemadmodum ea
me libere profiteor nemini debituram libentius alteri) laetari me serio
eum me nactam adversus[.] Celsissimos principes rerum mearum Inter-
pretam qui per ea qua est prudentia, mollissimorumque Regiorum adi-
tuum intelligentia, haec quae mitto parum sua vi specieve freta, ea
saltem gratia ornabit, quam afferre rebus offerentis fides et benevolentia, et recta atque opportuna eorum quae destinantur exhibendi tra-   20
dendique ratio solet. Crescat tibi (Illustrissime vir) cum vita decus et
gloria. Ab Aula Regia Theobaldi .15. July. 1607.

A6
TO KING CHRISTIAN OF DENMARK

Secretary's copy, BL Harley MS 7003, f. 54. Addressed "Augustissimo Principi
Christiano quarto Dei gratia Daniae, Norvagiae, Vandalorum, Gottorumque
Regi, Duci Schlesvici, Holsatiae, Stormariae, et Dittmarsiae, Comiti in Oldenburg et Delmenhort, Patrono suo observandissime./." (For a translation, see letter 60.) Written 15 July 1607.

🌿

Augustissime, Serenissime ac Potentissime rex, praeelectis Augustissimae Majestatis vestrae literis maximo profundetur gaudio, quam me a
tanto rege diligi honorarique perspicerem, cuius in me favenda constan-
tiam si per merita mihi augere liceret pleniori voto cum ambirem: At
cum praeter animi propensionem nihil aliud supersit, fida voluntate
obsequii pro[p]riu[s]plebo quod debitis officis adimplere nequeo.
Tamen in quocunque fortunae statu fuero, Augustissima Majestas vestra
pronam mihi semper fore mentem et defixum in sua obsequia animum
sine fuco comperiet; praesertim cum tam benigne Majestas vestra ad
meos usus et commoda immensam suam benignitatem offerat; quam   10
non dubitanter amplector, certa eam (exoriente occasione) mihi nec
inutilem, nec defuturam. Caeterem Deum Optimum Maximum ut

semper florentem incolum[n]emque Augustissimam Majestatem vestram quam diutissime conservet submissis genibus rogo. Ab Aula regia Theobaldi. 15. July. 1607.

> Majestati vestrae
> devotissime et devinctissime
> Ar. Stuarta./.

A7

TO SIR ANDREW SINCLAIR

Secretary's draft, with autograph address in Stuart's informal hand, BL Harley MS 7003, f. 50. Addressed "Illustrissimo viro Domino Christiano Frisio Regni Daniae Cancellario./" (For a translation, see letter 63.) Written February 1607/8.

✻

Accepi literas Illustritatis vestrae quas mihi postremas dedit, quibus me certiorem fecit, literas quas ad [*invictiss*] <Augustissimum> Regem [*ded*] haud ita pridem dederam, et exigua quae serenissimae Reginae [*desti-naveram*] <miseram> munuscula, Potentissimis Principiis [*vestrae ope*] Illustritatis vestrae opera reddita, haud ingrata extitisse, quod mihi sane jucundissime accidisse fateor, et, in eo, quid ab illustritate vestra prae-stitum fuerit facile agnossco, sed cum non hoc nunc primo humanitatis officio me sibi devinctam teneat, jure suo optimo, Illustritatis vestra, a me, eas vices repetet, (si quando occasionem fors obtulerit) quas et Illus-
10 tritatis vestrae [*in m*] summa in me merita postulant, et ego deberi numquam non libere profitebor. neque enim caelare possum post mutuam hanc officiorum contestatam vicissitudinem, invitam me ab Illustritatis vestra benevolentia atque humanitatis argumentis [*semper*] vinci. Optabo semper ut Illustritati vestrae succedant [*omnia*] omnia faeliciter, [*ut in te valetudo in semper comitem habeat gloriam gloriam, gloria felicitatem perpetuam*]. Data.   die.   february apud .<u>1607</u>
    Precabor Illustritatis vestrae constantem valetudinem et perpetuam faelictatem quibus mihi [*nihil*] <vix quicquam> accidere posse optabil-ius Intelligere Illustritatem vestram non diffido

---

Letter A7. Line 16. **Data:** After this word, the secretary has left space for the location to be added; similarly after *die* space has been provided for the day of the month to be inserted.
Line 18. **<vix quicquam>:** a revision which weakens the *nothing* of *nihil.*

A8

TO KING CHRISTIAN OF DENMARK

Secretary's copy, the James Marshall and Marie-Louise Osborn Collection, the Beinecke Rare Book and Manuscript Library, Yale University, Osborn Files 37.88. (For a translation, see letter 64.) Written 28 February 1607/8, dated in the docket.

꙳

Augustissime ac Potentissime Rex

Ex postremis Majestatis vestrae unis litteris, duo quae mihi in votis maxime serene sunt ut intelligerem [*factum*] <datum> est. Primun Gratiae qua me apud celsissimam Majestatem vestram florere glorior non modo nihil decessisse, sed etiam accessiorem (si fieri possit) factam. Alterum Majestatis vestrae res omnes ita prospere et faeliciter comparatas esse ut laetari omnes jure possent amici (quos ego universum orbem Christianum interpretor) quibus id innotescat. Addam etiam cum Serenissimae Majestatis vestrae bona venia tertium, quod mihi jucundum sane advenit, non indignam scilicet me habitam quam tantae laeticeae   10
participem faceret Invictissima Majestas vestra, quibus rebus ita <me gaudio> exultare [*acce*] fateor, ut quam inde voluptatem ceperim nullis litterarum notis exprim[*ere*]<i> posse[*m*] <credam>. **Et quanquam fortunae meae jure succenseam quae in hisce debitorum meorum cumulis et accessioribus [*(non* [   ] *sim*] saltem unde non indigna tanti Regis patrocinio et gratia videor, nihil plane suppeditet, tamen aeque mihi ferendum esse non censui, si cum animom (qui mihi unus est) in obsequium vestrae Majestati successisse utrum mihi probe conscia sim, aliud quippiam quod pro summis Majestatis vestrae in me meritis devote offerem non habeam; Nam et [*ipsis*] Principibus Magnamimis   20
ipsa est magnificentia pro praemis, et me jure non dedeceat si quam gloriam Invictissima majestas vestra ex animi magnitudine et beneficentia iam dudum adepta et eam ego ex obsequio quaeram atque observantia** supplex Oro summum Deum ut hanc pergat Majestati vestrae fortunare faelicitatem ut rebus omnibus <vobis> ad [*Majestatis vestrae*]

Line 15. [**(non** [   ] **sim**]: I cannot read two deleted words in this phrase.

animi sententiam prospere fluentibus universa Majestatis vestrae Regna
tanto Rege ego tanto Patrono quam diutissime gaudeamus incolumi.

The sentence that follows, written in the margin, may have been a postscript or
a replacement for the section deleted above.

❦

quod si in hoc tempore officio meo non videbor satisfecisse, Rogo,
obtestorque ut id potentissima Majestas vestra illustrissima proaviae
30 meae comitissae salopiensi deferet quae nuperrime vita functa triste tum
suis omnibus tum mihi imprimis ejus desiderium relinquens omnem
abstulit ejus obsequii exprimendi facultatem quod ego vestrae Majestatis summis in me meritis deberi semper non possem non profiteri.

A9
TO KING CHRISTIAN OF DENMARK

Secretary's copy, BL Harley MS 7003, f. 37. No formal address. (For a translation, see letter 65.) Written 1607/8, likely 15 March, since it appears on the
same sheet as the copy of letter 67.

❦

Augustissime ac Potentissime Rex

Pauci dies praeterlapsi sunt, postquam superiores meas ad Augustissimam Majestatem vestram dederam, cum Celsissimae ac Serenissimae
Reginae nostrae allatae <ad me> litterae sunt, ex quibus intellexi, cupere
Majestatem vestram ut famulus meus Thomas Cottinges, qui has nunc
(nisi Deus non vult) perfert, ad eam mitteretur, ut ejus opera inter pul-
sandae Cytherae peritos uti posset. Ac profecto, quanquam et is mihi
gratus inter paucos illius artis peritos existat, et non nesciam, in fortuna
Regia, ad quam potissimum omnia exquisitissima studia, vota, ingenia,
10 et operae tum in hac, tum in caeteris artibus, expeditissima diriguntur,
facilius esse [*numerum adhibere*] eorum qui maxime in quavis arte excel-

---

Letter A8. Line 27. **ego:** an error for *et.*

Line 29. **proaviae:** an error for *aviae.*   Line 30. **salopiensi:** a Latinized form of *Shrewsbury.*

Letter A9. Line 7. **Cytherae:** an error for *Citharae.*

lunt, numerum adhibere, quam modum, Tamen cum nihil ipsa dilligentius investigaverim, aut ambitiosius, quam eam occasionem, quae mihi exprimendi officii mei, atque animi in obsequium vestrae Majestatis addictissimi, facultatem suppeditaret, han[c] demum, quantulamcunque, opportune sese offerentem, libentissime arripui, et quem, exquisitissimis magistris traditum, et in meam gratiam, in hac arte instructum, haud cum levi, tum artis, tum morum ingenuitatis, comendatione accepi, hunc eundem, haud levius (modo id cum vestrae Majestatis bona venia fiat) comendatum vestrae Majestati mitto, mis-   20 sura (si aeque possem) Orpheum, aut Apollinem[.] Precor sumum Deum ut ad animi sententiam non in choro tantum et Aula, sed in vita, etiam [*ac*] <et> Regno omnia Majestati vestrae consonent ac conspirent. Dat: die: 1607.

Line 15. **han[c]:** The writing runs off the paper.   Line 21. **sumum:** an error for *summum*

Appendix B
LETTERS TO LADY ARBELLA STUART

BI

FROM KING JAMES

Copy, BL Add. MS 35844, f. 235. No address; docketed "Inclossd Copie of a letter to Arabella from the Kinge". Undated; likely his earliest to her, dated in BL *Catalogue of Additions* as 23 December 1591.

It is unclear whether this letter was sent; it may have been a draft of the letter that follows.

❧

A letter to Arabella from the King.

As the straict band of nature and blood, whereby we ar linked to other, craveth a most entier good will and mutuall intelligence to be inter-teyned betwixt us: so have we of longe tyme caried a most earnest deseir to contract that acquentance by lettres, as witnesses of the conjunction of hartes, [*with*] <which> our so far distant bodyes will not permit; being frome our harte most glade of this first occasion offered, aftir knawledge had of the more sure place of your abode; the incertantye quhairof till now must serve for excuse of our so long silence, with hav-
10 ing resolved, for our pairt, to recompense by a more frequent inter-course and reciproc correspondence/ these presentes shalbe to utter, with what great joy and contentment we have hard of the rare partes it hes pleased God to endew you withall, to your no small praise, and the great honour of that house wherof we ar both yssued; augmenting thairby so farre the obligation wherinto we stand bound, that we thinke it not sufficient to mak offer of all freindlie offices, and whatsumever can be expected from a most assured freind, and kyndlie affected kinse-man: wherof you may [*be*] <rest> assured insu[ch]sort, as yf occasion offer (whiche shall fall out to our desired wishe) in anye thing wherein
20 our favour may be showen, as may [*your*] <give> large [*promise*] <pruif> and testimonye of the Loving affection we carye towards so deir a Cousine

Line 9. **quhairof:** whereof.

B2

FROM KING JAMES

Secretary's copy, BL Stowe MS 158, f. 31. Addressed "To Our dearest Cousine The Lady Arbella". File copy in State Papers, Scottish, Eliz., vol. 47, f. 123. Written 23 December 1591.

✣

Although the natural bande of bloode my deare Cousine be sufficient for the good Intertenements of amitye yet will I not absteine from these common Offices of Letters having now so long keeped silence till your fame and report of so good parts in you have interpelled me, And as I can not bot in hearte rejoyse so can I not forebeare to signifye to you hereby what contentment I have receaved hearing of your so vertiouse behaviour wherein I pray you most hartelye to continew not that I doubt thereof being certified of so full concurse of nature and nouriture, bot that you may be the more encouraged to proceade in your ver- tiouse demeanour reaping the fruit of so honest estimation, the   10 encreasse of your honour and Joye of your kindelye affected freinds, speciallye of me whome it pleaseth most to sie soe vertuouse and honor- able Syons arise of that race whereof we have our discent. Now having more certane notice of the place of your abode, I will the more fre- quentlye visite you by my Letters, which I would be glade to do in per- son expecting also to knowe from time to time of your Estate by your owen hand which I looke you will not wearye to doe being firste sum- moned by me, and knowing how farre I shal be pleased thereby, In the meane while to next occasion of fordor knowledge of your State, after my hartiest comendaccion I wishe you my deare Cousine of God all   20 honour and hartye contentment.

From Halroude house the xxiii of December 1591

Your Loving and affectionatt Cousin

James R.

Line 4. **interpelled me:** interrupted me, come to my attention.
Line 22. **Halroude house:** Holyroodhouse, the palace in Edinburgh.

B3
FROM JOHN DODDERIDGE

Autograph, Cecil Papers 135, f. 108; docketed "1602 Daudrig letter to the Lady Arbella". Undated; written 30 December 1602, according to the report in Cecil Papers 135, ff. 179–80.

Stuart was not permitted to receive this letter from her grandmother's distressed servant, and Dodderidge was imprisoned for his part in her attempted engagement. Upon his release, he joined Stuart's household and was one of the yeoman servants who remained with her after her marriage and imprisonment.

🜊

May it please your honour, my Entertainement here, is Contrarye to all expectacion, soe that except your honour fully Satisfye this bearer, my Lord willnot think otherwayes of me, but that I am som Counterfet, and soe am in daunger of Trouble,./ for I have Signifyed to his Lordship that I am sent by m^r henry, and m^r william Cavendish, wherof [*they*] my Lord must be fully Satisfyed, and til my Lord be Resolved therof, I must Rest his honours pleasure,./ I beseech your honour therfore to Consider the Estate I am in, for I would be sory to doe any thing that may be offensive any way, to anye./

Your honours in what I
may without offence to
[*ay*] anye./
John Daudridge

10

B4
FROM GEORGE CHAWORTH

Autograph, Cecil Papers 135, f. 169/2. Addressed "To the Right honorable my verye good Ladye the Ladye Arbella at Hardwicke/ speedelye./" Written Tuesday, 15 March 1602/3; other contemporary texts indicate that Chaworth was correct about the day of the week as he wrote this letter, but confused about the date, which he twice noted as 17 March and once altered to 16 March.

This letter from Stuart's gentleman servant about affairs in London was written a little over a week before Queen Elizabeth's death. Despite Sir Henry Brounker's protestations to the contrary when he spoke with Chaworth,

---

Letter B3. Line 3. **Lord:** the Earl of Hertford.

Line 5. **m^r henry...Cavendish:** Stuart's maternal uncles.

Brounker indeed was riding toward Hardwick Hall. Stuart had attempted on 10 March to escape with her uncle Henry Cavendish and a group of supporters, as a result of which Brounker was ordered to investigate and to ensure that the north country remained secure. He intercepted Chaworth's letter and forwarded it to Sir Robert Cecil.

Chaworth remained close to Stuart for many years afterwards; nearly a decade later Stuart requested that Lady Chaworth, presumably his wife, the former Mary Kniveton of Derbyshire, be allowed to attend her in the Tower (BL Harley MS 7003, f. 72). The Chaworths named their children *Gilbert* and *Arbella*.

🜨

my servis remembred in all humiletye to your worthe honor
Maye yt please your honor to understand. that I presently after the recept of your honores letteres (whic was the 15th of march presently after dinner) I went and delivered them in al the speede possible to Sir Henrye and had delivered your honors [*letters*] letter which came by Ned Franke before Travis had delivered his letter from my old Ladye. what he sayed I leave till the next messenger. but he appoynted me to come to him the next daye and I should have aunsuer with out fayle and that I should fynd him within with out fayle—I went the next daye beinge this nowe present Tusedaye the 17th of march—and found him   10
gone from court, I went to my cosen Carres she was with the Queene for she ys sicke though courtiers saye contrarye—I was there asured that yf I spoke to [*her*] my cosen for your honor I should be hard and yt would be well accepted and that she would doe any thinge she could for your honor and the rather because my old Ladye sayed her naye in disgrasefull sort when she presented to her servis my cosen Quarles[,] this her c[h]ambermayed told me—and I meane to goe againe

---

Line 3. **15th of march:** an error for 14 March.   Lines 4–5. **Sir Henrye:** Sir Henry Brounker.

Line 6. **Travis:** Henry Travis, one of Bess of Hardwick's servants.

Line 6. **old Ladye:** Stuart's grandmother, Bess of Hardwick.

Line 10. **17th of march:** an error for 15 March.

Line 11. **cosen Carres:** Bridget Carr was a Gentlewoman of Queen Elizabeth's Privy Chamber.

Line 13. **hard:** heard.

Line 16. **cosen Quarles:** likely one of the Quarles of Ufford in Northamptonshire; Bridget Carr's sister Catherine had married into that family.

tomorrowe to move my selfe for your honor what I can and so assure
your selfe—but to the matter. I better bethought me of Sir Henryes
20 goinge from court against his promise made to me—I presently
departed posted to the howse with all speede at Lambeth—he was gone
from thence post as they told me into the cuntrye—I followed him to
knowe the cause of his sudden goinge—I overtooke him and as I perseved against his will—I feyned to him that I had matteres reported of
his goinge downe (which in deede I had not) as that he went to fetch
your honor to Toware—or to London, or to procure your honors
streight keepeinge in the cuntrye and hard usage from my old Ladye—
all which he with solleme protestations denyed—sayinge he went nott
to your honor but about her magestyes busines in to Nottinghamshire
30 not to Hardwicke except he went in kyndnes to see my old Ladye els he
protests he hath nothinge to speake to your honor nor will not anye
more of this matter. because he hath you not at anye certentye but in a
hundred myndes and that you saye and unsaye and divers severall
thinges, he protestes to me there ys noe hurt meant to your honor but
all good—as I [*thinge*] thinke (by his askinge me how far yt was to Haddon) he goeth to master Maneres and whether to bringe master George
up or noe I knowe not—or els to give chardge that you be nott suffered
to passe through the cuntrye or to give chardge to the gentle men in the
cuntrye or els northward that none helpe your honor awaye <(these be
40 only my foolishe conjecturs.)>—for as I heare the poste northward be
stopped all redye—I thought yt not amisse to certefye your honor thus
much yf yt was possible before his cumminge to the cuntrye—which I
hope I doe though this messenger I am assured was at his furst settinge
forth as I thinke at least 10 myles behynt him: but I gave him streight
chardge to poste nyght and daye with out rest as I hope he hath donne
or els I would he was hanged. his name ys Hutchinson—I have

Lines 23–24. **perseved:** perceived.   Line 26. **Toware:** the Tower of London.

Lines 35–36. **Haddon:** Haddon Hall, about fifteen miles from Hardwick Hall, was the family
seat of Sir George Manners's mother, the former Dorothy Vernon. Chaworth's comments
indicate that he feared George Manners was suspected of aiding Stuart.

Lines 39–40. <(**these…conjecturs.**)>: The addition is written in the margin along this section
of text.

delivered him 3^{l} 5^{s} for his chardges referringe his labor as he shall deserve by his hast—my good will to your honor made me write thus much which peradventure your honor will thinke needeles: but in my foolishnes (yf your honor so terme yt) I thought yt not amisse but con- 50 venient, because of the suddennes of his cominge downe but let this suffise your honor that yf yt be my follye my love to your honor made me foolish—Thus in all hast

Your honores true servant
to death
George Chaworth

I wish your honor all happines this present Tusedaye in the afternoone, halfe an howre past 4 a cloke—beinge the [*17*]<16>th of march—I will ansuer your honor for other matters in letteres tomorrowe by Dringe— in the interim let yt suffice your honor master Holford is well and at lib- 60 ertye and will be with your honor so soone as his ague will suffer him— I will write more of him by dringe

B5
FROM JAMES HUDSON

Autograph, Folger MS X.d.428 (36). Addressed "To the Right honorable and My very singullar good lady My lady arrebella hir grace dede at the Courtt." Written 24 February 1605/6.
   James Hudson was a Groom of King James's Privy Chamber.

�につい

Right honorable and my very good lady
It mae pleas your grace
This bearer is the power man namid Richard lassye, upon whome your grace hath bein so long dessyruss to showe sume part of your honorable piettye and charetty whome by chance this dae I mett in the streits and becaws your grace hath dyverss tymes sent to me to inqwyer of hime I

Letter B4. Line 60. **master Holford:** a friend who had been called to London for examination of his part in Stuart's attempted marriage.
Letter B5. Headnote. **dede:** Latin, the imperative form of *deliver.*
Line 3. **power:** poor.

have takin this boldness to signeffye thus muche to your grace by wryt-
ting and so praing god to presserve your grace I humble taek my leave
and ever Remayne

10   London this 24 of   your grassis most
    February /<u>1605</u>/   humble to Comand
                                       with service
                                         Ja. hudson

B6

FROM SIR ANDREW SINCLAIR

Autograph, BL Harley MS 7003, f. 41. Addressed "To the Ryght honourable
The Laydy Arabella." Undated; written August 1606.
    While King Christian IV of Denmark was in England, he made a comment
disparaging Lady Nottingham, to which she objected in a letter to Christian's
Lord Chamberlain, the Scottish Sir Andrew Sinclair. For Stuart's response, see
letter 51.

※

Madame, the Kinge my maister hes comandett me to vrett his gratious
commendations to your Laydyship and to advertis your Laydyship that
my Laydy Nothingeheme, hes vretten to me this morninge ane letter
that hir Laydyship [*Layd*] hes maid, [giving] the Kinge my maister
Notice of sum spitches his magestie sould heve spoken of hir to hir
desadvantage, as your Laydyship may perceve be the letter chi hes
vretten to me, the which the Kinge hes send to the Queinnes Magestie
his suster, since <his> Magesties Desayr is that your Laydyship vell
Defend his Magesties Innocencie in sutche thinges as his Magestie is
10   assured that hi is unjustly accussett of. the Queinnes Magestie vell chau
your Laydyship the letter sune[.] I rest ever and allwayes

                               Your Laydyships humble
                                    and faithefull
                                    frind to do your
                                    Laydyship Service
                                    Andres SinClar

vretten in grett haist

Letter B6. Line 1. **vrett:** write.   Line 6. **chi:** she.   Line 10. **chau:** show.

B7

FROM SIR ANDREW SINCLAIR

Autograph, BL Harley MS 7003, ff. 46–47. Addressed "To the Ryght honourable The Laydy Arbella." Written 26 August 1606.

❧

My humble Deutie being Remembered maist vordy Laydy, it hes plaisett bothe thair Magesties to command me to vrett thair Most gratious
Recommendations to your Laydyship and to thank your Laydyship for
the honnest favours it hes plaisett your Laydyship to bestou on bothe
thair Magesties. the Queene in speciall estimes Mutche of that present
your Laydyship hes send hir Magestie and sayes that hir Magestie vell
vair it for your Laydyships saike[,] the Kinge hes commandett me to
assure your Laydyship that thair is no honnour advancement nor plais-
our, that his Magestie kand do your Laydyship bot hi sall do it faithe-
fully, and vellingly, as one of the beste frends your Laydyship hes in the   10
varld, Surly I man confesse vithe verretie, that I never hard no Prince,
speik moire vordely of a prinsses, than hi does, of your Laydyships good
qualeties and rare vertus, veill I say no more bot I salbe ane faithefull
Instrument to Interteny that holly frindchep betuix his Magestie and
your Laydyship. as tutchinge My Laydy Nottinghams the Kinge is nou
verri veill content vithe hir Laydyship becaus hir letter vais vretten of a
laytell colerique passion, grundett on ane fekless Raporte for his Magestie dede Never think that hir Laydyship haid offendet him, bot only
thois that vais the Raporters of sutche fulliche vords to hir, for if so haid
beine that hi ded speik sum merry vordes in gesting it vais <not> the   20
Deutie of men of honnour (as hir Laydyship makes mention in hir Letter) to heve Rapportet againe to hir sutche thinges of no effek, and as
for my part Madame, I protest befor the living god I cheu not the Kinge
hir letter be Malice, bot be Deutie touards my gracious maister, for if I
haid not chauen him the letter I haid bine in Denger of a perpetuall

---

Line 1. **vordy:** worthy.   Line 7. **vair:** wear.

Line 11. **Surly:** surely.   **hard:** heard.   Line 13. **veill:** well.

Line 14. **Interteny:** entertain; maintain.   **holly:** holy.

Line 17. **laytell:** little.   **grundett:** grounded.   Line 19. **fulliche:** foolish.

Line 23. **cheu:** shew; showed.   Line 25. **chauen:** shown.

Desgrace, sue I pray your Laydyship (that if onny speik to my Desadvantage in this matter in Deschergine my oblist Deuti to my maister) at your Laydyship vell ansour for me as for one that hes alluayes Dedicat him self to do your Laydyship all the honnour and service that layes in
30   my pouer[,] as I confess my self to be perpetually oblist to your Laydyship sue in this Inviolable honnest Devotion I taik my live and commettes your Laydyship to the lords eternelle protection From Court at Kioffenhaffn the .26. agust .1606.

your Laydyships oblist treu frend
to do you Service
Andres SinClar.

B8

FROM QUEEN ANNA

Secretary's hand with the queen's autograph signature, BL Harley MS 6986, ff. 74–75. Addressed "To our Most honorable and Welbeloved Cousine The Ladye Arbella Stuart". Written 9 March 1607/8.

King Christian IV of Denmark, a well-known patron of musicians, may have requested that Stuart's lutenist be sent to him, as Queen Anna indicates here; or he may have requested any good lutenist and it was Queen Anna who selected Stuart's, as Prince Henry suggests in Appendix B, letter 9. For Stuart's replies, see letters 65–67.

꙳

Anna. R.
Weelbeloved Cousine We greete you hartlye well. Udo Gal our deere brothers the king off denmarks gentleman servant haith insisted with us, for the Licensing your servant Thomas Cottings to depart from you but not without your permission to our brothers service. and therefor we wryte these fewe lynes unto you, being assured your Ladyship will mak no difficultie, to satisfie our pleasour and our deere brothers desires. and so geving you the assurance off our constant favours, with

---

Letter B7. Line 27. **oblist:** obliged.   Line 31. **live:** leave.   Line 33. **Kioffenhaffn:** Copenhagen.
Letter B8. Line 2. **Udo:** Guido.   Line 4. **Thomas Cottings:** Thomas Cutting.

our wishes for the conteneuance or convalescence of your helth, exspecting your returne we committ your Ladyship to the protection of   10
god. from Whythall 9. March 1607

B9
FROM PRINCE HENRY

Autograph, BL Harley MS 6986, ff. 76–77. Addressed "A Madame Arbelle ma Cousine". Undated; written early March 1607/8, as was his mother's letter, Appendix B, letter 8.
     Prince Henry was fourteen years old.

🌿

Madam, the Queenes Majesty hath commaunded me to signifie to your Ladyship that shee would <have> Cutting your Ladyships servaunt to send to the King of Denmark because he desyred the Queen that shee would send him one that could play upon the lute. I pray your Lady-ship [*tha*] to send him back with ane answere assoone as your Ladyship can. I desyre you to commend me to my Lord and my Lady Shrewsbury and also not bethink me anything the worse scrivener etc that I write so ill but to suspend your jugement till you come hither then you shal find <me> as I was ever.

Your Ladyships loving   10
cousin and assured
freind
P Henry

BIO
FROM SIR JOHN ELPHINSTONE

Autograph, Arundel Castle MSS, Autograph Letters 1585–1617, no. 158. Addressed "My Lady Arbella The coart". Written 9 March 1607/8.
     This letter almost certainly was written by Sir John Elphinstone, Gentleman Usher to Queen Anna; he was a friend to Stuart and a cousin to Sir Andrew Sinclair, with whom he also corresponded.

Letter B9. Headnote. **A...Cousine:** To Lady Arbella my Cousin.
Line 6. **Lord...Shrewsbury:** Stuart's uncle and aunt, Gilbert and Mary Talbot, whom she would see, since she was visiting in the north after the death of her grandmother.

🦋

Madame this day I resavit your ladyships letters frome hardwick wrettne
the 23 of februarii hafing the day befor mad ansr to your ladyships
frome sheffeild the last therof wherby your ladyship may<t> know how
far yow ar beholdne to the carier if it had bene of any Importance. I haf
wrettne in my former letter this mater concerning maister cuttines your
mane that hes fallne out better nor I lukt for hafing her majesties letter
of request with the prmies to haf your ladyships good will to him to go
wher I know yow will think him well bestowit, with good advyce cuttines hes careit him self well in this mater and deserves your ladyships
10   spetiall favour of recommending him to his majestie of denmark as your
ladyships mane and of your sending wherne I hoip your ladyship will
wrett to his majestie if your helthe and layser may srve altho yow have
alredde wrettne this occasione cuming so suddenlie one letter more for
as also to recommend him being your ladyships mane to my cowsing sr
andrew sinclare who for your ladyships respect wilbe his good frend as I
shall do my best to the same effect for my dewtie to your ladyship and
his good cariage of him self in this mater and I think poore mane may
do your ladyship sim agreable srvice ther herefter for I think your ladyship may be ansrable for his good conditiones his uther qualeteis will
20   say sufficientlie for thame self[.] I am glad be this last letter of your ladyships being here at palme sonday whiche I beseik your ladyship not to
alter bot upone grett occasione and the farthest aganes ester for your
ladyship will have many turnes al this terme with king, law, frendes, and
sillie scheip who [*never*] will never have perking in Ingland bot for your
ladyships respect I wrett so muche of this in <my> former letter that I

Line 3. **sheffeild:** Sheffield, in Yorkshire, where the Talbots had two homes.

Line 4. **carier:** the letter carrier, who had been slow.

Line 5. **maister cuttines:** Thomas Cutting.

Line 7. **prmies...him:** promise that Cutting will leave for Denmark only if Stuart agrees.

Line 12. **layser:** leisure.   Line 14. **cowsing:** cousin.

Line 18. **sim:** some.   Line 19. **qualeteis:** qualities.

Line 22. **aganes ester:** against Easter.   Line 24. **scheip:** sheep.

Line 24. **have perking:** have parking; be enclosed in a park. The reference is unknown, but
likely alludes to one of Stuart's projects to obtain money, perhaps by raising sheep.

cane say no more bot, cing, cing, for I say in god all shall go well and your ladyship have helthe and be carefull to conserve the same without the whiche all the rest fare well. This day I delyverit to a carier send here be mr hamre your ladyships oncles mane a Barrele of salmons another of herrings and the thrid of dillis for my lady chatsworthes sake, as for fresche salmond ther was none to be had in our cuntre whene ther wer derect away for all was frossne Bot now evere day I luik for thame with the frestsches cumes frome our cuntre the carier promesis to have thame at chefeild this day senitt I pray god tha[*t*]<y> may gett <the> fiche and we here the fresche agane that tyme, her majestie the next weik gois to tibolles and meittes his majestie and palm sonday evine returnes together here I wrett this in grett hest as this berar cane shaw whiche makes me letter trublsim to your ladyship nor willinglie I wald be my hertlie srvice In all humeletie presentit I kis your ladyships handis and restis ever

30

40

your ladyships to be commandit
with srvice
Elphinstoin

I am wrayting one with your ladyships mater in law and my owne helthe whiche hes not bene very good sine your ladyships parting bot hoipis schortlie shalbe better with godes grace whythall the 9 of marche <u>1608</u>

Line 26. **cing:** sing.   Line 28. **all…well:** i.e., farewell to all the rest.

Line 29. **mr hamre:** perhaps William Hammond, servant to the Earl of Shrewsbury (Jamison, 231–32).

Line 30. **dillis:** dill pickles.   **lady chatsworthes:** Lady Chatsworth was Grace Cavendish, whose husband Henry had inherited Chatsworth when Bess of Hardwick died in February.

Line 32. **frossne:** frozen. The rivers where salmon came in the autumn to spawn would have been frozen in winter, when he had had a direct way to obtain the fish, presumably through a reliable carrier.

Line 33. **frestsches:** freshest.

Line 34. **chefeild:** Sheffield.   **this day senitt:** this day sennight; a week from today.

Line 35. **agane that tyme:** against that time; by then.

Line 36. **tibolles:** Theobalds, a royal residence in Middlesex.   **evine:** even; evening.

Line 38. **trublsim:** troublesome.   **wald:** would.   Line 44. **one:** i.e., another letter.

Appendix B

BII
FROM MARY MARKHAM

Autograph, Arundel Castle MSS, Autograph Letters 1585–1617, no. 170. Addressed "To the Ryght honorable My very good ladi, the ladi Arbella give thies". Written 11 April, no later than 1608. No year is indicated, but the letter must have been written before 1609, because William Markham was on Stuart's payroll in January 1610 (Seymour Papers 22). During the years Stuart was at court, 11 April fell after Easter (as Markham notes below) only in 1604, 1605, 1607, and 1608.

Mary Markham was the mother of eleven children, one of whom, Griffin, had participated in the Bye and Main plots in 1603, and another of whom, William, joined Stuart's entourage as a gentleman servant. He remained loyal to Stuart and was the man with whom she walked away from confinement in East Barnet when she attempted to escape to France.

☙

Ryght honorable

My homble dewte remembred with most homble thanks for your honorable favors to me And myn, I humbly besech your honor to pardon me, that I did not Send in eastar weak, Such was my bisynes As I was forsed to be from hom, I humbly besech your honor If It So pleas you that hi may have no man, bot be direkted And correkted, by eny It shalt pleas your ladiship to Apoynt, As also that It wilt pleas you to Apoynt my Sone <in> what collers and how It wilt pleas your honor to have him go, and It shalbe doon acordingly[,] Upon my knes I humbly
10 thank your honor It wilt pleas you to tak him, And what Serves I And myn be Able to dew, I humbly besech your ladiship to comaund us, and So resting At your honors Serves I humbly tak my leve praying god to preserve you In helthe with increas of honor

Rofford the xith
of aprill

your ladiships to
comaund
In all dewte And
Thankfolnes
mary markh<a>m

Line 4. **eastar weak:** Easter week.   Lines 6–7. **hi...Apoynt:** i.e., that he not have a personal manservant, but expect to obey those supervising him.

Line 8. **collers:** the colors of his livery, or uniform.

Line 14. **Rofford:** Rufford, in Nottinghamshire.

B12
FROM SIR JOHN HARINGTON OF EXTON

Autograph, Arundel Castle MSS, Autograph Letters 1585–1617, no. 169. Addressed "To the right honorable hir speciall good Lady the Lady Arbella Steward at the Court./" Written 19 November. No year is indicated, but the letter likely was written between 1604 and 1609, when Stuart was in favor and had access to Queen Anna, and perhaps toward the end of that time, when Harington would have been most involved in negotiations for Princess Elizabeth's marriage.

Queen Anna hoped that Princess Elizabeth would make a Roman Catholic marriage, and Sir John Harington of Exton, to whose care Elizabeth had been encharged, participated in protracted negotiations with Charles Emmanuel, Duke of Savoy, a Catholic. At the time Harington wrote this letter, negotiations either had broken down completely or appeared to have done so.

※

Most noble Lady

Geve mee leave thus boldly to put your honor in mynde of my humble suyt for acquaynting her Royall Majestie, with my endevor and proceeding, in the busynes concerning Duke Charles, allredy in part notyfyed to her highnes, though not in that fashion perhaps as I wold have wyshed.

I know soch affayrs are comonly wayed by the successe, and those that fayl that ys imputed allways to the execucion rather then the direccion But for meaner censurers I will not discorage my selfe, among whome I may bee styled a busy offycer withowt an offyce or soche lyke. Only I desyre that my soveraygn King and Queen may conceave, as the truthe ys, that my endeavors heerin have no other prospect nor retrospect, but my Loyall affection and dewty to them and theyr most deer Children whose good I wold purchase not with paper and Inke but with my best blood, as knoweth God to Whose holly proteccion I commit your honor remayning ever

19. Novembr: At your honors Comaundment.

                                                          John Haryngton./

Line 7. **wayed:** weighed; evaluated.

B13

FROM LADY ISABEL BOWES

Autograph, BL Harley MS 7003, ff. 55–56. Addressed "To the righte noble and moste worthie Lady the Lady Arbella these bee". Written 5 December 1609.

Stuart had visited her friend Lady Bowes at Walton Hall, Derbyshire, earlier in the year, and asked for help in locating a house in the country, away from court.

❦

Exelent Lady

I humbly thanke you that you woulde bee pleased to remember mee by your letter, I did hope I shoulde have seene your Ladyship in that place before this tyme but some occasion fell out to hinder my comminge upp for a while; I would bee gladd to heare howe your Ladyship proceedes in your Irishe sute: but I longe more to heare howe you keepe your health this weett winter./ I did not forgett to wryte to my brother St:Poole to knowe what house, or when it shalbee fitted for your Ladyship but I have receaved noe certayne answere yett; but I will not fayle
10 to bringe your Ladyship one my selfe; for I hope eare it bee longe to wayte on you there; if the dayes woulde growe a litle longer for travell, in the meane tyme and ever I cannot forgett to pray for your Ladyships health and happinesse acknowledginge my selfe more bounde to your Ladyship for your manifoulde favoures then to all the worlde besydes, and soe humbly take my leave, but will never leave to love and honour your Ladyship and soe ever reste./

Walton .5. of   Your honors in all
December. 1609   things
                                                   Issabell Bowes

B14

FROM MR WILLIAM SEYMOUR: A MESSENGER'S NOTE

Autograph, Seymour Papers 6, ff. 1–3. Docketed in the hand of the first Lord Weymouth, who married Seymour's granddaughter Frances: "A message sent by Mr William Seymour after Marquis of Hertford to a Lady (supposed to be Lady

---

Letter B13. Line 6. **Irishe sute:** the suit on Irish wines, in which Stuart was associated with Lady Bowes's brother, mentioned below.   Line 8. **St:Poole:** Sir George St. Paul.

Arabella:) that it was unfit to proceed further in the matter between them".
Undated; written between mid-February and May 1610.

Seymour had been called before the Privy Council on 10 February and said that while he and Stuart had discussed marriage, they would not have proceeded without King James's permission. It is unclear whether this message was ever delivered.

❦

I am com from Mr William Seymour with a message to your ladyship [*he hath w*] which was delivered unto me in <the> presence of this gentleman your servant and therefore your ladyship may be assured I will neyther add nor dimynish, but will truly relate [*what*] unto you[*r ladyship*] what he hath dyrected me to do. which is Thus; he hath seriously considered of the procedings betwene your ladyship and hym selfe and doth well perceve, if he should <go> on therein, it would not onely prove exceeding prejudiciall to your Contentment, but exstreame dangerous to hym, first in regard of the inequality of degrees betwene your Ladyship and hym, next the kings majesties pleasure and Comandment   10
to the Contra[r]y. which [*was meant intended sythe*] neyther your Ladyship or hym selfe did ever intend to neglect[.] he doth therefore [*he*] humbly desier your ladyship since the proceeding that is paste, doth <not> tye [*neyther*] hym nor your ladyship to any necessytie but [*the*] that you may Freely Comitt each other to [*theyr*] your best fortunes, that you would be pleased to desist from your intended resolution concerning hym, <who likewyse resolves not to truble you any more in this kinde> not doubting but your ladyship may [*gayne*] have one more fitter for your deegree (he having alredy presumed to hygh) and hym selfe a meaner match [*of*] <with> more securyty./   20

B15
FROM LADY JANE DRUMMOND

Autograph, BL Harley MS 7003, ff. 64–65. No address; docketed by Stuart's secretary "The Ladie Drummonds Letter to my Lady". Undated; likely written summer 1610.

After Stuart's marriage, she asked Lady Drummond, one of Queen Anna's Scottish attendants, for her appraisal of the situation (letter 78). For Stuart's response to the comments below, see letter 84.

❦

Madame

I resaivit your ladyships letter, and withit ane uther paepper which was just the sam words that was in the letter, bot your ladyship did not comand me to do anie thing with it, so as I can not imagin to what euse yee sent et, aluays I shall keip it to I know your ladyships plessur, yisterday being sonday I could have litle tym to spek with her majestie, bot this day her majestie heth sin your ladyships letter, her majestie sayes that when she gaive your ladyships pettition and letter to his majestie, he did taek et wellanuch, bot gaive no uther ansur then that yee had
10   etne of the forbidne trie, this was all her majestie comands me to say to your ladyship in this porpos, bot withall did remember her cyndly to your ladyship and sent you this litle tokne in wotnes of the contineuence of her majesties favor to your ladyship[.] now whar your ladyship dessyrs me to dell opnely and frily with you, I protest I can say nothing on knowleg, for I never spak to anie of that purpos bot to the quin, bot the wosdum of this stait, with the exsample, how sum of your qualitie, in the lyk caus hes bein uset, maeks me fer that yee shall not find so essie end to your truble, as yee expect, or I wisch, this is all I can say, and I should think my self happie if my notions could give better
20   testimonie of my truly being your ladyships

affectionat freind
to do you servic
Jane drumond

B16

FROM SIGNORE PROSPERO GORGES

Translated from an eighteenth-century transcript of the Italian original, Alnwick Castle MS 93A/35, Part 3. Docketed "Signor Prospero Gorges to the Lady Arbella". The British Library sold the unpublished original letter to W. Bindley on 25 October 1898; it is currently unlocated. Written 6 January 1610/11.

Stuart was in custody when she received this letter from Prospero Gorges, an Italian jeweler; she sent his bill for her husband's silk and amber points to her brother-in-law, and asked him to forward it to her aunt Mary Talbot (letter 92).

Letter B15. Line 5. **to:** until.   Line 9. **wellanuch:** well enough.

Line 10. **etne...trie:** eaten of the forbidden tree; an allusion to Eve's and Adam's sin of disobedience in the Garden of Eden.   Line 16. **quin:** queen.

🦎

Most illustrious and most excellent lady and patron
I did not believe, most excellent lady, that my illness was going to be as
long and serious as it has turned out to be. It has been close to five
months since I first tired from colic, then from a serious paralysis from
which my arms and hands remained crippled. I have been forced to stay
in bed, and in such a state, that except for my voice, I can call myself a
dead body. This, most excellent lady, was the reason I was not able to
make the visit I owe your excellence. I recognize that the great obliga-
tions I have towards you oblige me to make such a visit. The long illness,
the avarice of the doctors, the expensive services of this city, have drained   10
me in such a manner, both in body and in the little endurance that I had,
that now I find myself in need to count on all my friends, and patrons,
among whom I did not forget the loving-kindness of your excellence. I
resolve to kiss your hands, and to beg you to be my mediator with the
most excellent lady the Countess of Shrewsbury your aunt, who gives
many alms to the poor. I know that if she is assured by your excellence of
the miserable state I am in, from which I will not recover without a mira-
cle of God, I hope that she will assist me with some help. I am very sorry,
most excellent lady, to disclose my needs, but if I can not do so to your
excellence, I do not know to whom I may disclose them. I am including a   20
bill of six pounds and eight shillings and six pence—regarding the rest of
the bill that I have with your excellence, and may God be my witness that
if it were not for my extreme financial difficulties I would not trouble
her, I have hopes in your kindness, who will find me sensible of it, and in
your forgiveness for the trouble I give you. May God provide your excellence with the content that you and your servants desire, and may He lib-
erate you from your troubles. With a devoted heart, I pray to your divine
majesty, from this poor home on the 6th of January 1610.

Most illustrious and most excellent
Your humble servant   30
Prospero Gorges

B17

FROM ALICE COLLINGWOOD

Autograph, SPD, James, vol. 62, f. 26. Addressed "To the most noble and
renowned Lady, the Lady Arbella her Grace. humbly theis dede." Written 7
March 1610/11.

Alice Collingwood likely was the wife of Francis Collingwood of Newcastle, a recusant imprisoned for having slandered the king late in 1606 (Bradley, 1:274). In early March 1611, Stuart was in custody at Lambeth.

🏵

Most honorable and renowned Lady.

That which to the most seemes great presumption, for me (though thus dejected) to attempt this kinde of enterprise unto so high a personage, the more noble and illustrious that you are (most honorable Lady,) I presume you will the lesse take notice of my faulte, as only lookinge to the thinges wherin your vertues may be exercised, which is the truest noate of that same disposition all-dispos'd to vertue, holdinge all things else impertinent, or not immageninge that they have any beinge. And surely fame hath not ben sparinge to make knowne your honours wor-
10   thines, comprisinge both the vertues of this nature, as yt doth most worthely conteyne the vertues of the highest qualities. Wherby restinge confident that as Charity is not usually seperated from the rest; so I doe assure my selfe yt cannot be the least of them your honour is endowed with. Which joynctly leade me nowe to offer upp my humble suite unto your honour, an occasion for your pietie and pittye to be seene, the one in pardoninge my boldnes, the other in releevinge my necessity. Unto both wherof your honour may the rather be induced, beinge that as want hath priviledge to seeke for succoure every where, so yt carryeth reason to be more lamented when yt is occasioned by adversities; which
20   fareth nowe with me whome fortune hath ben such an enimye unto my birthe, as hath brought my state to be unequall to my callinge, and keepes me from my lawfull husband and all rightes by him, which are of extraordinary value: Wherin beinge loath to be offensive to your honour by a tedious discourse, I humbly leave yt to your wisdome, which is hable to considder well of such distresse. And both I and my poore Children will dayly pray for your honours wished happynes./

Your honours most humble Suplicant at commaund.
this .7th. of March   Alice: Collinwood.
<u>1610</u>.

TABLE OF CORRESPONDENTS

Letters are indicated by number.

INDEX OF PERSONS AND PLACES

Persons are indexed when they are discussed in the introductions, letters, or notes, but not when their writings are cited as sources. Titled persons are listed by title and in most cases cross-referenced by family name. Numbers refer to page and note numbers, rather than to letter numbers.